The *Other* Europe

The *Other* Europe

Eastern Europe to 1945

E. GARRISON WALTERS

SYRACUSE UNIVERSITY PRESS

First Edition
92 91 90 89 88 87   6 5 4 3 2 1

The paper used in this publication meets the minimum requirements of American National
Standard for Information Sciences—Permanence of Paper for Printed Materials, ANSI
Z39.48-1984.♾

Library of Congress Cataloging-in-Publication Data

Walters, E. Garrison.
   The other Europe: Eastern Europe to 1945/E. Garrison Walters.—1st ed.
   p. cm.
   Bibliography: p.
   Includes index.
   ISBN 0-8156-2412-3
   1. Europe, Eastern—History. I. Title.
DJK38.W35 1988
947—dc19   87-28560
                                                                     CIP

MANUFACTURED IN THE UNITED STATES OF AMERICA

For my parents

E. GARRISON WALTERS is the director of Graduate and Special Programs at the Ohio Board of Regents and is an adjunct Assistant Professor of Slavic and East European Languages and Literatures at Ohio State University. He is co-author of *Imi place limba Romana, A Romanian Reader.* Walters received his Ph.D. from Ohio State University.

Contents

Acknowledgments   ix

Introduction: What Is Eastern Europe?   xi

1   The Lands of Eastern Europe: Physical Survey
and Resource Base   1

2   History to 1800   16

3   History, 1800–1848   32

4   History, 1848–1914   47

5   Why Is There an Eastern Europe?   110

6   The Great War: From Origins to Settlement   132

7   Interwar Eastern Europe: An Overview   150

8   Interwar Poland   171

9   Interwar Czechoslovakia   189

10   Interwar Hungary   205

11   Interwar Romania   219

12   Interwar Yugoslavia   237

13   Interwar Bulgaria   251

14   Interwar Albania   261

15   Eastern Europe in World War II   270

16   The Soviet Example   308

17   The Eastern European Communist Parties to 1945   325

Afterword: Eastern Europe on the Eve of a New Vassalage   359

Appendix: Maps   365

     East Europe After 1947   366–367

     Peoples of East Europe   368–369

     Albania   370–371

     Bulgaria   372

Czechoslovakia   373
German Democratic Republic   374–375
Hungary   376
Poland   377
Romania   378
Yugoslavia   379
Habsburg Empire, 1278   380
Habsburg Empire, 1526   381
Habsburg Empire, 1699   382
Habsburg Empire, 1740   383
Habsburg Empire, 1780   384
Habsburg Empire, 1815   385
Habsburg Empire, *Ausgleich*   386
Habsburg Empire, 1914   387
East Europe, 1914   388–389
East Europe, 1922–1938   390–391
Notes   393
Suggestions for Further Reading   407
Index   417

Acknowledgments

*T*HIS BOOK WAS WRITTEN over a period of about five years while the author worked as a full-time administrator and part-time volunteer teacher. Many colleagues gave up time from their own research to contribute advice and encouragement and thereby to make an otherwise impossible project feasible. There is not sufficient space for me to acknowledge fully the debt owed to them or to mention all who assisted. Nevertheless, the author wants to signal his gratitude to those who worked especially hard on his behalf.

Richard Burks, Bob Donia, Stephen Fischer-Galati, Radu Floerescu, Chuck Gribble, Jiri Hochman, Jerzy Kryzanowski, Ken Naylor, Michael Petrovich, and Carole Rogel all offered suggestions and encouragement. In addition, Fred Chary, Duncan Perry, and Scott Seregny all read the manuscript with particular care and offered invaluable advice on organization and style. Ljubica Acevski, Shari Lorbach, and Robert Gross all made crucial contributions to the preparation of the manuscript.

Arthur Adams, Jan Adams, Michael Curran, and Diether Haenicke are former administrative colleagues who offered not only the flexibility needed for me to pursue teaching and research but also the inspiration of their own continuing scholarly activities. A current colleague, Elaine Hairston, has maintained this environment of support. I am especially grateful to all of them.

Finally, my greatest debt is to my wife, Noelle Van Pulis, who endured with grace and good humor the frequent distractions from household and parental duties which I visited on her during the preparation of this study.

Introduction
What Is Eastern Europe?

*I*T HAS BECOME something of a cliché for authors and journalists discussing Eastern Europe to preface their texts with threats that go more or less as follows: "Since this is the region in which both world wars began, it would be best for us to achieve a fuller understanding of the area before it gives birth to a third (and possibly final) conflict." This argument has lost most of its appeal in a world in which the term "balkanization" is more often applied to Africa or Southeast Asia than to the Balkans, but it is certainly true that most Westerners, and particularly Americans, are remarkably ignorant about the large, populous, and increasingly industrial area that lies between the Soviet Union and Germany, the region that the American writer Philip Roth refers to as "The Other Europe."

Eastern Europe is far more of a political expression than a geographical one. It is an area in which very few of the important physical features, such as rivers and mountains, have had a major role in determining boundaries between peoples, cultures, and nations. This is true both within the area itself and in its relationship to the surrounding regions. It is not surprising, therefore, that there are many conflicting definitions of just what comprises Eastern Europe (indeed, some scholars reject the term entirely). Perhaps the only definition that could approach unanimous support is one that simply points out that the solidly Russian areas to the east and the solidly German and Italian lands to the west are *not* a part of Eastern Europe.

If it is relatively easy to say what Eastern Europe is not, it is far more difficult and much more controversial to say what it is. The most widely accepted definition states that Eastern Europe consists of the territories of the present-day countries of (from north to south): Poland, Czechoslovakia, Hungary, Romania, Yugoslavia, Bulgaria, and Albania.

But many would disagree. A substantial number of Poles and Czechs would argue that their lands and peoples are geographically, culturally, and historically more western than eastern European.* This is a point of view that is also shared by a number of Slovaks, Hungarians, and also by two of the Yugoslav peoples—the Slovenes and the Croats. Many Romanians, although scarcely in a position to base a claim on geography or history, have often thought of their nation as an outpost of western culture in the east.

If only the Serbs, Bulgarians, Macedonians, and Albanians can be said to be fairly content with their status as East Europeans, it must be noted that there are representatives of other peoples who object to being left out. Thus, it is certainly true that a traditional definition of Eastern Europe between the two world wars would have included the three independent Baltic states of Estonia, Latvia, and Lithuania. Similarly, although an independent Ukrainian state has made only the briefest of appearances in modern times, many Ukrainians believe that their land should be an independent East European nation. Some authors would also include Finland and Greece in the region, but this is decidedly a minority view.

Since compromise (and controversy) are inescapable, the author has chosen a definition that is deemed most likely to appeal to the probable audience. It is assumed that most readers will have developed their interest in the history of Eastern Europe in consequence of being intrigued by the complexities of the area as it is now defined. Thus, this text will consider Eastern Europe from the standpoint of contemporary political realities: the Baltic states and the Ukraine will be excluded in view of their *de facto* integration into the Soviet Union proper rather than into its bloc; Yugoslavia and Albania, no longer in the bloc, will be retained because they are still a part of the same communist political-economic milieu as their neighbors. Greece, non-communist after a near miss, will

---

* The brilliant Czech novelist Milan Kundera argues eloquently that the term "Eastern Europe" is incorrect both culturally and politically: "My country . . . is an old West European country and it wishes to retain this identity." Kundera thinks it more appropriate to describe Eastern Europe as a "colonized form of Western Europe." This author strongly agrees with Kundera on the cultural identity of Eastern and Western Europe (see Chapter 5), and to a very considerable extent on the political-economic relationship as well. But, since the latter does connote important differences, and since repeated use of the phrase "colonized region of Western Europe" would be most awkward, the term Eastern Europe is retained as a convention if not an ideological declaration. For Kundera's remarks see A. Finkelhaupt, "Milan Kundera Interview," in Ladislav Matejka and Benjiman Stolz, eds., *Cross Currents: A Yearbook of Central European Culture* 1(1982):18.

be mentioned frequently simply because the Greek people and their culture had such a profound impact upon the Balkans. By contrast, the present day state of East Germany will not figure in the historical treatments, but as one of the nations of the Soviet sphere, its communist background will be examined.

In effect, this definition of Eastern Europe is a compromise from every relevant point of view: political, ethno-linguistic, and historical. The result appears to be extraordinarily awkward on the surface but after a time should begin to make sense. The student of Eastern Europe must accept the fact that this is a part of the world in which the simplest problems suddenly become complex.

This work is not intended for the specialist in East European history. The author hopes that scholars in that discipline will find some interesting new interpretations but is reasonably certain that they will not discover new information. The endnotes and the bibliography have been designed, therefore, to provide reference and bibliographic information for the general reader. Further, these citations emphasize sources on domestic issues rather than diplomatic affairs, for which numerous studies are widely known and available.

Whatever the reason for approaching it and however the definition is determined, "The Other Europe" deserves to be better known and understood. This volume attempts to serve as an introduction to those purposes. If the reader concludes with a sense of Eastern Europe's place in the framework of Europe, as well as an interest in further pursuing some aspect or another of its history or culture, that purpose will have been achieved.

The *Other* Europe

1

The Lands of Eastern Europe
Physical Survey and Resource Base

T HE MAP of Eastern Europe at first glance presents four striking physical phenomena. To the north there is the broad North European
(sometimes called North German) Plain which forms the southern coast
of the Baltic Sea. This region ranges from about 250 to 350 miles in
depth and is open to both east and west. The southern perimeter of the
plain is marked by the northernmost extension of the Carpathian Mountains, a huge serpentine chain which traverses the central part of Eastern
Europe from north to south in a broad, eastward-sweeping curve. To the
west of these mountains begins the great Danube River valley which,
with its tributaries and attendant plains, runs first north-south and then
eastward to cut through the Carpathians and enter the Black Sea. The
fourth region is the rugged landscape of the Balkan Peninsula, delineated
on the north by the Danube valley, to the west and south by the Adriatic
and the Aegean seas, and to the east by the Black Sea.[1]

Poland

Poland is one of the few countries of Eastern Europe which has a fairly
uniform landscape. Of the country's 121,000 square miles (roughly the
size of New Mexico), about 90 percent is in the North European Plain;
the remainder, at the extreme southern edge, is in the Carpathian and
Sudeten Mountains. Poland has well-defined frontiers to the north (the
Baltic) and the south (the Carpathians). To the east and the west, however,
Poland has no obvious physical boundaries.

The absence of natural east-west barriers has ensured that the ethnic
and political frontiers of Poland have been without historical continuity.

Since this text is concerned with the contemporary state, only those lands that are now a part of Poland will be discussed here. However, the section on history will provide some information on the adjacent areas which were at one time or another included in the Polish state.

The open nature of the landscape and the consequent vagueness of Polish frontiers have affected even the regional definition of Poland. Unlike all but one of the other East European countries, Poland lacks a reasonably well delineated set of provinces or geographic zones which are easily distinguished from each other and clearly and consistently associated with Poland. Even so, there are five regions which can be effectively identified with historical and geographical reference to Poland. They will be discussed in a south-to-north sequence, a pattern which follows the flow of the major river systems.

The southernmost part of Poland is the region called Galicia. Historically, this is only the western half of the area—the eastern half is now in the Soviet Union; the Poles usually call this area Małopolska, "lesser Poland," but because the term Galicia was used when the region was in the Habsburg Empire it has become the standard in the West. Galicia has the greatest topographic diversity of any of the five areas, for it includes the Polish section of the Carpathians (the High Tatra or Tatry Wysokie range) as well as rolling foothills and a portion of the great plain. The mountains of Galicia contain the headwaters of the Vistula (Wisła) River, which forms the nation's major drainage system. Although the rivers and streams in this area are not for the most part navigable, their valleys provide easy south-north and to a lesser extent east-west communications.

Galicia is fairly rich agriculturally, for there are many fertile valleys in the mountains, while the foothills and plains contain soil of above average quality. In addition to important livestock production, grains and root crops such as potatoes and beets are produced with comparatively high yields. The natural resources of the area include timber and some oil, iron, zinc, and other minerals. The principal city is Cracow (Kraków), with a population of 705,000 (1979). The agricultural and mineral resources account for a population density that is considerably higher than the Polish average.

To the west of Galicia, still along the southern border of Poland, is the region known as Silesia (Śląsk). The Polish part of Silesia (portions are also in East Germany and Czechoslovakia) extends along the east bank of the Oder (Odra) River, which is the second most important river system of Poland. The topography is similar to that of Galicia, although the southern mountains, the Sudetens, are much less rugged than the Tatra secion of the Carpathians. The foothills to the north are also much lower, and the region includes more plains than the land to the east. Although the mountains in this area are more easily cultivated, the plains are generally less fertile than the uplands, and Silesia is much less important agriculturally than Galicia.

What Silesia lacks in agriculture, however, is more than compensated for in industrial strength. The area has some of the most significant coal deposits in Europe, and these reserves, as well as other related mineral resources, make it a region of large urban industrial complexes and therefore of high population density. The most important of these are Wrocław (Breslau in German; pop. 608,000 in 1979), Katowice, and Opole. The Oder and its valley assure reasonably easy access for raw materials and manufactured goods to the rest of the country and for export via the Baltic.

The central part of Poland, usually called Mazovia (Mazowsze), is the only area which has remained continuously and indisputably Polish. Lying entirely in the plain, its major topographical feature is the Vistula which, with its numerous tributaries, bisects the region from southeast to northwest. The central location and the good communications account for the area's importance, since it lacks natural resources, and the soils in the plain are generally less productive than the European average. The capital at Warsaw (Warszawa; pop. 1.5 million in 1979) is the most important city, although Łódź to the west and Lublin to the east are also significant urban and industrial centers.

The west-central part of Poland is known as Wielkopolska ("Greater Poland"); its chief city is Poznán (pop. 544,000 in 1979; German name Posen). The topography of the region is not distinct from that of the Mazovia, but the area is defined economically by an orientation toward the Oder rather than the Vistula valley, and by a historical connection with the German lands to the west. Otherwise it bears a close geographic and demographic resemblance to the eastern section of the plain.

The fifth and most northern region of Poland is called Pomerania (Pomorze), a term which has been used rather loosely over the centuries to describe part of the German as well as the Polish littoral of the Baltic Sea. This area, which varies in depth from some 125 miles in the west to less than 50 in the east, is markedly different from the plain to the south. The effects of recent glaciation have marked Pomerania with low hills, lakes, and marshes. Much of the land is rocky and forested, and the soil is generally poor. Mineral resources are not significant.

The economic importance of Pomerania is to be found almost exclusively in its Baltic ports, although these have serious natural problems. The combination of prevailing winds and tides have left few good harbors, and those that are in operation require constant dredging. The major cities are Gdansk (Danzig in German) and Gdynia, both located near the mouth of the Vistula, and Szczecin (Stettin in German) at the mouth of the Oder. Although there are many miles of excellent beaches along the Baltic, the northern climate permits only a very short tourist season.

Czechoslovakia

Czechoslovakia, unlike Poland, is composed of regions that are geographically and historically well defined. Overall, the nation has some 49,000 square miles (about the size of New York). Although a considerable portion is heavily wooded mountains and hills, more than 55 percent of the land is classified as agricultural, providing one of the highest ratios of arable land to population in Europe. Moreover, the area available for agriculture is for the most part quite good and is complemented by a significant resource base. Together these factors give Czechoslovakia the strongest economy of the traditional states of eastern Europe—well balanced between industry and agriculture.

The Czech lands of Czechoslovakia are divided into two provinces which have long been distinct historical entities. The larger of the two is Bohemia (Čechy), which is the westernmost region of the state. The northern, western, and southern frontiers of Bohemia are marked by an arrowhead-shaped curve of low mountains (or high hills) which are geographically distinct and are defined as three separate areas. These are, from northeast counterclockwise to south-southeast, the Sudeten Mountains, the Ore Mountains, and the Česky Les (Bohemian Forest, which in usual Western terminology includes a range known in Czech as the Šumava). The area is separated from Moravia (Morava) to the east by a line of low hills.

The geography of Bohemia is notable in that virtually the entire region is drained by a series of rivers and streams that converge near the center and then flow northward as the Vltava and then the Elbe Rivers. Thus, Bohemia, although a part of Eastern Europe, has very easy water and land connections across Germany to the North Sea port of Hamburg. This factor has been most important in assisting the economic development of the region. The soils are of high quality in both the central plateau and in a large part of the northern mountain areas. Coal and lignite are also relatively abundant in these two areas, and they are consequently the most densely populated parts of the province. The regional (and national) capital is Prague (Praha), which had an estimated population of 1.1 million in 1979. The central and northern areas have no other large cities but include instead a great number of smaller towns. The southern part of Bohemia, which is less hospitable to agriculture and has few natural resources other than timber, is sparsely populated and has no important cities.

Moravia, about half the size of Bohemia, is essentially a long north-south valley that drains southward through the Morava River, which first forms the border with Austria and then connects with the Danube. The Morava valley has soils of mixed quality, but overall the area is quite prosperous agriculturally. The capital city, Brno (Brünn in German; 369,000 in 1979), is both a market town and a center of textile manufacturing. The extreme northeastern part of Moravia, about 20 percent of the province, is geographically a part of Silesia (this particular area is often called Teschen Silesia). Like its counterpart in Poland, this area has the natural resources for heavy industry. The principal city is Ostrava (pop. 322,000 in 1979).

Slovakia, the third region of Czechoslovakia, includes most of the northernmost extension of the Carpathian Mountains. Since the mountain range defines the area, it follows that internal communications are exceptionally poor: Slovakia and the Carpathians run east and west, but the rivers and valleys run north and south. Communications must therefore go either around or through the mountain ridges. Except for a few streams in the High Tatras (Vysoke Tatry in Slovak) that drain north into Poland, most of the Slovakian watershed looks south to the Tisza River in Hungary and from there to the Danube.

The capital of Slovakia is Bratislava (pop. 368,000 in 1979), which lies on the bank of the Danube at the westernmost extension of the Carpathian foothills. Bratislava is well located for trade purposes, but it also serves as a market town for the least elevated and therefore the agriculturally most productive part of the province. The lands to the east are divided into mountains along the north and a fringe of plains to the south. The mountains contain important mineral resources (iron, copper, gold, silver, and lead), but access is difficult. The plains contain some excellent farmland, but here also communications are much better south to Hungary rather than north and west to the rest of Czechoslovakia. There are no important cities in the area.

Hungary

Hungary is the most geographically unified of all of the states of Eastern Europe. Of the country's 35,900 square miles (about the size of Indiana), all but a very small part is in a fairly flat basin which is known as Pannonia, an ancient name which in modern times has been synonymous with Hungary. The topographical unity of the area is illustrated by the fact that about two-thirds of the land has an elevation of less than 650 feet, while the highest mountain peak is only a little more than 3,330 feet.

Despite the homogeneity and geographic cohesion of the present-day Hungarian state, the country's borders do not for the most part coincide with natural features. Thus, although the frontier which defines the north of Hungary follows (from west to east) Alpine foothills, the Danube, and Carpathian foothills, the eastern-southern frontier is a purely arbitrary line which crosses open plains until it reaches the Drava River in the west. It is not suprising, therefore, that the lines of ethnic and political Hungary are frequently at variance.

There are numerous ways of approaching the regionalization of Hungary, but the simplest and most effective is one which divides the country into only three areas. The principal feature in this division is the Danube River, which separates Transdanubia in the west from the Great Plain and the Northern Mountains in the east. Before discussing these lands individually, however, it is important to emphasize that the differences are entirely based upon geographical convenience rather than the separation of areas with particular historical-political significance.

Transdanubia (Dunántúl, meaning simply the land beyond the Danube) comprises roughly the western third of Hungary. In addition to the ubiquitous plains, the topography of this area is relieved by a fairly dispersed series of hills and mountains which cover perhaps half of the surface. The region is notable because it contains one of the few major lakes of Eastern Europe—Lake Balaton. For the most part, Transdanubia is not an area of significant agricultural productivity.

Transdanubia is, however, richly endowed with mineral resources. In addition to one of the world's largest reserves of bauxite (aluminum ore), there are also important quantities of uranium ore (mined under the direct control of the Soviet Union). Coal, iron, copper, manganese, and lead are also mined, and some oil and natural gas are found as well. Until quite recently, however, the availability of these resources has not caused the establishment of towns or cities for processing—this role was served by Budapest. As a consequence, Transdanubia has only a moderate population density.

The city of Budapest is almost a distinct region by itself. With a population of nearly 2.1 million (1980), this single city has nearly half of the country's urban population and about a fifth of its overall population. Located at a fairly easy Danube crossing point, the city is a recent combination of two separate towns. Buda, on the west bank, served the hill country of Transdanubia, while Pest, on the opposite side, was the focus for the Great Plain to the east. The proliferation of major, permanent bridges in the nineteenth century led to the effective fusion of the two towns into one large urban center.

The Great Plain (Alföld in Hungarian) has a role in Hungarian history and economic development proportionate to its size—more than half of the country. In part, the Great Plain is endowed with the extremely fertile black earth (chernozem) soils which can support a wide variety of crops. To a large extent, however, the region resembles a true steppe land: a treeless, grassy plain (similar to the plains of the American west). The Hungarians call this area the puszta, and it long served the same role as its American counterpart—the cultivation of grains and the grazing of cattle. Modern agricultural techniques, however, have permitted a more varied use of the land.

The eastern part of the Great Plain is drained by the Tisza River (Theiss in German) which in its meandering has left extensive deposits of sand as well as some marshlands. Careful development, however, has made much of this land suitable for fruit and vegetable cultivation. The northeast, in particular, has extensive vineyards. There are two small cities on the plain, Szeged in the extreme south, and Debrecen in the northeast.

The third region of Hungary, the Northern Mountains, is part of the foothills of the Slovak Carpathians to the north. The area has extensive reserves of timber, as well as a number of mineral resources. The agricultural productivity of this hilly area is limited. The chief city is Miskolc (pop. 210,000 in 1980—Hungary's second largest city), which is an industrial processing center for the nearby mines and forests. The population density of both the Great Plain and the Northern Mountains is low and, except as noted, quite dispersed.

Romania

Romania has an integral physical link to two of Eastern Europe's major geographic areas: the Carpathians and the Danube. The mountains are in the country's interior, but they have had an important role as a dividing line until quite recently. The Danube, although for the most part on a frontier, drains the entire country and is therefore a necessary focus for a major part of national life. Romania, with an area of 91,000 square miles (somewhat smaller than New York and Pennsylvania combined) is about half mountain and hill country, and about half river plain.

Romania's southern frontier follows the Danube eastward from the gorges known as the Iron Gates (where the river flows through the mountains), but the border then goes straight toward the Black Sea rather than following the river's sharp northward turn. The Black Sea coast and the Prut River form nearly the whole of the eastern border area. The northern frontier follows the line of the westward sweeping Carpathians, and then for a short distance the Tisza River, which rises in that part of the mountains. The western border is not naturally defined but cuts through the Pannonian plain to the west of the Transylvanian Mountains and eventually rejoins the Danube north of the Iron Gates.

Romania can be divided into four regions and two subregions, all of which have both historical and physical identities. These are: Transylvania (including the Banat); Moldavia (including Bucovina); Wallachia, and Dobrogea. In considering Romainian geography, one should note that the Carpathians, although quite high in places, are cut by numerous low passes and do not pose a significant obstacle to population movements or trade.

Transylvania is well defined on the south, east, and north where the border follows the line of the Carpathians. To the northwest the Tisza River forms a natural frontier for only a short distance, since it veers westward far into the Pannonian plain. The western border is thus artifical, cutting through plains and foothills according to ethnic and strategic considerations following World War I. The Banat, the major subregion of Transylvania, lies along the south-western border, north of the Danube and west of the Carpathians.

The terrain of Transylvania is generally mildly hilly except for the mountain ranges of the far north and central west, regions known respectively as Maramures and Muntii Apuseni. The diversity of the region is emphasized by the fact that the three major river systems all drain in different directions: the Someş northwest to the Tisza; the Mureş southwest to the Tisza (near its confluence with the Danube); and the Olt south directly to the Danube. The soils are generally poor, and the climate is too cold for vineyards and fruits, thus the predominant agricultural focus in Transylvania is on livestock and grains.

Transylvania is rich, however, in other resources. The area has extensive timber reserves as well as valuable deposits of iron ore, lead, zinc, copper, bauxite, and smaller sources of gold, silver, and uranium. Easy access to hydroelectric power and to reserves of natural gas and coal provide the fuels necessary for heavy industry. An exception to the general pattern for Transylvania is the Banat, which lacks minerals and fuels but has some of the finest agricultrual land in all of Europe. The principal cities of Transylvania are Cluj-Napoca (pop. 210,000; the capital), Timişoara (in the Banat), Sibiu, and Braşov. The latter two cities owe their prominence to location at the northern end of the trans-Carpathian trading routes. The overall population density of Transylvania is moderate.

Wallachia (Tara Românească—"the Romanian Land") is easily defined by the Carpathians to the north and west and the Danube to the south and east. The land is a rolling plain, traversed by streams and rivers that flow from the mountains to the Danube. Except for the Olt, which cuts through the Carpathians from Transylvania, all of the rivers are fairly small and shallow. The very high quality of the soil as well as the land's flatness provide an excellent base for agriculture, principally grain production. Very large petroleum deposits are found under the foothills just south of the mountains. Although there are few other resources, these are sufficient to support a larger than average population, including a number of urban industrial centers. The largest city is Bucharest (Bucureşti: pop. 1.9 million in 1980), which is also Romania's capital.

Moldavia (Moldova) is set apart by the Carpathians (now to the east) and a river—the Prut—on the west. The region's very short southern boundary is on the Danube. The northern frontier is in the subregion of Bucovina and represents a political rather than a geographical line. Overall, Moldavia resembles Wallachia except that it is hillier and thus somewhat more difficult to cultivate. The principal river, the Siret, flows south along the mountain foothills to the Danube. Together the Prut and the Siret drain the entire area. Natural resources include substantial reserves of timber in Bucovina. The principal cities are Iaşi (pop. 195,000), which is the regional capital, and Galaţi, a large industrial center on the Danube.

The Romanian part of Dobrogea (Dobrudja in Bulgarian) is the area between the northward-flowing Danube and the Black Sea. The soils of this fairly hilly region are quite good, but the very low rainfall limits agricultural productivity. The chief city, Constanţa (population 279,000 in 1980), however, is a good port, and the excellent beaches permit a lucrative summer tourist season.

Yugoslavia

Yugoslavia, with an area of 91,700 square miles (somewhat smaller than New York and Pennsylvania combined), is geographically the most diverse country in Eastern Europe. It has mountains of many types, hilly areas, plains, seacoast, a lake region, and a number of different river systems. The frontier, which touches seven other nations, is impossible to describe briefly. Yet all of this fits into a country considerably smaller than Poland. The regionalization of this complex area must of necessity follow the political subdivisions provided for in Yugoslavia's federal organization. Even so, these divisions are not enough. To the officially recognized six republics and two autonomous regions, one must add yet another area which has a separate historical-geographical identity (Dalmatia).

The smallest and most unified of the republics is Slovenia, which lies in the Alps and the Alpine foothills at the extreme northwest. The political lines here follow ethnic ones for the most part, and the region is not endowed with natural frontiers except where it touches the Adriatic at the southwest. Slovenia is poor agriculturally, but has a strong industrial base as a consequence of ready access to timber and hydroelectric power; iron and coal are found also in workable quantities. The republic capital is Ljubljana (pop. 300,000 in 1980).

Croatia (like Slovenia and the other areas of Yugoslavia) has borders that reflect historical and ethnic patterns rather than natural barriers. Much of the area is in the rolling valleys of the Drava and Sava rivers, which flow to the Danube from northwest to southeast. This region has much good farmland devoted to a variety of crops, primarily grains; orchards and vineyards are found also in quantity. West of this long valley system is an area of rugged hills, which connect the Alps of Slovenia to the north with the Dinaric Mountains to the south. These hills provide a break in the rocky wall that otherwise separates the Danube valley from the Adriatic. It is therefore not suprising that Croatia's captial city, Zagreb (pop. 700,000 in 1980), lies near this pass.

Croatia also includes almost all of Yugoslavia's Adriatic coast. This thin strip, known as Dalmatia, has a historical and geographic identity of its own, although it is ethnically and politically a part of Croatia. Dalmatia is easily distinguished because the coast is separated from the interior by the rugged Dinaric Mountains. The coastal strip varies in depth from little more than the width of a road in parts of the south to some seventy-five miles in the north. Only in the extreme north (the

Zagreb to Rijeka Pass) and south (the Neretva River) is there easy access to the interior.

Croatia is not particularly rich in mineral resources, but Zagreb's strategic location and good access to fuels have made it an important manufacturing center. In addition to industry, Croatia's economy is supported by strong agriculture in the interior and by fishing, trade, and very highly developed tourism along the coast.

The republic of Bosnia-Hercegovina forms the center core of Yugoslavia. Nearly the entire area is in an eastward extension of the Dinaric Mountains. The land is almost exclusively limestone, the porous nature of which drains water to underground streams and leaves the surface dry. Thus, there is little vegetation and scant opportunity for agriculture. The population density is consequently low. The principal city, Sarajevo (pop. 400,000 in 1980), owes its importance to its location along a trade route that connects the Danube valley with the Neretva River corridor to the Adriatic. Trade, handicrafts, and small-scale agriculture provide the basis of the economy. Most of the inhabitants of Bosnia-Hercegovina are Serbs and Croats, mixed together in such a way that the area cannot be reasonably divided between Serbia and Croatia. It is this complexity, rather than any historical or geographical unity, that permits Bosnia-Hercegovina to exist as a separate political entity.

The smallest of Yugoslavia's republics is Montenegro. Although the population speaks Serbian and borders on Serbia, Montenegro is politically distinct because its uniformly rugged and almost inaccessible mountains allowed it a separate historical development. Agriculture is poor as might be expected, and there is virtually no industry or natural resources other than timber. The largest city, Titograd, has fewer than 50,000 inhabitants.

Macedonia, the fifth republic, is in the extreme southeastern part of the country, bordered on the west by Albania, on the south by Greece, on the east by Bulgaria, and on the north by Serbia. None of these frontiers is natural or historic, but instead each reflects ethnic and political considerations. The capital, Skopje (pop. 440,000 in 1980), is in the center of the Vardar River valley which, together with the valley of the Morava River, forms a corridor from the Danube to the Aegean. Trade along this route has always been a principal factor in Macedonia's economy.

The terrain varies from mountainous to the west and east to hilly in the center along the river valleys. Agriculture is generally weak, although the climate and the terrain favor fruits and vineyards. The two large lakes along the Albanian-Greek border, Ohrid and Prespa, provide income from fishing and tourism. There are few natural resources and very little industry. Even so, the population density is much higher than in neighboring Montenegro, and Macedonia is thus quite poor.

Serbia, the largest and most populous of the six republics, also includes two autonomous regions, Kosovo and Vojvodina. Serbia proper is well endowed for both agriculture and industry. The land is mostly hilly, but the soil is fertile and well watered. Grains, fruits, and vines are all extensively cultivated, and there is a strong emphasis on livestock breeding, primrily of pigs. Copper, lead, bauxite, zinc, and other metals are mined in substantial quantities, and there are extensive reserves of timber.

Because of the rich agricultural and other resources found nearby, and thanks to its location at the confluence of a number of major trade routes, Belgrade (Beograd; pop. 1.3 million in 1980) became an important city quite early. It is a major manufacturing center as well as both re-publican and national capital. The extensive network of smaller cities and towns surrounding Belgrade gives Serbia a higher than average population density.

The two autonomous regions are exact opposites. Vojvodina, just north of Belgrade, is a part of the Hungarian (Pannonian) Plain and has soils of exceptional quality. In addition to high agricultural productivity, there are important reserves of oil and natural gas. Kosovo, on the other hand, is at the extreme southern end of Serbia where the soil is poorer, the climate drier, and where there are few natural resources. The predominantly Albanian population of Kosovo is very poor.

Bulgaria

Bulgaria (42,000 square miles—about the size of Ohio) has a highly varied landscape like its neighbor Yugoslavia. Bulgaria's frontiers, however, are clearer and easier to explain. The country is roughly rectangular, with the Black Sea and the line of the Danube forming the eastern and northern borders. On the west the frontier with Yugoslavia does not follow a clear natural line, although it does approximate the eastern side of the Morava-Vardar valley system. The southern border with Greece follows an arbitrary line through the southern foothills of the Rhodope Mountains. The shortest frontier, with Turkey, also follows an unnatural line from the Rhodopes to the Black Sea.

Bulgaria does not have regions that stand apart for important historical or ethnic reasons. There are, however, four distinct geographic zones which cut the country from west to east. The northernmost of these, the Bulgarian Plain, is part of the Danube River valley and resembles Wallachia to the north although it is hillier. The soils in this area are generally very good, and wheat and corn are the predominant crops. There are very few other resources, however, and the two principal cities, Ruse (pop. 173,000 in 1980) and Varna (pop. 291,000 in 1980), are primarily ports.

The second region of Bulgaria is the Balkan Mountain Range (*Balkan* is the word for "mountain" in Turkish, thus the name for the entire peninsula), which constitutes an east-west barrier running the length of the country. Although not particularly high, these mountains are fairly rugged and can only be traversed easily at a few major passes. Despite the difficult terrain, there are a number of large towns in this area, of which the most important are Turnovo to the north and Gabrovo to the south. In addition to the expected timber, the Balkan Mountains also contain some coal, iron, and other minerals.

The central part of Bulgaria is a long valley, quite narrow at the west, which opens gradually eastward toward the Black Sea. This region has most of the population and industry, and a very large part of the agricultural production of the country. Although it has no official name, it is often referred to as the Maritsa Valley, after the river which drains all but the extreme western and eastern areas. An old and important trade route follows the riverbed from Istanbul to Sofia and beyond.

This central valley of Bulgaria produces wheat and corn, but it is better known as Europe's largest garden. Onions, tomatoes, beans, peppers, and other products are grown in great quantity. There are also extensive vineyards, and cotton and tobacco are important crops. The cultivation of roses for their oil (an essential part of many perfumes) is also a major industry. Fruits—particularly apples, plums, and cherries—flourish in the orchards in the northern and southern foothills.

The largest city of the central plain is Sofia (pop. one million in 1980), which is Bulgaria's capital and only large urban area. Sofia is at the narrowest point of the valley system, where the Balkans and the Rhodopes almost touch. The city is important because of the its location on major trade routes, as a marketplace for the central valley, and as an industrial center that draws on the mineral and energy resources of the two mountain ranges. At the far eastern end of the central plain, Burgas (pop. 168,000 in 1980) is Bulgaria's second port after Varna and before Ruse.

The Rhodope Mountains on the south form the fourth region of

Bulgaria. These mountains are higher and more difficult than the Balkans, and there is only one easy corridor to the south. This route follows the Struma River valley as far as the Aegean. The mountains are rich in minerals, particularly lead, zinc, and copper, and of course there are reserves of timber. There are very few large towns in the area, however, and the raw materials are shipped northward for processing. Agriculture is scattered and weak, and the population density of this area is low.

Albania

With only 11,000 square miles (slightly larger than Maryland), Albania is Eastern Europe's smallest and least populous country. About 80 percent of its area is rugged mountains, while the remainder is hills and a few lowland areas not far from the coast. The nation's borders are obvious only to the west along the Adriatic. The northern, eastern, and southern frontiers with Yugoslavia and Greece follow lines that reflect political, ethnic, and historical factors, although in many areas the border does follow a watershed. The frontiers nevertheless cross some mountain ridges haphazardly and give Albania only a part of three major lakes, Scutari, Ohrid, and Prespa.

The mountains of Albania are for the most part an extension of the Dinaric range in Yugoslavia, and thus are largely limestone, dry, and barren. This condition is not complete, however, and the typically high precipitation combines with different types of rock to create areas that have some natural vegetation and the potential for small-scale agriculture. Almost every drop of rain that falls in Albania drains westward through the country to the Adriatic. The rivers that result are nonetheless little more than large streams and are not navigable to any meaningful extent.

Although it is to be expected that the mountainous regions would be poorly suited for agriculture, one would assume that the coastal plain would be much better. In fact, the difference is slight. The coastal area is marshy and does not have good soils. The wild streams from the mountains tend to change their course frequently and make agricultural work in the plains difficult and even dangerous. Overall, only about 5 percent of Albania's land is arable, and there is no crop of major importance produced above the subsistence level.

The mineral resources of the mountains include natural gas and oil in exportable quantities. Other resources include significant reserves of chrome and copper as well as smaller quantities of less valuable minerals.

Industry is poorly developed. Fishing in the Adriatic does not provide food beyond that required locally. The only city is the capital, Tiranä (pop. 198,000 in 1980), while the largest town, the port of Durrës, is less than half as large.

The Climate of Eastern Europe

Most of Eastern Europe is too far east to experience the moderating effects that the Atlantic Ocean produces on the climate of Western Europe. Thus, the usual weather pattern is that officially known as "continental" (i.e., cold winters and warm summers). Precipitation continues throughout the year with considerable snowfall in the winter and rainfall peaking in June and July. As one would expect, the northern area is cooler than the southern, but the differences are more important in the winter than in the summer. Overall, the climate is quite similar to that of the midwestern United States.

The only exception to the weather pattern occurs in the extreme south. The Adriatic coast of Yugoslavia (Dalmatia), all of Albania, and the southeastern part of Bulgaria are in the "Mediterranean" climate zone. This means that the winters are generally mild and the summers somewhat milder and less humid than in the inland areas. In contrast to the continental zone, most precipitation occurs in the winter, and takes the form of rain rather than snow.

2

History to 1800

*E*ASTERN EUROPE is an area of considerable ethnic diversity. The population of some one-hundred million people is composed of fourteen major nationality groups and nine smaller ones. The absence of natural features that presented serious barriers to population movements, together with the historical predominance of multinational political organizations, ensured that the various ethnic groups were mixed together over much of Eastern Europe. The savagery of the Second World War and the political decisions that followed the end of the fighting did much to simplify the ethnic map, but considerable complexity remains.

Since it is almost impossible to describe the peoples of Eastern Europe without also discussing the historical events that formed them, this section will survey the period from the beginning of history to about the year 1400. By the start of the fifteenth century, the last of the present-day nationalities was firmly established in the area, and the history of Eastern Europe began to be integrated into European history as a whole.

The first historical records about Eastern Europe were provided by Greek chroniclers.[1] In addition to their own Hellenic tribe, these writers recorded the presence of six other groups: Germanic, Celtic, Scythian, Illyrian, Thracian, and Dacian. Of this group, contact with the first three was sporadic. The Germanic tribes were weak and scattered in early times, and their usual habitat was far to the north of the Greek world. The Celts, who appear to have ruled once over most of Europe, were in decline at the beginning of recorded history, with their remaining strength shifting westward. Evidence of their earlier importance in Eastern Europe is to be found in the name of Bohemia, which is of Celtic origin.

The Scythians, who did not inhabit Eastern Europe proper, were loosely settled in the steppe land of southern Ukraine (from about the eighth to the first centuries B.C.). A semi-nomadic people, the Scythians frequently raided westward but disappeared from history without leaving any trace of their language. They were the last group to establish any sort of settlement on this plain for nearly a thousand years. After the Scythians, for century after century the steppe was to serve as a broad east-west highway bringing one savage invader after another from central Asia. Until these invasions ceased, East European history was even more turbulent than that of the rest of Europe.

The other three peoples noted by the Greeks, the Illyrians, the Thracians, and the Dacians, all inhabited the Balkan Peninsula to the north of Greece. The three were apparently closely related, but not enough remains of the languages of the latter two to provide much information about them. The Illyrians, however, did survive in a sense, as they are usually considered to be the ancestors of the Albanians. Given the geography of the Balkans, the tenacity of the Illyrian peoples is not surprising. Surrendering the lowlands to stronger groups, they occupied the most remote mountains of the area. Very few invaders attempted to conquer this inhospitable land, and those that did were either repulsed or, like the Romans, were content to occupy the coast and to control the major passes through the mountains.

The Albanian language is part of the Indo-European group that predominates in the Western world, but it is not closely related to any other language. Over the years it has been heavily influenced by Latin, Greek, south Slavic, Turkish, and Italian, without losing its distinct character. But the separation of groups occasioned by the difficult terrain, and the fact that no unified Albanian state existed until the twentieth century, led to considerable local variations. Today, the language has two major forms: Gheg (spoken by about two-thirds of the population, mostly in the north) and Tosk (the official literary language), as well as a number of lesser dialects.

The Thracians, who occupied present-day Bulgaria, were conquered and destroyed by the Romans as they advanced northwards from Greece. Nothing remains of the Thracian language and, except for a number of remarkable relics worked in gold, all records of their culture were obliterated as well. Following the conquest of the Thracians, the Romans moved across the Danube and attacked the Dacians. After a fierce struggle lasting more than six years, the emperor Trajan won a decisive victory in A.D. 107. This achievement was commemorated in Trajan's column, which still stands in Rome.

The Romans colonized Dacia (roughly present-day Romania) because it was valuable for its mineral resources, principally gold and silver. The region was on the fringes of the rapidly weakening empire, however, and the occupying army was withdrawn to the more easily defended line of the Danube after less than two centuries. Nevertheless, contacts with the Romanized native population continued for another hundred years, until worsening barbarian invasions from the east forced the colonists to take refuge in the Carpathians. There they were finally cut off from regular contact with the southern bank of the Danube. The subsequent collapse of the Roman Empire severed connections altogether and began the separate development of the Romanian people.

Romanian is a Romance language, in some respects closer to Latin than to its western relatives. Despite its isolation and the acquisition of a considerable number of Slavic words, the core of everyday speech is clearly Romance. Romanian does not have any major dialects, a fact which is probably a reflection of its origin in a fairly compact mountain region—a habitat which was inaccessible enough to discourage outside attack but which still permitted easy internal communication. The origin of Romanian must of necessity be based on speculation, however, for there are virtually no written records of the area from the time of the withdrawal of the Romans (around 300) until the end of the barbarian invasions nearly a thousand years later (around 1300).

The Slavs may well have been among the first inhabitants of Eastern Europe, but their original home, probably in the region of Poland, was too far north to be known to the Greek chroniclers. There are scattered early references in some Greek and Roman sources to what were undoubtedly Slavs or proto-Slavs, but it was not until after the end of the invasion of the Huns (A.D. 450) that the Slavs moved south of the northern forest line and into recorded history. The reason for this expansion is not known, but it was unquestionably facilitated by the enormous destruction wrought by the Huns, whose savage horsemen eliminated the peoples as well as the political organizations they found in their path across the plains.

The southward movement of the Slavs began toward the end of the fifth century and was complete about one hundred years later. The invasion was largely peaceful, because the Slavs were a pastoral people in search of good farmland, utterly unlike the rapacious Huns. The hills of Bohemia and Moravia, and the mountains of Slovakia were occupied first, while the plains of Pannonia, Wallachia, and Moldavia were bypassed because they were too exposed. Transylvania and the southern Carpathians were penetrated, but any Slav settlers that remained were eventually absorbed by the more numerous Romanians.

In the northern Balkan Peninsula, the Slavs occupied all but the mountains of Albania. They even moved into Greece as far as the Peloponnesus, but never took control of the ancient Greek cities. After the shock of the initial invasion, the urban areas in most of today's Greece gradually reasserted their control of the countryside and Hellenized the neighboring Slavs. In the vast majority of the peninsula, however, the Slavs quickly absorbed the scattered and weak native populations. Besides the Albanians, another group, a people of Latin origin known as Vlachs, also survived by moving to the mountains. Most of the Vlachs, whose language is similar to Romanian, have since disappeared, although a few remain in the more remote areas of Macedonia and Greece.

While some of the Slavs moved south, others remained, and still others moved north and east into areas that are now known as Russia and the Ukraine. As the Slavs moved farther apart and put more physical barriers between themselves, what had probably been a single Slavic language began to separate into dialects that eventually became new languages. When the migrations ceased in the seventh century, there were three major groups of languages: West Slavic, East Slavic, and South Slavic.

West Slavic includes the three present-day languages known as Polish, Czech, and Slovak. The differentiation between the three is probably a consequence of demographic separation into different geographic zones: the plains of Poland (Polish), the hills of Bohemia and Moravia (Czech), and the mountains of Slovakia (Slovak). The natural linguistic phenomena that tend to separate languages would probably have been restricted to dialectical differences had not later political developments kept the three areas apart for long periods. As it is, West Slavic has three distinct but closely related languages.

South Slavic has from three to five languages, depending upon one's point of view. Slovene, spoken by the inhabitants of the southeastern part of the Alps, is uncontestably one language. Slovene is fairly close to Slovak, even though they are in different language groups, because the two mountain peoples maintained contact long after the main bodies of West and South Slavic had separated. Serbo-Croatian is considered by most linguists to be one language, despite the fact that Serbs and Croats use different alphabets.

Bulgarian is similar to, but quite distinct from, Serbo-Croatian. The reasons for the major differences between these two languages are unclear, but linguists note that the western dialects of Bulgaria shade gradually into the eastern dialects of Serbia. The existence of Macedonian as a separate language is much debated. It is very close to Bulgarian, and most Bulgarians disagree with its status as an independent language. The situation is complicated by the fact that Macedonian itself has dialects, some of which are very close to Bulgarian and some closer (but not as close) to Serbo-Croatian. Whatever the validity of the arguments, Macedonian has been generally accepted as a separate language since World War II. Thus, most specialists compromise between three and five and agree on four South Slavic languages.

East Slavic probably remained as one language longer than the other groups. Gradually, however, different customs, political problems, and enormous distances separated the Russian speakers of the northern forest from the Ukrainian speakers of the lands along the fringe of the steppe. Byelorussian (White Russian) emerged as a transitional language between Russia to the east and Polish to the west.

The last of the major peoples of Eastern Europe to appear were the Magyars, whose name in the other languages of the region, Hungarian, evokes memories of the Huns. This comparison was not casual, for the Magyars, who arrived in Europe in the ninth century, were also nomadic horsemen from Central Asia. Unlike their predecessors, however, they settled down on the land when their westward drive was stopped. The area they seized, known to the Romans as Pannonia, was probably only sparsely occupied when the Magyars arrived. Few before them had dared to try to survive on the unprotected plain.

The Magyars spoke a language that was totally unlike that of their neighbors. Hungarian is one of the few languages of Europe that is not a part of the Indo-European family. (The other exceptions are Finnish and Estonian, which are distantly related to Hungarian, and Basque.) The appearance of the Magyars drove a wedge between the West and South Slavs and left only two areas of Eastern Europe—the plains of Moldavia and Wallachia—unoccupied.

The first of the native states to emerge in Eastern Europe was that of the Bulgarians. The Bulgars, who conquered the Slavic tribes of the lower Danube at the end of the eighth century, were actually a Central Asian people, related to the Huns and the Magyars. Numerically inferior to their Slavic subjects, the Bulgars were quickly assimilated, and the only distinct element that remains is their name. Even so, the Bulgarian state was a strong one and was able to remain independent and even to threaten Byzantium (the eastern remnant of the Roman Empire) throughout most of the ninth and tenth centuries.

The Bulgarians accepted the eastern form of Christianity, Orthodoxy, but they were strong enough to insist on their own autonomous church. The most important feature of the Bulgarian church was its use of the native language (instead of Greek). A new alphabet, known as Cyrillic, was derived in part from Greek and formed the basis for the

Serbian and the Russian as well as the Bulgarian scripts. This new language, which developed into Church Slavonic, also greatly influenced Russian vocabulary and grammar, since this derivative form was for centuries the official church language in Russia. The Romanians also received Orthodoxy from the Bulgarians, and their language was strongly affected by Church Slavonic as well.

The Bulgarian state eventually succumbed to the dual pressures of the Byzantine Greeks on the south and the endless stream of barbarians on the north. At its height, the Bulgarian empire included Serbia, Macedonia, Albania, Thrace, and, for a short time, Wallachia. Though it reappeared only briefly in early times (the Second Bulgarian Empire, 1190–1393), the Bulgarian state had an important impact on history.

Shortly after the Bulgars began to organize their expansion, another Slavic state took shape in the north. Known as Greater Moravia, this state expanded from an unknown base to include most of present-day Czechoslovakia, southern Poland, and northwestern Hungary. Beset to the north and west by Polish and German enemies, it finally collapsed under the additional pressure of a Magyar attack in 907. Most of the history of the Moravian state's century of existence remains a mystery, but it is known that this was the period when the brothers Constantine (Cyril) and Methodius introduced Christianity to the western Slavs.

The Moravian state disintegrated into three separate parts, none of which was truly independent. Slovakia became a part of Hungary early in the tenth century and remained so for more than a thousand years; at about the same time Southern Poland became a part of the embryonic Polish state, and Bohemia-Moravia retained autonomy but not independence as part of the German-dominated Holy Roman Empire.

The Polish state took shape in the middle of the tenth century around the area of Poznán, and entered history in 963 as a consequence of conflict with eastward-expanding Germans. This event was but the first recorded step in what has been an almost unbroken political and cultural struggle between the two peoples.

The Polish situation was reasonably good in the early years; however, for there was no organized power to the east, and they only had to fight on one front. By accepting Christianity in 966, the Poles deprived the Germans of the rights of holy crusaders, and thereafter more or less held their own in the west while they expanded to the east.

The Hungarians also began to form a state in the tenth century. When their westward expansion was stopped by the Germans in 955, the Hungarians finally settled permanently in Pannonia and their first king, St. Stephen, accepted Christianity in the year 1001. From the beginning, the Hungarian state included lands that were inhabited primarily by non-Hungarians. Slovakia, as noted before, was conquered very early, while Transylvania was incorporated in the first years of the eleventh century. Just a century later, Croatia, too, was added to what the Hungarians (somewhat anachronistically) called the "crownlands of St. Stephen."

In the southern part of Eastern Europe a new Slavic state arose less than a century after the final defeat of the Bulgarians (1014). Based at first in Montenegro, this new political entity was Serbian in character. Beginning in 1168, all of the Serbian lands, as well as Albania and most of Macedonia, were united in a single Slavic state which eventually conquered renascent Bulgaria, secured its own independent Orthodox church, and then, like the early Bulgarian Empire, tried to destroy Byzantium. When a final attempt to take Constantinople failed in 1355, the Serbian state began to fall apart.

The last areas of Eastern Europe to achieve political organization were the regions of Wallachia and Moldavia. At the beginning of the fourteenth century, the great wave of barbarian invasions from the east appeared to be over, and the Romanians descended from the mountains and cautiously began to settle on the plain. At first clinging to the foothills (where the capitals long remained), the two states gradually extended their power south to the Danube and east to the Dniester. This process may well have begun centuries before; but if so, it was surely stopped, and its foundations totally destroyed, by the terrible savagery of the Mongol invaders in the middle of the thirteenth century.

The fifteenth century was to be a time of momentous change for Eastern Europe, and its beginning is therefore a good place to stop for a historical review. In order to help clarify the situation for the student of contemporary affairs, the review will be based on the modern states.

The Northern Tier in 1400

Poland

Poland in 1400 was quite different from the Poland of today. Mazovia, Wielkopolska, and Galicia were in the Polish state, but Silesia was ruled by the Czechs, and most of Pomerania and the Baltic coast as far as Lithuania was in the hands of the Teutonic Knights—a German military—religious order. The Poles were involved in a constant struggle to regain the vital seaports and had just created a dynastic alliance with Lithuania, which was then a great state stretching from the Baltic south across the Ukraine almost to the Black Sea.

Internally, the Polish king was increasingly forced to rely upon the landed nobility and the Church for his strength. The manorial system was rapidly becoming a dominant form of organization in the countryside, as the needs of the embattled state required serfs or indebted tenants to produce an agricultural surplus and to be available in time of war. A number of towns were beginning to develop into trading centers, their rapid rate of growth assisted by large numbers of German colonists. A University at Cracow, founded in 1364, soon acquired a solid European reputation.

Czechoslovakia

As mentioned earlier, the Czech lands of Bohemia and Moravia were separated from Slovakia in the tenth century. The Czech state (known as Bohemia, and at this time including Silesia as well as Moravia) was ruled by a foreign king, but most power rested in the hands of the Czech nobles. German influence was strong, and Bohemia had become a part of the loosely organized Germanic confederation known as the Holy Roman Empire. As in Poland, large numbers of German colonists had settled in the towns, and trade with the west flourished. Feudalism was growing in importance in the countryside, but Bohemia could rely also upon mines that produced iron, copper, silver, and gold in abundance. The Charles University at Prague was one of Europe's great centers of learning.

Hungary

Medieval Hungary was a relatively large country that held the entire center of Eastern Europe. The organization of this state varied somewhat from that of its neighbors to the north. Because the Magyar kingdom included Slovakia, Croatia, and Transylvania, with large numbers of Slovaks, Croats, and Romanians, the king came to rely upon German colonists and specially organized frontier guards as well as feudal lords to support his power. As a consequence, a number of predominantly German cities appeared in Transylvania, and many Magyar peasants were spared enserfment in return for their loyalty. The Hungarian rulers were ambitious and often engaged in the dynastic intrigues and the consequent military conflicts that plagued nearly all of Europe. Overall, however, Hungary was a poor state with little more than subsistence agriculture as its economic base.

The Southern Tier to 1400

For the southern part of Eastern Europe, the dividing line for the changes of the fifteenth century should begin a little earlier than 1400. The year 1389, which marked the great Turkish victory over the Serbs at Kosovo Polje, was a critical date in history.

Yugoslavia

The south Slav lands were weak and divided just before 1389. Croatia, an independent state in the tenth and eleventh centuries, had been a part of Hungary for nearly three hundred years, while Slovenia, cut off from its independent Slav neighbors, had fallen to Austria in 1278. The weak Serbian state included parts of Montenegro, Albania, and Macedonia, but control of these outlying areas was tenuous at best. Serbia, like the rest of the southern islands, had not developed a feudal system when it fell to the Turks. This was partially due to the fact that the lands were not well suited to large estates, and partly a consequence of the constant turmoil and warfare that inhibited the growth of towns and highly organized social structures.

Bulgaria

The situation in Bulgaria was much the same as that in Serbia. Loosely organized politically and lacking an economic base capable of producing surpluses, the state grew stronger or weaker according to the relative skills of its leaders and the power of its neighbors. In the latter part of the fourteenth century, Bulgaria was about the size of today's Bulgaria, but its internal strength was at a low ebb.

Romania

The word "Romania," like "Czechoslovakia" and "Yugoslavia," did not exist in the year 1400. The Romanian peoples lived either in Hungarian Transylvania or in one of the two independent states of Moldavia and Wallachia. These latter had made remarkable progress since their founding in the thirteenth century. Several of their princes had shown great political skills, and increasingly important contacts with the west were spurring further development. Feudal institutions had not yet made an appearance, although there was a significant amount of trade moving between Transylvania and Byzantium. Despite this progress, neither state had developed the power to resist successfully a well-coordinated attack.

Albania

Albania in the late-fourteenth century was nominally controlled by Serbia, but even this weak influence extended only to a few lowland areas. In the mountains, the most important form of political organization was the clan, whose traditions of feuding kept the Albanians in conflict with each other.

History, 1400–1800

The four centuries of East European history between 1400 and 1800 saw the entire area, except for tiny Montenegro, fall under the domination of foreign powers. The different systems of the imperial states, together with the different periods and conditions of control, served to increase the already considerable political and cultural variation within Eastern Europe.

The Ottoman Turks

The appearance of the Ottoman Turks was the first step in this destructive sequence of events. These invaders quickly dominated the southern tier and then forced sharp changes to the north. The Austrian Habsburg family had already taken effective control of the Czech lands (Bohemia), but its rule had been weak and indirect. Now, facing a powerful Turkish threat, the Habsburgs consolidated, strengthened, and ultimately extended their sphere of dominance. Only Poland, protected by buffer states, had a historical development that was not entirely preoccupied with the Turkish danger.

The Turks first crossed into the Balkans from Asia Minor in about 1350, and first defeated the Serbs in 1372. But it was the crushing Turkish victory at the battle of Kosovo Polje in 1389 that opened the way for the complete subjugation of first Serbia, then Bulgaria, Albania, and most of the rest of Southeastern Europe. Because the Turks retained their control in this area for some four hundred to five-hundred years, it is essential to understand their system of governing and the enormous impact that it had upon the peoples caught up in it.

The most important aspect of Turkish rule from the historical perspective is that its influence was principally political and economic but was quite limited in religion and culture. That is to say, the Turks rarely attempted to destroy the religious, cultural, and ethnic identities of the subject peoples. All of the nationalities that lived in Southeastern Europe before the Turks came were still in existence after their withdrawal. The Ottoman rulers were Moslems, but they did not usually force their subjects to convert. Some people chose Islam anyway, for there were advantages in belonging to the official faith, but the overwhelming majority of the population remained Christian. The Turks, for the most part, respected and protected religious freedom.[2]

The Ottomans imposed a sort of feudal system on the Balkans. Turkish military leaders were given estates, and in return they paid taxes and provided soldiers and their own service to the central authority (the sultan) in time of war. The landlords in turn taxed the peasants who lived on this land. Though scarcely a blessing to the masses, Ottoman feudalism was not nearly so onerous at the beginning as its Christian European counterpart. Peasants did not become bound serfs or slaves, and, so long as the central government at Istanbul was strong, their taxes were kept within reason. An important side effect of Ottoman rule was that most of the Balkan peoples never developed a *native* class of landowning aristocrats (the Turks were later expelled), and thus in modern times have been spared some of the social problems that have plagued other societies.

Nevertheless, the advantages of Turkish rule were relative and abstract, for the people fiercely resented their subjugation. Even though the Turks respected the Christian religion and allowed a great deal of autonomy, they considered themselves and other Moslems to be superior. A dispute between a Moslem and a Christian would most likely be settled in favor of the former. There were also some real evils. The most notorious was the *devshirme* (child levy), in which carefully selected Christian children were taken from their parents and brought up as Moslems and professional soldiers in the sultan's personal army.

The effectiveness of Ottoman rule began to disintegrate over the centuries. In the early years, a flourishing economy and a carefully controlled system brought a degree of prosperity to all the people, even the peasants. But when the Turkish war machine lost its momentum, the economy slumped and the central authority became weak and corrupt.[3] By the late-eighteenth century, Istanbul was frequently powerless to control the landlords who had begun to exploit ruthlessly the peasantry. Internal revolts then began to reinforce the external pressures on Ottoman sovereignty.

Serbia

Serbia was the first of the states to be defeated by the Ottoman Turks and probably suffered more than any of the other lands. The Serbs' troubles stemmed partly from their own rebelliousness and partly from the fact that their territory lay right in the center of the thrust of Turkish military operations—northwest from Istanbul toward Vienna. The cities and towns of Serbia became Moslem fortresses and trading centers. The hills and forests remained Serbian, however, and they were usually infested with *hajduks,* Christian bandits who preyed upon the Turks.

Montenegro

The people of Montenegro remained in their mountain strongholds and fought one long, continuous war with the Turks. Though they did lose some battles, the Montenegrins were never really conquered. They developed a unique form of government in which they were ruled by a *vladika,* a man who was both prince and bishop, both spiritual and secular leader. Yet despite these differences, and their isolation in the mountains, the Montenegrins did not lose contact with the Serbs of Serbia proper.

Albania

The Albanian experience was similar to that of Montenegro. The Turks, desiring secure access to the Adriatic ports, mounted a tremendous struggle and eventually subjugated most of the country by about 1400. But some fifty years later, an Albanian chieftain, the legendary Skanderbeg, successfully cleared the land of Ottoman forces for twenty-five years. After his death, however, the Turks reasserted their power. Many Albanians, particularly in the lowlands of the south, then converted to Islam and joined the Ottoman army and administration. In contrast, the mountains of the far north were much less affected by Islam and the Turkish system.

Bulgaria

The Bulgarians, like the Serbs, were weak and disunited when the Turks arrived, and were thoroughly defeated only a few years after the battle of Kosovo. The suffering of the Serbs and Bulgarians under Ottoman rule was similar. Even so, the two Slav peoples retained their distinct identities during nearly half a millennium under the Turkish yoke largely because of the tenacity of their separate Orthodox churches.

Wallachia and Moldavia

The experience of the Romanians in the two Danubian principalities during the Ottoman period was markedly different from that of the other Balkan peoples. These lands lay on the right flank of the main Turkish thrust; consequently, the sultans preferred to keep them as buffer states rather than to garrison and defend them. To some extent this arrangement was won by the Romanian princes, who resisted Ottoman control throughout the fifteenth century; nevertheless, it is clear that the Turks ultimately had the power to impose whatever system they wished.

The arrangement between the Turks and the Romanians was fairly simple. The Romanians were allowed to keep their own rulers and to control their own internal affairs. In return they agreed to remain loyal and to pay an annual tribute to the sultan. The system worked badly from the start. The Romanians were frequently disloyal, and the Turks began to sell the thrones of the traitorous Romanian princes to the highest bidders. This led to a sort of large-scale tax-farming. The Romanian peasantry thus had the doubtful distinction of being enserfed and impoverished by their own rather than a foreign nobility. Aside from this, the material condition of the population in Wallachia and Moldavia was little different from that in the rest of the Balkans.

Hungary

The Hungarian kingdom, still including Transylvania, Croatia, and Slovakia, had to bear the full force of the Turkish attack after the Balkan states succumbed. The Hungarians fought valiantly for more than a century, frequently going on the offensive, but were finally crushed by the Turks at the crucial battle of Mohács in 1526. The Ottoman victory was so complete that they then went on to occupy nearly all the Hungarian state except Slovakia and Transylvania (Transylvania then became an independent state under Turkish protection).

Hungary was ruled by the Turks for more than a century and a half, but the feudal system reemerged after the liberation that took place between 1683 and 1699. An important change, however, came from the fact that, upon the death of the Magyar king at Mohács, the Hungarian crown had been added to the growing collection of the Austrian Habsburg family.

The Habsburg Empire

The character of the Habsburg Empire was largely defined by a fact that it was put together primarily through marriage rather than conquest. As new territories were acquired, the Austrian-based Habsburg family gathered new responsibilities as well as new titles. As an example, the monarch in Austria was also king of Hungary, but in contrast to Austria, Hungary had a limited monarchy in which the noble landlords were to be consulted on taxes, wars, and other important measures. Similar restrictions prevailed to a greater or lesser extent in other areas such as Bohemia.

Even so, in the period from 1400 to 1800 the Habsburg rulers were not greatly affected by local restrictions. Their empire was vigorous, expanding, and held together in part by its own momentum. Moreover, the feudal landlords usually considered their interests to be consistent with those of the monarchy. Except for a brief period in Bohemia, nationalism was not yet an important factor in politics.

The Turks besieged Vienna twice, first in 1529, and then again in 1683. The second effort was very nearly successful, but the Viennese were saved when Poland came to Austria's aid at the crucial moment. The Ottoman power declined rapidly after the failure of their last all-out effort, and the Habsburgs soon drove the Turks to the south bank of the Danube. The sultan formally acknowledged the loss of Hungary, including influence over Transylvania, by the Treaty of Karlowitz in 1699.

In the succeeding century, the Habsburgs added Romanian Bucovina, Polish Galicia, and parts of the Dalmatian coast to their empire, and consolidated their control over most of northern Italy (though Silesia was lost to Prussia). At the turn of the century, only France rivalled Austria as a European power.

The Czech Lands

The placid flow of history in Bohemia came to an abrupt end in the fifteenth century. A Czech, Jan Hus, who was a founder of the Protestant Hussite movement named after him, started a revolt against the Catholic establishment in about 1400. Hus and his followers were defeated after a protracted struggle, but the conflict had assumed a Slav-against-German character that smoldered for two centuries until it reemerged in the general religious conflict of the seventeenth century. The problems were exacerbated in 1526 when the Bohemian crown was lost to the German Habsburgs.

The Thirty Years War (1618–1648) began in Bohemia for religious reasons, but once again assumed a Protestant Slav-against-Catholic German orientation. This time, however, the Czechs were clearly committed to one side, and when they were crushed by the Austrians (Battle of White Mountain, 1620), it was much more of a national disaster than the defeat of the Hussite rebellion two centuries earlier. The victorious Habsburgs replaced the disloyal Czech nobles with Catholics from all over Europe. As a consequence, the Czech people, though still an overwhelming majority of the population, no longer had any real voice in the affairs of the kingdom of Bohemia. The totality of the Habsburg conquest had the effect of suppressing Czech national consciousness for nearly two centuries.

Poland

The Polish state, unlike the rest of Eastern Europe, began the fifteenth century on an ascending note. The Union with Lithuania continued, and in 1410 the Germans were defeated and driven from most of the Pomeranian coast. Poland-Lithuania then turned eastward once more, asserting its control over nearly all of today's Ukraine. After a formal union in 1569, Poland emerged as clearly the stronger partner and eventually submerged Lithuania. The apex of power for the Polish state came at the beginning of the seventeenth century, when Poland briefly controlled the capital of the Muscovite (Russian) state. But when the effort to seize Russia failed, the momentum quickly shifted against Poland. Most of the Ukraine was lost to Russia in 1654–1667. After that, all expansion ceased, and Poland remained fairly stable until it disappeared in 1795.

The decline of Poland was largely a consequence of internal weaknesses exacerbated by geographical vulnerability. Feudal institutions had prospered from the start, and the central power was never able to crush the independence of the local landlords. The result was a limited monarchy similar in some ways to that of England under the Magna Carta. But Poland lacked the security of an English channel; her neighbors to both east and west found it easy to intervene in the struggles between king and nobles. Finally, in 1772, 1793, and 1795, Prussia, Austria, and Russia were able simply to eliminate Poland by partitioning it among themselves.

History, 1800–1848

*T*HE NINETEENTH CENTURY added a vital new factor to the history of Eastern Europe: nationalism. Although there had been some national consciousness and even some national conflicts in earlier times, nationalism in its new form was a purer and more powerful phenomenon. In the past, dynastic questions (e.g., Poland), religious differences (e.g., Czechs and Germans), or the simple desire to overthrow a burdensome ruler or system (e.g., the Balkan peoples and the Turks) had always been the dominant factors. National feelings, where they existed, were always vague and secondary. After 1800, however, the situation was reversed, and nationalism became the key element; other issues were ancillary to this main theme. Because of nationalism's extreme importance in contemporary as well as historical Eastern Europe, it is appropriate to spend some time discussing the nature of the phenomenon together with the manner of its impact.

There are many definitions of nationalism, some of them quite complex, but all have a basic goal and a fundamental definition at their core. The goal is the fusion of a people and a state in a nation-state. Nationality is narrowly defined; it is more than a cultural group—it is a linguistic group. Thus, although a number of people may have a nearly identical history and culture, they are not a part of the same nationality if they speak different languages (or different mother tongues in the case of those who speak more than one language). The fusion of nationality and state in a nation-state—the goal of nationalism—is then simply the idea that people of certain nationality should have more or less complete control over the land that they inhabit. While the principle is fairly clear and straightforward, the further assumptions made by nationalists are many and diverse, and in specific cases, particularly in Eastern Europe, conflicting.

Nationalism in its most modern form is fundamentally an outgrowth of the French Revolution. The original internal struggle that began in France in 1789 was not itself nationalistic, but it became so when the other states of Europe attempted to suppress the successful revolutionaries. The French, who no longer had a dynasty to rally around, made an appeal to the masses—to the *French nationality*—to save *France*, the nation-state, as well as the revolution from its enemies. France, the country, was not actually in danger (the revolutionary government was), but for whatever reason or reasons of human psychology, it was easier and more successful to plead for aid to a concept based on a physical entity (France) rather than for a more abstract concept (the revolution).

The strategy of the French leaders (which was spontaneous and conceived out of desperation rather than design) was extremely effective. The aroused masses produced a popular army, backed by an entire population, that destroyed the feudal forces of the other European powers; nationalism and a new type of war were created at the same time. As the French armies moved across the frontiers of France, they took a new philosophy with them. The effect was considerable. The French fostered other nationalisms in a direct sense. For example, Napoleon recreated a Polish state (and thereby received substantial military assistance in the war against Russia) and created an Italian state. The French built nationalism in an indirect sense as well, for opposing peoples like the Spaniards and the Germans turned toward nationalism as a vehicle to rally people to resist a conquering foe, the French.

The defeat of France by the coalition of Europe did not diminish the growing power of nationalism. The ideas associated with this concept became a predominant intellectual force, especially among younger educated people throughout Europe. In France, nationalism was normally and naturally associated with the revolution and thus was strongest among those who leaned to the left in politics. But this leftist orientation was neither necessary nor universal, even extreme supporters of autocracy could and did consider themselves to be nationalists. This became one of the many contradictions of nationalism.

Even as the capital of a defeated nation, Paris was still the center of the developing ideology (or ideologies) of nationalism. This was even more the case after a second French revolution in 1830 overthrew again the old monarchy. Young people from all over Western and Eastern Europe came to study in Paris, and few returned home without being affected to some extent by the French.

Aside from study in France, the peoples of Eastern Europe came into contact with nationalism from a number of other sources. The Poles, because of their long association with France and early experience with nationalism, became living symbols of revolutionary nationalism.[1] Many of them traveled about Eastern Europe and offered encouragement and sometimes direct assistance to leaders of other national groups. Two peoples who had long had extensive contact with France, the Greeks and the Russians, also helped to spread the new ideas (though not, of course, as deliberately as the Poles). The German universities, particularly Berlin, also were strongly influenced by nationalism and were host to large numbers of East European students.

Given the extremely diverse backgrounds of the peoples of Eastern Europe, it is not surprising that the speed and depth of penetration of nationalist ideas varied considerably by area. It is worth noting, however, that nationalism affected first and most strongly those peoples who had the strongest traditions of national independence: Poles, Greeks, and Hungarians. Since these peoples in turn effected changes in the reactions of others in their areas, it seems most appropriate to look at the history of the period 1800–1848 on a regional basis.

The Peoples of the Russian Empire

The Poles

The only East European nationality in the Russian Empire was the Polish, but as a people the Poles were second only to the French in the intensity of their nationalism. In fact, the close ties between France and Poland had persisted for several centuries. It was thus not surprising that the victorious Napoleon decreed the revival of a Polish state in 1807. But the subsequent defeat of imperial France was also the end of Poland, and many Polish leaders fled to Paris. The Congress of Vienna (1815) returned the Poles to their captors, and the nation's future looked bleak.

In view of the bitterness that prevailed between Poles and Russians, it seemed probable that the returning overlord would severely punish what (from the Russian point of view) had been treason of the most flagrant sort. Yet this did not happen. Tsar Alexander I of Russia was endowed with a liberal education and was heir to an erratic temperament. He chose to provide Poland with a constitution—something denied to Russia proper. This document, though far from advanced, was nonetheless remarkable for the time and place.

Under Alexander's constitution, the Polish people had no voice in foreign affairs, and the army was controlled by a Russian grand duke (Alexander's brother), but an elected assembly of nobles had considerable autonomy with respect to domestic problems. Most important, Polish cultural freedom was virtually unrestricted; Polish schools and a Polish university functioned without serious interference from any quarter. Poles could travel freely and trade where they liked. The Poles, and particularly the Polish gentry who dominated society, were almost a privileged group within the Russian Empire.

Yet Polish nationalism had advanced to the point where even these exceptional concessions were insufficient. The Poles wanted complete independence.[2] Thus, when a successful revolution occurred in France in 1830, the Poles quickly followed suit and rose up against the Russians. The expected assistance from France never came close to materializing, however, and only a cholera epidemic delayed the crushing Russian victory. A new tsar, the grim Nicholas I, revoked Alexander's constitution and replaced it with the Organic Statute of 1832, a law that made Poland an integral part of the Russian Empire.

The defeat of Poland was complete. All internal autonomy was abolished and cultural freedom was greatly restricted. The leaders of the revolt, the best educated and most dynamic leaders of the nobility, were either killed or driven into exile. The effect was so devastating that when the revolutionary hurricane of 1848 swept across Europe, many Poles were involved in foreign lands, but in Poland itself the heavy hand of Russia kept a firm grip.

The Jews

The situation of the Jews in Eastern Europe, always precarious, could only be made worse by the emergence of nationalism.[3] The Jews had traditionally looked toward the central power for protection against the prejudices that frequently afflicted the surrounding masses, and they were now faced with a movement that threatened that relationship. Moreover, the alternative of becoming nationalists themselves was not usually open to them. Though many Jews were as much native speakers of Polish, Czech, Hungarian, or other languages as anyone else, and even though religion per se was not a fundamental element in nationalism, the emphasis on traditional peasant values and culture as the core of nationality tended to exclude the overwhelmingly urban, cosmopolitan Jews. Nor did East European nationalists show themselves to be any less vulnerable to the varying forms of anti-Semitism than the peasantry from which such ideas usually emanated.

The Peoples of the Habsburg Empire

The Habsburg Empire had suffered greatly in the quarter-century of struggle with France, and the dominant political figure of the empire, Prince Metternich, was determined to do everything possible to eliminate the new ideas and restore the old order. This reactionary philosophy spread throughout the Habsburg lands, and thanks to the Habsburg emperor's special position in the Germanic confederation, to much of Germany as well. In a sense Metternich was successful, for one could argue that his policies were largely responsible for delaying changes that appear (at least in retrospect) to have been inevitable.

On the other hand, it seems that the isolation and the tendency to be suspicious of new things had a very negative effect on the modernization of the empire. While the industrial revolution grew and expanded throughout western Europe and even in Russia, the Austrian lands fell further and further behind. Although the Habsburg Empire appeared to most contemporaries to be the strongest state in Europe, internally it was beset by the twin challenges provided by an awakening national consciousness and simultaneous economic stagnation. However, the extreme seriousness of these problems did not become apparent until much later.

The Czechs

The political history of the Czech lands from 1620 to 1800 is largely written in German, so complete had been the defeat of the Czechs. Nevertheless, despite fairly systematic oppression, the Czech language and culture survived. For many years only the peasants were truly Czech, but an economic upturn and consequent rise in population in the mid- to late-eighteenth century helped to revive a Czech middle class and weaken the German dominance of the towns and cities. Since the Czech area was the most suitable part of the Habsburg Empire for industrial development, its prosperity continued into the nineteenth century. The new Czech middle class developed a strong interest in education, and thus became the nucleus of a renascent national movement.[4]

By the first years of the nineteenth century, the Czechs had a small but significant intelligentsia of their own. In its approach to nationalism this group naturally tended to follow the German pattern, which stressed the study of peasant culture in order to find the essence of nationality. Historical studies were of key importance as well, and the historian František Palacký was the most influential of a number of skilled students of the Czech's past. Interestingly, the leaders in Prague tended to be preoccupied with the Slavic peoples as a whole, and the Czech capital was long the center of a pan-Slav movement.

By the middle of the century, the Czechs had succeeded in reestablishing their language in many areas; they had also revived their literature and generally restored the stature of their culture—at least in their own eyes. Their national development had not yet taken on any coherent political form, however. When the revolutionary storm broke out in 1848, Czechs took part but not as an organized national force. In the cities, the Czech national interest was often confused with the demands for liberal reform, which were also shared by many Germans. In the countryside, the peasants were far more interested in practical matters such as tax and work obligations than in abstract questions that had little impact on daily life.

The Czechs were not ready to make a strong national effort in 1848; nationalism had not yet become the major factor in political life. But the process had clearly begun, and the general dislocation of that revolutionary period served to accelerate the movement.

The Slovaks

The Slovaks, like the Czechs, were under the political and cultural domination of a foreign nobility. But the Hungarian control of Slovakia had lasted longer than the German ascendancy in Bohemia and Moravia and had always been more complete; the Slovaks had never really had a state of their own.[5] This inhibiting factor in national development was reinforced by two other problems. First, the economic revival that was affecting the Czech lands did not penetrate the remote hill regions of Slovakia. And perhaps more important, those Slovak leaders who were first influenced by nationalism were unsure as to which direction their efforts should take. There were compelling reasons for viewing the Slovak language as simply a dialect of Czech, and casting the Slovaks' lot with their more numerous and powerful brethren to the northwest. On the other hand, the approach to nationalism that stressed peasant culture as the true soul of a people precluded such an association because differences at the village level were significant. Taken together, these weaknesses and contradictions explain why Slovak nationalism was still in its infancy in 1848.

The Hungarians

The situation of the Hungarians within the Habsburg Empire was quite different from that of their Slavic neighbors. Until their defeat by the Turks in 1526, the Hungarians had been the dominant nationality in a large state that had had considerable influence in Europe for more than five hundred years. Though the Turkish conquest had been followed by rapid absorption of the Hungarian state by the Habsburgs, the native aristocracy and political institutions had remained basically intact. Technically, Hungary was linked to the Austrian Empire only by the fact that the Habsburg emperor was also the Hungarian king.

Despite the importance of this independent framework, the Hungarians had not made any major effort to assert autonomy before 1800.[6] This was in part a consequence of relative weakness. But much more significant was the fact that the dominant political element in Hungary, the aristocratic owners of large estates, was quite content with Habsburg rule. Aside from occasional and short-lived aberrations, the emperors in Vienna had effected a sort of symbiosis with the Magyar leaders, in which imperial protection of the economic interests of the nobility was rewarded with political loyalty.[7]

Thus, although the structure for the development of nationalism existed in Hungary, there were extremely powerful elements inhibiting its full development. Since a country as closely connected to the West as Hungary could not remain immune to such an important trend, nationalism did begin to develop, but at first along exclusively cultural lines. The overwhelming focus of this change was an intense interest in the revival of the Hungarian language. Though never actually suppressed, the Magyar tongue had yielded in commerce and literature to German, and was not even used in the national assembly, where the delegates still spoke Latin.

While the chief outward appearance of Hungarian nationalism in the first half of the nineteenth century was the flourishing literature in the native language, other changes were maturing quietly below the surface. Not all Hungarians were either owners of large estates or downtrodden serfs. The population of Hungary also included a significant number of nobles who owned relatively small plots of land. Worsening economic conditions and Vienna's exclusive concern with the large estate owners gradually produced a social element that was attracted to the political as well as to the cultural side of nationalism.

The Slovenes

The very small size and population of Slovenia effectively precluded a nationalism that was oriented toward national independence. Nevertheless, German, Italian, and French influences were strong in this relatively prosperous area, and a group of Slovene intellectuals made important contributions to the cultural development of their people.[8] Initially associated with Catholic organizations, this movement was not opposed by the Habsburgs.

The Germans

The philosophy of nationalism had a generally divisive impact on Germans within the Habsburg Empire. Nationalism did have the expected effect of sharply increasing all Germans' consciousness of their identity as a nation, but the idea of national-territorial identity was obviously directly contradictory to the raison d'être of a multinational empire. A few Germans reacted to this dilemma by accepting as inevitable the disintegration of the Habsburg realm and the creation of national states, including a united Germany. A far larger number accepted the idea of a German state but opposed the aspirations of the other nationalities and favored the forced Germanization of the peoples of the empire. The official Habsburg view, for obvious reasons, rejected entirely the idea of national states, as well as forced denationalization. This defense of the status quo was betrayed, however, by an increased emphasis on the use of the German language in official affairs. Overall, the lack of a unified German view had the inevitable effect of exacerbating the growing confusion.

The Croatians

The situation of the Croatians was in many ways analogous to that of the Slovaks. Long dominated by the Hungarians, their process of national development was confused by debate as to the nature of their relationship with the Serbs, who spoke essentially the same language, but who had an acutely different cultural-religious background. On the other hand, the Croatians did have an important national history, and they were not nearly so isolated and impoverished as the Slovaks. Croatian national development was thus at first largely cultural, although political questions were never far from the surface.[9]

The Serbs, Romanians, and Italians

Although the Habsburg Empire contained a significant number of Serbs and Romanians, the great majority of these peoples lived in the Ottoman Empire, and their affairs will be discussed in the next section. It should also be remembered that there were large numbers of Italians under Habsburg rule at this time and that, taken as a group, they were the most nationally conscious and consequently the most disaffected people in the empire.

The Peoples of the Ottoman Empire

The Ottoman Empire had ceased to be a great power at the end of the seventeenth century; by the beginning of the nineteenth, it was coming to be known as the "Sick Man of Europe." While western ideas penetrated this isolated area less easily than elsewhere, the rapidly decaying administrative system of the Turks provided fertile ground for political movements which favored change.

The Serbs

The first people to throw off the Ottoman yoke were the Serbs, who carried out a successful revolt that led to the limited autonomy of a large part of Serbia in 1816. This movement was not a reflection of the new nationalism, however. Instead, it represented the continuation of a struggle that had never really stopped since the battle of Kosovo in 1389. The Serbian tradition of resistance had long been manifest in the ceaseless effort to maintain a Serbian national church, and it was reinforced and encouraged by the unbroken independence of Montenegro. In later years, the Serbian cause was strengthened by the large contingent of refugees who lived on the Habsburg side of the frontier and gained valuable military experience in that empire's army.[10]

Ultimately, however, the most important factor for the Serbs was the backing of Russia. The tsars often professed support for their Slavic brethren, although they frequently broke their word when expediency led them to leave the Serbs suddenly in the lurch. But the situation stabilized long enough to create the Ottoman recognition of partial Serbian autonomy in 1826 (after twenty-two years of fighting) and then again at the end of a Russo-Turkish war that led to full autonomy in 1830.

It is important to reemphasize that this stage of the Serbian struggle was not really nationalistic. In addition to the tradition of resistance to Turkish rule, the key issue was quite pragmatic: security of the local population from cruel and despotic local governors. On several occasions, the Serbian forces were allied with the sultan in Istanbul against rebellious Turks living in Serbia. Moreover, very few Serbs were literate, and virtually none understood or cared about the theoretical niceties of nationalism. Nevertheless, the very fact of a quasi-independent Serbia served as a symbol for both the pragmatic and theoretical revolutionaries that were to follow.

The Greeks

While the Serbs were preoccupied with local issues, their Greek neighbors to the south were very much in the mainstream of the new nationalism. Even the harshest periods of Ottoman rule had not been able to eradicate the great tradition of Greek culture. In addition, many Greeks, especially those living abroad as traders, were in intimate contact with trends in the west. An explosion in Greece was only a matter of time.

The revolt finally began in 1821 and continued for years in a struggle of unrelieved bitterness in which Greeks and Turks engaged in wholesale massacres of the rival populations. The rebels were successful at first, but their own divisions prevented them from following through and permitted the Turks to recover and counterattack. The Greeks were on the brink of total defeat when Britain, France, and Russia intervened and defeated the Ottomans. The Treaty of Adrianople (1829) not only established the independence of Greece, but also guaranteed the autonomy of Serbia and put the Romanian principalities under Russian protection.

The Albanians

The Albanian situation in the first part of the nineteenth century was not really any different from the earlier period. The Turks were still in control of all the main centers, the economy was still extremely backward, and the Albanians were not on good enough terms with their neighbors to unite with them against the Ottomans. Education in the native language did not exist, and there was very little national consciousness, let alone nationalism.[11] Change would not come to Albania for many decades.

The Bulgarians

The outbreak of the Greek revolt had an immediate effect on the development of Bulgarian nationalism, albeit in a peculiar and indirect way. The Greeks had long dominated the Bulgarian Orthodox Church (and therefore also the schools) as well as much of the commerce in the Bulgarian lands. This had been so because the sultan in Istanbul had traditionally been advised on key matters by a class of Greeks who had become wealthy and powerful in exchange for their service to the Ottoman Empire. The Greek revolt of 1821 put an abrupt end to this system.

Freed of Greek control, the Bulgarians spent much of the decades of the thirties and forties patiently building a truly Bulgarian Church and school system.[12] This overwhelmingly peasant people worked hard and sacrificed much, with the result that literacy grew at an astounding rate. On the other hand, a Bulgarian commercial class also developed rapidly, aided by a reorientation of trade in which Bulgarian products replaced Serbian, Greek, and Romanian goods previously purchased by the imperial government.

The Bulgarians were exposed to nationalist ideas primarily through the presence of Bulgarian students at the increasingly radical Russian universities. This process was slow, however, and did not amount to much until the 1860s. In the interim, the Bulgarians, who of all non-Turks were physically closest to Istanbul and thus even more firmly under the Ottoman yoke, concentrated on exploiting the advantages that were available to them.

The Romanians

The Romanians, like the Bulgarians, also profited from the destruction of Greek power within the Ottoman Empire. This was particularly true in the political arena when in 1821 eleven decades of rule by corrupt Greek princes (known as Phanariots) was ended. Trade also shifted away from Greek hands. While the Romanians had long had the use of their own language in church and to a lesser extent in schools, before 1829 Greeks under Russian protection had continued to dominate much of the Romanian Orthodox Church.[13]

The Russian protectorate that began officially in 1829 (after the Russo-Turkish War) had a mixed impact. The Russians forced constitutions on each of the separate principalities, and these documents had the overall effect of legitimizing the economic and political rights of the landed aristocracy at the expense of the long-suffering peasantry. This greatly reinforced the existing feudal system, which was unique in the Balkans. On the other hand, the Russian officers in the army of occupation brought with them the idea of nationalism—direct from France where many had been stationed at the end of the Napoleonic Wars.

The irony of the act of officers of the world's greatest reactionary power spreading revolutionary ideas is matched by the other major source of Romanian nationalism. The Habsburg authorities in Transylvania had long sought to Catholicize the Romanian inhabitants of that province. The reasons were twofold: (1) the imperial authorities were devout Catholics; (2) more Catholics would serve as a counterweight to the largely Protestant Hungarians and Germans in the area. Through the device of the Uniate Church (Orthodox in ritual and most practices, but loyal to the pope) some conversions were achieved. The most important result, however, was not at all what was expected.

A number of Romanian Uniate priests were sent to Rome for training. There they developed a strong interest in the Latin origins of the Romanian people and language. Their research led them to propose the establishment of schools that concentrated on the native language and the study of ancient Rome and of sister Latin cultures. Since the climate for this type of instruction was better in Moldavia and Wallachia than in Transylvania, some of the teachers emigrated, and a substantial number of their Moldavian and Wallachian students were in turn inspired to continue their studies in France. Paris in the 1840s, when most of these students arrived, was a hotbed of nationalist and revolutionary ideas, and perhaps as a consequence of this sequence of events, the Romanians were second only to the Poles in their attachment to the new nationalism.

1848

As the nineteenth century approached its midpoint, serious societal tensions became more evident. The tremendous reaction that set in after 1815 was not able to eliminate the social and political aspirations raised by the French Revolution; instead it merely pushed them below the surface where they retained undiminished strength. The situation that would unleash these forces began with a serious agricultural crisis in the 1840s— known in Europe as the "hungry 40s" because of repeated crop failures. At the same time, the dislocation and instability brought about by the beginning of the industrial revolution created masses of starving workers in the cities.

The revolution that broke out in Paris in February 1848 was a reaction to the extreme nature of these tensions, and the spread of the revolution across much of the rest of Europe was very rapid. The focus of this text is, of course, Eastern Europe, but certain aspects of the revolution in the west had a long-term impact on the east. Most important in this context are the facts that: (1) the eventual defeat of the radicals in Paris had the effect ultimately of separating the political left from the ideology of nationalism; and (2) the various revolutions in Germany, though all defeated, added impetus to a previously immature German nationalism that was now to become a major factor in the future.

Of the three great empires that controlled all of Eastern Europe, one, the Russian, was unaffected by the revolutionary wave of 1848, while the second, the Ottoman, was only slightly disturbed by a revolt in the Romanian principality of Wallachia. Yet the Habsburg, the largest and, to external appearances the strongest, was nearly destroyed by unrest that penetrated even the remotest corners of its vast territory.

The revolution of 1848–1849 in the Habsburg lands was an extraordinarily complicated event in which conflicting social, political, and national forces were locked in a series of struggles marked by great bitterness and shifting alliances. The first phase of the revolt was primarily urban and largely involved the uprising of the German students and middle classes of Vienna and Prague. Faced with strong opposition at its very core, the weak imperial administration yielded. The Habsburgs granted a series of reforms comparable to those demanded by democratic revolutionaries in the West (representative government, freedom of press, assembly, and religion) and sent the unhappy Metternich into exile.

A brief period of apparent peace was followed by a revolt in the Italian lands—where nationalists had long been awaiting an opportunity and sensed that the time was ripe after learning of the first major concessions from Vienna. The Habsburgs sent troops into Italy, but many of those directed to move south were Hungarian. This unpleasant assignment had the effect of finally bringing to the surface the latent political nationalism of the Magyars. Ignoring the loyalist aristocrats, nationalist leaders rallied around the fiery orator Louis Kossuth and demanded full autonomy for Hungary.

The Hasburgs refused Kossuth's demands and prepared to fight in Hungary as well as in Italy. This reactionary move again brought revolt to the cities where radicals, discontented with the failure to implement the reforms promised earlier, were sympathetic to the Hungarians. The imperial court was forced to flee Vienna and seek refuge in the Moravian countryside. At this point it appeared that the Habsburg Empire would disintegrate within a matter of weeks.

The Habsburgs were rejuvenated, however, by a new emperor, Franz-Joseph, whose youthful determination made a sharp contrast with the chaos fostered by his feeble-minded predecessor. New advisers appeared as well, and together they plotted a series of counterattacks. The first of these was the implementation of a sweeping land reform (actually promulgated before the accession of the new emperor), which had the effect of moving the majority of the peasantry from a neutral or occasionally antigovernment posture back into loyalty to the empire. The second was to play the nationalities off against each other.

From the very beginning, Kossuth and the other leaders of the Hungarian revolution had made it clear that their concept of Hungary embraced the Crownlands of St. Stephen (i.e., including Croatia, Slovakia, and Transylvania as well as Hungary proper) and that only Magyars would have rights to full social, economic, and political equality within this area. Non-Magyars were not denied access to these rights, but their achievement of full citizenship was to be dependent on a change of nationality. Thus, Kossuth offered the minorities the opportunity to become Magyars.[14]

The Habsburg authorities did not need to be told that this policy would not be popular with the Croats, Romanians, and Slovaks. Within a short period of time an army of Croatians loyal to the emperor had been organized, and under the leadership of General Jelačić had helped to subdue the rebels in Vienna and had then turned against the Hungarians. At the same time, a smaller but no less spirited army of Romanians under a leader named Avram Iancu was harassing the Hungarian rear. The Slovaks were not able to create an army of their own, but their open hostility also hampered the Hungarian efforts. The collective resistance of these nationalities destroyed the inertia of Kossuth's rebellion and put him on the defensive.

The Hungarians were brave, determined fighters, and the frustrated Habsburg armies were unable to apply the *coup de grace*. Indeed, under the leadership of the brilliant Polish General Joseph Bem, the Magyars were still fighting in the spring of 1849 and even seemed to have the potential to inflict a critical defeat on their enemies. Finally, the Austrian emperor appealed to the Russian tsar for aid, and in the summer of 1849, a huge Russian army swept into Transylvania and ended the Hungarian revolution—itself the final remnant of the storm that first appeared in February of 1848.

The popular phrase "spring of nations" is an accurate term for the events of 1848–1849 in Eastern Europe. Class struggle and the clash between liberal and conservative opinions were at the core of the original explosion, but these elements soon became secondary to the conflict of nationalities. The central authorities were able to gain some strength through social and economic concessions, but these were not sufficient to end the revolt. On the one hand they did not break the loyalty of the Hungarian peasantry to Kossuth; on the other, they did not provide the inspiration necessary to send Croats, Romanians, and Slovaks into battle against Hungarians of the same social class. Only nationalism appears to explain these phenomena.

While one could argue that the peasant masses themselves were not thoroughly nationalistic and had little more than a rather confused national consciousness, there is clear evidence that their leaders were nationalists to some extent and that these men were able to command the peasants' loyalty at least partly on the basis of nationalist sentiment. Despite the fact that the nationalist movements were vanquished in 1848–1849, defeat only seemed to make them stronger. The Hungarians were crushed but unrepentant. The Croats, Romanians, and Slovaks were not rewarded for their loyalty to the emperor and in frustration and anger became more inclined to think of their own independence as a goal. The Czechs and others who had been less directly involved as nationalities in nationalist movements began to wonder if they should have been more active. After 1848, nationalists were more often militant radicals than romantics.

$$\underline{\quad 4 \quad}$$

History, 1848–1914

The Russian Empire, 1848–1914

ALTHOUGH the Russian Empire was not directly affected by the revolutions of 1848, the Crimean War of 1853–55 provided an experience as shattering as a revolution. The Russians not only lost the war, but they were forced to realize that their system of government was corrupt, inefficient, and in need of a thorough overhaul. The 1860s were, therefore, years of reforms. In addition to the abolition of serfdom, the military, the legal system, local government, and other facets of the administrative structure were changed significantly. The drive for reform did not affect the status of the East European minorities (Poles, Ukrainians, and Jews). In fact, the Polish revolt of 1863 (see below) hardened not only the Russian governing circles but also the Russian revolutionary left against the minorities.

The Russians were now experiencing a strong nationalistic movement of their own. Although most reformers from the time of Peter the Great (d. 1725) had considered that Russia's future lay in modernization (synonymous with Westernization at least in this case), by the mid-nineteenth century an increasing number of official and unofficial thinkers saw Russia's future in her past. Accepting the West European concept of the peasantry as the heart and soul of the nation, they looked to the early communal form of village life as their ideal. The government itself tried to revive this tradition in the wake of the abolition of serfdom. Some revolutionary leaders went even further and claimed that Russia should renounce the evils of the industrial west in favor of a simple, harmonious, pastoral society. The government, anxious to strengthen Russia's stature as a world power (especially after the Crimean debacle), strongly opposed this; nevertheless, the ideology had considerable impact.

If one considers that the Russians, whose remote habitat had long fostered a sort of xenophobia, had now chosen to embrace traditional

47

nationalism as well, it is not difficult to understand that the political climate for the minorities was not good. The Poles, ancient enemies from medieval times, were thought of as simple traitors after they revolted in 1863. The Russians' interest in pan-Slav, pan-Orthodox cultural movements could not encompass the hostile, Catholic Poles. In addition to the prejudices of a backward Christian peasantry, the Jews suffered the misfortune of being associated in the Russian mind with the Poles. The Ukrainians, to the extent that their aspirations to be a separate nation were noticed at all, were also considered to be traitors.

As Russian industrialization picked up steam in the latter decades of the century, the minority peoples were affected differently. In Poland proper, industrialization was especially swift, and both Poles and Jews prospered (at least by comparison to the rest of the empire). The Ukraine was scarcely affected, however; even the massive railroad-building effort of the tsarist regime was unable to improve significantly access to the countryside and thereby failed to stimulate efficient, market-oriented agriculture. The awkward land settlement following the abolition of serfdom contributed to this problem, and most peasants lived in grinding poverty. The situation of the Jews outside of the purely Polish areas was very bad and continued to get much worse. Both Russians and Ukrainians were far less tolerant than the Poles, and the ugly word *pogrom* (massacre) made its way into the vocabulary of the west before the century was out.

With limited exceptions, the various Russian revolutionary groups were highly nationalistic and blind to the seriousness of the nationality problem. In addition to Poles, Ukrainians, and Jews, the Russian Empire had substantial numbers of Byelorussians, Romanians, Lithuanians, Latvians, Estonians, Finns, Georgians, and Armenians, as well as millions of people of Turkic origin. Even Lenin's Bolsheviks were generally ignorant of the explosive potential of the non-Russian nationalities until they confronted it in the civil war that followed the revolution of 1917.

Before turning to discussions of the individual nationalities, a very brief sketch of the origins of Russian communism is appropriate. Even though industrializing rapidly, Russia was still an overwhelmingly rural and agricultural state by 1914. Only two cities—St. Petersburg (Leningrad) and Moscow—had any appreciable concentration of workers, and most of these were men fresh off the farm and completely lacking in proletarian consciousness. This was to prove irrelevant for, as elsewhere, Marxist socialism took root first not in the working class for which it was intended, but in the ranks of the disaffected members of the intelligentsia (the highly educated intellectually oriented segment of the population). Many of these people (whose backgrounds were overwhelmingly middle-class—not agrarian and proletarian) were frustrated by the lack of progress toward social justice in their society.

Russia was in many respects in a peculiar situation. She was able to adopt rather quickly a superficial industrialization (railroads, textile mills, foundries) and with these came all of the abuses already experienced in the West: sixteen-hour days, child labor, unsanitary housing, and more. But where Britain, France, and Germany had moved within a generation to alleviate the worst of these problems and consequently to give hope of further progress, Russia lacked the infrastructure (particularly the honest, professional bureaucracy) to carry out such reforms. Russia had also failed to implement a successful system of primary education. On the other hand, there was nothing backward about the Russian intelligentsia. Many young Russians were educated in the west, and western books and newspapers were still obtainable despite censorship. Thus, Russia had on one side a chaotic, inefficient, and inhumane society, and on the other a small but talented and articulate group of critics. In the middle stood an inept bureaucracy guided by an unskilled and indecisive leadership.

In such a situation some revolutionary orientation was inevitable. In the 1860s and 1870s, all sorts of radical groups prospered, including those who hoped to avoid the perils of modernity by turning the clock all the way back to the beginnings of recorded history. Despite the allegiance in varying degrees of a large part of the educated youth of the country, these movements failed. Like the government officials they hated, they were unable to overcome the inertia of Russian society. In their frustration they turned to terrorism, eventually succeeding in assassinating Tsar Alexander II in 1881. But the fact that they had merely exchanged a moderately enlightened incompetent for a reactionary one, not to mention the subsequent police counterterror, left the revolutionary movement disillusioned and in disarray.

It was after this passionate saga had run its course that Marxism began to gather adherents. Two aspects of this new philosophy had a special appeal for those Russians seeking radical change: first, the idea of harnessing the fruits of industrial society for the good of all seemed a reasonable alternative to the vast differentials between industrialist and worker which characterized the West (and also reflected all too closely the noble-serf relationship that they had so detested in their own country); second, the scientific pretensions of Marxism had enormous appeal. In all of the Western world the latter part of the nineteenth century was a time of acute rationalism and infatuation with science—the very word science carried the same connotation as magic had in earlier and more innocent times. The turn to rationalism and science was particularly strong among Russian radicals who had just witnessed the spectacular failure of a quasi-romantic revolutionary movement in their own country.

It is important to emphasize that even as late as 1917 there were very few Marxists in Russia. Other parties such as the liberal reformers and the agrarian radicals were far stronger. Yet the Marxists made a virtue of their small size by emphasizing organization and discipline. Their faith in the inevitable realization of their "scientifically" planned objectives also gave them a zeal and a determination that their opponents were hard pressed to match. Yet if Marxism were to succeed in Russia, it would somehow have to speak more directly to the problems of a Russian society which was still very different from that of the west. It took the creative genius of Lenin (see below) to solve this problem and thereby put the Marxists in position to seize power in the chaos of a nation suffering from war and revolution.

Poland in the Russian Empire, 1848–1914

As mentioned above, the Poles, considered by their contemporaries to be the most revolutionary of peoples, were unprepared and did not participate in the struggles of 1848. In part this was a consequence of the fact that the wounds from the battles of 1830–31 had not yet healed, but another factor also contributed. The voice of Poland in that most recent revolution, as well as in the entire history of the nation, had been that of the great landed aristocracy (the magnates) and the lesser nobles— referred to collectively as *szlachta* (nobility). After 1831, however, social changes began to have an effect. The peasantry developed a small but significant tendency to act independently. The growing middle class and the numerically small but politically powerful student-intellectual group were often actually hostile to noble leadership. Polish nationalism continued to be a vital, dynamic force, but it had lost the coherence imposed by a semi-feudal society.

In the decade and a half after 1848, a number of external forces alternately raised and lowered the hopes of nationalistic Poles. The defeat of the revolutionary movements of 1848 and the ensuing reaction in all of Europe was depressing and had the immediate effect of limiting the freedom of action of the Polish leaders in exile. Less well known, but certainly more important in the long run, was the abolition of tariff barriers between Russia and Poland in 1851. This helped to accelerate the growth of the already vigorous Polish industry, although it also tied the nation more closely to the East.

The hopes of the Poles were raised by the turn of France's Napoleon III from reaction at home to a sort of evangelistic nationalism abroad, by the Crimean War, by the unification and independence of Italy and Romania, and most important by the death of Tsar Nicholas I and the succession of the liberal Alexander II in 1855. But there were setbacks even here, however. The developing group of moderate and liberal thinkers and politicians in Russia proper had initially been sympathetic to the Poles. The revolt of 1830–31, directed against an oppressive tyrant, could be understood even by those who felt themselves to be loyal Russians. But obvious Polish sympathy for the British and French during the Crimean War (which included offers of military assistance) was another matter. Modern Russian nationalism was born in the struggle with the West in 1855–56, and as a consequence, the Poles were henceforth seen as simple traitors to Russia, unworthy of sympathy or assistance.

The Russian action that helped the Poles the most was one that was intended to hurt them: the repression of the Roman Catholic church. Though never outlawed, the Church after 1831 was subject to continuing harassment from St. Petersburg. Always a strong force in Polish society, Catholicism now acquired what the historian Piotr Wandycz describes as a "halo of martyrdom."[1] Thus the Church, which also had the advantages of strong organization and close ties to the West, became the rallying point for Polish nationalism. In many ways, this helped to minimize the impact of the growing social tensions in Poland.

Polish society in 1860 had four social classes. Two, the magnates and the gentry, were both a part of the *szlachta*, but their interests were increasingly divergent. The magnates, who had retained an amazing grip on their land and privileges after the revolution of 1830–31, were intensely nationalistic but also dependent economically on the feudal system; their counterparts elsewhere in the Russian Empire were the bedrock supporters of conservative autocracy. The magnates thus found themselves in a dilemma. Some Polish magnates abandoned the Polish cause for fear of its social and political consequences, while at the same time a large number gradually accepted the inevitability of the emancipation of the serfs. The majority attempted to ignore the issue, however, urging that it be suppressed until independence had been won.

The members of the gentry were also divided on the issue of land and freedom, the great majority favoring abolition or at least some compromise and only a fairly small percentage openly opposing an early resolution. Since of the eight to ten percent of the population that belonged to the *szlachta* only about five percent were magnates, the gentry attitude was particularly important. This class, deeply affected by nationalism, but also interested in the changes in the structure of society and economy that were taking place in the West, became the most dynamic in Polish society. From it came the political and intellectual elite that was to guide Poland for nearly a century.

The bourgeoisie was small in 1860. The original urban trading classes had been largely German or Jewish. As industry began to develop, more ethnic Poles from the gentry and some from the peasantry moved to the towns and participated in the new economic life. The gentry, many of whom owned enough land to provide some capital but not enough to assume an easy living, were especially prominent in the developing urban trades. Since at that time Poles were generally staunch advocates of equality for the Jews, Polish independence movements usually had the support of the Jewish townsmen. But the Russian or Russified bureaucrats in the towns were of course hostile, and they more than outweighed the importance of the Jews.

Below all of the other classes was the huge dark mass of the peasantry. For the most part politically inert, the peasants—as peasants everywhere—tended to react to direct stimuli rather than to abstract concepts. A consequence of this was a certain amount of resistance to revolutionary activity. To most of the peasants, struggle against the Russians was associated with the loss of life and destruction that occurred in 1830–31; to the extent that advantages were seen to emanate from such conflicts, they were perceived to accrue to the landlords and not to the peasantry. The most important factor in maintaining Polish national consciousness in the peasantry was the arrogance, corruption, and inefficiency of the Russian administration. Oppression of the Church served as a catalyst for other forms of resentment and made it possible for the *szlachta* to appeal successfully to at least some of the peasantry.

The relationship of lord and peasant was in fact crucial to the development of the plans for the next revolt in Poland. There was a general understanding in the nationalist leadership after 1831 that a battle not a war had been lost. When the situation at home became impossible, many Poles went into exile to sharpen their skills by helping others in their struggles. The revolutionary torch was passed from one generation to the next; there was tacit agreement that there would be another revolution when the time was right. As mentioned earlier, 1848 was too soon. But by the early 1860s, the sons of the young men of 1830 were reaching maturity. Thus, Alexander II's declaration of intention to liberate the serfs, promulgated in 1861, triggered a new explosion in Poland.

The Russian imposition of reform effectively removed the major obstacle preventing political collaboration between whites (the conservative landowners) and reds (radicals) in Poland. Both sides began to prepare for a revolt. The reds, better organized (primarily by students) and more determined than the whites, even went so far as to begin collecting taxes. Their preparations could not be secret, however, and the Russian administration struck back in late 1862 by reinstituting military conscription of Polish youth. If carried out, this action would have preempted revolutionary possibilities for some time; the Poles had no choice but to begin their insurrection immediately. Fighting began in January 1863, and continued through the spring and early summer of 1864. Although the Russians were hard pressed at first, no unbiased observer could have doubted the inevitability of their victory.

The Polish rebels were far from incompetent. Their planning process ensured a considerable amount of coordination, even a remarkable amount if the long period of occupation is considered. Most important of all, however, was the revolutionary land program. Manifestos promised all peasants the land they tilled and also offered grants of land to peasants who had none; the state, not the peasantry, would be responsible for indemnifying the landowners. Although this declaration and the accompanying appeals did not cause the peasants to rise as one, more of this class took part in the revolution than in any of the previous Polish revolts. Perhaps tragically, peasant support was sufficiently strong to keep the insurrection going, but not powerful enough to make the countryside untenable for the Russians.

There were a number of internal failures that counterbalanced the successes of the revolutionary leaders. The reds, who early asserted control over the movement as a whole, did not have good and consistent ties with the whites, nor had they begun any serious military (as opposed to general organizational) planning. They did make the bold and potentially decisive move of attempting to provoke a general peasant revolt within Russia proper, particularly in the neighboring Ukraine. However, the timing was wrong (the confusion produced by the 1861 declaration would have been better) and the appeals to the non-Polish peasants were superficial. The Ukrainian peasants, many of whom had suffered miserably under Polish landlords, could not be moved by a few speeches alone.

The most important factor in dooming the 1863 rebellion, however, was the international situation. For the Poles to be successful, it was imperative that there be a foreign diversion which either distracted the Russians or somehow shifted relations in such a way as to facilitate foreign aid. In fact, the situation in 1863 was the reverse of what it should have been. Emperor Napoleon III of France, logically Poland's most valuable ally, was bogged down in Mexico. Britain and Austria were willing to give moral support but nothing more. The decisive role was thus left to Prussia, which could dramatically affect the outcome by either opening or closing her frontiers to the Polish rebels. They were closed. The recently appointed Bismarck openly supported the Russians—a service for which he was to be handsomely rewarded in 1866 and again in 1870–71.

The Polish revolution of 1863 affected the historical development of the nation in several important ways. The Russians carried out a land reform in Poland that was far less favorable to the landlords than elsewhere in the tsarist empire. This had the intended effect of weakening the power of the Polish magnates, but it also provided Poland with a proportionately higher number of independent peasant farmers than elsewhere in the northern tier of Eastern Europe. Large estates (particularly those owned by the Russian crown or Russian nobles) also continued to exist, however, and thus Poland had both extremes of agriculture strongly represented.[2] A second major factor was the harsh repression that followed. The Polish kingdom was abolished; even the name Poland disappeared (in favor of "Vistulaland"), and the country was ruled as simply another Russian province.

For a generation after 1863 political life in the Polish lands was comparatively subdued. Given the devastation of 1863 and the disillusionment and repression that followed, this is hardly surprising. In the 1890s, when memories of sorrow and sacrifice had faded in the old and a generation of energetic patriots had reached manhood, a new strain of political life developed. Unlike its elders, the new generation was more pragmatic, more willing to look calmly and rationally at the realities of international political life. This is not to say that they were less passionate in their nationalism for, if anything, they were even more ardent. But in the harsh Russian schools, in which simply speaking Polish was an offense that provoked immediate punishment, they had learned to control their emotions and to bide their time.

The most important of the new political parties was that which came to be known as the National Democrat Party. Based in autonomous Austrian Galicia, it nevertheless had its strength in Russian Poland, where it had to operate illegally. In Prussian (now German) Poland, it also functioned illegally, although there the more efficient repression slowed its initial growth. The leader of the National Democrats, Roman Dmowski, was an intense nationalist to whom all other things were secondary.[3] Searching for a practically based philosophy he attacked the *szlachta* as degenerate, the Jews as hopelessly alien, and even criticized the role of the Catholic Church. His views appealed to the intelligentsia and to the Polish industrial-mercantile middle class, both of which were becoming numerically more important. Unfortunately, his extreme nationalism, almost racist in character, also attracted those who were in competititon with Germans, Jews, Ukrainians, Lithuanians, and Russians for business, jobs, or education, and this negative nationalism of the National Democrats became ever more prominent.

Fundamentally opportunistic in nature, Dmowski's National Democrats moved gradually toward a cooperation with Russia. There were two reasons for this surprising choice. First, the growing strength of Germany concerned the Poles living in that country, and they joined the National Democrats in disproportionate numbers. This gave the party a strongly anti-German cast. More important, Russia's defeat in the 1905 war with Japan, and the ensuing revolution and semiparliamentary government, convinced Dmowski and his followers that a structural transformation of Russia was imminent, and that the Poles could work from within to secure a solution that was favorable to Poland. Russia's alliance with Britain and France reinforced Dmowski's optimism, for he believed that those nations would influence Russia in favor of Poland. The National Democrats, therefore, hung on to Russia until the end.

The opposite current in Polish political life was that of the PPS—the Polish Socialist Party, led by the charismatic Józef Piłsudski. The PPS was more nationalist than socialist (the real Marxist party, the SKDPL, is discussed in a later chapter), but it differed from the National Democrats in a number of important ways. Besides appealing to the workers, the PPS eschewed Dmowski's tendency toward racism and favored the return of a "great Poland"—a federation with Lithuania and possibly also with the Ukraine.[4] Such an approach obviously offered no possibility of reconciliation with Russia, from which it contemplated taking an enormous amount of territory. In any case, Piłsudski and his followers were ardent Russophobes. The PPS retained its base in Galicia after 1905, and while its rivals participated in the Russian parliaments, the PPS undertook rather different activities in Russian Poland: terrorism, bank robberies, and revolutionary agitation. Piłsudski was inevitably forced into an accommodation with his Austrian hosts and their German allies. At first not as sanguine as Dmowski about the value of such foreign assistance, Piłsudski nevertheless found himself organizing Polish legions to fight for Austria-Hungary as the war drew nearer.

The two major Polish political parties were obviously bitter rivals, as evidenced by their radically different choice of allies. Yet the schism was fortuitous in the long run. When three great empires clashed on Polish soil, the Poles had cannily covered all bets on the future.

A Note on Prussian (German) Poland

The history of Russian Poland has been sketched above, that of Austrian Poland is described below. Prussian Poland has not been accorded a separate section since there is much less to describe. The situation in this region was different in that the Poles in Pomerania, Wielkopolska, and Silesia had scattered among them a strong German minority (a majority in Silesia). The Germans in this area were overwhelmingly Protestant and the Poles almost totally Catholic, so that religious discrimination paralleled the national. Since Prussia-Germany was determined to integrate the Polish areas as quickly as possible (for example in Bismarck's *Kulturkampf*), the Poles as a nationality had virtually no political freedom. Their national aspirations were further reduced by the enormous industrial development which disturbed and disoriented traditional peasant and village-based nationalism. Those Poles who wished to be politically active emigrated to Galicia or (after 1905) to Russia. It should be emphasized, however, that Polish cultural (as opposed to political) life remained strong despite the repression.

The Ukrainians in the Russian Empire, 1848–1914

No East European people has had a more confused and chaotic history than the Ukrainians (usually referred to as Ruthenians in the context of the Habsburg lands). In the introduction to this text the Ukraine was excluded from the definition of Eastern Europe, largely because that area is now de facto (and in its entirety) a part of the Soviet Union. Even so, at various stages of history large numbers of Ukrainians were included in East European domestic as well as foreign affairs. The Ukrainians had little importance as a nationality, however, until after 1848, when nationalism finally began to have a significant effect upon them.

The Ukraine, with its capital at Kiev, was the home of the first Russian state, and its rulers were the first Russians to become Christians. Like the Bulgars, Serbs, and Romanians, the Kievan Russians adopted the Greek Orthodox variant of Christianity. Their state was strong in the early medieval period, but it soon fell prey to internal weaknesses and external pressures. The internal problem centered around the practice of allowing each son an equal share of the inheritance, which meant that one state became many smaller ones, and which in turn caused either great fragmentation of power, or civil war, or both. Externally, the Kievans soon found themselves too exposed geographically, their population centers too close to the broad steppe highway which brought one savage central Asian invader after another to their doorstep. It was the combination of these factors that eventually shifted the locus of Russian power northeastward to Moscow, where a new state, protected by the deep forests and the long winters, developed a tradition of unity, and, ultimately, of expansion.

In the meantime, however, the Kievan Russian population continued to survive. The turbulent times and continually exposed position prevented the resurgence of political power, but the people clung to the land and especially to the patches of forest that offered refuge. They developed a tradition of freeholding (as opposed to serfdom), and their bands of more or less democratically organized fighters, the famous Cossacks, resisted invaders from all directions. Gradually, the dialects of the area of the Ukraine separated from those of the Moscow region. It is hard to say when they became different languages, but a clear divergence seems to have taken effect sometime before the middle of the seventeenth century.

Following the end of the barbarian invasions, the surrounding states attempted to expand their influence over the Ukraine. Poland-Lithuania (later just Poland) was the most successful at first, eventually conquering all except for the southern fringes, which were held by the Turks. But, as described earlier, this eastward expansion of Poland was stopped by the vigorous, Moscow-based Russian state in 1667. Most of the Ukrainian-inhabited lands thus fell to Russia. The process of Russification was continued in the late-eighteenth century by the partitions of Poland in which many more Ukrainian lands were added to Russia. All Ukrainian territory not in Russia was in the Habsburg Empire: in the eastern half of Galicia where Ukrainians were a large majority around a Polish and Jewish minority, and in Carpatho-Ruthenia, a small isolated, sparsely populated, mountainous area in which they were a solid majority; and in Bucovina, where they were mixed about half and half with Romanians.

The Poles and the Russians brought the institutions of serfdom with them to the Ukrainian lands. The peasants disliked this, of course, and the situation was made worse by the conqueror's practice of routinely giving estates as rewards to their favorites. Thus most of the landlords were foreign (i.e., Polish or Russian). The Ukraine has great agricultural potential, but the disincentives of serfdom kept the area overwhelmingly poor and backward. Internal communications were so difficult, particularly in the Russian regions, that surpluses from the few efficiently managed estates had to be sold for export because they could not be transported to domestic markets. Ironically, the growth of this grain trade in the nineteenth century (based on the Black Sea port of Odessa), helped move Russia and Germany (also a grain exporter) from close friendship to agricultural and finally political rivalry.

Ukrainian nationalism had a slow and painful growth. It was not easy to draw a clear line from the glory of ancient Kiev to a Ukraine that was distinct from Moscow's Russia. There was no Ukrainian literary language by the mid-nineteenth century, and vigilant Russian, Austrian, and Polish authorities did their best to frustrate its development. The goal of Ukrainian unity was further hindered by the fact that a majority of the Ukrainians in Galicia and Carpatho-Ruthenia had adopted the Uniate compromise between Catholicism and Orthodoxy (see the section on Translyvania above). This meant that the Ukrainians did not even have the sort of religious cohesion that facilitated national consciousness in other foreign-dominated areas such as Bulgaria and Poland.

The Ukrainian national movement did not, in fact, become an organized force of any significance before the Great War. Yet its potential was there. Men who looked at the flow of history could not help but notice that no one had yet succeeded in arresting, let alone eliminating, a movement toward national consciousness. They were also aware of the fact that the Ukraine, even by the most conservative of definitions, was larger in area and population than any state of Eastern Europe. The Ukrainian "problem" was therefore always in the leaders' minds as a potential, if not an actual, factor.

The Habsburg Empire, 1848–1914

The crisis of 1848 both revealed and exacerbated the weaknesses of the Habsburg Empire. The social reforms carried out in the midst of the struggle did produce some important improvements, particularly in the economy, but much remained to be done. The emancipation of the peasantry, for example, only made the need for land reform more acute. The government in Vienna was aware of the problem but was not willing to consider the only possible solution—redistribution of the land—because such a course was anathema to the landed nobility, the class which provided the political base for the monarchy. Similar contradictions on other key issues resulted in official inaction with respect to social tensions, and a slow and uneven rate of economic growth.

The nationality problem was clearly aggravated by the events of 1848. The defeated rebels, the Hungarians and the Italians, were sullen and unrepentant. The peoples who had cooperated with the imperial forces, the Croats, Romanians, and Slovaks, were unrewarded and increasingly bitter. The remaining major nationalities, the Czechs, Poles, Ruthenians, and Slovenes, had neither rebelled nor assisted in an important way, but all were strongly affected by the wave of nationalist fervor and were increasingly inclined to seek significant changes in governmental policy.

Faced with powerful hostility and strident and often conflicting demands, the Habsburg administration reacted by attempting to suppress all manifestations of nationalism—even the German. The young emperor, Franz-Joseph (who reigned until 1916), appointed a series of heads of government who were inflexible in most matters and fanatically opposed to any compromise on the national question. The best known of these, Alexander Bach, created a system of government which one critic referred to as "a standing army of soldiers, a sitting army of bureaucrats, a kneeling army of worshippers, and a sneaking army of informers."[5] The advantage of historical hindsight makes it easy to see that this repressive policy was doomed to failure. The reactionary measures of Bach and others might have been somewhat effective a century earlier (although even that is doubtful), but by 1848 national feeling was too well developed to be destroyed. Thus, it is not surprising that the next major crisis for the Habsburg Empire was occasioned by a nationality problem.

The Italians, as mentioned earlier, had long been the most intensely nationalist and consequently the most disaffected people in the empire. Their defeat in 1848 was followed immediately by planning for a new revolt. The revolutionaries were assisted by Count Cavour, the leader of the independent Italian state of Piedmont-Sardinia. A master diplomat, Cavour was able first to establish an alliance with France, and then to provoke a conflict which led to war with Austria in 1859. The Habsburg leadership had the opportunity to avoid this situation through some rather inconsequential compromises but chose instead to fight. This tendency toward a thoughtless rush to battle was to be an unfortunate characteristic of Habsburg foreign policy right down to the final blunder of 1914.

The French and the Piedmontese defeated the Austrians, but not decisively. The peace treaty provided for cession of the province of Lombardy to Piedmont-Sardinia and put an end to Habsburg domination in southern Italy, but it allowed the Austrians to retain Venetia. This latter area was important to Vienna because of its ports and also because it was an emerging industrial center. In the long run, however, saving Venetia turned out to be an expensive victory. Cavour rapidly unified Italy, and the strong state that emerged was determined to redeem all Italian lands. Italy thus became an enemy of the Habsburg Empire, and the word "irredentism" (from the Italian for "unredeemed") entered the languages of the world.

The next crisis for the imperial leadership was far more serious and led to important domestic changes. In 1866 Franz-Joseph again allowed himself to be provoked into conflict, this time by Bismarck of Prussia. The immediate problem was a disagreement over the Danish-German provinces of Schlewswig and Holstein, although the real issue was whether Prussia or Austria should have predominant influence over the German lands. The military verdict in this case was decisive; in just seven weeks the Prussians crushed the Habsburg army at Königgrätz; the road to Vienna was wide open. The Austrians were hampered by fighting on a second front with Italy, but the war clearly revealed the technical and organizational inferiority of the Habsburg state; Austria was now no longer preceived as a major power.

The outward costs of the defeat were not that great. Prussia asserted her control over the German lands, and a united German state was created under her leadership only four years later. Italy got Venetia, but this was the only territorial loss for Vienna, which also escaped having to pay reparations. Far more significant, however, were the internal changes that now became necessary. The imperial government had realized before the war began that it was impossible to undertake such a major struggle without the loyal participation of the strongest of the nationalities—the Magyars. A revolt in Hungary during a war with Prussia and Italy would surely have been fatal.

The Hungarian leaders were assured, therefore, that important compromises would be made on the national question in return for their cooperation. Defeat, even though not the intended result of the deal, made it all the more necessary for the weakened Habsburg state to keep its word. The result was the *Ausgleich* (compromise) of 1867, which fundamentally restructured the government of the Hasburg monarchy.

After 1867, the empire was divided into two parts, one ruled by the Austrians from Vienna and the other ruled by the Hungarians from Budapest. The new state was known as Austria-Hungary (often referred to as the Dual Monarchy); the term "Austria," frequently used before 1867 for the entire Habsburg Empire, now applied only to one-half.

The new governmental organization had three separate structures. First, the old imperial administration, still based in Vienna, had severely restricted responsibilities, the most important of which were foreign and military affairs. The emperor and his staff had a great deal of flexibility in these areas, but final decision-making power was limited by the need to secure approval of the other two structures—separate Austrian and Hungarian governments. Thus, major diplomatic and military actions had to be approved by both Budapest and Vienna. To underscore the balance of power, it should be noted that a large part of the military forces from the Hungarian half of the empire remained in the *Honvéd*, a sort of Hungarian national guard, which only joined the imperial army in times of crisis and then only with the explicit authorization of the Hungarian government.

The strange pattern of organization of Austria-Hungary is outlined in the following chart. The Austrian and Hungarian structures were entirely separate from the imperial administration except for the position of the emperor-king in the respective constitutions. But even the role of the sovereign was different on the two sides, since the Austrian constitution permitted the emperor an important role in Austrian governmental affairs while the Hungarian constitution limited the king to a more or less ceremonial position in the government in Budapest. In other words, Franz-Joseph was a key figure in Austrian domestic affairs but not in Hungarian. The mechanism by which the two halves managed their joint affairs was carefully designed to preserve their separateness. Each parliament elected a delegation empowered to negotiate on matters of common interest. These met alternately in Vienna and Budapest, but (here the theory was carried to the limit) were forbidden to meet in the same room at the same time. The only exception was if they had disagreed three times, in which case they could meet together but had to vote without debate.

These extreme measures were included in the *Ausgleich* on the insistence of the Hungarians. They feared, and probably with some reason, that regular joint sessions of the delegations would establish a de facto Austro-Hungarian parliament. In such a situation, interest groups on the two sides might coalesce into alliances that could endanger Hungarian interests. In practice, the reverse occurred, since the Austrians had a far more liberal franchise than the Hungarians and were consequently far more divided internally. Thus, Budapest was able on occasion to interfere in Vienna's domestic affairs.

AUSTRIA- HUNGARY

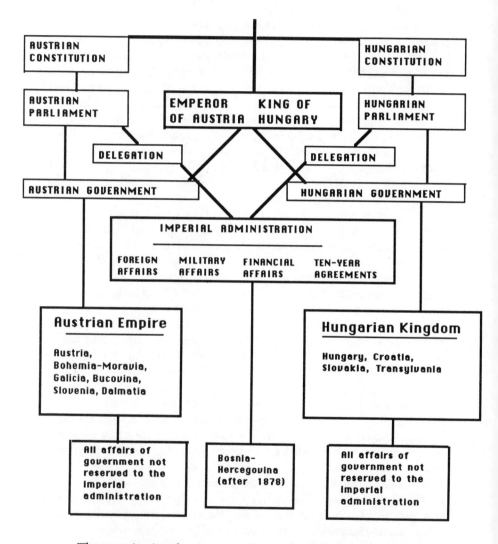

The constitutional structure of the *Ausgleich* was in practice un-
alterable. The careful mirror-imaging at the top ensured that no changes
could be made without the unqualified approval of both sides. Thus, as
we shall see, even if the emperor and the Austrian government could be
convinced that fundamental constitutional reforms were necessary in

Austria, these could not be effected without Hungarian acquiescence. Budapest even took this duality to the extreme of asserting that the Austrian and Hungarian constitutions were both component parts of the *Ausgleich* (and thus of the overall constitution) and that even these could not be changed without mutual consent. This view, which was never challenged on a major issue, effectively implied a Hungarian veto over basic Austrian law.[6] Even though Vienna rejected the Hungarian argument, the dispute hindered reform movements in Austria because of the fear of provoking a major crisis of unity.

Although both sides agreed that foreign and military affairs were the only essential and permanent common interests (the financial ministry simply supported the other two as well as the imperial court), they also recognized that there were a number of other matters that ought to be jointly administered at least on a temporary basis. Thus, the delegations negotiated Ten-Year Agreements to cover such matters. Typical of the more important issues were such affairs as tariffs, posts, and telegraphs. The first time around negotiations on the Ten-Year Agreements were fairly easy, but as time passed and the two halves of the empire developed different interests, they became progressively more difficult.

The Structure of Imperial Hungary

In domestic affairs the organization of Hungary was quite similar to that of Great Britain. There was no written fundamental law; instead the body of common law and tradition together formed a constitution. There were two parliamentary bodies, an upper house which included the higher nobility, and a lower house which was representative, although the franchise was severely limited according to a number of complicated factors relating to wealth, population, and nationality. The lower house had the sole right to initiate legislation and elected the various ministers who were responsible to it. The head of government was the prime minister; the king (the Austrian Emperor Franz-Joseph) could dismiss parliament and call for new elections, but in law and in practice his power was very limited. Local government, based on a system of counties, had some authority in local matters, but the government was, in fact, highly centralized.

The most important exception to absolute Magyar dominance in imperial Hungary was the special agreement with Croatia, the *Nagodba* (compromise) reached in 1868. Under this system, the Croatians had their own unicameral parliament and control over education, religion, police, the courts, and the territorial army; they were expressly forbidden, however, to raise any taxes. The Croatians also had specially designated places in the upper and lower houses of the Hungarian parliament and a guaranteed place in every ministry. Croatian representatives in Budapest were exempt from the laws that required the use of the Magyar language in all official matters.

The Magyars made this important concession to the Croats because they recognized the absolute necessity of appeasing this large, compact, strategically located, and nationally conscious people. The memory of the key role played by the Croatians in defeating Kossuth and the Hungarian revolution was still fresh only twenty years after the fact. Thus, the *Nagodba* was grudgingly agreed to, not freely given, and the Hungarians honored the letter rather than the spirit of compromise.[7] The governor of Croatia was appointed by Budapest, and could not be removed except by a two-thirds vote of the Croatian parliament. The balance of power in the province, despite the many apparent concessions, was clearly controlled by Hungary and Magyars.

The leaders in Budapest made every effort to ensure that the *Nagodba* did not set a precedent for further concessions. This attitude was made clear by the enforced union, also in 1868, of Transylvania with Hungary proper. As mentioned earlier, Transylvania had developed a tradition of autonomy after the Turkish conquest of Hungary. The union of 1868 was partly a reflection of the feeling of a majority of Magyars that Transylvania was an integral part of Hungary, and partly a means to discourage any ambitions of the Romanians, who comprised most of the province's population, toward achieving a voice in governmental affairs at the local or national level.

Hungarian Politics to 1914

Imperial Hungary was dominated by great landlords, or magnates, fewer than two thousand of whom owned almost a third of the arable land of the kingdom. The most important of the magnate families, that of Esterházy, owned an estate larger than many of the independent princedoms of pre-1870 Germany. Although the peasantry had been legally free since 1848, the transition from serf to freeman had not eliminated economic bonds. The Hungarian magnates owned entire villages and even towns, and the treatment meted out to their dependents was often no better than that suffered by serfs before 1848. Famous for arrogance, venality, and corruption, the Magyar aristocracy nonetheless produced many great leaders and statesmen.

More numerous than the magnates were the gentry, distinguished from the peasantry by a traditional right to nobility, and usually also by ownership of small estates. While the great landowners predominated in the northern part of Hungary, where the Ottoman occupation had been brief if it had occurred at all, the gentry were strongest in the south and west, where they had often received grants of land in return for service against the slowly retreating Turks. The gentry, the social class most deeply affected by nationalism, had formed the backbone of Kossuth's forces in 1848–49.

The peasantry existed everywhere in this overwhelmingly agricultural kingdom, and as a class the peasants were almost all poor. Precise statistics are unavailable, but the evidence suggests that all but a few of the peasants were either dwarfholders (not self-sufficient) or landless. The Magyar peasantry was perhaps slightly better off than the Slovak, Ruthenian (Ukrainian), Romanian, Croat, and Serb, but the differences were not great. The towns of royal Hungary were quite small and tended to have a high proportion of Germans and Jews. This was true even of the capital of Budapest.

In the first years of imperial Hungary, tradition, assisted by the structure of parliament and of the franchise, gave predominant political power to the aristocracy. Represented by the three brilliant negotiators of 1867, Gyula Andrássy, Istvan Deák, and Jozsef Eötvös, the aristocratic leaders were political conservatives, favoring the maintenance of the status quo as spelled out in the *Ausgleich* and the other arrangements of 1867–68. Two opposing currents in political life favored either a revision of the *Ausgleich* to leave only personal union without any common institutions, or, alternatively, total independence (the party of the still-exiled Kossuth). The other major domestic issues, in addition to relations with Austria, concerned trade and tariffs, church-state relations, and, increasingly, the status of the minorities.

The initial government, led by Deák, favored a separation of church and state, protectionism and close economic ties with Austria, and a fairly liberal treatment of the minorities. This moderate government was largely successful in its efforts, even passing a law on the rights of minorities (1868) that guaranteed equality in most areas. Deák's party ruled largely by virtue of its prestige, however, and his death and the ill health of other key leaders brought an end to its dominance in 1875. From that time until 1890, a member of the gentry by the name of Kálmán Tisza served as prime minister. His administration completely reversed the moderation that had marked the first years of modern Hungary.

Tisza had originally been opposed to the *Ausgleich,* favoring instead a simple personal union. He had not changed this view until just before his accession to power. But even though he joined with the Deákists to form the Liberal Party, Tisza jettisoned their moderate approach. Under Tisza, the renewals of the Ten-Year Agreements became crises, as the Hungarians fought for a smaller share of the cost of common expenditures as well as preferential trade and tariff arrangements. The generous approach to minority rights enacted into law in 1868 was ignored, and Hungary's approach to Austro-Hungarian foreign affairs seemed to have as its sole purpose the avoidance of situations that might encourage non-Hungarians to resist assimilation.

This desire to force the minorities to change their nationality, known as Magyarization, became stronger as the years went on.[8] The principal attack was focused on the schools, and legislation was passed that made the primary language of instruction Hungarian. This, of course, made teaching in the minority languages extremely difficult. As in Russian Poland, children could be expelled from school for speaking their native languages. Cultural and religious organizations that were not purely Magyar in language were regularly suppressed. Even danger signs in public places were posted only in Hungarian.

The fall of Tisza in 1890 was directly precipitated by an upsurge in the popularity of the separatist approach advocated by the followers of Kossuth. Since the independence-minded faction was not strong enough to assume control of the government, yet not weak enough to be ignored, Hungarian politics degenerated into chaos during the final decades of imperial Hungary. Relations with Austria suffered as the Magyars consistently refused to pay their share of the expenses of the central government. The occasion of the third Ten-Year Agreement precipitated a mini-tariff war between the two states. Even though the eventual compromise was favorable to Hungary, the prime minister was unable to secure parliamentary support and had to put it into effect by decree. The final straw was the Kossuthist insistence that Magyar be the language of command for those units of the imperial army that came from Hungary. This was not subject to compromise. Franz-Joseph stood firm, and the Budapest radicals had to give in.

The situation finally changed in 1905, when a coalition of independence-minded parties emerged victorious from a bitter election struggle. Since Franz-Joseph was unwilling to sanction the creation of a ministry composed primarily of individuals who favored the abolition of the monarchy, a serious crisis developed. The king appointed a loyalist ministry, and the coalition promptly gave it a vote of no-confidence in parliament. The ministry then chose not to resign but continued to govern. The Hungarian constitution was flagrantly violated in this step, but the opposition, aside from fostering a tax revolt, was unable to assert its legal place.

The opposition coalition, despite its strong electoral victory, was operating from a seriously flawed political base. Only a minority of the population could vote, and of that group only a minority were actually interested in a violent separation of Hungary from the structure established by the *Ausgleich*. Franz-Joseph and the Hungarian loyalists, sensing the weakness of their opponents, threatened them with the establishment by decree of universal manhood suffrage. This would have been an illegal act, of course, but once established it would have been impossible to reverse. Faced with the danger of the minorities (who were actually a majority of the population) voting equally with the Magyars, the coalition fell apart, and a constitutional government was restored. Nevertheless, deep divisions remained, and Hungary staggered into the conflict of 1914 with a unity of purpose that was purely superficial.[9]

The Structure of Imperial Austria

The Austrian superstructure resembled that of Hungary, but both in law and in practice there were fundamental differences between the two states. Austria did have a written constitution, although as in Hungary, much of the basic law was derived from tradition. There were also two houses of parliament, an upper composed of nobles, and a lower designated to represent the rest of the population. The role of the sovereign (emperor) was much different in Austria, however. Franz-Joseph appointed the nobles of the upper chamber, while in Hungary they served by birthright. The lower chamber, moreover, was (at first) not directly elected. Instead, it was composed of representatives selected by the assemblies of Austria's seventeen provinces. This house did not have the sole right to initiate legislation, as did its equivalent in Hungary, although it was charged with first consideration of all matters.

The crucial difference between Hungary and Austria was in the matter of ministerial responsibility. In the former, the government was in law and (usually) in practice subject to the will of the lower house of parliament. In the latter, however, the law was ambiguous, but the practice was clear: the emperor controlled the government by appointing and dismissing ministers, and most legislation was, in fact, initiated at the executive level. The emperor's authority was buttressed by an emergency clause in the constitution which allowed government by decree in the event that parliament was not in session. Since the emperor could dismiss the legislature without holding new elections for six months, this clause gave him considerable legal authority.

The seventeen provincial assemblies had an ambiguous function in government. On the one hand, their presiding officers were appointed by the crown (as were provincial governors), and all legislation had to be approved by the emperor. Moreover, general policy in most areas was set by the imperial parliament, with the provincial assemblies limited to defining the method of implementation. On the other hand, those matters not expressly reserved to the central government fell to the provinces, with the consequence that ambiguity or inaction in Vienna could give a considerable boost to those groups favoring local initiative. The very existence of conflict tended to make the provincial assemblies into meaningful bodies.

Austrian Politics to 1914

The social-political dynamics of Austria were also quite different from those of Hungary. A large landlord class did exist in Austria, but it was much smaller in number, distribution, and importance. Although there wre no equivalents of the Esterházys, there was a number of magnates who controlled the bulk of the land in Bohemia, Moravia, Silesia, and Galicia; in many ways, they also continued to rule their estates in a manner reminiscent of feudalism. Usually German (or Germanized in the Czech lands), these nobles were favored by the emperor. Nevertheless, their power was largely regional, and they had nothing similar to the influence their Hungarian colleagues had on imperial policy.

In the areas controlled by the magnates there were large numbers of economically dependent, landless, or dwarfholding peasants, comparable to perhaps half of their equivalents in Hungary in that they were of different nationality than the landlords they served (largely Czech in Bohemia-Movavia, and Ukrainian in Galicia). This factor was of increasing importance as both national and social problems became more acute.

The number of lesser nobles was much smaller in Austria than in Hungary, but this was more than counterbalanced by the large numbers of free peasants and townsmen. Many parts of Austria, particularly the mountainous areas, had never been subjected to feudalism, and in many other areas the emancipation of 1848 had been successful in freeing the peasants of de facto as well as de jure dependence. Thus, unlike Hungary, Austria had an important population of peasants who were, in fact, fairly efficient small farmers.

The Austrian half of the empire also differed in the extent to which it had developed an urban and industrial society. Not only did Vienna make Budapest look like a village, but there were other cities such as Prague and a whole host of urban complexes based on manufacturing in the Czech lands and elsewhere. Hungary also lacked the industrial and trading centers (except on a much smaller scale in Budapest alone) that existed in Austria. This disparity was a major cause of the disagreements on tariffs and trade cited above.

The political dynamics of Austria in the period 1867-1918 were extremely complex. Aside from the greater power of the sovereign, which waxed or waned according to the extent to which matters interested him, the greatest instability was to be found in the role of the provincial assemblies. Since these at first elected deputies to the lower house, that part of government was as representative as the franchise of the respective assemblies allowed it to be. In fact, the various provinces had traditions that ranged from very liberal to very conservative. Some areas, such as Galicia, returned primarily landowners, while others, such as Lower Austria (which included Vienna), sent primarily townsmen of the professional classes.

Political power within Austria tended to split three ways. First and most important were the German liberals, representing the trading, industrial, and urban professional classes that had sparked the Austrian part of the revolution of 1848. Generally in favor of a strictly limited monarchy, the full range of traditional constitutional freedoms (press, assembly, etc.), the German liberals also opposed the extension of the franchise to the masses. The liberal philosophy was socioeconomic at its base, and closely resembled similar movements elsewhere in Europe. But in Austria it also acquired a complexion of German nationalism, at least in the sense of favoring political and cultural dominance for the German lands and the German language. This seemed to be primarily a reflection of the fact that Germans made up the overwhelming majority of the bourgeoisie, rather than a consequence of the sort of cultural insecurity that generated Magyarization in Hungary. Very few Germans showed an interest in trying to destroy the culture of the minority nationalities.

Second in importance were the minorities themselves. Though Poles,

Czechs, Slovenes, Italians, and others managed to be elected in significant numbers to both provincial and imperial chambers, they failed to act consistently as a unified political coalition on matters of mutual interest. In part this reflected different class values; the Poles tended to be aristocrats, the Czechs bourgeois, the Slovenes peasants. In part the separate roads were a consequence of different objectives: the Poles thought in terms of keeping alive the idea of an independent Poland; the Czechs aimed for a arrangement like that given to the Magyars; the Slovenes had modest cultural aims; the Italians simply wanted to join Italy.

The final political power center in Austria was that of the aristocratic-bureaucratic elite. The old imperial Austria, like most other aristocratic empires, had cultivated a tradition in which government service was the most important aim in life for the nobility. The restructuring of the Habsburg lands could not suddenly destroy either the individuals or the tradition. Drawn primarily from the aristocracy, these leaders nonetheless displayed the attitudes of noblesse oblige that were common in similar classes on the continent, and therefore supported many "liberal" reforms in matters such as the condition of the working class—despite opposition from the regular liberal politicians. The aristocratic-bureaucratic elite owed its loyalty to the emperor and was largely unaffected by nationalism. Because of the emperor's support, as well as the prestige generated by tradition, it played a role out of all proportion to its numbers.

In the first years after the *Ausgleich*, the role of the Catholic church in the state was a major political issue. The Habsburg family had long identified itself with the Church, and Austria had always fought on the Catholic side in the religious wars of earlier times. Though Protestantism had made some inroads—among Hungarians and the Germans of Transylvania—it never was treated with more than the minimum of toleration. The Habsburgs, as mentioned earlier, had attempted to draw as many of the Orthodox as possible to Catholicism through the device of the Uniate Church and had had some success among the Romanians of Transylvania (see above). This tradition of identifying church and state now came into strong conflict with German liberal anticlericalism.

The struggle in parliament was intense. In addition to history and tradition, the Catholics had the help of the devout Poles and Slovenes. But the ultimate victory of the liberals was less a consequence of their own strength than of the fact that the emperor and his closest advisers decided not to intervene forcefully on the side of the Church. This showed that there were more than purely religious issues at stake: some questions, such as civil marriage, were obviously religious and symbolic, but others, such as that of the schools, had at their core the key issue of modernization.

The Austro-Prussian War had shown the Habsburg lands to be weak and backward. Reforms, including much technical and scientific progress, were essential if this situation was to change. Franz-Joseph realized that some modernization was necessary, and it is not surprising that he chose not to support the ultraconservative church school system. Reforms of the military, the courts, and in the areas of freedom of speech and the press then followed under the first liberal governments. Austria seemed to be struggling to catch up.

Industrial development was obviously crucial to the modernization of the state, and every effort was made to force the pace. As elsewhere in Europe, railroad building led the way and was accompanied by widespread speculation. The familiar problems of overconfidence and under capitalization made the system ripe for crisis, however, and the European financial crash of 1873 hurt the Austrian economy very badly. Recovery from this debacle was slow, and the process did much to damage relations between Austria and Hungary. The former needed a secure, protected market in which to sell the products of its young industry, manufactures which were not yet able to compete on the world market. But the Hungarians did not want to do as the Austrians wished, partly because they did not want to pay higher prices for inferior products and partly because they hoped to develop industries of their own. These fundamental differences contributed to the bitter struggle over renewal of the Ten-Year Agreements, since the agreements were the means by which internal and external tariffs were established.

Foreign affairs played a far more important role in the domestic politics of the Austrian half of the Habsburg Empire than in the Hungarian. Of the several reasons for this, two stand out. First, the imperial government and the imperial bureaucracy were still located in Vienna, and many individuals continued to have multiple interests. Further, it should again be stressed that Franz-Joseph, who as king of Hungary had very little authority in Budapest, was an important factor in Austrian domestic politics, a leader who could and did play a consistently active role. If the emperor could not control Hungary's approach to foreign policy, it was all the more important that he control Austria's. Otherwise, he would become a politically insignificant figure. Also, Austria's developing industrial and mercantile interests demanded vigorous involvement in foreign affairs. On the other hand, Hungary, which was overwhelmingly agricultural and preoccupied with forcing a solution to the national problem, simply favored the status quo.

Following the *Ausgleich,* the first event in international affairs to affect Austrian politics was one in which Austria-Hungary had no direct role: the Franco-Prussian War of 1870–71. The Prussians' crushing victory, and their subsequent creation of a united Germany under their control, had a profound effect on the Habsburg Empire. Having dominated the affairs of the German lands until their own defeat by Prussia in 1866, the rulers in Vienna had not easily given up hopes of reasserting their control. But the events of 1870–71 ended those hopes forever. If Austria-Hungary were to play a role in international affairs in the future, it would not be in German affairs. That door was closed for good.

The war of 1870–71 and the creation of a unified German state for the first time in modern history provoked a new burst of German nationalism. This emotional explosion easily penetrated the frontiers of Austria, where it caused real problems. The Czechs, like their brother Slavs in Poland, were strongly francophile, and had openly cheered for the French during the war. This might have led to real ugliness had not the French defeat been so speedy and so complete. Even so, Franz-Joseph and the upper levels of the imperial administration had mixed emotions at the outcome. They were glad at the success of their fellow Germans but sad about losing any possibility of renewed influence in the German lands. Most important, however, was the emerging fear that the new Germany would reverse the pattern of the past and attempt to control or even annex the predominantly German parts of the Austro-Hungarian Empire.

It was this fear that compelled Franz-Joseph to appoint a ministry that attempted to placate the Czechs and to strengthen the Slavic elements of the empire at the expense of the Germans. The failure of this effort in the face of intense German and Hungarian pressure (see the section on the Czechs, below) forced the emperor to restore a liberal government. Nevertheless, the underlying fears remained. The financial troubles of 1873 increased the emperor's lack of confidence in the liberals and gave urgency to his search for alternatives to German nationalism. His concern, combined with Austria's continuing tradition of great power behavior, led to the empire's rapidly expanding involvement in the affairs of the Balkans.

The dynamics of foreign policy in this period will be discussed in greater detail in a subsequent chapter on the origins of the Great War. At this point, it is appropriate to stress only the domestic linkages of the Austro-Hungarian foreign policy. In this context, it should be remembered first that the Habsburgs did have a tradition of involvement in the Balkans; second, there was a clear tendency, subconsciously if not consciously, for the Austrian leadership to see foreign adventures as a means for diverting attention from apparently insolvable domestic issues; finally, the narrow, mulish attitude that characterized the earlier policy of Franz-Joseph and his advisors continued to lead the government into hopeless, unforeseen situations from which it was unwilling or unable to retreat.

The Balkan problems and Austria-Hungary's involvement can be sketched as follows. The peoples of the Ottoman province of Bosnia-Hercegovina (Serbs and Croats primarily) rose in revolt in 1875. The reasons for their insurrection were largely local and immediate—raised taxes at a time of bad harvests—but the revolt soon spread to the other Slavs still in Turkey (Bulgarians and Macedonians). Further, the independent Slavic states (Serbia and Montenegro) were drawn closer to conflict through obvious sympathy for their brethren, as were also the neighboring Orthodox states (Romania and Greece). Most important, however, was the fact that the "great Slav brother" to the north—Russia—was obviously being pulled into battle by the force of its own rhetoric. The Russian leadership, which had attempted to divert the attention of its oppressed and miserable population through pan-Slav and pan-Orthodox propaganda, now found itself prisoner of its own public opinion.

The Austro-Hungarian leadership viewed all this with the traditional alarm. Even a fairly calm and rational person could foresee a situation in which Russia, allied with the Slavic and Orthodox states of the Balkans, would drive the Turks out of Europe. Russia would then control the entire southeastern part of the continent directly through her own troops or indirectly through weak satellite states. This would have the effect not only of preempting further Austro-Hungarian expansion, but in the long run it might also threaten the existence of that state by flanking it on three sides with a powerful Slavic alliance that would constantly act as a magnet for the Slavs of the empire. Vienna acted swiftly to prevent this nightmare.

In several diplomatic meetings prior to the outbreak of hostilities, the Austro-Hungarians promised to maintain a benevolent neutrality (i.e., to do nothing) if the Russians would: (1) promise not to create a large Slavic state in the Balkans (this meant Bulgaria—Vienna feared that whether from gratitude or direct control or both any Bulgarian state would be a puppet of Russia); and (2) allow Austria-Hungary to occupy Bosnia-Hercegovina as "compensation." The Russians agreed to this, primarily because they knew the British were also extremely suspicious of their motives and that an Austro-British-Turkish coalition against Russia was not only possible but probable if Moscow pushed too hard.

The Russians had a much more difficult time against the Turks than they expected, winning only after a long, bitter struggle through 1877–78. Nevertheless, the tsar was so flushed with victory that he ignored his

earlier promises and, in the Russo-Turkish Treaty of San Stefano, proclaimed the creation of what came to be known in diplomatic circles as
a "Big Bulgaria." The other powers, particularly the British and the
Austro-Hungarians, were outraged at this, and there was much rattling
of sabers. Finally, the German chancellor, Otto von Bismarck, called the
nations to a conference at Berlin (1878) in order to settle matters and
prevent war. Here the Russians were forced to back down and reduce
Bulgaria to a much smaller state. The Austro-Hungarian occupation of
Bosnia-Hercegovina was ratified, albeit after much haggling over frontiers.

The events in the Balkans had long-term foreign and domestic repercussions. In foreign affairs, to be discussed in more detail later, Austria-
Hungary and Russia became more bitter enemies than ever before, and
their rivalry in the Balkans simmered until the explosion of 1914. Domestically, a more complex struggle began. Since it was obvious that the
new province of Bosnia-Hercegovina could not be added to either Austria
or Hungary, the imperial administration proposed that it be administered
directly by the imperial finance ministry. This solution was simple enough,
and the proposal was ratified by both the Austrian and the Hungarian
parliaments. Nevertheless, the opposition was strong and deeply rooted.
Neither German liberals nor the overwhelming majority of the Magyars
were in favor of adding more Slavs to the empire. Their point was reinforced, and their criticism made more vigorous, by the fact that many of
the "liberated" peoples of Bosnia-Hercegovina (mostly Orthodox Serbs
and Moslem Serbs and Albanians) waged a bitter struggle against the
occupying troops.

Franz-Joseph acted quickly to resolve the problems posed by a
foreign enemy and domestic critics. In 1879 Austria-Hungary concluded
an alliance with Germany. Though technically defensive, the treaty was
in fact aimed against Russia. It was also supposed to be secret, but since
the major objective (cooling Russia and thus quieting domestic opposition) had to do with public opinion, the general terms were immediately
leaked and became common knowledge. The alliance was in truth popular
with the German liberals and with the Magyars, both of whom saw it
as an anchor that would prevent the empire from drifting too far from
the status quo which they so strongly favored. With this support in hand
Franz-Joseph swiftly moved to counter-balance what was seen as a powerful increase in Austro-German influence in the empire.

In 1879 the emperor dismissed the German liberal government,
dissolved parliament, and called for new elections. Franz-Joseph then
confirmed as the new prime minister a Czech nobleman, Count Taaffe,
who based his power on a coalition of autocrats, clericals, and slavs

(primarily Poles and Czechs).[10] Just as his appointment was part of an overall balancing act for the empire as a whole, so was Taaffe forced to maintain a juggling act in the Austrian half. He was remarkably successful in this, since he continued to govern until 1893. Taaffe's skill was in making a seemingly endless series of compromises that appeased one party without driving the other into revolt. Thus, the Catholics won many victories, but the fundamental secularization of the empire was not reversed. Similarly, the Czechs improved their situation bit by bit, but what they really wanted—a trialist empire—eluded them (see below).

Taaffe's government, like that of Tisza in Hungary, was symbolic of the systemic disease of the Dual Monarchy. Extravagant acrobatics were necessary on almost a daily basis just to keep the whole structure from collapsing. Yet these continuous adjustments rarely approached real solutions to the more fundamental problems. The backward, patchwork mode of organization had acquired an inertia of its own. The last real attempt at reform came in 1897 when the prime minister, Count Badeni, published ordinances which would establish that, by July 1901, Czech and German would have equal standing in the administrative affairs of the provinces of Bohemia and Moravia. Since this meant that many Germans would have to learn Czech (not to mention the symbolic value it would have on the latter), it met the same sort of furious German opposition as the Hohenwart plan of 1871 (see below). Badeni, like Count Hohenwart, was forced to resign when Franz-Joseph decided that the German and Magyar pressures would destroy the empire. The ordinances were withdrawn.

After 1897 there were no further attempts at major reconciliation. The nationalities became ever more radical—not least the Czechs. Economically the empire prospered, but the increasingly affluent middle classes did not provide the cement with which to hold the foundation together. Even the social democrats organized their party along national lines. In Vienna the Christian Socialist party espoused an anti-Semitism that was to be an unpleasant precursor of tragic events to come. The establishment of universal manhood suffrage in 1907 merely reinforced the existing fractionalization: some fifty political parties put forward candidates for the 1911 parliamentary elections. The Austrian half of the empire, like the Hungarian, stumbled into war blindly, without any real cohesion.

The Czechs

Although the Czechs, as a nation, had not played a major role in the struggles of 1848–49, the Czech national question emerged afterwards to become one of the two or three key problems in the Habsburg empire. Its importance was partly strategic, since the Czech lands included most of the industrial strength of the empire, and partly a result of the fact that large numbers of Germans lived among the Czechs and had been there for many centuries. For these reasons the relatively simple solution of local autonomy accorded to the Poles in Galicia could not be given lightly to the Czechs.

The burden on the imperial authorities was somewhat lightened by the fact that the Czechs were themselves increasingly divided on goals and methods. The senior group among them, the men responsible for the cultural renaissance of the first half of the century, had limited objectives. They wanted to extend and consolidate their cultural achievements, and they were aware that some political role for the Czechs was necessary if they were to be secure from German pressures in the future. These "Old Czechs," as they were soon called, did not, however, look to a solution that would remove them from the Habsburg aegis. Palacký, the great historian and political leader, summed up the point of view of the Old Czechs at the time with his famous statement that, "If Austria did not exist, we would have to invent her."[11]

Implicit in this loyalist position was, of course, the assumption that a satisfactory compromise could be worked out with the imperial authorities and with the Germans residing in the Czech lands (Bohemia was then 60 percent Czech and 40 percent German; Moravia was 70–30). This proved to be difficult to achieve. In the first years after the revolution of 1848, the harsh repression emanating from Vienna was such that there was no opportunity for the formulation of reform plans that had any realistic possibility of approval. The Old Czechs gradually moderated this pressure through an alliance with the local aristocracy, however, and some progress was made in the acceptance of the use of the Czech language in administrative affairs.

The *Ausgleich* of 1867 caused a radical change in this situation. The Czechs were shocked that their interests had been totally ignored in the restructuring of the state. They believed that their claims to a share of the government were better than those of the Magyars and that a trialist Austrian-Czech-Hungarian arrangement was the minimum that they should receive. Traditional Czech sympathies toward pan-Slavism were also offended by the abandonment of the Croats and the Slovaks to absolute Magyar control. In immediate practical terms the Old Czechs responded to the insult by refusing to cooperate with the government in Vienna. They also found that their leadership was severely challenged by a more radical group (dubbed, of course, the "Young Czechs"), which accused them of complicity in the defeat of 1867 by virtue of their excessively conservative and passive tactics.[12]

The furor in the Czech lands, both in the sudden intransigence of the Old Czechs and in that they might soon be replaced by even more radical types, was watched with great concern by the authorities in Vienna. Though neither violent action (aside from tossing inkwells in parliament) nor revolution was in sight, there was a possibility of short- and long-range disruption that could severely weaken what was now seen to be a rather frail ship of state. The various governments in the first years of the post-*Ausgleich* period made a number of awkward and confused gestures to the Czechs. Their lack of success and the failure to even begin to develop a coherent policy was largely a reflection of the fact that all of the cabinets had important contingents of German liberals who opposed any significant concessions to the Czechs.

The aftermath of the Franco-Prussian War and the subsequent creation of Germany changed this by making Franz-Joseph suspicious of the German liberals to the point of wanting to establish a Slav-based political entity which would offset them in governmental affairs. The Hohenwart ministry, appointed in February of 1871, brought to power a group charged with creating a federal arrangement with the Czechs. Following new provincial elections throughout the Austrian half, the provincial parliament of Bohemia was asked to state on what terms Franz-Joseph could be crowned king in Prague. The Czechs quickly responded with a proposal that would have given them a status essentially the same as that of the Hungarians. The emperor and the government were prepared to accept.

The Czech proposal aroused a storm of opposition from the German liberals and the Magyars. The former objected because this new change in the state structure, unlike the *Ausgleich,* would place large numbers of Germans under foreign cultural domination. It was one thing to permit Czechs to use their own language in schools and social affairs, but it was quite another to force Germans to use it as well. Many Germans thought of Prague (and other Bohemian and Moravian towns) as inherently German and regarded a transfer of administration to the Czechs as a form of treason. This extreme view of the situation was fueled by the fact that German nationalism was an increasingly important factor—especially strong in the immediate aftermath of the creation of Germany.

The Magyars saw the Czech proposal as a direct and indirect threat to their power. The direct challenge was obvious, since one-third of a voice in the imperial government was less than one-half. Of equal, if not greater, concern was the long-range danger of formally recognizing a

Slav entity within the empire. It did not require any great leap of the imagination to foresee a time when Prague would take Budapest to task on the subject of the latter's treatment of the Slovaks and the Croats—in effect interfering in Hungary's internal affairs. And when such conflicts appeared, it seemed probable that Vienna would side with Prague against Budapest. The economic interests of Czech and German would override their cultural rivalry (or so it seemed to the Hungarians at the time—the reality might have been quite different).

Faced with vehement, implacable opposition, Franz-Joseph gave in and refused to sanction the Czech proposal. The Hohenwart ministry fell, and German liberals returned to power in Austria. The Czechs, shocked once again, reacted in a surprisingly mild manner to this great defeat.[13] Since the Battle of White Mountain in 1620, the Czechs have seemed to roll with their opponents' punches, and the aftermath of 1871 was no exception. The Czechs continued to press on the issue of official language use, chipping away here and there at German exclusivity. They boycotted the Austrian parliament until 1879, when they returned to support the Taaffe government. They were patient even then, however, and it was only after a decade of little or no progress that the Young Czechs first outnumbered their more conservative rivals in the Bohemian parliament (1889). Hostility between Czechs and Germans then increased quickly, and in 1893 martial law had to be declared briefly in Prague.

Violence was still exceptional in the Czech-German struggle, however, and the real effect was a deepening alienation of the Czechs, who came to display a fundamental distrust of the Germans. There were further attempts at compromise, but these foundered on the rocks of German-Magyar hostility or failed to break past the suspicions of the more radical Czechs. As the empire drifted into the violent summer of 1914, the imperial authorities in Vienna had little fear of revolt or widespread treason in the Czech lands, but neither were they so foolish as to expect loyal and enthusiastic support in the time of trial.[14] Their judgments were correct, for the Czechs gave the empire in war as much as the empire had given them in peace—as little as possible.

The Hungarians in the Habsburg Empire

Hungarian political affairs have been discussed in some detail above; therefore, this section will concentrate on cultural and economic problems. Yet since both of these factors directly affected the political sphere and cannot be separated from it, those linkages will be discussed as well.

Hungarian cultural awareness, as described earlier, emerged with great energy in the first half of the nineteenth-century. Its rapid growth inevitably encountered similar movements on the part of other nationalities. Contact quickly became conflict. Differences were already sufficiently strong to send non-Magyars into battle against Magyars in 1848–49. After the *Ausgleich*, the Hungarians soon returned to the most extreme of their earlier positions: the minorities must themselves become Hungarian. The following incident illustrates the depth of feeling. At a meeting in 1848, Kossuth told a Serbian delegation that concessions would be made to the minorities but that all must accept the Magyar language as their own. "Then," replied a Serb, "we must look for recognition elsewhere than at Pressburg [Bratislava—then the Hungarian headquarters]." "In that case," answered Kossuth, "the sword must decide." "The Serbs," came the reply, "were never afraid of that."[15]

It should be emphasized that the Hungarian position was more extreme than that of others. Cultural independence, including the right to teach, write, and publish in another language, was rarely rejected elsewhere at this time. The Czechs of Bohemia and Moravia, for example, won these rights with very little opposition from the Germans. Even the use of a language as a second (as opposed to an equal) vehicle for administration and politics was usually tolerated elsewhere in the Habsburg lands. But the Hungarians were adamant: the minorities were to use the Magyar language or they were to be silent. This implacable stand was probably a consequence both of the fact that the Hungarians were a minority in their own country and of their relative insecurity with a recently revived language and culture.

The results of the policy of forced Magyarization were catastrophic. The more the Hungarians insisted, the more they were resisted. The minority opposition infuriated the Magyarizers, who pushed all the harder and were then resisted even more. This vicious downward spiral helped to make the Hungarian kingdom perpetually unstable and thus also contributed to the ultimate failure of the Dual Monarchy.

The nationality problem even had a profoundly negative effect on the economy. Hungary desperately needed land reform. The estates of the magnates were inefficiently operated, and the subsidies and special treatment that the landlords provided to themselves acted as a drag on the entire economy. Nevertheless, the official view was that to weaken the magnates would be to strike at the center of the Magyar spirit, and thereby to make the country more vulnerable to the inroads of the destructive nationalities. Even though some of the leading magnate families were unusually and outspokenly tolerant toward the non-Magyars, and even though the locus of power shifted away from the magnates as a class, this fear of tampering with the system held back vital reforms.

Without withdrawing any of the above, it should be said that the overall picture is probably unfairly bleak. Hungary made progress in many areas in the years 1848–1914. Nowhere was this more apparent than in Budapest, which became a sophisticated, culturally alive capital city. Graceful literature continued to flow from Hungarian pens, and great wines were matured in the vineyards of the northeastern counties. It is regrettable that grace and maturity were not more apparent in politics.

The Germans in the Habsburg Empire

In the years after 1848 the Germans of the Austro-Hungarian Empire became more aware of and more supportive of German nationalism but also more aware of and less tolerant of other nationalisms. Yet this generalization should not be taken to mean that all Germans were affected in the same way. In the solidly German lands of Austria proper, many Germans still thought of themselves first of all as Catholics. These people, mostly peasants, villagers, and aristrocrats, were largely unconcerned about a possible threat from the other nationalities and cooperated in parliament with other strong Catholic groups such as the Poles and the Slovenes. The combination of relative isolation and prosperity made the Austrian hinterland perhaps the least politically volatile part of the empire, particularly in the first half of this period.

Those Germans who felt their national status most strongly were those who were in daily contact, and often in daily competition, with other peoples. This was particularly true of the Germans of Vienna, a city which was already nearly as multinational by mid-century as was the empire as whole. The Vienna Germans, moreover, had been in the forefront of the revolution of 1848, and had been in frequent contact with the revolutionaries of the various German states. They were thus both less inclined to be loyal to the Habsburgs and more aware of and interested in the cultural if not always the political side of the emerging German nationalism. Economically, however, they were relatively content. As merchants, traders, bankers, manufacturers, and professionals, the German middle classes of Vienna were living fairly well and generally favored protection against competition from Germany.

Those Germans living outside of Austria can be divided roughly into two groups: the Germans of the Czech lands, and those of other areas. In the Czech lands, and particularly in Bohemia, the Germans were spread fairly evenly across all levels of the population: city, town, and village. Some areas were almost entirely German (the Sudeten fringe), but generally Germans were scattered as a fairly consistent minority of 20 to 40 percent throughout the population. The Germans of the Czech lands had long been secure in a dominant role and, being neither oppressed nor challenged, they were not at first especially nationalistic. The Czech revival changed this quickly, however, and the surprised Germans fought back bitterly as described earlier. The tension in Bohemia was particularly acute because the Czech national sentiment was carried to a great extent by a rising middle class that was in direct economic conflict with the Germans. Boycotts and counter-boycotts were a frequent feature of the national struggle in Bohemia.

The other group of Germans in the empire were those who had settled, for one reason or another, in non-German areas—overwhelmingly cities. For the most part these people were urban traders, bureaucrats or former bureaucrats, and the like. (An exception were the Germans of Transylvania, who had been settled there by Hungarian kings in early medieval times to help defend the frontiers against the Turks.) These Germans had developed prosperous communities far from the traditional German lands. It is difficult to generalize about the national attitudes of these smaller German groups: while some intermarried and assimilated (particularly in the Hungarian areas), others became the most fanatical of nationalists and were the ancestors of those East European Germans who welcomed Hitler with enthusiasm.

Overall, the situation of the Germans was confused. Thrilled by the successes of the new German state, they were proud to see their own people on the brink of building a great new civilization. Yet this did not mean that most or even many wanted to join Germany. Regional, religious, and dynastic loyalties did not vanish overnight. On the other hand, being *kaisertreu* (loyal to the emperor) ought not to mean giving control over politics to non-Germans, whom many believed to be culturally inferior. This dilemma did not particularly disturb the first groups of Germans mentioned—the Austrian village clericals and aristocrats—but it was of deep concern to others. Two political expressions of German feeling will thus be sketched briefly below.

The Christian Socialist was a German political party based overwhelmingly in Vienna. Although pro-Catholic and pro-Habsburg, it was not sponsored by either and was even frequently an embarrassment to both. More anti than pro, the Christian Socialists were opposed to Jews, liberals, socialists, and non-Germans, roughly in that order, but contradictions were not infrequent (e.g., dislike of the Magyars sometimes fostered sympathy for the minorities in Hungary). Led by Karl Leuger, who was mayor of Vienna for many years around the turn of the century, the vague, grab-bag philosophy of the Christian Socialists drew strong support despite its obvious weaknesses. In large part a reaction to the infatuation of German liberals with the German state, its ambivalent nature demonstrated the lack of clear alternatives.

Far more coherent as a political party and a political philosophy was that of the Social Democrats Party (SDP). A Marxist party (for its relation to communism, see below), the SDP was focused on the rapidly expanding working class. Quickly abandoning the concept of inevitable violent revolution, the Austrian SDP was also imaginative in nationality theory. The party dropped the national self-determination idea in favor of a federal state in which minorities would have full cultural but not political independence. The SDP was itself organized along these lines. But even this promising idea came too late; in 1911 the embittered Czechs formed their own separate SDP, effectively splitting the proletarian parties in two. The Austrian SDP was still strong, however, and is the ancestor of the governing party of today's Austria.

The Slovaks in the Habsburg Empire

The situation of the Slovaks changed little after 1848, except that Magyar persecution from 1867 on increased Slovak national consciousness and stiffened the resolve of those who considered the Slovaks to be a separate entity from the Czechs. Although the Czechs and the Slovaks, separated historically for such a long period, had developed a strong sense of cooperation and kinship in the period around 1848, their division into two different parts of the empire after 1867 arrested this trend. The Czechs were hard pressed to maintain even minimal national rights of their own and were in no position to help the Slovaks. The necessity for the latter to go it alone therefore limited the possibilities for cooperation and development.

Slovakia did not share in the industrial prosperity of the last years of Austria-Hungary. Not only was there less in the way of investment capital available in the Hungarian half, but the bleak hills and mountains still had little appeal for developers.[16] Bratislava blossomed as a river port and trading center, but the population of that city was primarily Hungarian and German throughout this period. The hardships in Slovakia were such that a disproportionately high percentage of the population (as compared, for example, to the Czechs) decided to emigrate to the United States.

The Romanians in the Habsburg Empire

The Romanians of Transylvania, like the Croats, were sufficiently upset by the extreme nationalist views of Kossuth that they chose to fight for the emperor and against the Hungarian revolutionaries in 1848–49. Also like the Croats, they were not rewarded for their loyalty and turned instead to fight by whatever means necessary for their national rights. The *Ausgleich,* and the subsequent annexation of Transylvania to Hungary, was a real blow to them. Surprisingly, however, they at first chose to try to work within the existing system and did not begin to turn to their co-nationals south of the Carpathians until it was obvious that their grievances would not be listened to.

Continuing a tradition of many years, the Romanian national movement at first centered around the Uniate Church. But this compromise organization, accepted originally as a vehicle to wring concessions from the Catholic Habsburgs, was of no importance in dealing with the secular Hungarian officials after 1867. The failure of the Uniates to effect changes of any significance caused many to disown this hybrid church, and a number of parishes reverted to Orthodoxy.

The effort to Magyarize was stronger in Transylvania than in any other part of the Hungarian kingdom. This province, which the Magyars considered to be an integral part of their homeland, was of prime importance to them. The Romanians were given no quarter; the moderate provisions of the Hungarian Nationality Law of 1868 were never made available to them. The campaign was nonetheless as much a failure in Transylvania as elsewhere.[17] The reasons, at least in retrospect, are obvious: it is difficult to stop an idea from spreading, and it is all but impossible to eliminate one that has already gained wide currency; illiterates cannot have their nationality changed except by extensive education—an extraordinarily expensive and time-consuming process that does not guarantee success; and finally, a nationality that has ready access to culturally free co-nationals in a neighboring county almost certainly cannot be suppressed.

As the Romanians of Transylvania became more frustrated, and consequently more radical in their nationalism, they drew increasing attention from the Romanians of Romania. By the turn of the century, the press of Bucharest was constantly filled with stories of Magyar repression in Transylvania. More and more Austro-Hungarian Romanians went to jail or emigrated or both. But the Hungarians refused to moderate their views, and their behavior kept the relations between Austria-Hungary and Romania (allies on paper) in a constant state of tension and bitterness.

The Slovenes in the Habsburg Empire

The situation of the Slovenes in the Habsburg monarchy did not change materially until after the *Ausgleich* of 1867. Then, following the creation of an Austrian parliament, the Slovenes had the opportunity to express themselves officially for the first time in history. The early German liberal governments were not inclined to listen, but beginning with the Taaffe period in 1879, the Slovenes became a small but important cog in the aristocratic-clerical-Slav coalition. The strong and consistent Catholicism of the Slovenes was an essential factor in this. The Church repaid their support on religious issues with assistance on national ones. This relationship was especially important in educational affairs—an area in which the Slovenes and the Church worked together to secure religious schools with instruction in Slovene. This alliance was quite successful in maintaining primary schools in the solidly Slovene areas, but the Germans blocked the creation of most higher schools as well as expansion to districts with larger German populations.

The Yugoslav idea (see below) penetrated Slovenia quite early, and many Slovene intellectuals were in favor of union with their fellow south Slavs. The leading Slovene political party, the Slovene Peoples Party, was in favor of cooperation (and possibly, union) with the Catholic Croats but balked at the idea of making common cause with the Orthodox Serbs.[18] Within the framework of the Habsburg Empire this conservative viewpoint was dominant. Following the collapse of the monarchy, however, a broader sentiment in favor of Yugoslavism prevailed.

Slovenia's rich national resources facilitated fairly rapid industrial growth beginning in the last decades of the century. This development, in addition to the fact that Slovenes were a major part of the population of the vital Trieste seaport-industrial region, made Slovenia a very important part of the Habsburg Empire.

The Croats in the Habsburg Empire

The Croats, it should be remembered, played a crucial role in preventing the collapse of the Habsburg Empire in 1848–49. With great courage and considerable sacrifice in blood, they had recaptured Vienna from German liberal rebels and had then engaged Kossuth's armies in a series of sharp battles that forced the Magyars eastward and thereby allowed the imperial leadership the opportunity to reorganize and go back on the offensive. As a nationality, however, they received nothing for their efforts. The Croat leader, Joseph Jelačić, was decorated, but his people were not. It was thus a striking blow to the Croats when they discovered that the *Ausgleich* would place them totally under Hungarian control.

The situation in Croatia in 1867–68 was so volatile that even the Hungarians realized that some compromise was essential. Thus the *Nagodba* (compromise) of 1868 was negotiated (see above). This agreement was important in that it recognized a high degree of autonomy for the Croatians in their own lands, and also permitted them limited national rights in Hungary proper (e.g., Croatian could be used in the parliament in Budapest). Two flaws in the *Nagodba* surfaced immediately, however. The issue of the vital seaport of Rijeka (then known as Fiume) was unsettled. The Hungarians held it by virtue of *force majeure,* but the Croatians never recognized this solution. Even more important than the territorial issue was the fact that the Hungarians never honored either the letter or the spirit of the *Nagodba.*

The Hungarian leader in the first years after the *Ausgleich* was Deák, a statesman and a moderate on the nationality issue who was chiefly responsible for the *Nagodba.* Unfortunately, this settlement, like the nationality law of 1868 for which Deák was also largely responsible, did not have the support of the vast majority of Hungarians, both politicians and others. Deák and his party were able to force these issues through parliament because of the enormous prestige that they, the authors of the *Ausgleich,* held in Hungary. But they were not able to force their people to behave as they wished. The weakness of these moderates grew as the Magyar politicians realized that the *Ausgleich* was solid, that it did not depend on the goodwill that Deák commanded in Vienna.

Hungarian bad faith was met with Croatian intransigence. Although an important segment of the Croatian political spectrum (the large land-owners) would have been happy with an honest application of the *Nagodba*, there were many Croats who wanted a more radical solution. Some favored a south-Slav trialist program in which a Croatian-led state would assume equal status with Austria and Hungary. Others wanted nothing less than a fully independent Croatia. Altogether, the opposition was sufficiently strong to elect an overwhelming majority in the Croatian parliament, and even a small armed revolt was mounted by the more extreme enemeies of the *Nagodba*.

The Hungarians reacted to this opposition by appointing a governor of Croatia who was instructed to ignore the constitution if necessary to maintain order and (above all) Magyar rule. The governor was reasonably successful in preventing a continuation of the earlier rebellion, but he could not improve the legitimacy of Hungarian authority in Croatian minds. One governmental tactic, the setting of Croat against Serb (about one-fourth of the population), had some immediate effect in creating divisions and probably also had some long-term effect in encouraging those of the two peoples who were disinclined to cooperate with each other. But overall, the tendency of Croats and Serbs to think alike was very strong. This trend affected the Austrian half as well, since not only Slovenes but also the strong Croatian majority in the Austrian province of Dalmatia were influenced by concepts of south Slav unity.[19]

Parts of Croatia prospered in the general economic upswing of the late-nineteenth–early-twentieth century period. Zagreb developed considerably as a trading center and also experienced some industrial growth. Rijeka, though technically a part of Hungary proper, made great progress as a seaport, and its economic strength helped to improve conditions in the nearby countryside. Croatia was still an overwhelmingly rural and agrarian area, however, and there was little improvement in agriculture. Land reform was urgently needed in the north, where Hungarian and Croatian magnates held huge estates. There was a strong contingent of small peasant farmers in the south and east, but these suffered from the all-too-common problems of lack of capital and access to markets, as well as ignorance of modern agricultural techniques. Significantly, a party primarily concerned with the problems of these small farmers (the Croatian Peasant Party led by Stjepan Radić) emerged as an important voice amid the welter of exclusively nationalistic political groupings.

Overall, however, Croatian politicians were like those of the rest of Eastern Europe in their preoccupation with nationalism. On the eve of the war, those favoring outright secession from the empire were probably still a minority. But, as in the Czech lands, the loyalists were distinctly unhappy and clearly unwilling to be satisfied with the status quo for the indefinite future.

The Serbs in the Habsburg Empire

The Austrian Empire acquired a significant Serbian population in the last years of the eighteenth century. As the Habsburg armies pushed the Ottoman forces south through Hungary after the failure of the last siege of Vienna (1683), many Serbs, always ready to fight the Turks, flocked to their banners. But when the military struggle ground to a halt in 1699, the vast majority of the Serbian homeland was still in the Ottoman Empire. Rightfully fearing Turkish reprisals, thousands of Serbs fled north across the Danube to seek refuge in the Habsburg lands. There they settled along the frontier and were given special privileges, including a limited autonomy, in return for their service as border guards.

The creation of an independent Serbian state in the early nineteenth century drew some Serbs back to the south, but most remained in the southern Hungarian Plain, where they built villages and farms in addition to towns and forts. These Habsburg Serbs, with their access to Austrian culture, were far more educated than their co-nationals in the south, and were responsible for much of the cultural progress and national awareness of their people. Later, when the pressures of Magyarization drove them to resistance, many made common cause with the Croats. They also helped to serve as a bridge between the unity-minded south Slavs of the Habsburg lands on the one side and the stronger and more militantly expansionist independent Serbian state on the other.[20]

The Carpatho-Ruthenians in the Habsburg Empire

The smallest of the regular Habsburg nationalities were the Carpatho-Ruthenians. In fact, they were simply Ukrainians (the Habsburgs preferred to use "Ruthenian") living in the extremes of the Carpathian Mountains. Their habitat, geographically an extension of Slovakia, was in the Hungarian half of the empire. The Carpatho-Ruthenes had been converted to the Uniate Church many centuries earlier, and thus had little contact with their Orthodox co-nationals in Galicia or in Russia. They were subjected to a fierce Magyarization campaign after 1867, and although they offered little in the way of organized resistance, were nonetheless largely unaffected.

The Poles in the Habsburg Empire

The Poles were a relatively recent addition to the Habsburg lands, not having been present in significant numbers until the empire acquired the province of Galacia in the first partition of Poland (1772). In the initial century of Habsburg rule, the Poles were ruled from Vienna with a heavy hand. While it is true that their leaders were predominantly aristocratic and that the people were as Catholic as their Habsburg overlords, it is also true that the Polish reputation for revolutionary nationalism was well deserved. In Metternich's Austria (1815–48), they were thoroughly distrusted, and even the local affairs of Galicia were administered by bureaucrats sent from Vienna.

The position of the Habsburgs vis-à-vis the Poles in Galicia was greatly strengthened by the ruler's ability to exploit class and national conflicts in the province. As typically arrogant landowners, the Polish aristocrats were hated by the oppressed peasantry. Since some 40 percent of the masses were not Poles, but Ukrainians who suffered religious and national as well as social and economic discrimination, the situation was especially explosive. The poorly organized Polish revolution of 1846 illustrates this.

This insurrection, which was of necessity planned and organized by men of the gentry class, met its inevitable defeat more quickly than expected because of a betrayal. Nevertheless, the Austrian authorities were not content with a crushing defeat of the Polish revolutionary center in Cracow. Instead, they carried the struggle into the countryside and incited the peasants against their landlords. The violence was awesome: in one district more than 90 percent of the manor houses were destroyed and large numbers of landowners and members of their families were killed. The Austrians, who wanted to set a local rather than a national example, had not intended things to go so far. In particular, they were surprised when the peasant violence spread from the Polish areas of western Galicia to the overwhelmingly Ukrainian areas of eastern Galicia, where it acquired fury that it was especially hard to bring under control.[21]

The events of 1846 helped to keep Austrian Poland, like Russian and Prussian Poland, quiet during the trauma of 1848–49. The emancipation of the peasantry throughout the empire in 1848 improved the social situation, but only slightly. As elsewhere, the peasants were free, but the landlords still held the land. The leaders of the Polish aristocracy in Galicia became increasingly conservative as they became aware of some of the lessons of 1846 and 1848: they realized that the national question could not be raised without reopening the social question and, further, that Polish aspirations were certain to run directly counter to those of the ever more nationally conscious Ukrainians. Galicia was thus comparatively tranquil in the period 1848–67. The Austrian Poles, as discussed above, did not attempt an insurrection on their own territory during the Polish revolution of 1863.

Thus it can be said that the interests of the Polish leadership in Galicia and of the Habsburg government were coalescing, so that the Austro-Hungarian *Ausgleich* of 1867 was followed quickly by a similar Austro-Polish compromise. In effect, the Poles won autonomy in local affairs in return for loyalty to the empire. The policies of the governing Polish aristocrats in autonomous Galicia were predictable. The interests of the landowners were supported to the maximum possible extent, with the result that there was very little industrial development. Since most of Galicia lacked the natural resources for heavy industry, some backwardness was to be expected, but government policy clearly made the situation worse.

In cultural affairs, the new leaders followed in the wake of the Magyars. Every attempt was made to "Polonize" the minorities (Ukrainians and Jews). Polish was declared the official language of the province and was the only language used in education above the primary level. The authorities acted forcibly to break up Ukrainian cultural organizations. The results, as elsewhere, were counterproductive. The Ukrainians became more and more hostile to the Poles. Their bitterness was enhanced, of course, by the social situation in which predominantly Polish landlords lived lives of ease and luxury in areas inhabited by masses of extremely poor Ukrainian peasants.

As the century drew to a close, the leadership of the Polish aristocracy was subject to increasingly intense pressure. Many Poles objected to what were clearly reactionary social and economic policies. Others (with some overlap of course) were frustrated by the comparatively passive attitude of the Galician *szlachta* to the overall problem of Polish nationalism. This was especially obvious since the *szlachta* from Russian Poland, whose wealth had been destroyed in the aftermath of the 1863 revolt, had dropped their class interests in favor of national ones.

Many of the leaders from Russian Poland had sought refuge in Galicia, and their voices were clearly heard. The declaration of universal manhood suffrage in the Austrian half of the empire (1907) broke the conservative stranglehold on the provincial government, but it led, predictably, to chaos rather than to a coherent new approach to politics. No group or stable coalition could assume a leading position. As elsewhere in Eastern Europe on the eve of the Great War, political fragmentation was the order of the day.

The Balkan Peoples and the Ottoman Empire

The Ottoman Empire escaped relatively unscathed from the storm of 1848 (the brief revolt in Wallachia was suppressed without difficulty), but this was more a sign of the empire's isolation than of its strength. Even so the ideas of nationalism continued to percolate through the rocky landscape, and it was obvious that the only large nationality still under Turkish control—the Bulgarian—was restless and simply biding its time. Within the Ottoman administrative structure there was widespread recognition of the need for rapid reform. Yet the inertia of many centuries without any real precedent for systemic change frustrated those desiring fundamental reorganization. Eventually, some reform did occur and some interesting possibilities emerged. But since this was a classic case of too little too late, we must turn our attention to the complicated political event first of the Balkans as a whole and then of the Balkan peoples themselves.

The Crimean War was an extremely bloody conflict fought for reasons too obscure to mention. It is sufficient to point out that the Ottoman Empire, despite being on the winning side with France and Britain against Russia, emerged even weaker in victory. This occurred because the powers (Britain, France, Prussia, Austria, and Russia) took control of the Danubian principalities from the vanquished Russians but realized that the Turks were too feeble and too lacking in public respect to reassert even their nominal authority. The principalities were therefore placed under the aegis of the powers as a group. Since this sort of rule was necessarily indirect and ineffectual, the Romanians were able to secure independence and unity in 1859—despite the fact that only the French were in favor of this step. The Romanians showed themselves to be as good at timing as the Habsburgs were bad—they took advantage of the Italian crisis of 1859 to divert attention and permit a fait accompli.

The other independent Balkan states, Serbia, Montenegro, and Greece, began negotiations on an alliance to clear the Turks from the

Balkans. Their objectives conflicted, particularly in the region of Macedonia, which all claimed more or less in its entirety, and they were slow to come to a consensus. The ideal time would have been 1866, when the Austrians were at war with Prussia and Italy, and the Russians, only a decade after the Crimean defeat, were preoccupied with domestic affairs. But the Balkan states were not prepared, and a golden opportunity was lost. By 1867 a stronger Austria-Hungary was created, and Russia was showing more confidence. Only the clever Romanians, who exchanged a domestic dynasty for a more prestigious foreign one, were able to take advantage of 1866.

The next crisis escalated into a major conflict in which nearly everyone in the Balkans was involved. As recounted earlier, the inefficient and corrupt Turkish administration in the province of Bosnia-Hercegovina tormented the local population to the point of rebellion in 1875. The issues were primarily local, but it was also clear that the independent states of Montenegro and Serbia had incited the Serbs in the province, while some of the Catholic Croats, hoping for annexation of the province by the Habsburgs also threw oil on the fire.[22] Things then quickly got out of hand. Russia, abetted by Serbia, Montenegro, and Romania, offered the rebels arms as well as moral support. The tension quickly spread, and the Bulgarians, reacting to long-simmering passions, rose in revolt in April 1876. The Turks, who had had difficulty in suppressing the rebels of isolated and inaccessible Bosnia-Hercegovina, turned quickly against the neighboring, poorly armed Bulgarians. The Bulgarian revolt was put down ruthlessly, and the civilian population was subjected to horrible atrocities, including mass murders of entire village populations.

Turkish inhumanity in Bulgaria did much to seal the ultimate Ottoman defeat. Foreign reporters, notably the American J. A. MacGahan, provided all the gory details to the British press. The massacres made front page news in the sensation-oriented papers. The British government, which had as its natural inclination the support of Ottoman power in order to block the Russians from Constantinople (which would give them year-round warm winter ports and the potential to challenge British maritime supremacy), was forced by public opinion to sanction a war against the Turks.

Serbia and Montenegro quickly declared war on the Ottoman Empire and were as quickly defeated. Although the Serbs lacked nothing in zeal and determination, their armaments and military training were woefully inadequate. The Russians, sensing a Slavic holocaust, had no option but to intervene. After first paying a price for Austro-Hungarian neutrality (see above), the tsar also found that he had to negotiate with the Romanians. The latter insisted on a guarantee of their territorial integrity (important since Russia had lost some Romanian territory after the Crimean War and clearly wanted it back), full payment for the transit costs of the Russian army, and the right to participate in the war as an ally of Russia. The confident Russians ceded on the first two points but refused the final one. The Romanians, who had little desire to fight an obviously hopeless war against Russia over this issue, yielded.

The Russians' initially powerful offensive bogged down after a few months (in the winter of 1877–78) in front of the strategically located Turkish fortress of Pleven. Fearing a major tactical defeat that would lead to a long, humiliating struggle, the Russians asked for Romanian assistance. The latter responded with alacrity, and, following enormous sacrifices of human life, the seige of Pleven was broken. With the road to Constantinople wide open, the Russians then told the Romanians to stay home and plunged ahead alone. As noted above, the Russians ignored their promises to Austria and created, in the treaty of San Stefano, a large Bulgarian state. Since this solution had the support only of the exhausted Russians and the powerless Bulgarians, it is not surprising that it was scrapped at the Berlin Congress of 1878.

The outcome of the 1877–78 war had important repercussions for all of Southeastern Europe. Russia and Austria-Hungary, as described earlier, settled into new roles as sworn enemies. But the liberating power had made other enemies as well. The Romanians were furious at a blatant Russian double cross: the tsar ignored his treaty obligations and took territory (Bessarabia) from his Romanian ally. The Serbs, who had long thought of themselves as Russia's special friends,, were also alienated. The "Big Bulgaria" established at San Stefano would have taken territory coveted by Serbia. Further, it appeared that the Russians had intended that Bulgaria, not Serbia, become the dominant power in the Balkans. The anger of the Serbs and the Romanians was such that they drew closer to Austria-Hungary; the latter even joined the Dual Alliance (Austria-Hungary and Germany).

The alliance structure that evolved from the Russo-Turkish War of 1877–78 was unnatural and consequently warped the international politics of the area for decades. The alliances were unnatural because both Serbia and Romania, though they had legitimate short-term grievances against Russia, had more serious long-term conflicts with Austria-Hungary. Romania had a valid claim to Russian Bessarabia, but this province was less strategic, smaller, and had fewer Romanians than the Austro-Hungarian province of Transylvania, where Hungarian rule was becoming increasingly unpleasant for non-Magyars. Serbia also had a right to feel jilted, but, as of the date of its agreement with Austria-Hungary, neither Russia nor Bulgaria held a large amount of Serbian territory, while Austria-Hungary controlled Bosnia-Hercegovina, the Serb-populated parts of southern Hungary, and Croatia. Further, Austria-Hungary was just as likely as Russia/Bulgaria to prevent Serbian seizure of Macedonia. The fact that Habsburg diplomats had worked hard (and successfully) at Berlin to keep Serbia and Montenegro from having a common frontier was evidence of the Austro-Hungarian desire to prevent any increase in the size or influence of Serbia.

The Russian situation became even worse when the Bulgarians proved to be restive and uncooperative allies. The Russians had a record in Bulgaria of good deeds and good intentions, but they were also obliged, in the tense international atmosphere after 1878, to maintain the status quo. Thus, Bulgarian plans to seize territory from Turkey were usually frustrated by the Russians before they could get to the point of an international incident. This behavior, together with the traditional arrogance of the Russian advisers in the country, produced a gradual estrangement. The death of Tsar Alexander II, the "Tsar Liberator," (1881) also contributed to this process by breaking the strong personal ties that the Bulgarian people had felt for the Russian leader. Russian influence, therefore, was minimal when in 1885 the Bulgarians took advantage of a revolt in the Turkish-administered part of Bulgaria proper (not including Macedonia) and quickly annexed it.

The Russians protested vigorously, in part because they disliked the Bulgarians acting independently and in part because the action was in violation of the Berlin settlement which the Russians had sworn to uphold. The Serbs were more forceful. Noting the Bulgarian isolation, they launched a sudden attack in the hope of forcing the Bulgarians to give them some territorial "compensation" (compensation for what was never clear). The Bulgarians, fighting without their Russian advisers, who had been withdrawn in protest of the annexation, surprised everyone by thoroughly defeating the Serbs. Indeed, Serb's odd choice of friends proved to be useful on this occasion, for it was only Austro-Hungarian warnings that prevented the victorious Bulgarians from invading Serbia and annexing part of its territory.

Russia continued to meddle in Bulgarian affairs after 1885, even going so far as to kidnap the Bulgarian prince. The Russian intrigues were notable for their incompetence, however, and the tsar soon found himself without any influence whatsoever in Bulgaria. This produced a fundamental disequilibrium in the Balkans, with predominant influence in the hands of Austria-Hungary. Tension was eased when Bismarck, who had always tried to maintain some ties with Russia, was forced to resign and the new German government allowed relations with its eastern neighbors to harden. Russia was very much on the defensive at this point, and although bitter and hostile, she was forced to turn her attention elsewhere and to bide her time until the situation in the Balkans changed. As a consequence, there was more than a quarter of a century of peace in Southeastern Europe.

Astute observers were aware of the fact that this peace was superficial. They realized that the Russian withdrawal was only temporary, and they also knew that there were powerful forces working to upset the precarious balance. Overall, these currents were a part of the general tide of nationalism which was tearing at Eastern Europe. The complexity was enormous, but two major aspects require separate discussion: the Macedonian problem and the phenomenon of "Yugoslavism." Other factors were important, but these two were sufficient by themselves to provoke destabilization and, ultimately, war.

The problem of Macedonia, which has had enormous appeal for the authors of international thrillers, drove diplomats mad. Macedonia, which in 1885 was defined roughly by what is now Yugoslav and Greek Macedonia, as well as some parts of contemporary Serbia and Bulgaria, was still under Ottoman rule. The province's population was so diverse and so intermixed that a French chef named a complicated salad after it. The nationalities of the non-Slavic peoples were easy to identify: Greek, Turk, Albanian, and Vlach. The Slavic peoples (a solid majority of the population) were either "south Serbs," "Bulgarians," or "slavophone Greeks," depending on whether one was listening, respectively, to the official line of Belgrade, Sofia, or Athens. Linguistically and historically, the Bulgarians had the best case in this argument for control of Macedonia, and they also generated the most local support. The Greeks and the Serbs yielded nothing in zeal and determination, however, and a vicious three-way contest ensued.[23]

The vehicle for the overt struggle for control was the Orthodox Church. The willingness, in the early days of Christianity in the Balkans, of the patriarch in Constantinople to gain converts to Orthodoxy by permitting autonomous churches once again facilitated conflict. The separate Serbian and Bulgarian churches, long dormant under Ottoman rule which had favored a single Greek authority, had been revived in the latter part of the nineteenth century. Now backed by their national governments, they competed with the Greek church for the allegiance of the Macedonian villagers. The chief weapon in this battle was the church school, which, of course, provided instruction in the literary language of the sponsoring country. Even the Romanians joined in the fray, setting up schools for the scattered, pastoral Vlachs. Among those Slavs who were not clearly Serbs (and who will later be known simply as Macedonians) the Bulgarian campaign was the most successful.

In the 1890s the struggle in Macedonia took a more openly political turn as a group known as IMRO (Internal Macedonian Revolutionary Organization) proclaimed "Macedonia for Macedonians." IMRO had as its most immediate objective autonomy for Macedonia: to be achieved through the forcible elimination of Turkish rule. This fourth side (as opposed to Bulgarians, Serbs, and Turks) was quite successful in gathering local support and in 1898 went on the offensive in a campaign of terror against the Turks.[24] IMRO kept the pot boiling in this fashion until 1903, when a mass rising of the Macedonians was put down by the Turks with extreme cruelty and much bloodshed. After this, IMRO drifted under the control of the Bulgarians. Or, one might also say that Bulgaria fell under the sway of IMRO, since the number of Macedonian refugees (many of them armed and prone to violence) that congregated in the Bulgarian capital of Sofia was so great as to influence strongly that country's policy.

The Macedonian problem was particularly important in that it kept the independent Balkan states from forming alliances either for protection or for common gain. They could not even agree on a war against their universal enemy, the Turk, since that would involve action in Macedonia. The Balkan states had much to offer each other in economic as well as political cooperation, but the Macedonian issue kept them apart. Later, when external pressures forced a brief unity, the legacy of hostility and distrust over Macedonia quickly brought common action to an end.

The other major factor of nationalism in the Balkans, the "Yugoslav idea" was more hopeful than the Macedonian issue, although in the long run it proved to be more explosive. In the early section on the Slavic languages, it was noted that the south Slavic languages (Yugo-Slav means south-Slav) were very similar to each other. In particular, the dialects of the Serbs and the Croats are so close that they are now considered as one language. Slovene and Bulgarian (and later, Macedonian) on either side are less similar but still closely related. The nonlinguistic differences between the four nationalities are religious (Slovenes and Croats are Catholic; Serbs and Bulgarians are Orthodox) and historical.

In the middle of the nineteenth century, a new generation of scholars, increasingly aware of the linguistic similarities, began to build bridges, particularly between Serbs and Croats. The idea was to create a larger nationalism, embracing more than just one small group. The Yugoslav movement was at first largely cultural and received an enormous boost in the early eighteenth century when the great Serbian writer, Vuk Kar-adžić, chose a dialect that was in the middle of the range of Serbian and Croatian dialects as the Serb literary language.[25] A century later the Croat, Bishop Strossmayer, preached cultural unity as a precursor to political unity. Not all Serbs and Croats (and even fewer Slovenes and Bulgars) accepted the Yugoslav idea, but it always retained a powerful hold on many influential men. Indeed, modified to include provisos for Serbian leadership, it became the state ideology of Serbia, and thus a part of the rationale for Belgrade's interference in Croatia, Bosnia-Hercegovina, and Macedonia.

Shortly after the turn of the century, Austria-Hungary's favorable position in the Balkans began to collapse. The Romanians were more and more unhappy about the status of their brethren in Transylvania and had a bitter trade dispute with Austria-Hungary. The treaty between the two states had been renewed, but its validity was weakened by the fact that Romanian leaders were so afraid to let it become public that only a handful of people knew about it. Serbia had similar trade disputes and was also upset about the treatment of Serbs and Croats in Hungary and in Bosnia-Hercegovina. The change in the Serbian dynasty in 1903, and Austro-Hungarian opposition to Serbian and Bulgarian action against the Turks in the wake of the Macedonian rising of the same year, combined to make relations even worse. Finally, Russia's defeat by Japan in the Far East, and Tsar Nicholas' decision to look once more to the Balkans for an outlet to his nation's interest in foreign affairs, again heated up the situation.

The first crisis in the new period came in 1908, when the Young Turk movement in the Ottoman Empire carried out a successful revolution. The Russian foreign minister, A. P. Izvolsky, thought this development would make a useful diversion for his country's desire to force the Ottomans to give Russian ships freer access to and from the Black Sea. Realizing that Russia could not act alone, Izvolsky met with his counterpart in Austria-Hungary, Count Aehrenthal, and proposed that Austria-Hungary annex (as opposed to merely occupy) Bosnia-Hercegovina in return for support of Russia's plans. Aehrenthal agreed, or at least Izvolsky thought he did. But before the Russians could complete their negotiations with the Turks and the other powers, the Austro-Hungarians announced annexation. In the genral excitement that followed, Vienna held on to its fait accompli and Russia got nothing.

The "Bosnian Crisis," as it came to be known, seemed to be a great victory for Austria-Hungary; Vienna had once more successfully double-crossed its eastern neighbor. Yet the long-term results were otherwise. The Serbs and the Bulgarians now came to see Austria-Hungary as their real enemy (Austria-Hungary had made her control over a large number of south Slavs permanent.) With considerable Russian prodding, the two Balkan states forged over a four-year period (the Macedonian problem accounted for the delay) a secret alliance against Turkey, with certain provisions that were also clearly aimed at Austria-Hungary. Shortly thereafter the Bulgarians signed a pact with Greece, and the bellicose Montenegrins signed with all three.

The First Balkan War began in October, 1912 when four of the five Balkan states (Romania did not participate) attacked Turkey. Russia did not take part directly, but saber rattling on the Russo-Turkish frontier in the Caucasus tied down many Turkish troops. The stoic Bulgarians, closest to the Turkish center of power, had to do most of the fighting, but all of the allies distinguished themselves, and the Turks were thoroughly defeated by March of 1913. The great powers then called the Balkan states to London and dictated a peace which included the creation of an Albanian state. The settlement of this First Balkan War really satisfied no one (Bulgarians, Greeks, and Serbs all wanted a larger share of Macedonia), and thus soon led to a second conflict.

The Bulgarians felt that their allies had not honored the prewar agreements, although in truth these were rather vague. An unfortunate series of misunderstandings between Russia and Bulgaria resulted in a serious estrangement between the two and caused the latter to decide to strike while she still had an army in the field. The Bulgarians thus attacked the Serb and Greek positions in Macedonia. Unfortunately for the Bulgarians, however, the Serbs, Greeks, Montenegrins, and even the Romanians and the Turks had all joined in a new alliance. Surrounded, the Bulgarians were quickly crushed in the ensuing brief (three months) Second Balkan War. At the end, all of the allies (except Montenegro) chopped off parts of Bulgaria.

On the eve of the Great War, the focus of the perennial Balkan crisis shifted northwards. The Serbs, having won most of what they wanted in Macedonia, were stronger, more confident, and increasingly interested in the problems of their Slavic brethren in the Habsburg Empire. The Romanians, though technically still allies with Austria-Hungary, were more and more outspoken about the plight of the Romanians of Transylvania. The seeds of further conflict had already taken root.

Independent Serbia, 1848–1914

The Serbs had the misfortune to have a serious dynastic conflict embedded into their national history. From the early days of the successful nineteenth-century risings against the Turks, two families had been prominent: the Karageorgevich and the Orbrenovich. The first Serbian national leader was a Karageorgevich followed closely by an Obrenovich. The latter was the first recognized prince of Serbia (1815), but when he was forced to resign (1839), members of his own family were unable to hold on to power. In 1842, a Karageorgevich became prince, but he too was forced to resign in favor of the previous Obrenovich ruler (1858). This family then hung on until 1903. The dispute between the two groups had more serious consequences than the shuffling of people on and off the throne: the rivalry produced intrigue, bitterness, and a number of assassinations and murders. All of this had a strongly negative effect on Serbian politics.

One of the ablest of the leaders of Serbia was Michael Obrenovich (1860–1868). Michael increased his power vis-à-vis the freely elected parliament to the extent that he became more an independent executive than a limited constitutional monarch. He used his authority to institute many badly needed reforms (particularly in modernizing the army) and also in trying to create a coalition of the independent Balkan states against the Ottoman Empire.[26] This important diplomatic project was slowed by mutual suspicion but eventually succeeded in producing an alliance. Unfortunately, agreement was reached too late to take advantage of the great opportunity of 1866, and Michael's death (by assassination) in 1868 ended the effort.

Michael's successor was his dissolute cousin, Milan, who referred to Serbia as "that damned country." The new prince was nonetheless intelligent, and he managed to hold on to the strong executive position won by his predecessor. Unfortunately for Milan, however, he began his reign on bad terms with the Russians. The tsar had hoped to unite Serbia and Montenegro under the latter's ruler and was therefore not pleased with Milan. This factor may help to explain Russia's extreme favoritism for Bulgaria over Serbia after the war of 1877–78. In any case, Milan felt that he had no choice but to align his country with Austria-Hungary.

Part of the price for the diplomatic tie was a trade agreement. Inevitably, this deal between states of such widely varying strengths proved to be unequal. Serbia became, in effect, an economic colony of Austria-Hungary. The lack of tariff protection prevented the growth of domestic Serbian industry and left the country in a comparatively backward position even in the Balkans. Serbian agricultural products could be marketed at a reasonable price in Austria-Hungary, but even this had its drawbacks. Serbian farmers soon became used to producing for a single market and thus developed an almost total dependence on their northern neighbor. Overall, the unequal economic relationship was a calamity for

Serbia, particularly because the political side of the relationship was inherently unstable.

Milan (who declared himself king in 1882) made a terrible mistake in the disastrous attack on Bulgaria in 1885. After that his position became untenable, and he abdicated in 1889. The new king was Milan's son, Alexander, who was considerably less skilled than his predecessors. Personally erratic, he outraged nearly everyone by insisting on marrying a woman who was older and divorced, not to mention a commoner. This decision clearly demonstrated his political insensitivity, which was reflected in the rapid degeneration of royal authority in the country. Alexander survived for only three years after his marriage. In the summer of 1903, the king and his queen were brutally murdered in a coup carried out by army officers, and Peter Karageorgevich was proclaimed king.

This last dynastic turnabout had important domestic and foreign repercussions. The conspirators in the army led a provisional government that called new elections under a new, liberal constitution. Henceforth, the new parliament, not the king, controlled the government. The dominant political party was the Radical, which, like the Croatian Peasant Party, evinced a strong interest in the welfare of the small peasant farmer (although second to none in its strong nationalism).

Austria-Hungary, which had served as a sort of sponsor for the Obrenovich dynasty, was deeply worried by the events of 1903. As it turned out, the concern was most appropriate. The new Serbian government was anxious to end its dependent economic relationship with its northern neighbor. The motivation for this was partly just what it seemed, but there was also a strong undercurrent of dissatisfaction with the nationality and foreign policies of the Dual Monarchy. The diplomats in Vienna sensed the significance of the Serbian demand for renegotiation of the trade agreement and did their best to frighten the Serbs into submission. One part of this struggle was the "Pig War" (1906), in which Austro-Hungarian imperial authorities turned back Serbia's most important export by claiming that the animals were diseased.[27] These tactics failed, as the Serbs quickly found new markets and new allies in France and Russia.

Freed from the constraints of the Austro-Hungarian alliance, Serbia became far more aggressive in Balkan politics. The old Serb desire was for Serbia to be the magnet for the creation of a new and larger south Slavic state. Austria-Hungary's annexation of Bosnia-Hercegovina thus reinforced and sharpened an existing sense of rivalry, and Serbia, ever closer to Russia, took the lead in organizing the alliances that led to the Balkan wars of 1912–13. The Serbs were also deeply involved in the affairs of the Slavs of the Dual Monarchy, and they offered aid, comfort and perhaps also leadership to the revolutionary and terrorist groups that now seemed to be everywhere.

The Bulgarians, 1848–1914

In the middle decades of the nineteenth century, Bulgarian economic development lost much of the impetus that it had gained after the Greek war for independence. The reason for this was not a sudden reversal of Ottoman trade patterns, but rather the slow but accelerating penetration of foreign manufactured and agricultural products into the empire. In the early period of Ottoman military weakness, the western powers had forced the sultan to give foreign nationals extensive commercial concessions which amounted to the right to import and export duty free. This arrangement became particularly important in the 1860s, when a flood of cheap manufactured products seriously upset the village economy of Bulgaria by destroying its handicraft industries. In addition, steam-powered vessels made it possible for the Ottoman elite to import at low cost foodstuffs that had previously been hauled overland from the Bulgarian farms.[28]

But the weakening of economic progress did not adversely affect the national revival. Instead, dislocation and discontent clearly favored those advocating change. The cultural development of the earlier years proceeded at a rapid pace and culminated in the restoration of the independent Bulgarian Orthodox Church in 1870. The Ottoman leaders probably hoped that by permitting the revival of the Bulgarian Church they would alleviate the growing nationalist pressure. If that was indeed their hope, they were quickly disappointed. Bulgarian revolutionary groups had been organized by the early 1860s, and their development did not slow until independence was won.

The Bulgarian revolutionaries were forced to operate primarily in exile. Most lived in Romania, which was not only convenient to Bulgaria, but also in whose cities a number of prosperous, patriotic Bulgarian merchants could be found; most of the Romanian governments were also highly sympathetic. The greatest influence on the Bulgarians, however, was Russia. The similarities of the two languages, the common Orthodox faith, and the growth of pan-Slav sentiments all contributed to a close relationship between the two peoples. But it is important to remember that there were levels to this friendship. Thus, for example, official Russian scholarships brought Bulgarian students to Russian universities, where, contrary to plan, many of these young men were deeply influenced by the revolutionaries who seemed to dominate student life in the last decades of tsarist rule.

The four great leaders of the Bulgarian liberation movement were: George Rakovski (d. 1867), a writer and poet; Vasil Levski (d. 1872); Christo Botev (d. 1876), also a poet; and Ljuben Karavelov (d. 1879), a writer and a political leader, and the only one of the four to see his country free and independent. Levski, who was a skilled organizer of revolutionary forces, was killed after a colleague betrayed him to the authorities in 1872. Botev was one of chief forces behind the famous April Rising of 1876. Though this revolt failed to drive out the Turks and instead cost Botev and thousands of other Bulgarians their lives, it did, as described above, pave the way for the Russian intervention that created a Bulgarian state in 1878.[29]

The Russians were not nearly as shocked and upset by the decisions of the Congress of Berlin as were the Bulgarians. The Bulgaria established in the Treaty of San Stefano was reduced by two-thirds. Macedonia was separated entirely, while the southern part of Bulgaria, known as Eastern Rumelia, was given a Christian governor but remained a part of the Ottoman Empire. At first the Bulgarians refused to recognize the Berlin settlement and, instead of proceeding to write a constitution and set up a government, concentrated their energies on petitioning the European powers for reconsideration. This embarrassed the Russian officials in the country, who were only too aware of the fact that the Bulgarian actions only annoyed the powers and led to suspicions that the Russians themselves were responsible. The Russians, therefore, were themselves forced to apply pressure to the Bulgarians, thus producing considerable friction between liberators and liberated.

In the debates leading to the creation of a Bulgarian constitution, the majority of the delegates ignored Russian pressure and opted for a liberal approach which severely limited the power of the prince—thus offering a sharp contrast to the role of the tsar in Russia. The person selected to be prince, Alexander of Battenberg (Germany), was not happy with the Tirnovo Constitution (named after the town in which it was drawn up), but he also developed serious conflicts with the Russians. The latter were on the one hand careful to avoid conflict with the other powers on the Macedonian question, while at the same time they were anxious to exploit their influence in Bulgaria in much the same way that other nations treated their colonies. As a consequence, Alexander soon found himself in opposition to both the Russians and the domestic liberals, receiving the support of only the relatively weak Bulgarian conservatives.

Alexander at first did well, taking advantage of the rightist reaction to the murder of Alexander II of Russia by forcing a suspension of the Tirnovo Constitution. Severe problems appeared, however, when the Bulgarians in Eastern Rumelia (Southern Bulgaria) revolted against their Ottoman rulers (1885) and voted to join Bulgaria. The Russians had no choice but to oppose the violation of the Berlin Treaty of 1878, and were severely vexed by the Bulgarian's failure to follow their lead. The Bulgarians, of course, had no alternative but to support the aspirations of their co-nationals. Russo-Bulgarian conflict might have been avoided at this juncture if the two sides had been accustomed to communicating openly and carefully with each other. As it was, the former allies saw very different interests in 1885, and now took sharply different views. The Russians, stung by the Bulgarian failure to consult with them over the Rumelian affair, became opponents of Bulgarian unification—a truly ironic turn of events.[30]

In the diplomatic turbulence that followed the events of 1885, the Serbs, sensing that the Bulgarians were entirely without allies, decided to attack Bulgaria. The official objective was "compensation" (never specified, see above), but it is obvious that the Serbian goal was to weaken Bulgaria and thus make it easier for Serbia to assert control over Macedonia in the future. With their Russian advisors withdrawn in the sudden chill between Russia and Bulgaria, the troops of the latter were undecided underdogs in their struggle with the Serbs. But in an amazing turnabout, the Bulgarians routed the attacking Serbs and might have occupied Belgrade if the Russians and Austro-Hungarians had not forced a halt.

The Russians now found themselves in a very odd position. Their supposed client state (Bulgaria) had been disloyal, and they were forced to assist an ally (Serbia) of their enemy (Austria-Hungary) in a conflict of significance. The only reasonable course in such a situation was for the tsar of Russia to claim that he had in fact supported the interests of Bulgaria, but that he had been frustrated by the prince (Alexander) who did not understand his country's best interests. Russian displeasure expressed in this way was sufficient to incite a military coup which forced Alexander from the throne. A countercoup restored the prince, but, faced with Russia's implacable opposition, Alexander abdicated and went home to Germany. The tsar seemed to be having his way.

The events of 1885–86, however, produced a strong anti-Russian current in Bulgarian politics. The key politician in the countercoup against the military, Stefan Stambulov, drew his support from those who objected to foreign (i.e., Russian) meddling in Bulgaria's internal affairs. Although unable to prevent Alexander's abdication, Stambulov succeeded in arranging the election of a new prince (Ferdinand of Saxe-Coburg in Germany) who was entirely free of Russian influence. Stambulov was then able to dominate the inexperienced foreign ruler for some seven years. But once the prince felt he had the strength and the skills to rule alone, he had his one-time mentor dismissed and then murdered. Ferdinand was a shrewd politician in a limited, short-term sort of way, and his rule saw Bulgaria oscillate between loyalty to and hostility toward Russia. Consequently, the superficiality of Bulgarian policy alienated the Russians even further, and the latter were pleased to make a deal with the Serbs after they broke with Austria-Hungary (1903). Bulgaria, in turn, drifted into an alliance with Germany and Austria-Hungary.

Two major factors dominated Bulgarian politics in the period before 1914: economic dislocation and pervasive corruption. The economic problems had to do with the collapse of the handicraft industry in the face of competition from cheap foreign manufactured goods, and the loss of centuries-old agricultural markets in Istanbul and elsewhere in the former Ottoman Empire. Since the Bulgarians were not troubled by an economic conflict between small farmers and owners of large estates—the latter did not exist—and since the Bulgarian political tradition leaned toward the democratic, there was a real consensus on solutions to these problems. Unfortunately, the Ottoman tradition of bribery and other types of corruption in all aspects of public life had been forcibly superimposed on the Bulgarian approach to politics. Thus, a politician such as Stambulov and a prince such as Ferdinand were able to purchase support for measures that went against the popular will. The result was chaos thinly veiled by nationalist pride.

Not only did Bulgaria fail to solve her economic problems, but she was also unable to achieve any solution to the problem of the "lost province"—Macedonia. Bulgarians could not accept the idea that this region was anything other than an integral part of the Bulgarian homeland, and their hostility toward their neighbors increased sharply as the latter not only failed to accept the Bulgarian view but also advanced ever stronger claims of their own. The influence of this issue on Bulgarian politics increased as large numbers of heavily armed fanatics from Macedonia chose Sofia as their place of refuge. Bulgaria's unhappy experience in the Balkan wars (see above) was in large part a reflection of the emotion generated by these irredentists.

The outbreak of World War I saw Bulgaria choosing to ally herself with her traditional enemy—the Turks—and with distant and unknown supporters—Germans and Austro-Hungarians—against kindred Slavs in Russia, Serbia, and Montenegro. This oddity is to some extent a reflection of charged emotions over Macedonia, but it is still unlikely that it would have occurred if the government in Sofia had been genuinely representative of the will of the people. Unfortunately, the crisis and sacrifice of war served only to deepen rather than to resolve the inherent conflicts in Bulgarian politics.

The Romanians, 1848–1914

Developments in the Romanian lands after 1848 did not have much in common with those in the rest of the Balkans. In large part this was a consequence of the relative weakness of Turkish power. On the one hand, the Turks had lost much of their influence in the principalities to Russia in 1829, and, as described above, the outcome of the Crimean War left the Turks with a role that was largely symbolic. On the other hand, the Romanians' historical freedom from direct Turkish rule now bore bitter fruit: unlike the Serbs and Bulgarians, the Romanians had a native land-owning aristocracy and the social and economic problems that were a natural consequence of this class. The situation in Transylvania was similar, except that the Romanians were peasants and the nobles were Magyar.

The social structure in the principalities resulted in a dual political party system. The strongest group was the conservative, which drew its support from the land-owning aristocracy. Opposed to them were the liberals who were not, as one might expect, based on the peasantry. Instead, the liberals represented the fledgling bourgeoise, although the leaders were mostly Parisian-educated sons of the nobility. The peasants, uneducated and oppressed, had no real representation except for the liberals (who were inclined more to use them than to represent them). A consequence of this structure was that the crucial socioeconomic question, that of land reform, was much debated but never really resolved.

The liberals owed their strength to the fact that they were radical nationalists par excellence. In exile after the defeat of the Bucharest revolt of 1848, they took good advantage of their Parisian contacts to argue their cause during the Crimean War. Their success in drawing French support gave them considerable freedom of action in the postwar situation. The arrangement of collective control of the principalities by the powers as a group greatly weakened the influence of the conservative Turks and Russians. It also diluted the influence of the pro-Turkish British, and the Romanians were able to take advantage of the confusion created by the Franco-Austrian war in Italy to elect a native Romanian, Alexander Cuza, as prince of both Moldavia an Wallachia (1859). This had the effect of a de facto unification and met with much hostility on the part of the powers (only the French were in favor). Without the diversion of the Franco-Austrian war in Italy, it is doubtful that the Romanians could have gotten away with their fait accompli.

Under the rule of Cuza, de facto unification soon became de jure as the powers saw little hope of agreeing upon a formula to redivide the country. By 1862, therefore, we can refer to Romania as a single country instead of two principalities (Transylvania was still in the Austrian Empire, of course). Despite Cuza's success in the international arena, the prince was never able to direct the flow of domestic politics. Neither a conservative nor a liberal himself, Cuza lacked the political skill to effect a solid compromise or to forge an enduring alliance with one side or another. Party strife and a rapid change of government was therefore the rule for the first years of his tenure.

Cuza's disenchantment with domestic conflict led him to effect a coup d'etat in 1864. The issue was land reform, about which neither party had done much, and Cuza seized power ostensibly to end the stalemate. In fact, the reform which he proclaimed was a substantial one in that much land was redistributed. Unfortunately, the peasants did not get enough land to become truly independent and prosperous and instead incurred debts which often made their situation worse. In many ways, the result was analogous to that of the Russian reform of the same time, for the landlords were hurt but not destroyed. In their hatred of Cuza, the nobles conspired with the liberals in a countercoup which sent the prince into exile in 1866.

The uneasy alliance between liberals and conservatives was weak to the point that both realized that it was impossible to make one of their own number prince. They agreed, therefore, to seek a foreigner for the throne. Their choice, Charles (Carol, in Romanian) of Hohenzollern-Sigmaringen, was a relative of the Prussian king. The idea of a foreign dynasty was promoted as a means of raising the prestige and thus the strength of Romania. Many of the great powers did not want this, and their opposition was strong, with Austria in the lead. But once again proper timing helped—the Austro-Prussian War of 1866 more than preoccupied Romania's enemies.

The first years of Carol's reign were not much different from Cuza's. Governments came and went with bewildering speed. Carol's personal attachment was to the liberals, but his ideology was conservative. A major issue was the tariff system: the liberals wanted higher tariffs to protect developing industry, while the conservatives wanted free trade for their grain exports and did not greatly fear dependency on trading partners who were also conservative in their beliefs (e.g., Austria-Hungary). Carol swayed back and forth, but finally in 1876, Romania, like Serbia, signed a treaty with Austria-Hungary that essentially opened the country to foreign manufactured goods.

The Russo-Turkish War of 1877–78 had important consequences for Romania. Conservative reluctance to participate in the conflict met with strong opposition from the adventurous prince, who quickly ordered a liberal government. The liberals stayed in power for more than a decade thereafter and used their position to effect many changes, including important incentives to industrial growth and the eventual nonrenewal of the trade treaty with Austria-Hungary (1885). The Russian double cross of the Romanians (the seizure of the province of Bessarabia) also had important consequences. Romania joined the Dual Alliance in 1879, but found it an uncomfortable relationship. Commercial ties were obviously not good, and as time went on differences about the treatment of the Romanian majority in Transylvania led to open hostility between the governments in Budapest and Bucharest. As noted earlier, Romanian leaders were so afraid of public objection to the alliance that only a few people knew of it. This extreme secrecy effectively negated the purpose of the alliance—joint planning was impossible, and when the Romanian people did become aware of the agreement, they did not feel bound to honor it.

In the decades before the Great War domestic political tensions lessened somewhat. The passing of highly controversial men like the liberal Ion Brătianu removed a source of friction (but also deprived the country of genuine leadership). The two political parties came to hold more similar socioeconomic views as both feared unrest from the peasantry and the growing proletariat. The plight of the Romanians in Transylvania also served as a unifying factor as first cultural, then political irredentism became popular.[31] Hatred of Russia over the Bessarabian issue did not so much disappear as take second place to anti-Hungarian feelings.

As the Great War approached, Romania, like all of her East European neighbors, had serious domestic social and economic problems. Unlike many of the others, however, the cries for change were not yet pressing enough to threaten political instability. Even an enormous uprising like the Peasant Revolt of 1907 in Moldavia did not produce major changes in the system. The real concern was in foreign affairs, as Romanians hoped for the return of both Bessarabia and Transylvania. Ironically, the surprisingly successful achievement of this foreign policy objective provided the catalyst necessary to bring the domestic problems to the surface.

The Albanians, 1848–1914

The Albanians have not received much attention in these pages. In part this is a reflection of their relatively small numbers, but a more important reason is the comparatively greater subjection of the Albanians as a nationality. After the heroic resistance of Skanderbeg in the fifteenth century, the Turkish victory in Albania had been thorough and crushing. To be sure, many of the mountainous areas of the north had remained more or less independent, but the very inaccessibility and isolation which made this possible also limited their importance. In the more developed central and southern parts of the country the powerful Turkish presence had effected large-scale conversions to Islam—a fact that contributed to cultural isolation from the West as well as to political dependence on the Ottomans. Given this domestic situation and the Turkish determination to hold onto what they perceived to be a very strategic area, it is surprising that any Albanian national movement occurred at all.

Ironically, it was the Ottoman system that facilitated the Albanian national awakening. The traditional lack of prejudice against other nationalities in the Ottoman Empire had made it possible for Albanians, Moslem and non-Moslem, to join the imperial service or to take up commercial duties in distant cities. It was these Albanians who first felt the winds of nationalism blowing from the West. Though many Albanians abroad had gradually become Turkish, many had retained their language and folklore and were captured by the new philosophy which looked to these elements of culture more than to any other. Gradually, centers of Albanian nationalism sprang up in such places as southern Italy, Bucharest, Istanbul, and even Boston.

But the Albanians were like the Serbs in that they had begun national political resistance before they developed cultural nationalism. The decay of the Ottoman administrative system produced continual turmoil in Albania from the beginning of the nineteenth century on. The Turks' inability to provide honest government and a stable economy revived the rebellious spirit of a people for whom the sword and the rifle were constant companions. If the Albanians had not been divided by religion and the lack of a standard dialect, it seems probable that a large-scale explosion would have occurred. As it was, revolts were scattered but bitter, and the conflict served to increase Albanian national consciousness.

The Russo-Turkish war of 1877–78 inspired increased political activity in Albania. The Russians' friendship for the Slavic peoples of the Balkans—particularly the Montenegrins who were long-time enemies of the Albanians—made many Albanians fearful of what a Turkish defeat would bring. The Treaty of San Stefano, by giving much land inhabited by Albanians to Bulgaria and to Montenegro, confirmed their worst fears. When the powers made clear their intention of establishing a new territorial settlement, just as the Bulgarians organized to defend the San Stefano treaty, so the Albanians gathered to oppose it. In this they were supported by the Turks, whose aims were synonymous, at least insofar as holding on to Ottoman territory was concerned. The Albanian movement which was formed in the summer of 1878 was known as the League of Prizren, after the town in which the first meetings were held.

The League of Prizren was a fairly conservative group, representing for the most part the Moslem landowners of the central valleys. These men were loyal to Turkey, but as time went on the more radical group which favored an autonomous Albania within the Ottoman Empire gained the upper hand.[32] A more immediate task accepted by all factions, however, was resisting the loss of what was perceived to be Albanian territory. The Albanian cause was partially successful at Berlin, though not for the most part because of anything the Albanians did. Rather, Austro-Hungarian and British opposition to the aims of Russia and her Slavic brethren was the most important factor. The role of a pawn in great power chess game was one that the Albanians were to experience frequently.

True to their tradition, however, the Albanians did not accede gracefully to the surrender of any land at all. They dug in and held on against intense Montenegrin pressure and, accordingly, won some further concessions on the frontier. But resistance of this kind could not endure. The powers rightfully suspected the Turks of indirectly fomenting Albanian intransigence, and when the patience of the West was exhausted, a show of force was directed against the Turks. The latter quickly sent an army to threaten the insurgents' rear, and Montenegro just as quickly got her land.

The Turks were obviously using the League of Prizren for their own ends (after all, it was still Turkish territory that was in dispute), and when everything possible had been wrung out of this cause, they dropped it. The fact that the League had come to favor autonomy particularly alarmed the Turks, who soon declared the movement illegal. There followed more than three decades of repression in which the leaders in Istanbul did everything in their power to suppress Albanian nationalism. But in part because the Albanians in exile were so important, the result was the reverse of that intended. From the rather disorganized, fragmented movement that still lacked an ideological base in 1880, the Albanian national case achieved a remarkable degree of coherence and unity in little more than a generation. Brilliant intellectuals such as Sami Frashëri (1850–1904) led the way, and by 1908 a standard alphabet had been chosen and accepted by all the major groups—the Albanians thus overcame an obstacle that was considerably more difficult than that faced by other East European peoples.

During the First Balkan War (1912) the Albanians took advantage of general confusion and Turkish weakness and established an independent state. Support from Austria-Hungary was again crucial, but the Italians, whose intentions were far from altruistic, were also helpful. The Albanians had their frontiers decided for them, established by a diplomatic conference meeting in London. The results were generally favorable to Albania, although the historically Serbian region of Kosovo, where half of all Albanians lived, was held by Serbia. The powers were determined to control most of Albania's affairs themselves and even went so far as to set up an international commission to oversee trade and administration. Further, the diplomats also selected a prince, Wilhelm zu Wied of Germany, who lasted all of six months before domestic turmoil forced him to return home. A few months later the Great War came to Albania, and for four years one army after another fought its way across the barren landscape. Incredibly, the onslaught was so sudden that the still disorganized Albanians never had a chance to take sides.

5

Why Is There an Eastern Europe?

BEFORE PROCEEDING TO THE STORY of the Great War, the reader is urged to put aside the building drama and to reflect upon a different question: why is there an *Eastern* Europe? Or, in other words, why isn't Europe seen as an essential whole? Why do we capitalize Eastern and Western when referring to Europe but not (usually) northern and southern? (At this point the reader is reminded that, as stated in the Introduction, Eastern Europe is defined as ending on the east at the frontier of the present-day Soviet Union. Thus, for the purposes of this discussion, Europe as a whole is considered to end at that place as well.) Is there really an important difference between orient and occident on this single continent and, if so, where is the dividing line? Is the source of the difference merely a political phenomenon (and thus by implication a transient one), or does it have deeper, more complex roots?

These questions and others like them have been much asked but very little answered. And of those responses that have appeared, few have garnered more praise than criticism. The subject is fiercely controversial, yet the author feels an obligation to attempt some explanation. The task in this case is more reasonable in that anyone who has come to this point in this work already knows more about Eastern Europe than all but a very small percentage of the world's population. Thus, the reader can be addressed as something of an expert, and has a fair opportunity to judge the evidence and the quality of the arguments and to accept them or to reach an alternative conclusion.

The thesis to be considered, therefore, runs as follows: there are important geographical differences between Western Europe overall and Eastern Europe overall (the "overall" is hereafter to be understood). These differences are sufficiently significant to have generated a different chronology of economic development. The economic disparity, together with

110

some of the geographic factors in a direct sense, created a different political environment as well. And, although it can generally be said that the east was doing the same things as the west only later, there came a point in history when the more advanced west tended to act in ways that would make the east's secondary position a permanent one. Finally, the political, economic, and social differences between east and west in Europe are *not* reflected in any major way in culture, an area in which it can be said that Europe is one.

To begin with the geography, it is possible to isolate three areas in which Eastern and Western Europe are quite different. They are: (1) climate; (2) access to navigable waterways; and (3) presence of natural, easily defensible boundaries. A quick glance at the map will tell anyone with a basic knowledge of geography that Eastern Europe will be colder and will have less and more variable precipitation than Western Europe. The principal reason is that, despite the comparatively northern location of Europe on the globe (Rome is as far north as New York; Stockholm is on a latitude with the city of Juneau, Alaska), it is warmed considerably by the prevailing wind (from the southwest) which comes off the warm water of the Gulf Stream. The air picks up moisture over the sea and tends to release it as it encounters the cooler landmass of Europe. But what is true for Western Europe is much less true for Eastern Europe. The farther east the wind goes, the more warmth and moisture is lost. There is no precise dividing line, of course, but east of a line running roughly from Berlin along the edge of the Alps to Trieste and then south just back from the coastal strip of Dalmatia and Albania and into Greece, the weather is noticeably colder and dryer than it is to the west of that line. In addition to the obvious role played by the mountains as barriers, a difference can also be seen on the North German Plain, where the weakening warm air currents from the southwest are more vulnerable to interference from polar air masses.

An obvious effect of these climactic differences can be seen in agriculture. In Holland, the growing season is longer and the rainfall is more bountiful and predictable than at the same latitude in southern Poland. The historian William H. McNeill, to whose brilliant short work, *The Shape of European History,*[1] this chapter owes a great deal, notes that the moldboard plow, which sharply improved the agriculture of northwestern Europe by breaking deep furrows that provided essential drainage, was much less effective in improving agricultural productivity in the lands east of the Elbe. There was less water to drain, and the soil was in any case harder to plow. This is not to say that Eastern Europe is uniformly infertile or that there is a sharp and consistent difference with the west, but rather that the region as a whole has a significantly weaker agricultural potential.

The second factor, access to navigable waterways, is as clear as that of climate. A careful look at the map shows that the lands of Western Europe not only have long seacoasts in both absolute terms and in proportion to their size, but are also penetrated to a large extent by navigable rivers. The situation of Eastern Europe is much different. There is much less seacoast in comparison to landmass and what there is, is qualitatively inferior: the eastern Baltic has a severe ice problem in winter; the Black Sea is almost an inland waterway beause its narrow exit is so easily blocked by hostile forces; and the Dalmatian coastline has few good harbors and equally few good access routes to the interior.

The river systems of east and west are also quite different. In northwestern Europe there are numerous points at which seagoing vessels can travel long distances inland without off-loading cargo. And even when it is necessary to shift to another vessel, portages tend to be short and to provide access to adjacent river systems which are capable of carrying smaller boats for long distances. In Eastern Europe, although the Danube is navigable for much of its length, seagoing vessels were, until comparatively recently, blocked at the Iron Gates and in practice rarely penetrated that far because of channel problems. The Danube's usefulness as an inland waterway was also limited until recently because of heavy concentrations of ice in winter. Elsewhere in Eastern Europe rivers are navigable for only fairly short distances and those of the north area are also affected by ice.

The historical importance of waterways for transport and hence economic development cannot be overstated. Overland transport relied on draft animals for locomotion until the mid-nineteenth century, and despite the gradual improvement of roads and bridges, this method was often slower and always more expensive than barges, boats, or ships. The heavier and bulkier the goods, the greater the disparity. Thus a commodity such as grain was rarely shipped by land for more than short distances. The wines of Burgundy, in the interior of France, were generally unknown in foreign lands, while those of Bordeaux, on the seacoast, were principally responsible for the international reputation of their nation's vintners. Until the railroad began to give overland trade a decided advantage in speed at a roughly competitive cost, the waterways of Western Europe offered that region a sharp advantage over Eastern Europe in commercial and subsequently in industrial development.

The subject of natural, easily defensible frontiers is the most difficult of the natural phenomena to describe as a dividing factor between east and west in Europe. In modern times water has been seen as a barrier to military activity. Coasts and rivers are viewed as easier to defend than any type of land other than rugged mountains. And in this sense it is clear that Western Europe has more defensible boundaries than the lands to the east. Yet this was not always so, since the same factors that make waterways valuable for commerce also for a long time made them inviting to fierce and destructive raiders. Growth in Western Europe was stunted for centuries by the persistent marauding of the Vikings, whose attacks on waterborne trade and coastal settlements prohibited progress in those areas most likely to develop along modern lines. It was the defeat of the Vikings, and the political and economic changes that made this possible, that marked a clear division between west and east in economic development.

The peoples of northwestern Europe were slow in meeting the Viking challenge, and it is easy to oversimplify this complex process. Even so, the outline is clear. The Vikings were successful because they were mobile and because they could bring superior force to almost any point against their disorganized rivals. To defeat them, the landsmen had to acquire greater mobility of their own and they had also to develop a system that could link scattered and isolated villages for rapid resistance. The defense which the westerners developed was the knight on horseback, backed by the feudal and manorial systems which were necessary to support this new type of warrior.

The knight was more than a match for the Vikings because his lance gave him great power, while armor on his and his horse's body made them difficult to injure. Moreover, the knight was more mobile than the Vikings, since the latter could not carry more than a few horses on their ships and those for only a short time. Putting knights in the field was no easy matter, however. Their support required a complex, specialized society. Knights in training could not also work in the fields, nor could those specialists who made their equipment: armorers, saddlemakers, etc. The horses themselves were used only for combat and related practice and eventually became a breed separate from their brethren pulling plows and carts. To feed, clothe, and shelter knights, assistants, and animals, it was necessary to turn from subsistence farming to larger scale cultivation that would make possible first a surplus of food and then an excess of labor as well. But there was something of a vicious circle operating in this case, since more effective cultivation required effective protection, and as a consequence progress in developing the new system was slow at first.

By 900, however, the new defenses were generally in place and the

Vikings had been resisted with sufficient consistency that their sources of support were denied them and their system had as a consequence rapidly begun to fall apart. The landsmen of the northwest had developed feudalism, essentially a network of relationships in which one man or a group of men (the knights) promised to protect other groups (the farmers and the artisans) in return for various goods and services (food, equipment, labor on fortifications, etc.). Gradually, these relationships hardened into social classes. Also, the dependency of the farmers led to the closely regulated ties of the manorial system in which those who tilled the land lost title to it and instead served a noble master who became both landlord and protector in the feudal system. There are many subtleties to feudalism and manorialism, and their development was neither chronologically linear nor geographically even. Nevertheless, from the point of view of this discussion, it is essential to grasp the outline of their origin and practice, since these systems did not develop in Eastern Europe until much later, and the consequences of this delay were enormous.

The new society in the west took full advantage of Western Europe's natural geographical advantages. Secure frontiers permitted cultivation that was both more extensive and more intensive than in the east and in a more favorable climate. This in turn allowed a more rapid population growth (severely checked on occasion by disease). Towns and cities began to appear, and more and more trade began to follow the natural waterways of the region. These developments, together with the superior shipbuilding skills that were acquired by those who had no choice but to sail the stormy North Sea, gave the West Europeans not only the strength to defend themselves but also the power to reach out and challenge distant civilizations. The basic mechanisms of the west's new society were in place by about 1300, but because of the plague, the system did not really begin to flower until about 1500.

What was happening in Eastern Europe while this new socio-economic system was beginning to develop in the west? In 1300, when the new society was already functioning to some extent in the west, the East Europeans were just beginning to recover from the enormous destruction wrought by the Mongol invasion of 1241. The only good thing about this invasion (although people did not know it at the time) was that it was the final thrust in a millennium of barbarian attacks. Trade, population growth, and state-building had all been impeded by these attacks, which had consistently devastated the fertile lowlands far more than the less productive hills, mountains, and northern forests. Unfortunately, although the Mongols were the last of the central asian barbarians, other, equally formidable outsiders were soon to challenge the East Europeans on their home territory.

By 1400, when the peoples in the west of Europe no longer had to fear conquest by an alien civilization (they fought among themselves, of course), those in the east now found themselves standing alone against the most powerful rivals to date: the Ottoman Turks. This new enemy was not as terrible as the barbarians had been in that the Turks had no desire to destroy for the sake of destruction. But the Turks effectively stunted in the east the development of the political and economic systems that were beginning to flourish in the west. The Turks were fighting not merely for booty, as the barbarians had done, but above all to impose their own ideas of society on new lands and peoples.

The Ottoman system itself has been discussed earlier in some detail. At this point the sole emphasis is on assessing the profound impact that the presence of Ottoman power had on the East Europeans and, because it had comparatively little effect in the west, on sharpening the already important political and economic differences between the two halves of Europe. In this context it must also be stressed that the Turkish thrusts altered the development of all of Eastern Europe, not only those lands that fell directly under the sultan's power.

The first Ottoman attack on Vienna (in September 1529) was a crisis for all of Europe, as there was a widespread understanding that the fall of this city would open up the lowlands of Germany and hence all of Europe to the "infidel" invaders. Even so, the nations of the west contributed little to the struggle. Instead, it was the peoples of Eastern Europe, including the Poles, the Czechs, and the Austrians of the Habsburg Empire, together with refugee soldiers from the conquered southeast, who rallied to save Vienna. And even though the kingdom of Poland and the Habsburg Empire had conflicts and problems that did not directly involve the Ottoman menace, it was a fact that they could not ignore, an ever-present danger that inevitably altered their development in nearly every way.

Let us turn now to what was happening in the west when the Polish army of King Sobieski saved Vienna from its second siege by the Turks (July 17–September 12, 1683) and thus paved the way for the gradual Ottoman retreat that was apparent by 1700. We find that in contrast to the exhausted if victorious east, Western Europe was flourishing, changing, and growing at the beginning of the eighteenth century. Sheltered from outside attack, the west had discovered a new world and begun to colonize it. Trade routes to the Far East were established and lucrative.

The old feudal and manorial systems were falling apart. They were no longer needed for defense and were ill-suited to the new commercial society which required strong central authority and mobility of labor to support its far-flung operations. Prosperity, together with improved sanitation and health measures, were fostering a rapid population growth, which in turn was a factor in increasing urbanization.

The eighteenth century was the time at which decisive developmental differences between east and west in Europe not only became apparent but also began to become linked together in a dependent relationship. Certainly, the states of the east were less powerful militarily: the disappearance of the Polish kingdom is the obvious example, but much more significant is the fact that the enormous Habsburg Empire was defeated by the much smaller and less populous Prussian kingdom in 1740. The disparity in power was mirrored by, and partly a consequence of, divergent political systems. Poland and the Balkans were mostly under non-European domination, while the Habsburg Empire tried and failed to restructure itself as a unified national state along the lines of France.

And just as the feudal and manorial structure began to disintegrate in the west, it began to grow in the east. Local landlords actually increased their power in parts of the Habsburg Empire, enhancing not only their political strength within the system but also (partly as a consequence) their ability to control the labor and the freedom of movement of the peasants who tilled their lands. In Poland, the presence of the Russian system did the same only more dramatically, while in the Balkans the rapid paralysis of the central Ottoman authority gave the landlords a freedom to control and exploit the peasantry that had not been possible before. Toward the end of the century the pressure to create large, directly managed estates increased in response to the possibility of exporting surplus food, especially grain. The market for these products was the expanding urban population of the west. And here one can clearly discern a relationship of leader and follower between west and east. The East European landlords were not economically dependent on the western markets, for they could survive and even retain their positions without them, but the lure of great wealth was irresistible. The pattern of production for export was not consistent either chronologically or spatially (many areas of Eastern Europe could not produce for the market), but in important ways the stronger and more advanced west was directing the development of the weaker and less advanced east. And, unsurprisingly, the thrust of that direction was to maintain and increase disparity and thus dependency.

The pattern that emerged in the eighteenth century continued throughout the nineteenth and was reinforced by some new factors, in particular the advent of the industrial revolution and the rise of the cult of the nation-state. The industrial revolution moved from Britain to the continent around 1800 and penetrated eastward for decades thereafter. But as the northwest of Europe was industrializing, Eastern Europe was affected only in an indirect way. Thus, while parts of the Czech lands and scattered areas of Poland and Hungary did industrialize, the role of most of Eastern Europe was to serve as a supplier of unprocessed materials (including some ores and fuels as well as foodstuffs) and as a market for manufactured goods. East-west trade increased as the century progressed and so did the investment of western capital in the east. But the thrust of these changes was to cement the earlier relationship of dependency. The surge in Eastern Europe's population growth that began in the nineteenth century was a consequence of roughly the same factors as in the west, including increased prosperity. But the better job opportunities fostered by trade with Western Europe were a short-lived phenomenon, while that of a rapidly increasing population was a permanent one. Eastern Europe was developing mass rural overpopulation and poverty at the same time as Western Europe was pioneering its urban counterpart.

The economic relationship between east and west should not be oversimplified, however. A principal reason for the comparative under-industrialization of Eastern Europe is the fact that the region as a whole was seriously deficient in the essential raw materials needed for basic industry (iron ore and coking coal), as well as in fuels and in access to efficient transport. Those areas of Eastern Europe that were close to raw materials (i.e., northwestern Bohemia) or which had good transport (e.g., the region of Budapest) experienced significant development. In the rest of Eastern Europe the situation was similar to that of the backward resource-poor areas of southern Europe: Spain, Portugal, and southern Italy.

It is a fact that the west tended to exploit its advantage. This can be seen especially clearly in the flow of capital. Western Europe, which was rapidly spewing out surpluses of an enormous range of goods and services, had money to invest. Eastern Europe, tied up with either an inefficient manorial system of agriculture or an even less efficient system of subsistence farming, did not. Foreign investment is, of course, not necessarily bad—French capital was instrumental in the industrialization of Germany, while European and especially British capital was crucial to the economic development of the United States. But where the lender holds both the economic and political cards, the borrower is affected in some significant ways. Railroads are built, but they tend to follow lines that reflect the economic and political priorities of those providing the funds. The same is true for mining operations and in agricultural investment. Little money goes to the development of local manufacturing for the simple reason that there is comparatively little profit in that area.

The effect of the cult of the nation-state in the relationship between eastern and western Europe was perhaps more striking than that of the economy. In the nineteenth century, Western Europe moved toward an organizing system of states which were based on a single nationality, usually defined by a single language (see the earlier discussion of nationalism). This process culminated in the unification of first Italy and then Germany. The changes in the west were scarcely painless, as every major modification required warfare and strong grudges always remained. Yet the determination of the East Europeans, who were very much in the mainstream of western thought, to do the same thing had catastrophic results. In the west nationalism tended to unite more people than it divided; in the east the reverse was true, or very nearly so. This does not mean, as some argue, that nationalism in the west was positive while in the east it was negative. Rather, it means essentially that the physical means of division and separation that allowed for solutions in the west were rarely possible in the east (it is also the case that many strong states had formed in the west *before* linguistic national consciousness became a major factor—France is a good example—while this did not occur in the east). If Frankfort and the region around it had been populated largely by French speakers, or if a large part of central France had been English speaking, Western Europe would have had the kind of problem that afflicted the east in such areas as Danzig and Transylvania. Nationalism in Eastern Europe was not necessarily evil, but it was certainly divisive, and it enhanced and reinforced the comparative political weakness that had its origins in economic differences.

Was there then, before the enormous suffering and consequent changes of World War I, reason to say that there was both an Eastern and a Western Europe? The answer has to be yes. One can agrue about the precise dividing line, and many will. But even if one maintains that Prague had more in common with Paris than with Sofia and that consequently the two should not be lumped together, the fact is that east and west of a line that follows roughly Churchill's Iron Curtain (from Stettin to Trieste) different kinds of generalizations about society applied in 1914. To the west, those living on the land were usually farmers who participated in a money economy. To the east very few had this status. To the west the economies could be described as urban, industrial, mercantile, and international. To the east society was characterized as rural, agricultural, closed, and provincial. The political structures of the west were moving toward increasing popular participation and were manifesting lower levels of internal class and national tension. To the east democratic tendencies were severely limited, and internal political tensions between classes and nationalities were growing. Only in the international scene does one see close parallels: a fierce hatred for neighboring states was the norm everywhere. But while those in the west were generally able to fight for the cause they believed in, those in the east usually either did not, or, even stranger, found that their cause of choice was not even at issue.

One must wonder, after reading this imposing list of dissimilarities, if both groups deserved the same appellation. Should the single geographical term "European" really describe both? Are there ties that transcend these differences? The answer again is yes. For even though there were important political, social, and economic differences between east and west in Europe in 1914, there was an essential cultural unity. People of similar backgrounds on both sides of the elusive dividing line tended to think about life in the same way. Basic philosophical systems, as manifested in moral values and approaches to understanding the nature of man and the world, were the same. There is, for example, no Eastern Europe and Western Europe in science, and there never was. Copernicus was a Pole, while Poles studying physics studied Newton. There was continuing debate in all of Europe about the origins and future of man, and these sometimes took violent form as witness the numerous religious wars. Yet the context of the quarrel was the same. Catholics, Protestants, and Orthodox debate in a common philosophic language the role of the papacy or any other theological question, but Christians and Confucians scarcely know where to begin their debate or how to articulate their differences. This line of argument could be carried further, but since few would argue against the proposition that Eastern Europe and Western Europe are both a part of what is known as Western civilization, there is not much purpose.

The real argument for a difference between Eastern Europe and Western Europe does not lie in the broad view of civilization but in the narrower context of culture. It is difficult to define "culture" since certain elements of culture are inherent in its definition. For the purposes of this discussion, however, culture will be defined as a common set of values in philosophy, art, literature, and music. Although it is theoretically possible to have the same values without exposure to at least many of the same writings, paintings, and musical compositions, in practice a significant amount of shared experience is essential. The question then becomes, do West and East Europeans have essentially similar values and experiences in philosophy, literature, art, and music? Before this question can be dealt with appropriately, however, a rather technical problem must be resolved. We cannot compare peasants in the east with bourgeois in the west. Yet it has just been stipulated that the east was largely peasant and the west largely bourgeois. How can this be resolved? First, we must consider not only absolute numbers but also relative proportions. Nearly all of Eastern Europe has always had a significant number of educated urban dwellers. One should remember that the question here is not the same as that of an island on which fifty Parisian-educated intellectuals rule over five million slaves with no education of any kind. Second, we must view Eastern Europe as a society tending to follow Western Europe in its socioeconomic development. Eastern Europe is becoming more industrial and more bourgeois all the time. The question then, assuming that Eastern Europe is generally successful in following Western Europe, is will the cultural development be parallel as well?

Our discussion from this point will follow two paths. First a survey of educational patterns will provide a framework. Subsequently, there will be a brief discussion of the culture of each Eastern European people and its relation to that of Western Europe. For reasons of manageability of the argument and of economy of space, the focus in the latter case will be on literature. Education in all of Christian Europe was initially based on the churches. Religious organizations maintained educational institutions principally for the training of their own officials. All three major types—Roman Catholic, Protestant, and Orthodox—stressed this to varying degrees. Protestants and Catholics consider education especially important, the Orthodox less so. Those affected by these different views were largely the lower clergy, so that the Orthodox village priest rarely had more than a rudimentary education, while his Catholic and Protestant counterparts were often not only literate but also familiar with a number of works in addition to the Bible and other religious writings. Since the local priests were usually the only available teachers for the rural poor until fairly recent times, this meant that literacy was generally less widespread in Orthodox areas. It was also the case that Catholic and Protestant churches tended to support educational institutions for laymen, up to and including the university level, while the Orthodox did not. This meant that in the Orthodox areas education at all levels was comparatively weak for some time. On the other hand, medium and higher level Orthodox theologians were like their Catholic and Protestant counterparts in that they were frequently sent to other lands to study and often learned foreign languages (the Catholics, of course, all learned at least some Latin).

The original Catholic and Protestant schools of Eastern Europe, both lay and theological, seemed to be equal in quality and in number (in proportion to population) to those of Western Europe. The universities at Cracow and Prague were generally considered to be among Europe's finest. There is no question that the content of religious education in Catholic and Protestant theological schools was the same whether they were located in east or west. This was also true for lay education, since for most of this period secular education was based on the churches. History, for example, would be taught as church history or would revolve around it. The Catholic schools used Latin as the basis for instruction until the end of the eighteenth century, while instruction in the vernacular was generally a Protestant innovation. Orthodox theological schools taught both in Church Slavonic and in Greek. Thus, until about the middle of the eighteenth century, there was little difference between education in Eastern and Western Europe except for the Orthodox areas (remember that a minority of East Europeans are Orthodox).

The increase in secular education in the west in the eighteenth century began to change things. During the Enlightenment, education in Western Europe, particularly France and Germany, pulled away from that of Eastern Europe, largely because the social forces in the west were demanding study of a broader range of subjects than the narrow religious and classical approach which had been and continued to be dominant in the east. Science, secular philosophy, and the study of the arts and humanities were given a prominent role in higher and even some secondary educational institutions of the west. With few exceptions the counterpart institutions in the east did not follow suit. The reason was the essential conservatism of the regimes then controlling Eastern Europe. A considerable cultural divergence might have occurred at this point except for one fact—students traveled from east to west to study. This factor was important not only in the northern Catholic and Protestant lands but also in parts of the Orthodox south.

The phenomenon of the westward-traveling student varied in strength from country to country and from time to time. In Poland, a tradition of higher education in the schools of France and Italy was long established by the beginning of the eighteenth century.[2] Students were typically sons of the nobility (as elsewhere in Eastern Europe), and even after the partitions their parents continued to find a way to give many of them a western education. Many Polish students studied in Vienna, but comparatively few went to Germany. Czech youths were typically educated in Catholic schools that used Latin and German until the national revival of the nineteenth century. Though education in the Czech lands suffered from the general conservatism of the Habsburgs and of the Roman Catholic authorities in the Habsburg Empire, it was nonetheless quite easy for Czech students to attend the secular German Universities.

Slovak students were usually taught in Latin in Catholic schools or in German or Hungarian in Protestant schools until the mid-nineteenth century, at which point education was exclusively in Hungarian. The other nationalities of the Hungarian crownlands—the Croatians and the Romanians of Transylvania—had a similar experience. Comparatively few of the minority peoples received an education at all, particularly since there were very few non-Magyar families who were wealthy. Nonetheless, those who were able to surmount the obstacles and move on to higher education did so in the west—typically in Vienna, Rome, or in the various German universities (France was an unusual destination for students from the Habsburg lands). The education of the Magyars themselves was similar to that of the other nationalities of the Hungarian half of the Habsburg Empire, except that there were many more wealthy families to support foreign education. Also, many of the rich landlords sent their children to the excellent Hungarian-language schools which sprang up in the early nineteenth century. Latin was the official language of administration in Hungary until 1848, and even after the *Ausgleich*, schoolchildren moving beyond basic primary education usually studied German as well as their own language.

The situation in the Orthodox areas of southeastern Europe was different from that in the north in that by 1800 very few Serbs, Bulgarians, Romanians, or Albanians had received an education similar to that available in the rest of Europe at the same time. Things changed rapidly in the nineteenth century, however. As noted earlier, by the close of the first third of the century it was very common for Romanian nobles to send their sons to France or (somewhat less frequently) to Germany for higher education. The need to prepare them for their foreign study resulted in the importation of western or western-trained (often Greek) teachers. There was also close contact with the Romanians of Transylvania, many of whom were not studying in Rome or Vienna.[3] By the last third of the century, Romanian education was firmly established on the pattern of France.

The situation of the Serbs and Bulgarians, both of whom lacked a native aristocracy, was somewhat different, yet the results were similar. Education became important early in the history of independent Serbia, and students' travel was often financed by the state. Although some went to study in Russia (often at the expense of the tsarist government) many also went to Germany and France. The presence of the Habsburg Serbs, and the influence of Yugoslav-oriented Croatians, ensured that the orientation of Serbian education was toward that of Western Europe. Thus, despite a strong Russian influence, education in Serbia was by 1914 structured along West European lines.

Traditional education in Bulgaria in 1800 was controlled by the Greek Orthodox Church. Much of the Bulgarian national awakening was, as described earlier, part of an effort to throw off Greek authority in both religion and education. Even so, many Bulgarians knew Greek, and many Greeks were familiar with Western European developments in education. This was also true of Russia, of course, and many of the Bulgarian students who studied in Moscow and St. Petersburg were as influenced by Voltaire and Rousseau as by the Russian slavophils. Interestingly, a significant number of Bulgarians also received a western education in Istanbul—at the American-founded (1863) and administered Robert College. Again, whatever the original influences, by 1914 the Bulgarian educational system had the same structure and general curriculum as that of Western Europe.

The growth of Albanian nationalism is all the more remarkable given the educational system that prevailed there prior to 1912. The few schools that existed in Albania proper were all religious, and they tended to change the nationality of those who attended them: Moslems became Turks, Orthodox became Greek, and even the Roman Catholics tended to be tied directly to Rome and to the Italian Church.[4] Given that the very few wealthy landlords who sent their sons away for education were Moslems and consequently usually sent them to Istanbul to religious schools, it was scarcely the case that in 1914 the Western European approach to education was well known, let alone dominant in Albania. Even so, western influence was significant. In addition to those trained in Greece and Italy, a number of Albanians also attended Robert College. The general direction was such that the educational system that the Albanians attempted to build in the interwar period was oriented toward that of Western Europe.

Thus, the overall structure of East European education was, with minor exceptions, formed along the West European model. The culture which this system reflected and propagated was much the same. In particular, literature, which encompasses all of human experience, can be shown to be essentially the same in structure and approach in both east and west. Though the fact of different languages meant that the content was not always the same (there were, of course, many translations and many could read foreigh languages), the themes of the various writers, and the larger literary tradition from which they drew their inspiration, was a common European one. The following is not meant to be a complete treatment of East European literature, but is rather an attempt to demonstrate the common roots of all the literatures of Europe.

The use of a Czech literary language dates to the fourteenth century, when written Czech was employed for lay poetry and prose as well as for religious writing. It was used, together with Latin, at the University in Prague (known as the Charles University), which was founded in 1348. The use of literary Czech received considerable impetus from Jan Hus (see above), who tried to make the written language as close as possible to that of the people, and whose orthographic system, developed around 1400, is essentially the same as that used today.[5] To emphasize the cosmopolitanism of medieval Bohemia, it should be remembered that Hus' Proto-Protestantism had its origins in the works of the English cleric, John Wycliffe, and that there is abundant evidence that many Czech speakers were familiar with writing in German as early as the fourteenth century. When the renaissance penetrated the Czech lands in the fifteenth and sixteenth centuries, Czechs wrote about man and his environment in both Czech and Latin. These texts reveal that their authors were knowledgeable about and participating in the new currents of thought that were sweeping the continent. There is no great literature from this period, however, and the development of culture in the Czech language was arrested but not destroyed by the Habsburg victory over the Czech Protestants at the Battle of White Mountain in 1620. For nearly two centuries thereafter, both education and cultural expression were either in Latin or, increasingly, in German. While this was a blow to specifically Czech culture, it emphasizes the fact that the Czechs were always closely tied to developments in Western Europe.

The achievements of the early period of Czech culture were never lost, however, and they became a solid foundation for the national revival of the nineteenth century. Part of the heritage was from Czechs living in exile in various parts of Protestant Europe who had kept the language alive in both religious and secular writing. The most important of these was the great John Comenius (Jan Komenský 1592–1670), whose contributions to philosophy and especially to the philosophy of education have earned him an important place in European history. Yet despite their accomplishments, the exiles' language inevitably became somewhat estranged from that of the people, and the writers of the national revival had to refine if not reinvent the literary langauge.

Literary themes in the Czech lands in the nineteenth century were diverse. Many writers were oriented to the classics, while an increasing number, particularly the younger writers who were influenced by the growing national struggle, adopted the interest in folklore and village life which had its origins in German romanticism. The prevailing nationalistic orientation makes it unsurprising that the greatest writer of the nineteenth century was a historian, František Palacký (1798–1876). It would be a mistake to think of Palacký as a chauvinist, however, for his greatness lies in his understanding of not only his people's suffering but also of the place of all nationalities in the broader context of history. Palacký advocated change but not conquest, and his elegant prose spoke of harmony between peoples.[6] A younger colleague of Palacký's, the historian Tamáš G. Masaryk (1850–1937), was interested in the status of the Slavic peoples as a whole. Masaryk's *Spirit of Russia* is a classic both as a work of history and as a study of the Russian state and people.

In the latter part of the century, as the cultural struggle with the Germans became more intense, many Czech writers sought inspiration in the literature of Britain, France, and other West European nations. The poet Jaroslav Vrchlický (1853–1912) is the most prominent representative of this school. In addition to his own work, he is known for his translations from many languages, particularly French and Italian. In concluding that the Czechs were in the mainstream of European culture, one should note that two of the greatest composers in the history of western music, Bedřich Smetana (1824–1884) and Antonín Dvořák (1841–1904), were Czech.

No one could seriously argue that Polish literature, like that of the Czechs, is less European than that of, for example, Italy. Polish writers, in fact, usually wrote in Latin until the seventeenth century and even after that, classical and other writings in Latin were known and appreciated by a large number of Poles. Polish ties to France dated to the premodern period, and Polish intellectual life had a tradition of cosmopolitanism in part because so many Poles had shared their lives between Paris and Warsaw or Cracow.

The development of a Polish literary language occurred in the fifteenth century largely as a consequence of the pressure of Protestantism.[7] Czech refugees frequented Polish territory, and the university at Cracow was for a time a center of Protestant thought. As in the Czech lands, the emphasis on the use of a language that the common people could understand spurred the use of Polish, both by the Protestants and by their Catholic opponents. This trend was weak at first, but by 1500 Polish was beginning to replace German as the language of commerce in the towns. The real impact of Protestantism on Polish culture appeared, however, in the sixteenth century.

The sixteenth century is known as the "Golden Age of Polish Literature." It was a period in which the Polish literary language matured and proliferated (although much important secular and ecclesiastical writing was still in Latin). It was also the period in which the Renaissance fully penetrated the country, opening up new channels of thought in which Polish writers took an important part. The best known of these was the brilliant poet, Jan Kochanowski (1530–84). Educated first at the University in Cracow, he traveled, studied, and wrote in Italy, Germany, and France over a period of some fifteen years. Kochanowski's themes were both classical and contemporary, and his writing, though comparatively little known outside of Poland, was a benchmark for generations of Polish writers to come. Other writers of the "Golden Age" include the poet Mikołaj Rej (1505–1569) and the Jesuit political and religious polemicist, Piotr Skarga (1536–1612).[8]

The seventeenth and eighteenth centuries were periods of comparative literary inactivity in Poland. There are, for example, no great Polish figures of the Enlightenment, for this was a time in which the Polish nation was struggling and failing to maintain its existence. It is perhaps as a consequence of that crisis that Poles figure so prominently in the romantic literature of the nineteenth century. Of the many great European writers of that time, one of the best known is the poet and playwright, Adam Mickiewicz (1789–1855). Born in what is now Byelorussia, Mickiewicz was educated at the University of Wilno (Vilnius). He taught school for a while, but his nationalistic tendencies caught the eye of the tsarist authorities, and he was forced to live in Russia proper for some six years (1823–1829). After a brief stay in Italy, he returned to Poland too late to participate in the revolution of 1830–31. From 1832 he lived in Paris and lectured at the Collège de France. Along with his French colleague, Jules Michelet, he personified the radical romantic nationalism of Paris at the time. In 1848 Mickiewiez organized a Polish legion to fight for the freedom of Italy from Austria, and died in 1855 in Istanbul while organizing volunteer groups to fight against Russia in the Crimea.[9]

Mickiewicz's verse is known for the sharpness and the elegance of its language and for the passion of its appeal to the tragedy of the Polish nation. His two best known works, *Dziady* (Forefather's Eve) and *Pan Tadeusz* (Mr. Tadeusz) are nostalgic yet vigorous and happy. The former is a symbol of Polish Russophobia, so much so that performances or attempted performances in Poland after 1945 have represented major political as well as cultural events. The latter, which is less overtly nationalistic, is generally considered to be the best writing in Polish and has a major place in world literature.

Other great Polish writers of the nineteenth century include Henryk Sienkiewicz (1846–1916), the first of three Poles to win the Nobel Prize for Literature; and Bolesław Prus (1845–1912). And one should not end this brief survey of the place of Poland in European culture without mention of Frederyk Chopin (1810–1849), the brilliant composer who was born near Warsaw and whose work also reflects the emotion of the Polish romantic nationalist movement.

The Slovak literary language, like the Polish, received much of the impetus for its development from Czech Protestant refugees of the fifteenth century. Though the Czechs continued to use their own language, the idea of the use of the vernacular quickly penetrated to the Slovaks. In the second part of the sixteenth century, for example, the leaders of the Catholic Counter-Reformation used a form of Slovak in their printed tracts. But development of a standard Slovak language was delayed by three factors: geographical barriers had led to many different dialects; Czech was sufficiently similar to pose an alternative; and the Hungarian authorities were strenuously opposed. It was, therefore, not until the nineteenth century that the contemporary literary language was developed. Its codifier, Ludovít Štúr, was a German-educated journalist and politician. Although two of the greatest Slovak writers of all time, the poet Ján Kollár (1793–1852), and the philologist Pavel Šafárik (1795–1861), wrote principally in Czech and opposed Štúr's language, it nevertheless developed many adherents in Slovakia and was used by a great many talented writers from about 1850 on.[10] Literary themes in Slovak, as in the other languages of Eastern Europe, were often inspired by folklore and by life in the villages. Even so, the general trends of European literature can be clearly discerned in that of the Slovaks.[11]

The official written language in the Hungarian lands was Latin until the nineteenth century, although Hungarian had begun to develop as a literary language much earlier, again particularly in consequence of the Reformation and Counter-Reformation. The use of the language was spurred by the nationalism of the late-eighteenth and early-nineteenth centuries, which in turn was in large part a reaction to the Habsburg emperor's attempt to replace Latin with German.[12]

There were many great Hungarian writers of the nineteenth century, but four stand out as clearly being of world stature. The romantic poet Mihály Vörösmarty (1800–1855) wrote first in Latin but went on to become a brilliant stylist in Hungarian. He was closely linked to the German romantics and knew their language well enough to collaborate on a German-Hungarian dictionary. The next writer, János Arany (1817–1882) was a realist and an epic poet, who in later life was secretary of the Hungarian Academy of Sciences and a translator of Shakespeare. The most brilliant of the nineteenth-century Hungarian writers was the realist poet, Sándor Petöfi (1823–1849), whose skill with the complex Hungarian language is considered to be unparalleled. Petöfi was a fiery nationalist (he was actually of Slovak origin; his father's name was Petrovics) whose principal theme was the Magyar people's desire for freedom. Appropriately, his life ended in battle while fighting under Bem in the closing weeks of the Hungarian revolution. Mór Jókai (1825–1904) differed from his colleagues in that he was a storyteller, not a poet, and his themes were less oriented to nationalism (although he was certainly a patriot). Jókai's work has been extremely widely translated, and he is better known outside of Hungary than his poetic colleagues principally because the nature of the Hungarian language makes translations of poetry very difficult. Jókai was personally involved in West European literary circles as well, and he was a regular correspondent of the great French novelist, Emile Zola.[13]

In nineteenth-century Hungary, literary criticism, which can almost be considered an art form separate from that of the writing of literature itself, flourished. In this area it is impossible to separate Hungarian trends from those of Western Europe. Hungary also maintained her share of the European achievement in music, as she numbered among her sons the great Ferenc (Franz) Liszt (1811–1886).

The story of the growth and interrelationships of the literatures of the Yugoslav peoples—Serbs, Croats, and Slovenes—is too complex for adequate treatment in a very brief summary such as this. Nevertheless, some basic trends can be outlined. The Serbs long used a variety of Church Slavonic as their literary language. Although it had probably been similar to popular speech when first adopted in the tenth century, it lost that congruence over the intervening years in which nearly all writing was religious. It was the great Vuk Karadžić (1787–1864) who developed a modern literary language. His version gained general acceptance in the middle third of the nineteenth century and became the official language of the Serbian state in 1868. Karadžić, who lived most of his life in Vienna and who often wrote in German, was much influenced by a Slovene, Jernej Kopitar (1788–1844).

The Croats had also used a variant of Church Slavonic early in their history but later dropped it in favor of Latin. A Croatian literary language of some importance developed in Dalmatia under the influence of the Italian renaissance in the sixteenth century.[14] There was no continuity of tradition from this, however, and by the end of the eighteenth century most educated Croats wrote in German, Latin, or occasionally Hungarian.

The spirit of nationalism and especially the Illyrian movement (see above) provided a motivation for a new literary language.[15] Under the leadership of Ljudevit Gaj (1809–1872), who was greatly influenced by the pan-Slav ideas of the Slovak Jan Kollár, the Croats decided to adopt essentially the same language as that chosen by Karadžić. This led to a remarkable event, the *Književni Dogovor* (Literary Agreement) signed in Vienna in 1850. In this document leading Serbs and Croats officially adopted a single literary language (but with different alphabets). Despite Kopitar's brilliant efforts (interestingly, he wrote only in German), as well as the presence of a large number of Slovenes in the Illyrian movement, a unified Slovene literary language was not developed in the nineteenth century.[16]

The literature of the Slovene and Serbo-Croatian speaking areas in the nineteenth century was, as elsewhere, typically first romantic poetry with a nationalist bent, then a turn to epic poetry more akin to the realist traditions that prevailed in the middle of the century, and finally a move to the novel. The emphasis in the Serb areas was principally derived from folklore, while classical themes were more evident in the Slovene and Croatian areas. Nationalism, revealed in tales of past glory, was ever present. There were no writers of the stature of Mickiewicz or Petöfi (although the Slovenes had a great romantic poet in France Prešeren [1800–1849]), but given the comparatively recent development of widely accepted literary languages, the pace of literary development was rapid and strong.

Writing in Romanian before 1800 was limited essentially to documents and to liturgical works. However, the Romanians' language was sufficiently unified that there were no important difficulties in establishing a standard literary version; the adoption of a single Latin-based orthography in 1850 solved the only real problem. On the other hand, the Romanians had from the beginning a real struggle between those who wished to make Romanian culture a derivative of that of Western Europe and especially of France, and those who sought to develop a specifically national culture within the general framework of Europe. A number of early nineteenth-century writers were francophile to the point of speaking as well as writing principally in French.[17]

An early supporter of the nativist school was the versatile writer Ion Heliade-Rădulescu (1802–1872). Romania also produced two brilliant poets, Vasile Alecsandri (1821–1890) and Mihai Eminescu (1850–1889). Both were romantics of a sort, but Eminescu was particularly brilliant, known for his lyrical portrayal of the life of the common people. A fine novelist and playwright, Ion Luca Caragiale (1852–1912) was acclaimed for his sense of humor and for his shrewd understanding of the pretensions and conflicts of Romanian bourgeois society. Titu Maiorescu (1840–1917) was an outstanding literary critic whose German education provided a valuable counterbalance to the Francophile current. Maiorescu's journal, *Convorbiri literare* (Literary Discussions), had a solid reputation on the continent.

The Bulgarians had the first real Slavic literary language, Church Slavic (called Old Church Slavonic before about 1100). But this language grew apart from the speech of the people over the centuries and even had to compete with Russian and Serbian versions in liturgical writing. When the Bulgarian nationalists of the nineteenth century sought a common language with which to communicate, there was none at hand. In their effort to construct a new literary language, they were inspired by the work of Father Paisi of the Hilandar Monastery of Mount Athos (1722–1797), whose writings on the early Bulgarian empires instilled a sense of pride and historical mission.[18] Paisi's own language was archaic, however, and it was only after much debate and discussion that a compromise emerged in the middle of the nineteenth century. With few exceptions, the new language conformed to the vernacular.

The literature that emerged in Bulgaria was much influenced first by that of Greece and then by that of Russia. A reaction to this foreign influence soon set in, however, and the best Bulgarian writers argued for the avoidance of foreign affectations. The previously mentioned leaders of the national liberation movement, George Rakovski, Christo Botev, and Ljuben Karavelov, were all important writers. The most important literary figure of nineteenth-century Bulgaria, however, was the versatile Ivan Vazov (1850–1921). Although he was a gifted poet and dramatist, Vazov is internationally famous for his novel *Pod Igoto* (Under the Yoke), which depicted the suffering of the Bulgarians under Turkish rule during the revolutionary struggles of 1876–1878.[19] A less acclaimed but even more popular novelist was Aleko Konstantinov (1863–1897) whose *Bay Ganyo* is a story full of wit and humor. Konstantinov traveled widely in the west, and acquainted his readers with cities as diverse as Florence and Chicago. A poet, Pencho Slaveykov (1866–1912), was chiefly responsible for bringing western concepts of literary criticism to Bulgaria.

In reviewing the literature of Eastern Europe before 1914, one can certainly find trends that are not entirely in harmony with those of Western Europe at the same time. This is particularly true of the Eastern European emphasis on portraying village life and folklore which, although not dominant, was strong even in the Czech lands. A difference in choice of themes should not be interpreted as a separation of culture, however. East European writers talked about the peasants because most people were peasants. As their nations become more urbanized, there were more stories of city life. One should not forget in this context that rural themes were also common in Western Europe and that the romantic approach to the peasantry, which characterized the initial period in Eastern Europe, had its origins in the work of Herder and the German romantics. Overall, one finds that the writers of Eastern Europe, though typically nationalistic and consequently wary of any and all foreign influence, were nonetheless very much attuned to the literary currents of Western Europe. The backgrounds of their literary characters often varied, but the themes and approaches were much the same. Also, in addition to the access made possible through translations, most East European writers knew several West European languages and a great many had traveled in the west. At most a tiny minority of the intelligentsia of Eastern Europe would have argued, in 1914, that their nation's culture was in any fundamental way different from that of Western Europe.

This chapter on the validity of the concept of an *Eastern* Europe is awkward and difficult because it argues the case from two different and contradictory directions. On the one hand, there is a claim that socioeconomic and therefore political development was sufficiently different to allow the two halves of Europe to fall into different categories. On the other hand, the essential cultural unity of the entire area is proclaimed. Does the latter negate the former? Can a coherent theory be formed? The answer to these questions is that the conflict doesn't really matter, certainly it has no great relevance to this text. The purpose is not to posit an unshakable theory of Eastern Europe (surely an impossibility in a practical if not in a scientific sense), but rather to ask the reader to pause and to think analytically about Eastern Europe in a larger context. It is not important that the reader develop a sense of unity and coherence, but rather that the diversity and contradictions of Eastern Europe be clearly understood. As we move forward to the fury of war and the continuing crisis of the peace that followed, we need to know not the answer to the question "Why is there an *Eastern* Europe?", but the reasons why such a question is asked at all.

6

The Great War
From Origins to Settlement

Eastern Europe and the Origins of World War I

*T*HE READER WHO HAS PROGRESSED to this point in the tangled history of Eastern Europe does not need to be convinced that the area had enormous potential for provoking conflict, both internal and external. The various national quarrels which separated the peoples of Eastern Europe were vastly more important than any unifying factors—indeed it is hard to find any integrative forces, real or theoretical. To this pervasive internal tension one must add the further stress of the great power rivalries in which the East European peoples were often pawns. Thus, before discussing the specific events that led to war, a brief survey of the major powers and their relations to each other and to Eastern Europe is necessary.

There were five nations that had active status as great powers just before the war: Austria-Hungary, Britain, France, Germany, and Russia. Two others which might be included, the United States and the Ottoman Empire, are excluded because the former had the strength but lacked the inclination, while the latter, "the sick man of Europe," owed whatever status it had to traditional courtesy rather than to any real influence. Italy was a factor, but a decidedly secondary one, and Japan had not yet begun to reach out beyond her distant power base.

It is noteworthy that of the five great powers, only two, Britain and France, were not physically involved in Eastern Europe. Yet even these states had important interests in the area. The British had a long-standing fear of Russian naval potential and had chosen to provide strong support for the Ottoman Empire. The leaders in London, with remarkable consistency, had concluded that the end of the rule of sultans in Istanbul would give Russia access to year-round warm water ports (the Black Sea would become a "Russian lake") and the British supply line to India via Suez would become vulnerable. The British people were not especially fond of the Ottoman system, but it took powerful misbehavior on the part of the Turks to cause them to shake their government's support. Such was the case in the Russo-Turkish War of 1877–78, when reports of atrocities in Bulgaria caused London to stand aside and let the Russians act. But even then, the British moved quickly and forcefully to overturn a settlement (San Stefano) which they felt made the Russians too strong.

The role of France is less easy to define. The French did have a traditional affinity for the Poles, which was originally based in religion. This relationship bore some political fruit in the Napoleonic period, albeit temporarily. After that time, France was much less active as a great power; aside from bizarre episodes in the reign of Louis Napoleon (e.g., the Crimean War), the French were rarely leaders anywhere beyond their own borders, and their lack of aggressiveness, combined with the lack of East European issues which directly affected France, made that country's role in the area appear to be secondary. Yet much occurred below the diplomatic surface. A great many of the East European nationalist leaders had drawn their ideological inspiration from France; many men had been educated in Paris, and many organizations had published their first manifestos there. It is hardly surprising that the East Europeans' affinity for France, its people and its institutions was warmly reciprocated. The widespread French sympathy for the peoples of Eastern Europe created a public opinion factor of great significance. A French government that, for example, favored Russian annexation of Romania, would have been very unpopular. Since France was a democracy after 1871, the pressure of public opinion prevented French governments from ignoring the national aspirations of the East Europeans. Policy from Paris was not openly, adventurously disruptive of the status quo, but it was a factor to be reckoned with in international affairs.

Germany, born out of the 1870–71 conflict with France, at first had few interests in the lands to the east. The Germans held a section of Poland, and they were only too happy to assist the Russians and the Austro-Hungarians in keeping the restive Polish nationality in line. For some time, Germany and Russia were close friends and allies. However, two factors gradually unraveled this relationship. Germany's increasingly close ties to Austria-Hungary inevitably forced Berlin to choose between her two allies, and this came to be almost invariably at the expense of Russia. Bismarck's frantic diplomacy and Russia's turn to the Far East after the frustration of 1878 kept the tension under control for quite some time, but Bismarck's fall from power (1890) and Russia's defeat by Japan (1905) sharply exacerbated the strains. In the meantime, Germany and Russia became commercial rivals in the international grain trade. By the turn of the century relations between the two countries were very strained.

Austria-Hungary's relations with Eastern Europe have already been discussed at length, as have Russia's. It is sufficient to state that both countries saw their own actions as inherently defensive and the other's as deliberately threatening. Thus, the Russians did not view their own activities in the Balkan Slavic states as inappropriate, meddling, or as a challenge to the security of Austria-Hungary; rather they saw their purpose as preventing Austro-Hungarian expansion which would endanger Russia's southern frontier and her grain trade through the Straits. The leaders in Vienna, on the other hand, felt that Russian support for the independent Slavic states was nothing more than an indirect attack on the integrity of their multinational empire; in their minds expansion in the Balkans was a purely defensive move designed to offset a particularly dangerous threat from the east. Given these attitudes, one can easily understand why the situation soon went out of control. When one adds the facts of markedly incompetent leadership in both empires to the emergence of the alliance system in Europe, it is not hard to see how rivalry led to conflict and finally to conflagration.

Alliance systems of sorts had existed throughout history, but modern technology made alliances far more important and more rigid than in the past. In an age in which standing armies with intelligence and planning staffs could launch a full-scale offensive by rail in a matter of a few days, diplomacy had to be very different. Foreign ministers could no longer react to the threat of war by embarking on a leisurely tour of foreign capitals during which they would try to line up allies in between visits to the opera. The French discovered this to their sorrow in 1870— Prussian guns could be heard in Paris while the government was trying to get organized to fight. In a sense this French defeat gave birth to the alliance system. France was so embittered by her defeat and so anxious to recover her lost territory that her leaders were obviously on the market for any anti-German alliance they could put together. Bismarck knew this and countered by setting up his own alliance first. Starting with Austria-Hungary in 1879, the Germans soon signed up Romania and Italy as well.

As noted earlier, Bismarck tried to balance his alliance by keeping an agreement with Russia at the same time. This was difficult, but while Bismarck was in power it was possible. When the Iron Chancellor had been dismissed, more confident but less competent hands took the helm in Germany. The deal with Russia (appropriately called the "reinsurance" treaty) was scrapped. Tensions then began to mount quickly. France and Russia became allies four years later (1894), and an arms race began. The Germans drove the previously neutral British into the enemy camp by launching a naval construction program that frightened London in reality far more than the potential Russian navy ever had. As the situation grew more tense, the alliance became closer. The Germans, with their continuing fear of encirclement, became more and more entangled with the affairs of their only major ally, Austria-Hungary. France, by the same token, knew that without Russian pressure from the east, Germany could destroy her long before the British could be of help.

Thus, the alliance system gradually permitted the two paranoid rivals, Russia and Austria-Hungary, to call the shots for their friends. Numerous crises occurred in the first years of the twentieth century, but although war was averted, the shocks were not like earthquakes which at least relieve stress. Instead, tensions began to increase again at a higher level immediately after each crisis passed. The Bosnian affair (see above) is a good example of this. The Balkan wars of 1912–13 were a remarkable exception. Since the issues were largely local, the great powers restrained themselves and watched while the small states carved up the remainder of European Turkey. Since Bulgaria had no close allies, even her crushing defeat did not cause much trouble. The Austro-Hungarians, nervous about the growth of Serbia, had their fears assuaged by the creation of Albania, which blocked Serbia's access to the sea. But the elimination of a major internal Balkan problem simply served to make the external problem more serious. Most important, the Serbs reacted to the achievement of most of their aims in Macedonia by looking elsewhere. Their attention was soon riveted anew on the plight of their brethren in the Austro-Hungarian empire.

We will probably never know the extent of official Serbian involvement in the Bosnian revolutionary movement, *Mlada Bosna* (Young Bosnia), which assassinated the heir to the Austro-Hungarian throne, Archduke Franz-Ferdinand, on June 28, 1914, in Sarajevo. Although we do know that the group had strong ties with important people in Belgrade, some of them official, there is no evidence that the group was controlled by the Serbian government or that the planned action was known, much less sanctioned, by anyone in authority.[1] In fact, there is every reason to believe that the leaders in Belgrade would not have approved. Another theory, that Hungarian leaders engineered the assassination because the Hungarians feared that Franz-Ferdinand would favor a "trialist" reorganization of the empire, has even less evidence to support it. The most likely explanation is that a band of fanatical youths simply decided upon the most dramatic possible act available to them. The government in Vienna, of course, made an important contribution by choosing to send a major public figure into an extremely restive area at the worst possible time—the Serbian national holiday.

The deed done, events moved quickly. The obtuse leaders in Vienna continued their tradition of blundering into war by attempting thoroughly to humiliate Serbia. Germany, lacking a coherent policy of its own and more inclined to react than to act at this point, did not restrain Vienna. Russia also felt her honor was at stake—no one should be allowed to humiliate her ally. Fearing that Austria-Hungary would move quickly to destroy Serbia, the tsar showed his determination by ordering his army to mobilize. This, in turn, caused Germany to act; the German General Staff had long had a plan, the famous Schlieffen Plan, for dealing with the nightmare of a war on two fronts. The idea was first to deal France a crushing blow, thus preventing British intervention, while merely holding the Russians off. Unfortunately, the plan assumed that war would start when the comparatively slow process of Russian mobilization began: the small German force reserved from the attack on France could not resist a fully mobilized Russian army. The Germans thus felt constrained to attack, and war thus began in August, 1914.

World War I in Eastern Europe

The First World War had three fairly separate fronts in Eastern Europe. The first was in Poland, where German and Russian troops faced each other in a campaign that, after an initial Russian push (stopped at Tanneberg, 1914), resulted in a steady German drive eastwards. When the war was over in this area (Treaty of Brest-Litovsk, 1918), Poland was completely in German hands. The second front was the central one, comprising Austrian Galicia and the central Ukraine. Here also, the Russians moved forward in the early months, capturing most of Galicia (including Lvov) and occupying part of Slovakia. Fighting was severe, and all sides took heavy casualties in a seesaw struggle. By 1917 Galicia was cleared of Russian forces, and by the time of the Treaty of Brest-Litovsk, the Germans had driven deep into the central Ukraine, taking Kiev and even Kharkov.

The final front was the Balkan one which, typically, cannot be described in a few words. The complexity of the struggle paralleled the political situation. The regime in Vienna resolved to crush Serbia quickly, partially out of vengefulness and partly because it too wanted to free troops for the Russian front as fast as possible. The hurried attack was a disaster. Repeated assaults were repulsed, and the imperial forces were defending their own territory after only a few months of enormous casualties. Then, late in 1915, Bulgaria joined the war on the side of the Central Powers; Sofia's compensation for entering the struggle was to be Macedonia. Faced with a war on two fronts, the Serbian forces staged a brilliant retreat through Albania to the Greek island of Corfu. After a rest, the remainder of the Serbian Army (much less than half) joined an Allied offensive based in Salonika. Serbia, however, suffered nearly three years of enemy occupation.

The other part of the Balkan front was the Romanian. Technically allied with the Central Powers, the Romanian leaders had nevertheless stayed neutral, and then, following public opinion, had joined the Allies in 1916. But with enemies on three sides, and only the faltering Russians available to provide assistance, the Romanians were quickly crushed. Most of the country was occupied, while a remnant of the army maintained a front together with the Tsar's army. The Russian capitulation at Brest-Litovsk forced the Romanians to follow suit a few months later (May, 1918). After the collapse of Austria-Hungary in the autumn of the same year, the Romanians repudiated their surrender and quickly captured Transylvania.

The First World War inflicted enormous human and material damage on Eastern Europe. Poland, Serbia, Montenegro, Romania, and Albania were all both battlegrounds and areas subject to at least one foreign occupation. And where the civilian populations did not suffer directly they suffered indirectly. For example, Poland did not exist, but Poles could be and were drafted by the powers that controlled their homeland; Poles fought in the armies of three empires and not infrequently had to aim their guns at their countrymen. The same was true of the south Slavs; tens of thousands of the Austro-Hungarian troops that attacked Serbia were Croats, Slovenes, and even Serbs. The Czechs were not at first forced to fight other Czechs, but they demonstrated their lack of enthusiasm for their government's cause by deserting to the Russians en masse. By the end of the war, some thirty thousand Czechs had changed sides and were fighting with the Russians.[2]

In addition to military and civilian casualties, the disruption of the war caused a breakdown in the rather weak public health systems. Epidemics swept through most areas and killed hundreds of thousands. Famine was everywhere a problem, as food surplus areas were cut off from foreign markets. Military confiscation of transport made it difficult to distribute supplies even within countries. The war effort did spur industrial development, but there was practically nothing available to consumers while the struggle continued and, as will be explained later, much of the new capacity could not be readily converted to civilian use even after hostilities ceased. Practically without exception, the countries and peoples of Eastern Europe were exhausted by the war.

The sacrifices and destruction of war did not in any way diminish diplomatic activity. Even before the first battles began a number of agreements about the postwar settlement had been reached by optimistic allies. The continuing struggle multiplied these activities, often without apparent regard to the fortunes of war. Even an overview of wartime diplomacy is beyond the scope of this study, so that only a brief analysis of the strategies of each of the countries-to-be is possible here. These will be linked as necessary to the policies of the non-East European participants, but it is assumed that the reader is familiar with the general issues and at least their ultimate resolution.

The situation of the Poles was particularly difficult since the lack of any form of Polish political entity—independent or dependent—deprived potential leaders of the natural base from which diplomatic action is usually launched. Further, the division of the Polish peoples into the three empires made a unified approach and a coherent policy focus extremely hard to achieve. As described earlier, different organizations had grown up which favored association with the various occupying powers. The pro-Austrian group was narrowly based on the aristocrats who exercised a limited autonomy in Galicia, and this factor, together with Austria-Hungary's increasingly obvious weakness, made affiliation with that country an impractical option. The real choice had to be either the pro-German approach of Piłsudski's Socialists or the pro-Russian approach of Dmowski's National-Democrats (it should be remembered, of course, that these groups were more opposed to one side than in favor of the other).

The course of the conflict did not give either group much cause for optimism. German victories failed to cheer Piłsudski, who quickly observed that Berlin's successes served only to eliminate that fleeting trace of flexibility which had earlier drawn the attention of his ardently Russophobic soul. Eventually, Piłsudski and his legionnaires (the only separate Polish force in the war), shifted from fighting with the Central Powers to openly resisting them; Piłsudski was imprisoned. Shortly afterward the March revolution in Russia produced a dramatic shift in that country's attitude toward the Poles: the revival of an independent Polish state was now an official war aim of the government (British and French pressure helped effect this change), and Polish officers and soldiers were gathered into purely Polish units for the first time. The Bolsheviks continued this policy after their revolution, but the Russian surrender at Brest-Litovsk forced Lenin to change his policy (at least his official one).

The months from Brest-Litovsk in February to the November armistice were grim ones for patriotic Poles—especially those living in Poland. The Germans had established a tiny "Kingdom of Poland" in a small part of the area formerly held by Russia, but this was obviously just for show. Berlin's grip on all of the Polish lands was absolute, and the nature of the occupation was anything but sympathetic to Polish nationalism. Yet all of this changed with amazing speed in November. One of the Allies' terms had been the evacuation of Poland. This was done quickly, but even before it could be completed, Piłsudski, released from prison one day before the armistice, had raced back to Warsaw and had established an independent government. The return of the Polish military units from Russia and the surfacing of an underground force organized by Piłsudski quickly gave the new government strength. Even earlier, Dmowski had taken advantage of his contacts in Paris (where he was in exile) to have Poland recognized by the Allies as a belligerent against the Central Powers. This move was to be extremely useful since it made it possible for Poland to be represented at the forthcoming peace conference.

The situation of the Czech nationalists was very similar to that of the Poles, perhaps even worse. The Czechs not only did not have a national state, they had never had one in modern times; moreover, all of the Czech lands and people were controlled by Austria-Hungary, whose government showed no inclination to compromise. The mass desertion of Czech troops mentioned above was an obvious reaction to this depressing situation. Despite these disadvantages, the Czechs fared amazingly well. In large part this was a consequence of the quality of their leadership, and particularly that of Thomas Masaryk and Edvard Beneš. These two pursued two goals at the same time: the unification of the Czech lands with Slovakia, and the creation of an independent Czechoslovak state.

The Czech-Slovak unification drive proceeded with surprising speed. The Slovaks, long-suffering under Hungarian domination, were sensitive about their newly-developed national consciousness and were consequently very suspicious of the motives of their more advanced neighbors. The tension was such that without the pressure of war negotiations might never have reached fruition. As it was, a declaration of agreement in principle was approved by Czech and Slovak organizations in 1915

(Cleveland, Ohio), and a more detailed arrangement, the famous Pittsburgh Agreement, was then signed by many key leaders, including Masaryk. The American location of these important milestones reflects the strong pro-unification sentiments of both Czech and Slovak emigrants to the United States.

The drive to secure Allied recognition of an independent Czechoslovakia also went remarkably smoothly. Operating from headquarters in Paris, the urbane and sophisticated Masaryk and Beneš made a great impression on the Western leaders. Despite the fact that they did not represent any government, they succeeded, like Dmowski before them, in securing recognition by the Allies for a political entity which had not heretofore existed (October, 1918). This move to independence had the strong support of the people at home. Although overt resistance to the war had at first been slight (aside from the desertions), in the waning days of the struggle open opposition had increased. A highly successful general strike in October of 1918 demonstrated popular support for independence, and subsequently a Czechoslovak Republic was proclaimed in Prague.

The attitude of Hungary was quite different from that of its East European neighbors. As the conflict opened, Budapest shared in the sustained burst of nationalist fervor that swept London, Paris, and Berlin—in fact, the people of the Hungarian capital were noticeably more enthusiastic than the residents of their sister capital, Vienna. The Hungarian government saw the war as an opportunity to stifle non-Magyar nationalist sentiment within its half of the empire by striking at irredentist troublemakers operating from the outside. Budapest's inflexibility toward Serbia after the assassination was indicative of this attitude. But as the conflict continued and the casualty lists lengthened, the depression that affected the other belligerents affected the Hungarians as well. Even so, two factors combined to keep them more grimly determined than the Austrians, and thus helped to keep the Dual Monarchy firmly in the war and on a collision course with disaster.

First, one should remember that for the Hungarians the war was far more of a struggle against hated rivals than it was for the Austrians. The Magyars had never forgotten Russian intervention against Kossuth in 1849, and they had also developed a sort of slavophobia which applied to Serbs, Croats, and Slovaks as well as to Russians. The Romanians were also in the category of ancestral enemies. A second factor dividing the leaders of the two halves of the empire was nationality policy. The Austrians had grown increasingly tired of fighting the national aspirations of their subject nationalities and, as described earlier, several proposals for reorganization had gathered widespread support in Vienna. But these had foundered on the rocks of Magyar intransigence: the principle of national self determination was not applicable to the Crownlands of St. Stephen. Thus, Allied initiatives, which asked nothing more than the granting of autonomy to the larger nationalities in return for a separate peace, met firm resistance in Budapest. The end of the war and the collapse of the empire produced an unsurprising result in Hungary: the government declared its independence and at the same time asserted its refusal to yield any territory.

Romania was late in entering the war partly for strategic reasons (a well-founded concern, as the military debacle demonstrated) and partly for reasons of diplomacy; the Romanians wanted to have the promise of as much land as they could before they joined the Allies. The desire to recover both Bessarabia and Transylvania was impossible, of course, since one of the two holders of these provinces must become an ally. That the Romanians opted for the Allies and the return of Transylvania is not surprising. The delay was occasioned by the need to negotiate the details, particularly since some of Romania's claims conflicted with those of Serbia, in the Banat, not strictly a part of Transylvania. The deal won by Prime Minister Ionel Brătianu (son of Ion Brătianu) was nonetheless exceptional. Romania was promised nearly everything she wanted.

The initially bright picture as Romania plunged into the war was greatly dimmed by her sudden, almost total defeat at the hands of the Central Powers. Of course, the Allies could not claim bad faith for a disaster that was largely a consequence of their inability to deliver promised military support, nor could they question Romania's acceptance of a dictated peace after the revolution in Petrograd forced the collapse of the Russian front. Yet the Bolshevik revolution was in the long run of great benefit to the Romanians, since the demise of tsarist Russia allowed them to revive their claims to Bessarabia. Following the end of the war and the beginning of the retreat of the German occupation armies, the independent Romanian government was rapidly restored and just as quickly had an army in the field to support its territorial aspirations.

For the Bulgarians, the First World War was essentially a sequel to their country's humiliating defeat in the Second Balkan War. The desire for revenge was great, and it was only the widespread sympathy for the Western democracies, the longstanding affinity for Russia, and the desire to drive the best possible bargain with the Central Powers that delayed Bulgaria's entry into the war. A rapid thrust into Macedonia assured Bulgaria of her most important objective. Later, Romania's entry on the opposite side allowed the Bulgarians to seize all of the Dobrogea (more than was lost in the Second Balkan War). Sofia controlled these territories and part of Albania until the summer of 1918, when a powerful Allied thrust from Salonika coupled with the collapse of Austro-Hungarian military effectiveness forced Bulgaria from the war. The armistice stipulated the immediate withdrawal of Bulgarian forces from lands seized from Serbia, Romania, and Albania.

The idea of a Yugoslavia gained acceptance slowly during the war. As a political concept it moved with difficulty from the primarily intellectual world of its origin to the arena of practical politics. Certainly it was not part of the original Serbian objective—the Allies were strongly opposed to the break up of the Habsburg Empire (restructuring it was another matter). Instead, Serbia looked for territory elsewhere, particularly at the expense of Albania. Since Serbia was one of the original belligerents, she was in a poor bargaining position. The Allies eventually broke their policy on the integrity of the Habsburg realm by offering Dalmatia and other territories to Italy in exchange for Italian participation in the war (1915). The Serbs had no such opportunity to bargain; at first their participation was assured and later even their surrender would have made little difference. It is important to remember that Serbia never actually capitulated; her army kept fighting to the end.

Montenegro's position was somewhat different. This tiny ally of Serbia fought bravely on the Dalmatian and Bosnian fronts, but the Serbian retreat left even their rocky and inhospitable terrain open to attack from three sides. The Austro-Hungarian command asked for unconditional surrender and the handing over of all Serbian troops in the country. The Montenegrins refused, and the country was occupied after fierce fighting. Like the Serbs, the Montenegrins never officially accepted defeat in any way.

The collapse of the Serbian military effort in 1916 made the leaders of that country think more carefully about the Yugoslav idea as a genuine policy for the future. The concept was becoming more popular in war-weary Slovenia and the Croat lands, and it had always had a strong attraction for the Serbs of Bosnia-Hercegovina. In this spirit of "unity as the best real alternative" as opposed to unity because it was the best idea, Croat and Serb representatives met on the island of Corfu in the summer of 1917. The agreement to seek a Yugoslav state under the Serbian Karageorgevich dynasty was an unenthusiastic one, as the two sides differed on many key issues. But they did agree on union, and their declaration was a powerful propaganda weapon against the Dual Monarchy.

When the armistice of November, 1918, was signed, Belgrade was in Allied hands, the Austro-Hungarian forces had melted away, and the German forces that had been added (as everywhere in the east) to "stiffen" the front were in full retreat. Since the Serbian army comprised the majority of the Allied force in the Balkans, that nation had the power to move into the other areas of present-day Yugoslavia. The complete break-down in civil and military authority in these areas facilitated the transfer, although there was some scattered resistance in Croatian areas. In ret-rospect, however, unification was one of the easiest things Yugoslavia has ever done.

Albania, ever the exception, was the only country of present day Eastern Europe not to have achieved de facto independence by war's end. In truth, the Albanians were helpless. Portions of Albania's territory had been overrun by Serbs, Greeks, Montenegrins, Austro-Hungarians, and even French. Most important, Italy had been promised the greater part of Albania as an incentive to enter the war. The end of Austro-Hungarian occupation signalled the beginning of an Italian regime. The only hope for the Albanians was at the peace conference.

The Settlement

Albania's hopes for a fair deal at the conference table rode largely on the shoulders of Woodrow Wilson, whose famous Fourteen Points had changed the character of wartime diplomacy. Even though Wilson called for the preservation of the Habsburg Empire, his support for the general principle of national self-determination was an inspiration to the peoples of Eastern Europe and a revelation to the British, French, and Italians. Wilson's initiative helped speed the recognition of the recreated Polish state and, when it was obvious that Habsburg glue would no longer hold, Wilson approved of Czechoslovakia. Wilson's ideas also helped to save Albania and unify Yugoslavia. On the other hand, the principle of national self-determination also contributed to tying areas of mixed ethnic pop-ulation into political Gordian knots, whose complexity defied solution while raising already inflamed passions.

The westerner is accustomed to thinking of the Treaty of Versailles as the document that defined the peace; in fact, this treaty dealt only with Germany. Other treaties dealt with other belligerents: Neuilly with Bulgaria, St. Germain with Turkey, and Trianon with Hungary. Overall, the peace treaties were a mixed bag of Wilsonian idealism, diplomatic quid pro quo, and fait accompli. The noble precepts of the American president were attractive but impractical; moreover, although the policies of the United States demanded attention, that country was not strong enough to insist on having its own way. The Europeans were put on the defensive by Wilson, but his ideas served more often as an excuse for wiping the slate clean and starting the bargaining afresh. Thus Italy lost the territory in Yugoslavia and Albania promised to the Italians during the war, but this change reflected more Italy's very weak position at the end of the fighting than it did romantic nationalism in the west. In other cases the peacemakers in Paris accepted the military status quo rather than going to the trouble of enforcing their wishes.

Settling the frontiers of Poland was far easier for the Allies than anyone had anticipated. Restoration of the boundaries that had obtained before the first partition was not possible, in part because the Poland of 1772 had included substantial non-Polish areas, and in part because nearly a century and a half of history had caused many changes. Even so, the methodical Germans had simplified the problem in the west: the census of 1910 gave clear guidelines for most of the area. The Prussian provinces of Poznania and Pomerania (including a corridor to the Baltic) were obviously still ethnically Polish. The key port city of Danzig was a special problem since the urban center was solidly German but the environs were solidly Polish (a not untypical type of pattern in Eastern Europe). The ultimate decision was to create a "free city" belonging to neither country, but serving, as did all such attempts to apply national self-determination on a small scale, to magnify local tensions and exacerbate national hatred.

The province of Silesia provided even more vexing difficulties. Though probably overwhelmingly Polish before the partitions, a century of rapid industrial development had drastically altered the ethnic map of the area. At the same time the enormous economic potential of Silesia made its disposition an especially emotional issue. The peacemakers decided on a series of plebiscites to guide them, but the results were not helpful. The German administration, which still controlled the entire region, did its best to manipulate the results. The Polish government was so occupied with the war in the east that it could not effectively protest. Even so, the Germans won less than 60 percent of the vote; an honest figure would have been closer to 50 percent. Confused by the outcome and alarmed by several Polish insurrections, the authorities in Paris decided to partition the area roughly in half along an east-west axis. Germany got the larger and richer share, but the Polish state nonetheless received an enormous economic boost.

The extreme southern part of Silesia (known as Upper or more commonly Teschen Silesia) was divided between Poland and Czechoslovakia. Here again, the pattern of settlement had effected a mosaic that defied a rational solution. The precise ethnic mixture of the area in 1919 is still a matter of disagreement between Polish and Czech scholars today, but even a clear cut majority for one side or another would not have showed the way to an obvious disposition, so intermingled were the peoples of different nationalities. The Allies' decision on a rough 50-50 split was thus highly controversial. Particularly aggrieved were the Poles who felt that their nation had far greater need of the industrial strength of the area than did Czechoslovakia. The issue of Teschen Silesia was sufficiently serious to prevent cooperation between the two countries during most of the interwar period.

The eastern frontiers of Poland occasioned much discussion in Paris, but the final decisions were made elsewhere. The principle of national self-determination, reinforced by the representations of Ukrainian and Lithuanian organizations, caused the Allies to commission studies of the ethnic distribution of the population with a view toward drawing a national frontier. Under the direction of a British diplomat, Lord Curzon, a careful analysis was done and the "Curzon Line" was proposed as Poland's eastern frontier. Though hardly perfect, the proposal was a good one which coped effectively with numerous, severe conflicts. The fates of the cities of Vilnius and Lvov were especially challenging. Both had the population patterns of Danzig, in this case Polish urban cores surrounded respectively by Lithuanian and Ukrainian countryside; to make the situation more difficult, both cities were major Polish cultural centers, and the Lvov region had significant oil fields. The Curzon Line left Vilnius in Lithuania and Lvov under temporary Polish administration pending a regional plebiscite.

The views of the diplomats in Paris were almost superfluous, however, for Poland's eastern border region was in great turmoil. The Allies' ability to enforce their decisions was practically nil. Pushing eastward, the Poles tried to bring order into the chaos of the Russian civil war, which always had at least three sides. After establishing control of the lands west of the Curzon Line, the Polish army continued to move east. Piłsudski, who had dreams of a giant Polish-Ukrainian-Lithuanian confederation which would both promote prosperity and lessen national tensions, made an alliance with the Ukrainian leader Simon Petlura.[3] Together they dominated vast areas of what had been the western part of the Russian Empire. But their supply lines were soon greatly overextended, and a Red Army counteroffensive destroyed Petlura's forces and drove the Poles back to the gates of Warsaw. Again, huge stretches of territory were covered in a short time, and again the offensive forces were overextended. The Poles rallied and with some French assistance defeated the Red Army in a battle known as the "Miracle of Warsaw." The cycle then began anew, but this time the Poles chose a prudent stopping point, Lenin agreed to an armistice, and Poland held de facto if not de jure both Vilnius and Lvov and large areas east of the Curzon Line. A new Polish state was born.

The situation of Czechoslovakia was less traumatic than that of Poland. This new nation achieved nearly everything it wanted in its frontiers. The settlement in Teschen Silesia was as good as the country could hope to get. Elsewhere, the leaders in Prague successfully argued against the full application of the principle of national self-determination. Particularly significant was the situation in the Sudeten region, where large areas of solidly German population bordered on Germany proper. The Czechoslovaks were able to argue against partition of the area on historical and strategic grounds. In the first place, Beneš and Masaryk argued eloquently that the lands had been Czech originally and that German settlement on a large scale had occurred only after the Czech defeat in the Thirty Years War (1618–1648). The Germans, they said, should not be rewarded for their centuries-long oppression of the Czech people. The strategic argument emphasized the fact that without the mountainous Sudeten border areas Czechoslovakia would have no natural defense against a German attack in the future.

The first of these arguments appealed to the more sentimental British and Americans, while the second had the undivided attention of the more practical French. The latter's foremost concern at the peace conference was the future of Germany; France wanted to see her rival as weak as possible. The strategic aspects of the Sudeten area were obvious to the leaders in Paris, who also noted its economic potential. The wrangling was intense, but Czechoslovakia kept the Sudeten region. A similar argument prevailed in the case of southern Slovakia. Here again Prague successfully argued for an ethnically foreign (Hungarian) area on strategic and economic grounds. Without the railroads running east to west in the southern Carpathian foothills, it would be almost impossible to administer and develop trade in Slovakia, a province whose territory runs east to west but which is cut by mountains which ran north to south. Czechoslovakia also received Carpatho-Ruthenia, but largely by default. Only the Soviets and the Hungarians wanted it, and these two counted for little at the peace conference.

Hungary's situation at the end of the war was indeed dismal. She was a defeated enemy state, and all of her territorial aspirations ran directly counter to the principle of national self-determination. Accordingly, Hungary lost every border dispute in which she was involved: Slovakia went to Czechoslovakia; Transylvania to Romania; Croatia, the Vojvodina, and the Banat to Yugoslavia. The Hungarians lost even the minor disputes, as ethnically Magyar areas on the fringes of the country were taken for one reason or another (e.g., Czechoslovakia's claim to the land south of Slovakia). Budapest also came out second best in a tug of war with Austria over a small area which was settled by plebiscite. The Hungarians were not only defeated, they were friendless and powerless.

No country was more successful than Romania in the acquisition of territory. First the Dobrogea was returned from Bulgaria. Then the much-disputed province of Bessarabia was incorporated into Romania after the power vacuum created by the Russian civil war made it possible to call an assembly representing the local population which then voted for union with Romania. Similarly, the province of Bucovina, which had been detached from Moldavia by Austria in the eighteenth century, was restored. Here again the collapse of the Dual Empire and the chaos of the civil war in Russia allowed the Romanians to include large areas inhabited primarily by Ukrainians. In fact, there was so little opposition to the Romanian advances into Dobrogea, Bessarabia, and Bucovina that borders were established without difficulty.

The case of Transylvania was somewhat different. Romanian troops swept into this province in pursuit of the retreating Austro-Hungarian and German armies. It was not a major campaign, but there was significant opposition, particularly in the areas inhabited by Hungarians and Germans. The borders were hard to establish. The Romanians wanted to press well to the west of the historic Transylvanian countries in order to seize strategic towns and rail lines. The Allies were unenthusiastic about this, but it was difficult both in ideological and in practical terms to force the Romanians to retreat. The Béla Kun revolt in Hungary (see below), and Romania's role in crushing it, eventually changed the situation, and the Romanians got pretty much what they wanted.

Under their aggressive leader Ionel Brătianu, the Romanians had a diplomatic struggle with Yugoslavia over the former Hungarian province of the Banat. This area was ethnically mixed but not unreasonably so, at least by East European standards. Brătianu, however, insisted on the entire area, including the bank of the Danube opposite Belgrade. Fortunately, these rather extravagant claims against an ally found little favor, and the area was divided by the Allies along fairly equitable lines. The dispute between the two was then quickly forgotten.

Bulgaria's situation was analogous to that of Hungary. Thoroughly defeated and lacking even the sympathy available so often in the past from Russia, the Bulgarians were unable to resist their enemies. The Dobrogea and Macedonia were quickly lost to Romania and Yugoslavia, respectively. Greece nibbled at the southern frontier. Only the border with the former ally, Turkey, reamined untouched. Bulgaria after World War I was not much smaller than she had been after the Second Balkan War, but she had in the meantime once again struggled mightily for nothing. Bulgaria continued to be an unhappy nation.

Yugoslavia, with more borders than anyone else, had more frontier disputes. With three countries (Greece, Romania, and Bulgaria) differences were resolved without undue difficulty. The remaining four frontiers, all of which were essentially brand new, presented serious problems. Yugoslavia wished to take virtually the entire northern and eastern part of Albania. In this she was opposed by Italy, which also had designs on basically the same area. The outcome was a stalemate since the prewar boundaries remained, but in the interim many words and not a few bullets flew through the air. The Yugoslavs and the Italians also clashed over the Dalmatian coast, including especially the two important ports of Rijeka (called Fiume by the Italians) and Trieste. The Italians had been promised the entire area, but were willing to concede the coastline south of Rijeka. Eventually the Yugoslavs got all but the city and the immediate environs of Trieste. From an ethnic point of view the solution was an extremely good one, but neither side was really happy.

The border with Austria in the Slovene lands was particularly hard to define. Slovenia had been an integral part of Austria for more than six centuries, and clear distinctions on a historic basis were not possible. Consequently, the plebiscite system was used extensively to make decisions. Interestingly, a number of heavily Slovene areas remained in Austria. Though many factors were at work, it seems that a significant number of Slovenes voted for their historic cultural and religious associations instead of the new linguistic nationalism.

Croatia's boundaries had been sufficiently clear, even under Hungarian rule, that little genuine disagreement was possible. But the same was far from true in the Yugoslav-Hungarian border province of Vojvodina. Here Serbs had been settled for centuries on what originally had been a part of the kingdom of Hungary. Budapest's later control of the area had reintroduced a Hungarian population, and the province was mixed up in a way that prevented simple division. Surveys, votes, domestic violence, and military and diplomatic threats were all used in a bitter campaign. Not surprisingly, the Yugoslavs got their way. Belgrade also acquired, however, a significant Hungarian minority.

Various secret agreements among the Allies during the war had carved Albania up so thoroughly that nothing was left. As stated above, Wilson's views had much to do with the scrapping of these treaties. Ultimately, however, a tactical switch by the Italians was of very great importance. Realizing that direct control of the country was impossible, the Italians decided to go for indirect control later on; given this objective it was not in Rome's interest that Yugoslavia and Greece should get anything at all. Italy thus resisted changes in Albanian frontiers. While all of this diplomatic infighting was taking place, the Albanian resistance movements were showing their views by making life extremely difficult for would-be occupiers. Albania emerged from the war with essentially the same frontiers as before, but the validity of her independence was a more important concern.

7

Interwar Eastern Europe
An Overview

THE ESTABLISHMENT of the independent states of interwar Eastern
Europe was possible only because all of the great powers bordering
on the area were defeated in the same war. In the hindsight of more than
half a century this seems an unremarkable fact. But for the peoples living
at that time and in those places, it was more than remarkable—it was
miraculous. If one considers that all of the neighboring empires were
engaged against each other in a bitter struggle, then only one outcome
of the war would seem possible: victory for one side or another, followed
by sharply increased control by that power (or powers). It would stand
to reason, in fact, that at least one empire would emerge far stronger
than before and in the absence of rivals would be extremely intolerant
of minority nationalities. Even those who pinned their hopes on a reorganization of the Habsburg realm could not be overly sanguine: a
victorious empire would have less, not more, incentive to reform.

The early years of the struggle dashed most of the hopes that remained. Two independent states, Serbia and Romania, were quickly
crushed; Albania simply ceased to exist. No one spoke of the revival of
Poland with any serious expectations. Calls for the autonomy of the
Czech lands were now labeled as treasonous in both Vienna and Budapest.
Those close to diplomatic circles in the west knew or sensed that the
desperate Allies were willing to make concessions affecting the national
aspirations of any East European people. Thus the defeat of one group
of oppressors would only cause them to be exchanged for a new set. To
residents of Eastern Europe, the nature of the postwar world was un-
certain, but the possibilities all seemed grim.

The outbreak of the Bolshevik revolution and Russia's subsequent
impotence and defeat were the darkest hours of the war for the Allies.
It was feared that enormous German reinforcements from the east would

be able to challenge the stalemate in the west months before American troops could restore the balance. Yet this cataclysmic event was the beginning of hope for the East Europeans (though few probably thought so at the time). For with Russia defeated and incapable of realizing her own aims in Eastern Europe, the miraculous became the possible. The defeat of Germany and the collapse of Austria-Hungary then created an enormous power vacuum in which nationalist schemes that had once seemed frivolous and romantic suddenly became realities. In assessing the interwar period this fairy-tale ending must always be kept in mind. No one really planned for independence; hardly anyone expected it. When it did come, no one was really prepared.

Before reviewing the international political developments of the interwar period, it is essential to construct an understanding of the economic situation. In the early parts of this narrative the connection between economic and political events has been treated as a secondary issue. This approach reflects the views of contemporary politicans who rarely had more than a superficial understanding of economic forces. Thus, for example, primary railroad building usually followed the dictates of military planners and comparatively little attention was given to its impact on industrial development (although marketing of agricultural products was often a concern of sorts). The events of the First World War and the subsequent national reorganization changed all of this drastically. Traditional patterns of trade were so severely disrupted that the national economies were at a standstill. Without careful reconstruction and development, the nations of Eastern Europe might have found their material situation growing continually worse rather than better.

There was another way in which the national-political reorganization directly affected the economies. For decades nationalist leaders had been preaching the glories of the unified national state. The influence of utopian nationalists, like the Italian Giuseppe Mazzini, who believed that a world of nation-states would mean the end of war, was strong in Eastern Europe. This quasi-religious, prophetic approach to politics naturally raised expectations far beyond the normal situation. The people, in fact, had been told to expect a sort of heaven on earth, that a new world of harmony and plenty would appear when nationalist goals were achieved. When this did not occur, the politicians were on the spot; they could claim that all was not yet resolved, and they made great use of irredentism as a means of distracting the masses. But it was nonetheless difficult to argue that, because country X did not yet control all of province Y, the standard of living was falling. The dilemma of the politicians was made more uncomfortable by the fact that all of the countries of Eastern

Europe were, at least in theory and to some extent, democracies in which the leaders could be held accountable for their policies.

If the politicians began to pay a great deal more attention to economic problems, one should not assume that solutions therefore suddenly became plentiful. The leaders were unsure of themselves and untrained, and their nations generally lacked the cadre of highly specialized people necessary for good planning. On the other hand, the problems were enormous: they were probably comparatively greater than those affecting Western Europe, where governments were also finding it extremely hard to cope. Perhaps the greatest tragedy of interwar Eastern Europe was the politicians' inability to take a broad view of the economic situation. One can argue that their failure to understand the crucial importance of multinational initiatives doomed the experiment in independence.

It is important to remember that, from the perspective of the interwar period, the prewar pattern of trade and economic development had been fundamentally multinational. Industrial products manufactured in Poland and the Czech lands were generally marketed outside the borders of the countries-to-be. Indeed, most of prewar Eastern Europe's manufacturing capacity had been created on the assumption of an extensive tariff-free trading area (the nascent industrial bases of Serbia and Romania are the only significant exceptions). The same problem applied to access to raw materials and technology. A typical factory in Budapest drew most of its natural resources from areas that were not a part of Hungary after 1918—coal would be a good example. It is also probable that many of the engineers and technicians in the same factory were either Austrian by nationality, or had been trained in Austria.

The situation of agriculture was essentially the same. Although most East European farms were not sufficiently productive to generate a surplus worthy of transporting, those that did export were typically dependent on what were to become foreign markets. The wines of Dalmatia and Slovenia, for example, had a strong natural market in the Austro-Hungarian Empire. When those regions became a part of Yugoslavia, the very small demand in the rest of the country could not begin to pick up the slack. Very high tariffs, combined with economic dislocation elsewhere, made export extremely difficult. In the case of agriculture, even the core areas of enlarged states like Serbia-Yugoslavia and Romania were adversely affected. An example is Bessarabia, whose produce for market directly competed with that of the old provinces of Moldavia and Wallachia.

All of the nations of Eastern Europe except Albania and Hungary carried out fairly extensive land reforms. The net effect, however, varied significantly by country, and the consequences were for the most part not very helpful. In Yugoslavia, the objective was to make the country as a whole similar to Serbia, a region of small farmers. Estates in Bosnia-Hercegovina, Croatia, the Vojvodina, and the Banat were dissolved and the land given to the peasants who tilled it. This reform was relatively easy since the dispossessed landowners were almost exclusively foreigners. Romania underwent a similar process as Russian and Hungarian nobles lost their possessions in Bassarabia and Transylvania, respectively; but in the Regat (the old kingdom, pre-1918) the ethnically Romanian landowners retained much of their grip. In Poland, the process was much less complete since in the vast eastern regions the peasants were usually Ukrainian or Byelorussian but the landlords were generally Polish. Thus the changes amounted more to a moderation than a radical reform. In Czechoslovakia, legislation gradually broke up the large estates, many of which were owned by Germans or Magyars.

Bulgaria did have a land reform, but it was on a small scale since fewer major changes were necessary. As in Serbia, there were no really large estates and no foreign-owned lands of importance. Thus the Bulgarian reform served only to reduce the extent of some of the larger farms. In Albania, a major change from an estate system to peasant ownership was put into effect, but a change in government restored the status quo. In Hungary, where the power of the land-owning nobility was absolute, a reform was proposed and enacted but never carried out.

East European agriculture, which could have served as the basis for a surplus that could modernize society, acted instead as an anchor holding the economies firmly in the past. The few land reforms that were fully carried out transferred ownership of the soil to those who tilled it and therefore, at least in theory, improved incentives. But that was the only positive effect. The new owners also acquired heavy debts for, as in the past, compensation had to be paid to the former landlords. And also as before, the peasants were on the whole in a very poor position to make payments. The average amount of land distributed to a family was not more than one or two hectares, even though five is usually considered the minimum for self-sufficiency with only the smallest possibility of a surplus for the market. Moreover, these dwarfholdings were often divided into many separate strips. Modern mechanized farming was thus impossible. Where large estates did persist, absentee landlords, lack of incentives for the peasants, and minimal access to credit and to education produced the same effect for a backward, isolated, and impoverished peasantry.

In a sense the land reforms made the situation worse. Instead of forcing the peasants out of the countryside and into the cities, the changes acted both as an inducement to stay and a hindrance to departure. The inducement to remain was the traditional peasant desire for land ownership; the hindrance to migration was the indebtedness that accompanied acceptance of the property coupled with the extreme difficulty of selling at a reasonable price. Ironically, the only good thing about the reforms was that they prevented the depression from having an even more severe impact. So many of the peasants were dwarfholders and therefore engaged in (at best) subsistence agriculture, that they were not seriously affected by the plunging prices for food in the depression era. Similarly, unemployed in the cities often returned to family living on the land in the hope of finding enough food to prevent starvation. This reverse migration resolved some temporary difficulties, but in the long run it exacerbated the endemic problem of rural overpopulation.

The prevailing trend in economic thinking in most of the world at this time was protectionist and autarkic. For the most part, and especially in Eastern Europe, this point of view was a reflection of nationalism. The models for the modern nation-state were the highly developed industrial countries of the west: Britain, France, and Germany. These models applied for a number of reasons: they were the first nation-states; industrial development was equated with modernity ("Westernization") and a higher standard of living; and a strong national industrial base was essential for survival in modern warfare. This last point was, unfortunately, the most important. All of the states of Eastern Europe were extremely insecure and had good reason to fear war. Industrial capacity was equated with strength. Imports of basic manufactured products had two disadvantages in the East European view: they stifled domestic development, and they were potentially unreliable in a national security crisis.

Based on these criteria, the nations of Eastern Europe generally put heavy taxes on machinery imports and tried to foster the development of key products in their own countries. Bulgaria, which was too underdeveloped to expect much effect in the short term, was a partial exception, and Albania was unable to attempt this approach because of foreign domination. Inevitably, however, these autarkic strategies could not succeed. None of the countries had the resource base necessary to achieve anything more than a very limited self-sufficiency. Moreover, the countries were poor and found it very difficult to sustain the luxury of domestically produced products that were far more expensive than (probably) superior items available for import.

Given the inapplicability of protectionism in the vast majority of industrial sectors, the East European leaders were forced to make at least some trade arrangements. Typically, they followed essentially political lines in their search for trading partners. Overwhelmingly, this meant that prewar markets and resource areas were ignored in favor of more distant options. It was therefore especially unfortunate that natural allies were rarely natural trading partners. Within the area, two moderately industrialized states (Poland and Czechoslovakia) and two predominantly agricultural states with small but growing industries (Romania and Yogoslavia) were grouped together in a rough alliance (see below). But the similarity of their economies, together with the geographical barrier, limited development.

The principal non-East European ally (France) of these four states also lacked the ability to solve economic difficulties for her friends. Although the French economy was still strong in the early years of the depression (partly because it was so slow in recovering from the war), Paris found it hard to transfer her strength elsewhere. The problem became particularly acute in the 1930s since the two fascist states, Italy and Germany, were astride the only east-west rail routes. The livestock and foodstuffs that the east Europeans exported to France were typically not well suited for shipping by the much slower sea route. On the other hand, French exports to Eastern Europe were all too often armaments, products which obviously did little to bolster the economies of the poorer countries.

The great depression of the 1930s hurt Eastern Europe more than Western Europe since changes in the terms of trade were generally beneficial to exporters of industrial as opposed to agricultural goods. Preexisting problems of unemployment, unequal distribution of wealth, shortage of investment capital, and inflation were exacerbated. Sympathetic nations of the West were unable to provide aid because of their own problems, and in fact were even less willing to accept imports than in the past. The shift from democracy to totalitarianism in Eastern Europe largely preceded the depression, but this is deceptive since the international economic crisis was for this region merely an extension and an emphasis of a long-term phenomenon.

The final state of the interwar East European economic situation was one of dependency. Though the countries of the region were anxious to develop commercial independence, they never came close to developing financial independence. The role of foreign capital had always been extremely important for Eastern Europe, and this did not change in the interwar period. Assets owned by the defeated countries (principally Germany, but also Austria and Hungary) were generally nationalized just after the war. Compensation was mandatory in such cases, and although the inflation greatly reduced the costs, foreign loans had to be floated in order to cover the total. The income from these loans helped produce a "mini-boom" in the early postwar period. Together with inflation, which sharply reduced fixed costs (e.g., labor), the new funds fueled heavy investment in producer and consumer goods. Inflation also protected domestic manufacturers, since devalued currencies made imports extremely expensive. And as people removed funds from rapidly eroding savings accounts and spent them on tangible items, the consumer market was for a time especially strong. Thus, despite all sorts of problems in the economic environment, sharp growth rates obtained for a few years.

But the bubble burst rather quickly. Very little of the money available from foreign loans was used to pay for genuinely productive purposes. Much, perhaps most, was used to pay off the debts. Large amounts were also spent for public works of a monumental nature and for armaments. Corruption siphoned off an unknown, but probably a large amount. A careful estimate suggests that no more than 20 percent of the amount borrowed went into investments that actually helped to produce new capital for the economy.[1] The results were disastrous. The new loans had been made at very high interest rates, and soon the countries found themselves in the worst possible position: old debts had been turned into new ones that were even more expensive, but at the same time the economy's ability to produce the surplus needed for debt service had not kept pace. Thus, even before the depression began, East European countries were forced to reschedule loans and to transfer assets to foreign (principally British, French, and American) owners. Hungary was even forced to accept an American banker as overall manager of financial matters.[2]

The structure of the East European economies made foreign penetration and control very easy. Small numbers of very large bankers owned much of industry directly. At the same time, cartels dominated most of the more important sectors of heavy and light industry. Thus a group of foreign investors could assert control over a large area by focusing their acquisitions on banks, or, using leverage obtained by buying bonds representing a country's indebtedness, could force the transfer of industries in return for settlement. These manuevers had the effect of making East European manufacturing capacity subsidiary to that of the west; the results were by no means beneficial, since the controlling companies usually preferred to prevent the weaker units from growing and competing with home industry, and since the transfer of technology was rarely effected. The use of mass production techniques, electrification, and other forms of mechanization that were fueling growth in the west, were available on only a scattered basis in the east. Even more significant, foreign investors concentrated their acquisitions on firms involved in the extraction of industrial raw materials. Thus, East European coal, ores, oil, and timber could be supplied at artificially low prices to western manufacturers. Overall, 50–70 percent of the East European economy was financed by foreign capital (Czechoslovakia is the only important exception).

Since foreign investment, whether controlled by foreigners or by natives, was not generally being put to productive use, it was of very little help during the depression. As countries shut their doors to trade and attempted (usually with considerable success) to substitute domestic agricultural production for imports, the situation of the East European economies became much worse: they had less income, while their ability to find domestic alternatives for machinery and raw materials imports was virtually non-existent. In the deep, politically explosive stagnation that followed, only one country, Nazi Germany, offered a solution. Its idea, "clearing," was not a new one, but in the skilled hands of the Nazi finance minister Schacht, it became a powerful weapon of German economic control and expansion.[3]

Essentially, clearing is a sophisticated form of bilateral trade. Two countries agree to promote the exchange of goods at a designated level for a limited time. Various mechanisms are used to simplify and facilitate payments (special bank accounts, for example), and in their negotiations the two countries may decide to ignore aspects of the world market. Thus exchange rates for currencies determined in multilateral trade may not be accurate when only two countries are involved. Another attractive aspect of clearing is the amount of control if affords. For countries which had gradually become committed to government management of trade and finance, clearing was far more efficient than the array of exchange controls, tariffs, and taxes then in use. In clearing, both the level and the commodity structure of trade can be determined in advance with considerable accuracy.

The Nazi proposals were quite simple: they would purchase agricultural products and raw materials and in return would provide finished industrial goods. Although this was not the ideal trade structure for the industrializing countries of Eastern Europe, it still seemed a real break. Without clearing they would have to continue to dump hugh quantities of foodstuffs which could not be sold on the world market; some exchange was better than none. The Nazis actually sweetened this deal by agreeing to pay more than market prices for some of the items they imported. They could do this for three reasons. First, it was cheaper for them to purchase goods on a barter basis that otherwise would have to be bought on the world market, something that was difficult for Germany since she found it difficult to export; also, low quality goods could be sold to the east for comparatively high prices. Second, the Germans didn't intend to pay; although they imported up to the limit of every agreement, they managed in one way or another to fail to deliver the appropriate line of exports. Germany was continually in a deficit position. Third, by buying in large quantities at high prices the Nazis created a dependency. Since breaking the agreements would create havoc in essential areas of their economies, the East European leaders found it very difficult to resist Berlin's demands.

Schacht used the Nazi propaganda machine to make it appear that Germany was making enormous sacrifices to help her poorer neighbors. In fact, just the reverse was true, as the people of Eastern Europe unwittingly used much of their labor to help Hitler's rearmament. This eventually became clear to the leaders of Eastern Europe, but by the time they saw the trap they were in it. The western powers, which disdained clearing themselves, were in no position to ease these countries over the extraordinary hardship that would immediately follow disengagement from Germany. Moreover, as Nazi military might grew, pressure to conform was ever harder to resist. In the years just before the war, the Germans even were able to order changes in the internal economic structure of some countries to better suit their own needs. Most affected by Nazi domination in this respect were Bulgaria, Hungary, Yugoslavia, and Romania. Poland and Czechoslovakia were not controlled but were by no means unaffected. The Nazi seizure of first Austria and then Czechoslovakia sharply enhanced Berlin's position in the first four nations, since the two annexed countries had extensive investments there.

Although international political developments in Eastern Europe ultimately came to follow the pattern of economic concerns, this was not the case at first. In large part this is due to the fact that for Eastern Europe all problems of diplomacy were related directly or indirectly to the national tensions within the region itself. Every country had fundamental and legitimate concerns about its national security. These dangers had an immediacy that made them rather different from those that worried most other nations. Thus, for example, French diplomacy in the 1920s demonstrated a real fear of Germany, but because of the latter's weakness it was essentially a long-term danger that the French were striving to make even more remote. For the nations of Eastern Europe, on the other hand, real enemies of comparatively great power were everywhere. It would have required a major crisis and probably a great conflict before France could lose even a square centimeter of territory, but by contrast an unprepared and friendless Poland might again have disappeared without out greatly disturbing the diplomatic waters. Since the internal conflicts of Eastern Europe so pervade its interwar history, a brief review of them seems appropriate.

Poland had five neighbors and among them only one friend. She had border conflicts with the Soviet Union over a vast territory, with Lithuania over the city of Vilnius, with Germany over a broad area but especially the corridor and Danzig, and with Czechoslovakia over Teschen Silesia. The only stable frontier was that with Romania, but both countries were so deep in the Ukraine at their meeting point that no national passions were aroused in drawing a line between them. Czechoslovakia disputed the Teschen area with Poland, the large Sudeten region with Germany, Slovakia and its southern fringe with Hungary, and Carpatho-Ruthenia with both Hungary and the Soviet Union. The border with Austria was the only one not contested.

Hungary did have differences, albeit minor ones, with Austria. The rest of Hungary's quarrels with her neighbors were far more serious: in addition to the disagreement with Czechoslovakia, she had fundamental differences with Yugoslavia on the entire Croatia-Vojvodina-Banat area, and with Romania over all of Transylvania. For Romania, in addition to the above, there were disputes with the Soviet Union over Bessarabia and with Bulgaria over Dobrogea. On the other hand, Romania's relations with Poland and Yugoslavia were unaffected by territorial problems. This was lucky for the Yugoslavs since otherwise all seven of their neighbors would have been enemies. The Yugoslav dispute with Bulgaria over Macedonia needs no further elaboration at this point. Yugoslavia's border with Greece was essentially a ceasefire line from the Balkan wars, and all frontiers with Albania were contested. Finally, in addition to the situation with Hungary, Yugoslavia had very bad relations with Italy (Trieste) and Austria (Slovenia). Bulgaria, in addition to the disputes with Romania and Yugoslavia, was also unhappy with her frontiers with Turkey and Greece (also basically ceasefire lines). Albania had running battles (sometimes literally) with both Greece and Yugoslavia over the twisting demarcation lines that separated her from her neighbors.

These conflicts divided Eastern Europe into two groups: the status quo states which had essentially what they wanted and were striving only to keep it; and the revisionist states which had lost much and whose hopes were pegged on major changes. In this latter category, of course, were the two defeated states: Hungary and Bulgaria. All the rest except Albania were oriented to the status quo. In a strange way Albania was in both categories: she wanted to keep what she had and get even more, but her neighbors thought she had too much. It would be a mistake to assume, however, that only the status quo countries had reason to be nervous about their territorial integrity. The Bulgarians and the Hungarians also had good cause to fear that frustrated rivals might attempt to resolve their concerns by dissolving their enemies. The Albanians, of course, had a real precedent of foreign intervention to worry about.

The conflict between winners and losers, between defenders and challengers, soon contributed to the growth of a new alliance system in Europe. The League of Nations was supposed to prevent this, but as with most other international problems of significance, the international organization was impotent. Indeed, it was only the extreme weakness of the two major malcontents, Germany and the Soviet Union, that prevented conflicting structures from appearing before the signatures on the peace treaties were dry. Yet by 1922, Berlin and Moscow had reached some basic understandings (the Rapallo agreements) and had thereby frightened France into creating an alliance system outside of the collective security mechanisms of the league. The French network had dual aims: on the one hand, it strove to encircle and thus weaken Germany; on the other, it sought to isolate the Soviet Union—to create a *cordon sanitaire* against the spread of communism.

The French diplomatic crusade had immediate and dramatic success. A treaty with Poland (1921) was followed by agreements with Czechoslovakia (1924), Yugoslavia (1927), and Romania (1926). The latter three, united in their hostility to Hungary more than in any concern about Germany or the USSR, had earlier allied with each other to form the famous Little Entente. Unfortunately, the deep rift between Poland and Czechoslovakia made it impossible for the Poles to participate directly in the Little Entente and thus served to prevent a genuinely East European alliance system from forming.

France's hopes in creating a network of alliances in Eastern Europe were brought to nothing for several reasons. Most important, France herself lacked the military and particularly the economic strength to make the alliances self-sustaining. Leaders in Warsaw, Prague, Belgrade, and Bucharest soon realized that ties with Paris were more glamorous than meaningful. The French could supply arms, but they could not buttress the budgets needed to pay for them. The economic well-being of the allied states of Eastern Europe was vital to the French, but the leaders in Paris were unwilling or unable to provide the necessary assistance. Eventually, as noted above, the financial weaknesses of France's allies to the east seriously weakened ties or in some cases even drove former friends into the arms of Germany.

Also crucial was the fact that France stood virtually alone in trying to maintain peace based on the treaties that ended World War I. The involvement of the United States in the affairs of Europe ended with Warren G. Harding's election to the presidency in 1920. Shortly afterward, the British decided that France was more of a threat to peace than Germany or the Soviet Union, and London ignored or resisted French initiatives.

After the first few years, interwar diplomacy became less and less dramatic; mounting confusion and even indifference made the work of the statesmen appear to be almost farcical. Particularly prominent in this black comedy were the efforts at collective security and disarmament. Both of these concepts grew out of the idealism that had led people in the west to call World War I "the war to end all wars." The League of Nations, the ultimate attempt at collective security, was, as mentioned above, of no particular significance in major problems. Yet the nations of Eastern Europe, more in need of security than others, embraced it with enthusiasm. Even the anti-status quo states, Hungary and Bulgaria, had great hopes for the League, which they saw as a forum through which they might effect a redress of their grievances. East European diplomats were generally very active in the various international organizations, treating their work seriously longer than did their colleagues from the West. This did not mean that they or their countries were naive (they did, after all, establish the alliances with France); it meant simply that their greater insecurity caused them to grab at every straw in the wind. Finally, however, the impotence of the League in dealing with the Italian invasion of Ethiopia led even the East European optimists to give up on the international organization.

The East Europeans were also interested in the disarmament conferences, but in these they had no opportunity to play a central role. The chief actors were necessarily those countries that were most heavily armed. The nations of East Europe had the same general interest in disarmament that they had in collective security, but they were disillusioned much faster in this case. The absolute failure of the great powers to make progress in their negotiations was clearly felt in the east. Within a few years, the pace of rearmament in Eastern Europe outstripped that in the rest of the world. The always-expanding military establishments were on a perpetual war footing after 1930.

In fact, before the peace treaties had been completed formally to end World War I, four of the East European states had been involved in armed conflict. The first of these was a real war, pitting Poland against the Soviet Union in a new version of a very old quarrel. The Polish leaders were unashamedly expansionist; as they looked eastward, they thought in terms of the boundaries which Poland had held at the beginning of the seventeenth century. Polish aggressiveness was not motivated merely by a fixation on the glory of the remote past, or even by the instincts of an eagle sensing easy prey. Poland did have an ethnic claim based on the solid but scattered areas of Polish population and often, where Poles did not live on the land, Poles owned it.

The Polish-Soviet war and its territorial results are described above. The long-term diplomatic consequences are themselves very important. The importance of French aid to the Poles, though frequently exaggerated, did serve to tie the two nations together. The French alliance gave Poland a sense of security which in the long run was probably very harmful. Relations with both the Soviet Union and Lithuania were extremely bad, and diplomatic relations were not restored for many years. The primacy of national defense and the security of frontiers as domestic political issues immediately began to have an unbalancing effect on the formation of an orderly democratic system.

The Béla Kun rebellion in Hungary brought three of the new nations of Eastern Europe into conflict. The decision of the communist Kun to attempt to reestablish the old "Great Hungary" led to attacks on both Czechoslovakia and Romania. The government in Prague was in a poor position to organize a defense of Slovakia, but the large Romanian army quickly showed an overwhelming offensive capability. The resulting total defeat of the now powerless Hungarians was not so important in her enemies' eyes as the fact that she had so quickly tried to overthrow the new territorial order. The association of Czechoslovakia, Romania, and Yugoslavia in the anti-Hungarian Little Entente was a direct consequence. These three powers maintained huge military establishments (of course, they had other enemies as well), and even though Hungary had virtually no military of her own, they kept large contingents on the borders ready to fight at a moment's notice. None of the three, by the way, had diplomatic relations with the Soviet Union until the 1930s.

Moscow was not completely isolated, however, for from 1921 she had been the beneficiary of cooperation with Germany. Even before the Rapallo agreement of 1922, the Germans were producing aircraft, tanks, and poison gas on Soviet soil. These factories armed the Soviet Union and at the same time permitted the Germans to experiment in the manufacture and use of weapons prohibited to them by the Treaty of Versailles. The cooperative relationship between the two outcast nations continued until the Nazi seizure of power in 1933. It is not surprising that, although the Soviet Union could establish close relations with Germany, she could make no progress with the two other revisionist states,

Hungary and Bulgaria, both of which had put down communist rebellions with considerable bloodshed.

A new factor in the diplomatic game of the 1920s was Benito Mussolini's Italy. The first fascist began by going off in many diplomatic directions at once, but he soon settled on a policy of support for the revisionists. By the close of the decade, Italy had established close relations with Bulgaria and Hungary—apparently going so far as to ship illegal arms to the latter. Also by 1930 Italy had established a virtual protectorate over Albania, thus removing that nation from the diplomatic game.

The 1930s were fundamentally different from the 1920s because the economic crisis loosened the diplomatic bonds that had been established earlier with so much effort. The French alliance system, as recounted earlier, was without strong economic roots, and it faltered as the East European states realized that total industrial collapse was a more present danger than attack from a revisionist enemy. This new preoccupation with the economy also weakened diplomatic relationships within Eastern Europe, for political leaders felt that the best response to a chaotic international marketplace was withdrawal. The level of regional trade, never very high, fell precipitously. When self-sufficiency was shown to be a failure, those leaders who sought new commercial arrangements found that Nazi Germany had the best options (see above).

If Nazi economic penetration of Eastern Europe was subtle and skillful, the same could not be said for Berlin's regular diplomacy, which was rarely so polished as to earn the adjective "blunt." Indeed, this behavior shows even more clearly the importance of the economic initiatives. The Nazis quickly wrote off three countries and one government as enemies. Of the three countries two were former enemies—Poland and Czechoslovakia—but one had been a friend—the Soviet Union. Hitler's motives in breaking ties with Moscow were partly ideological but largely practical. Since Germany intended to rearm openly, she had no further need for secret factories in the east; moreover, a country which had just suffered the staggering human and resource losses of the collectivization drive did not seem a power with which to reckon.

Hitler escalated hostility with Poland and Czechoslovakia in a number of ways, not least by using Nazis within them as constant threats to civil order. In Austria, these tactics were particularly successful, and the question of *Anschluss* (Austrian unification with Germany) became a key diplomatic issue. Berlin had only one ally on this issue (Italy—albeit with serious misgivings), but it was soon demonstrated that none were necessary. The French, faced down earlier on the issue of the remilitarization of the Rhineland, were more alone than ever and looked to strengthening their defenses. The Poles and Czechs were seriously alarmed, but their inability to work together inevitably weakened them as a factor. On several occasions the Poles proposed to the French a preemptive strike against Germany. Paris, although beset with internal problems, was tempted. But the dynamics had shifted dramatically since the 1920s. Of the Little Entente, Romania was economically vulnerable and internally chaotic, Yugoslavia was neutralized by Italy and distant from Germany in any case, and Czechoslovakia still had her feud with Poland. Further afield, the Soviet Union was no longer allied with Germany, but Joseph Stalin, just starting the purges, was obviously content to let the capitalists struggle with each other. In the meantime Britain, as John F. Kennedy said, slept, and the United States was clearly uninterested in matters not directly affecting trade. When Germany annexed Austria in March of 1938, protests were few and feeble.

The *Anschluss* was enough of a shock to awaken the Western nations to the reality of the Nazi menace. Hitler's rapid and unopposed strike to the south did more than impart his regime with the psychological momentum of a juggernaut: it also significantly strengthened the economic, demographic, and strategic position of the Reich. The takeover of Austria cemented the alliance with Italy, ending forever feeble hopes in London and Paris that tensions over ethnically mixed Italian and German areas in southern Austria might keep Hitler and Mussolini apart. Rome's decision to step under the shadow of the swastika was extremely important, since it ensured that any future conflict would affect southern as well as northern Europe.

Anglo-French appreciation of the Nazi danger was of no value in the short run. Hitler, emboldened by his success, immediately began to put pressure on Czechoslovakia. He instructed the leader of the Sudeten German Nazis, Konrad Henlein, to make demands on the government in Prague that would be unacceptable. This was done, as Henlein, backed by the hysterical propaganda mill in Berlin, insisted that Germans in Czechoslovakia be awarded de facto autonomy. The Czechoslovak leader, Beneš, appealed to his allies for help, but he soon realized tht he would get no assistance. The French were now committed to a static defense and had fixed their hopes on the Maginot Line. The British leader, Neville Chamberlain, had no sooner awakened to Hitler's aims than he made the equally shocking discovery that his country was all but defenseless. Rearmament then began at a frantic pace, but as a new crisis built in the summer of 1938, London held a weak hand and showed no inclination to bluff.

As Beneš looked to his neighbors the situation was no better. Nazi economic penetration of Romania and Yugoslavia, together with the gradual drift to the right in those countries, had made the Little Entente moribund. Czechoslovakia's earlier efforts to gain support from the Soviet Union also bore no fruit in the climate of crisis. A defensive alliance between Czechoslovakia and the Soviet Union provided for mutual assistance only in the event of overt aggression and only if preexisting alliances operated as well. Moreover, the two countries had no common border, and neither Romania nor Poland was willing to allow the Red Army to use its territory for either transit or actual military operations. Poland, in fact, was openly hostile to Czechoslovakia, as the leaders in Warsaw foolishly took this opportunity to seek revenge over the issue of Teschen Silesia. And finally, the Hungarians were waiting for the moment to pounce on Slovakia and Carpatho-Ruthenia.

Beneš made things surprisingly difficult for Hitler by agreeing to Henlein's demands, to which Britain and France had shown some sympathy on the grounds of supporting the principle of national self-determination. Since a compromise was an unacceptable diversion from Hitler's grand design, Beneš' move caused Berlin to drop all pretense and to begin clamoring for the dismemberment of Czechoslovakia pure and simple. Following a series of Anglo-French-German summit meetings, the last of which was held at Munich in September of 1938, London and Paris advised Beneš to give in. Reluctantly, he did so, and Germany occupied and annexed the Sudetenland without a shot being fired. In rapid order, Slovakia and "Carpatho-Ukraine" broke away to form autonomous governments which were de facto Nazi protectorates. Hungary was allowed, with the best wishes of Hitler and Mussolini, to make border adjustments in Slovakia and Carpatho-Ruthenia. Polish forces seized the disputed areas of Teschen Silesia. In March of 1939, the other shoe was finally dropped, and the remainder of the Czechoslovak state (essentially the province of Moravia and half the province of Bohemia) formally became a protectorate of the Third Reich.

The demise of Czechoslovakia continues to be one of the most debated events of the twentieth century. To date the weight of the evidence is with the critics of Britain and France; so much so that the word "Munich" has become a symbol for any unprincipled sellout. Although much of the critical position is based on purely speculative evidence (e.g., that an Anglo-French declaration of war would have triggered Soviet intervention and/or a military coup overthrowing Hitler), some consequences of Czechoslovakia's collapse and the manner in which it was obtained are undeniable. First, as with the *Anschluss*, the financial, military, and strategic position of Germany was greatly enhanced. Most important in this regard were seizure of the stocks of the very well-equipped Czechoslovak army and control over the Škoda Works, one of Europe's foremost arms manufacturers. Second, the effect on the states of southeastern Europe was striking. Already financially dependent (and even more so after the Nazi takeover of the very extensive Czechoslovak investments), the leaders of these states now saw the west as completely impotent and moved quickly to accommodate themselves to the reality of Nazi power. Berlin made enormous diplomatic progress between Munich and the attack on Poland: Bulgaria and Romania were snared, and Hungary and Yugoslavia needed only the smallest of pushes before they too fell into the führer's trap.

Finally, the effect of Munich on Hitler himself was most significant. Though the British leaders viewed Munich as nothing more than a strategic retreat, their public utterances gave the reverse impression. Chamberlain's references to "peace in our time" and disdain for "a faraway country of which we know nothing" led many people, Hitler among them, to believe that appeasement would continue until a German invasion fleet entered the English Channel. Accordingly, Hitler speeded up his plans for Eastern Europe, selecting Poland as his next target.

Munich also had an effect on Stalin, who came to the not necessarily unwarranted conclusion that the purpose of appeasement was to divert Hitler eastward while the British and the French tended to their defenses. Stalin countered this, or thought he did, by coming to an agreement with Hitler, known as the Molotov-Ribbentrop pact, in 1939. Publicly, this agreement was a defensive alliance, but secretly it was also a far-reaching accord which divided the area between the empires into spheres of influence in which they were to have a free hand. The Soviet Union received assurances of freedom of action in Finland and the Baltic States, in eastern Poland to the Curzon Line, and in Bessarabia. Germany got an effective guarantee of Soviet acquiescence in activities covering all of the rest of Eastern Europe, including the remainder of Poland.

The stage was thus set for the final act leading to war. Hitler began to pressure Poland over the status of Danzig and the corridor. The propaganda effort was from the start every bit as clumsy and lacking in pretense of a desire for compromise as the closing period of the campaign in Czechoslovakia. In the early stages London and Paris signalled Berlin that the two western powers had every intention of standing by their treaty obligations to Poland. Eventually, in the summer of 1939, these statements were put in the form of a public guarantee of Poland's frontiers.

Secure in his agreement with Stalin and confident that the spirit of Munich reigned, Hitler took no notice. Early in the morning of September 1, 1939, the German army fabricated a Polish military provocation in the Danzig area; later in the day German armor poured into Poland from every possible direction. Britain and France declared war on September 3. The Soviet Union was silent until she too invaded Poland on September 17.

The Polish forces fought bravely but not well. Like the French, the Poles had not altered their military doctrine beyond the lessons learned in the static warfare of 1914–18. Polish forces lacked the mobility to respond to the rapid thrusts of armor and aircraft which were to give the world the word "Blitzkrieg." In any case, the absolute inability of the British and French to offer any meaningful assistance, direct or diversionary, together with the Soviet attack, made an early defeat inevitable. Warsaw was captured by German forces on September 27, and all large-scale combat ceased less than a week later. In the circumstances, the fact that the Poles resisted for a full month is a great tribute to their heroism and tenacity.

Diplomatic activity in September of 1939 was intense. Romania and Yugoslavia, allied with Poland since the 1920s, decided on September 5 to ignore their obligations and remain neutral. Berlin did not have to use great pressure to obtain this result. The leaders of these countries had decided many months earlier that the most they could hope to achieve was to stay out of Hitler's way. Indeed, Berlin had to work very hard to restrain the Hungarians, who wanted an excuse to attack Romania, and the Bulgarians, who were awaiting the suitable moment to destroy Yugoslavia. Even as Europe crashed into flames around them, the leaders of Eastern Europe were still guided first and foremost by nationalism and irredentism.

The phase of the war between the invasion of Poland and the invasion of France (May, 1940), known in the West as the "phony war," was a time of consolidation of Nazi and Soviet power in Eastern Europe. The Soviets quickly asserted their control over the Baltic states (following some negotiations with Germany over the status of Lithuania) and launched the "Winter War" of 1939–40 against Finland. In December of 1939, Romania, facing rising domestic turmoil and fearing a Soviet attack on Bessarabia, effectively surrendered her economy to Germany. Guaranteed access to Romanian oil greatly boosted Hitler's confidence (the other principal source of supply was the Soviet Union). The vassalage of the Bulgarians, though not so dramatically effected, was nonetheless equally real. In fact, just before Nazi armor poured through the Ardennes into France, in Eastern Europe only Hungary and Yugoslavia showed any signs of independence of Germany.

Both Budapest and Belgrade continued to maintain diplomatic relations with the Western Allies after the fall of France, but the parties favoring open alliance with the Germans were greatly strengthened. The situation in Hungary became particularly acute in late June when the Soviet Union, putting into effect the final clauses of the Hitler-Stalin Pact, demanded that Romania cede Bessarabia, and the hapless government in Bucharest, which had recently officially joined the Axis, was ordered by her new allies to give in. There was strong feeling in Hungary, even among the anti-German party, that any serious crisis for Romania should become the occasion for a Hungarian attack with the aim of "liberating" Transylvania. The Bessarabian issue, which seriously damaged the prestige and authority of King Carol's government, was obviously such a case.

Hungarian preparations for war caused a certain level of panic in Berlin. Continued access to Romanian oil was vital to the Nazi military and industrial effort. A war in the vicinity of the oil fields must inevitably disrupt supply lines and might even cause damage sufficient to threaten overall Nazi strategy for years to come. Hitler had no troops in Hungary, and he feared that the Hungarian fanatics might ignore his warnings and start a war before the German military could effectively intervene. Accordingly, Berlin chose to appease the Hungarians. When direct negotiations between Budapest and Bucharest failed as expected, the two self-styled "great statesmen" of the Axis, Baron von Ribbentrop and Count Ciano (Italy's foreign minister who was also Mussolini's son-in-law), dictated a settlement known as the Second Vienna Award (August, 1940). Transylvania was partitioned in an extraordinarily awkward way (necessary because a large part of the Hungarian population was on the far side of the province from Hungary). About 40 percent of the land and people went to Hungary, but this was still much less than the Magyars expected. The net result, not suprisingly, was to exacerbate the existing hatred between Romanians and Hungarians.

The partition of Transylvania also paved the way for further Nazi penetration of southeastern Europe. King Carol was forced to abdicate and flee Romania a week after he agreed to the settlement (he had also been forced to return some territory to Bulgaria); the military leader who now took control, General Ion Antonescu, quickly agreed to the stationing of German troops in his country. In Hungary, the German takeover was not nearly so complete, but the country was now almost surrounded by the Axis, to whose good offices her leaders were greatly indebted. In October, Hungary was formally given permission to join the Axis (though she did not join the war against Britain and France).

Hitler was pleased with the situation he had created in the southeast: Hungary, Yugoslavia, Bulgaria, and Romania were all political and economic dependencies at the total military cost of a few divisions peacefully placed around the oil fields of Ploiesti. Further south, Greece and Turkey were hostile but terrorized into a neutrality which added even greater depth to the protection of the Nazi flank. Hitler would probably have left the status quo in southeastern Europe for some time, probably until after the planned conquest of the Soviet Union, had not the less than fine Italian hand of Mussolini intervened. Il Duce had never liked his change of status from first fascist to afterthought. His jealousy of Hitler reached its peak after the quick German victory over France. Determined to restore his prestige, Mussolini looked for an easy target for his own troops.

The Italian target of choice was Yugoslavia, but Rome's generals feared a difficult campaign and Berlin was explicit in its warnings of Hitler's ire should war begin in the central Balkans (again there was a fear that Hungary would be drawn in and that oil supplies would be disrupted). The Nazis were less clear about Greece, however, and Mussolini decided to attack first and ask for clarification later. Thus, entirely without the knowledge and approval of its German allies, the Italian army invaded Greece (from Albania) without a declaration of war. Mussolini broke the news to Hitler personally. The führer, fresh from an unpleasant conference with another uncooperative fascist (Francisco Franco), proceeded to have one of his most unrestrained temper tantrums.

The date of the Italian invasion of Greece, October 28, 1940, is thought by many to be a turning point in the war. Lacking a careful plan and completely without experience in guerrilla warfare, the Italian army soon found itself in headlong retreat; the Greek forces, mostly irregulars, threatened to throw the Italians into the sea and liberate Albania. The impending humiliation of his ally, together with the fact that British military units were assisting the Greeks and securing bases that threatened Germany's southern flank, forced Hitler to act. Berlin first tried to get the Greeks to abandon the British and forget the whole thing, but the leaders in Athens were too honorable and too brave for that. The only remaining alternative was a German attack. Berlin's agents thus spent the winter in the diplomatic preparations that must necessarily precede any direct thrust against Greece. First Romania, then Hungary and Bulgaria, agreed to the transit of troops. This might have been enough, but the German strategists concluded that, without at least Yugoslav non-belligerency as well, the operation would be unnecessarily risky.

Under intense pressure, the Yugoslav government agreed on March 25 to stand aside in a conflict between Germany and Greece. Wehrmacht planners had no sooner filed away their contingency plans for war with Yugoslavia, however, than they had to take them out again: on March 27 a military coup overthrew the Belgrade government and replaced it with one that was hostile to alliance with the Axis. The new leaders did not disavow the treaty of March 25, but Hitler concluded that they could not be trusted (they were negotiating with both the British and the Soviets) and ordered a simultaneous attack on Greece and Yugoslavia for April 6.

The plan for the move against Yugoslavia was code-named "Operation Punishment." More than in the name, the sentiment was made clear by the militarily purposeless air attack which destroyed Belgrade on the first day of the campaign. Within two weeks Yugoslavia was knocked out of the war. Greece was mastered only one week later. The Balkan campaign of the Wehrmacht and the Luftwaffe was almost a textbook exercise. Why then do some consider the beginning of the war in southeastern Europe a turning point in the war as whole? Simply because even conservative estimates agree that the campaign cost Hitler dearly in men, materials, and, perhaps most important, in time—all of which were badly needed for Operation Barbarossa (the attack on the USSR). The courage and the tenacity of the Greeks and Yugoslavs made necessary a campaign that delayed Barbarossa for some two months and deprived it of approximately seven divisions (5 percent of the attacking force). It is interesting to speculate what would have happened if the Nazis had reached the gates of Leningrad and Moscow two months *before* the snows of November with even more troops in reserve.

With the launching of Operation Barbarossa (June 22, 1941), the interwar period for Eastern Europe finally came to an end. All of the once-independent nations were now in the Axis grip, either conquered and occupied (Czechoslovakia, Poland, Yugoslavia, and Albania), or locked in political, military, and economic servitude (Hungary, Romania, Bulgaria). It is difficult to imagine a more complete disaster.

8

Interwar Poland

POLAND DESERVES TO BE the first state of interwar Eastern Europe to receive detailed treatment in these pages. Not only was she the largest, most populous, and most powerful state of the region, but her problems in the period reflect all of the social, economic, and political dilemmas that plagued all of Eastern Europe. A thorough exposition of Poland's situation provides a touchstone for analyzing the specific concerns of the other nations as well as a framework for understanding the status of the region as a whole.

Interwar Eastern Europe is usually characterized as having been created in a power vacuum, and such was certainly the case for Poland. The armistice of November 11, 1918, called for the immediate evacuation by the German military of all areas occupied since the outbreak of the war. Though the sheer volume of space controlled by Germany in the east made immediate withdrawal a logistical impossibility, civil authority in Poland, heretofore a responsibility of German occupation forces, disappeared almost instantly. Since there was no other stable political entity within hundreds of miles of Poland's frontiers, the Poles, after nearly a century and a half of foreign domination, had to begin to fend for themselves right away.

As it happened, the very sudden collapse of authority had the effect of considerably strengthening the position of one of the two principal Polish political factions: that of Joseph Piłsudski and (at least nominally) his Socialist Party. The story of Piłsudski's activities during the war is a complex one, but it is sufficient in this context to point out that, after organizing forces to fight with Austria-Hungary and against Russia, he had had the good fortune to become suspect in the eyes of the German authorities who came to control the sector in which he operated.[1] They put him in prison, a move which both kept him in Poland and freed him from eventual charges of collaboration with the enemy: Piłsudski was later able to demonstrate that he was officially an enemy of both Russia and Germany, that he had fought only for Poland.

Just before the conclusion of the armistice, Piłsudski was released from prison. Free, in Warsaw, and now recognized as a national hero, he immediately began to build a provisional governing authority around the remnants of the legions which he had earlier organized to fight on the Russian front. The rapid growth of Piłsudski's power alarmed his key political rival, Dmowski, leader of the National Democrats, who was by comparison greatly isolated in Paris. Dmowski was nonetheless a figure to be reckoned with, for he had come to be accepted by the Western statesmen during the war years as the voice of the future independent Poland, and he was in fact accredited as his nation's representative at the Paris Peace Conference.

The political forces that immediately emerged in the initial post-armistice power vacuum took some time to sort themselves out and to reach the point of establishing a legal and constitutional structure in which to operate. Before this new pattern is described, however, it is appropriate to survey the economic and social situation of the new country.

It is impossible to analyze the economic status of the nascent Polish state without first discussing the damage and dislocation brought about by the war and the shifting of frontiers. The eastern part of the country suffered most. The first great battle of the war, Tannenberg, was fought some one hundred miles north of Warsaw in the autumn of 1914. Though the Russians were defeated and never made further progress westward, it took the German and Austro-Hungarian forces more than a year of heavy fighting to drive the tsarist army out of Poland. In 1916, a Russian offensive regained a substantial amount of territory (primarily in Galicia) which was not entirely recaptured by the Central Powers until 1917. There was little fighting in present-day Poland in 1917 and 1918, though deprivation caused by the war continued to be severe. Loss of population during the First World War directly through military action and indirectly through disease, famine, and flight is estimated at four million, or some 13 percent of the total population.[2]

In addition to the loss of life, both industry and agriculture were exhausted. Mining and manufacturing enterprises which escaped destruction in the fighting were converted by the German and Austro-Hungarian authorities to war-related work and were run full blast with the absolute minimum of maintenance and investment. The work force, like that of Germany proper, suffered enormously from the Allied blockade on foodstuffs; most people were affected by malnutrition and many were on the verge of starvation. Farms were systematically stripped of produce, livestock, and human labor (conscripted for military and industrial work). Even when supplies were available, the peasants had little incentive to produce beyond what they could hide and use for themselves. No one wished to work harder for the privilege of making forced deliveries to foreign military authorities.

To the bleak picture of industry and agriculture one must add the image of disrupted communications and the virtual absence of administrative and support services. Though the Germans had rebuilt and even expanded some railroad and other transport and communication networks, much damage remained unrepaired, and maintenance ceased with the departure of German troops. Further, the civilain support bureaucracies, including their records and much of their personnel, had been a part of foreign systems and were largely lost to the local peoples. Reconstruction in many cases meant starting from scratch.

Interwar Poland was overwhelmingly agricultural. In 1919 more than 75 percent of the population was dependent on agriculture for its livelihood.[3] This figure changed to 63 percent in 1931, and to perhaps 60 percent on the eve of the war, but despite the significance of the shift, the rural and agrarian character of the nation was largely unaffected.[4] Indeed, most of the people working on the land were desperately poor, and most farm operations could by West European standards be described as "backward."

By 1931, when some reforms and improvements had been effected in Polish agriculture, the number of people per unit of cultivated land was 2.2 times that of France, but the average yield per hectare in wheat was only 75 percent of the French level. By another measure, overall per capita agricultural production in Poland was only 28 percent that of France. These data led a western economist to estimate that in 1930 about 30 percent of the total rural population was "surplus"—that is, not needed on the land if the level of Western European productivity could be reached. This would have amounted to a "surplus" of nearly six million people.[5]

There was considerable regional differentiation in Polish agriculture. In the western areas, which had been a part of the German empire and where rainfall and soils were generally better, per capita productivity was comparatively high; the formerly Russian and Austrian areas had about the same productivity and were below the national average.

Although there was a land reform in Poland in the early 1920s, it had little effect on the enormous disparity in the size and wealth of agricultural holdings. The land reform did break up many large estates, but overall only 6 percent of the land was affected and many large estates continued to exist.[6] Thus, although 20 percent of the land was in estates larger than fifty hectares, the proprietors who owned it represented only one-half of one percent of all proprietors. Land reform occurred largely in the west, where most of the former owners were German by nationality (and usually by citizenship as well). In the south and east the estates had typically been held by ethnic Poles who transferred their citizenship to the new Polish state when it was created. The government was reluctant to dispossess these men, often the scions of famous Polish noble families, and action was particularly unlikely when the peasants who would benefit were not themselves ethnic Poles. Thus, although there was always some redistribution of land in areas solidly inhabited by Polish peasants, Polish-owned estates continued to be large, and their owners continued to wield economic and political power. Also, as elsewhere in Eastern Europe, most owners of expropriated land received compensation from the state, which in turn was to receive payment from the peasants. This process minimized damage to the estate owners and kept the new peasant owners freeholders only in name. The indebtedness of the peasantry was rarely diminished as a consequence of land reform, instead it typically increased dramatically so that the peasants were often just as vulnerable to the landowner's exploitation of their labor as they had been before "reform."

There were in Poland some "medium farmers" (holders of 20 to 50 hectares) who resembled in many ways farmers in Western Europe and the United States, although as in Eastern Europe as a whole, they were less "modern" than their western counterparts. Their status will not be dwelt upon, however, since they were so few in number: perhaps 2 percent of the total holdings. Their political and economic impact was somewhat greater than this, of course, but overall the prosperous "medium farmer" was a relatively insignificant factor in the Polish equation.

The classic definition of the peasantry distinguishes it as a class from that of farmers in an economic sense: farmers see their occupation as a business engaged in for profit, but peasants are primarily concerned with producing enough to survive. If peasants should raise more food than needed for subsistence, their first reaction will be to consume more. Unless forced to do so, they will rarely attempt to produce more than they can use themselves. Of course, the state and the large landowners could and did apply pressure to produce more. Following the abolition of serfdom, this pressure took various forms, but in all cases it reflected the fact that the peasant, however much he wanted to be, was not really self-sufficient. The state created monopolies on items of actual or perceived necessity (e.g., salt and alcohol) and by keeping prices high effectively taxed the peasants. The large landowners took advantage of other weaknesses, notably the fact that they controlled the forests upon which the peasants depended for the wood used as fuel for cooking and for heat. Payment for firewood was usually in kind or in labor since the peasants did not have cash. The peasants also did not have either the money to pay for manufactured agricultural implements or the inclination to use them, so that industrial advances had little effect on agricultural productivity. Aside from the rare large purchase such as an iron plow, the peasants sought to use only those items that they or their fellow villagers could make on their own. But even one iron plow in every couple of generations is a huge expense, and the net effect of such a purchase, together with the need for salt, firewood, and alcohol, kept the peasants working harder because they were perpetually in debt.

But not much harder. Debts were an accepted part of life. It was very difficult for the state and the landowner to threaten people used to extreme hardship; the peasants would work hard enough to keep their land and, if possible, to put a little more food on the table. But no more. Neither their philosophy or the reality of which it was a reasonably good reflection suggested a purpose in harder work. Or perhaps it would be more accurate to speak for the most part about more *efficient* work, since in most cases and for much of the time the peasants worked to the point of physical exhaustion. A farmer, for example, might decide to send a son to agricultural school to learn new techniques and better management. But a peasant, even in the unlikely event that the idea should occur to him and that his son would have access to the necessary elementary and secondary schooling, would almost certainly not do the same. On the one hand the precariousness of the peasant's everyday situation would counsel against taking the risk of trying to survive even a short period without an extra pair of hands; on the other hand the concept of investment, of putting aside income from times of (relative) surplus, and of sacrificing in the hope of some radical change in the future, was alien to the peasant. Life (at least on earth) was a continuum of poverty interspersed with occasional joy and more frequent sorrow. One did not expect more; change was a concept understood with difficulty or more likely not at all.

This explanation of the world view of the peasant is important because peasants in interwar Poland held 47 percent of the land and were 60 percent of the population. This latter figure makes clear a fundamental dilemma faced by Poland and by all of the other East European countries: how is it possible to modernize a society in which a majority of the population is engaged in an occupation which produces little or no surplus and which lacks the resources, the incentives, and the philosophical motivation to change? How could a country cope with a situation so inefficient that more than 30 percent of its rural population was "surplus" (i.e., not needed to maintain the existing level of production)? One solution that was tried (but incompletely, as noted above) was land reform.

The peasants considered that land reform, which to them meant the breakup of large estates with distribution at no cost to the peasantry, was the solution to all problems. But even if it had been done just as the peasants wished, the results would probably not have been much better for anyone and might easily have been much worse. Even if one assumes that impoverishing the estate holders would have had a negligible effect on the economy (and there are a number of arguments that suggest otherwise), one must still make the assumption that the peasants would then become more productive on their larger holdings. Two factors, the system of inheritance and the demographic profile, together with the traditional peasant philosophy about surplus production, make it most unlikely that this increase in productivity would have occurred.

In a brilliant essay on the peasantry of Eastern Europe, the historian Hugh Seton-Watson describes the system of inheritance that paralyzed all of Eastern Europe:

> In Eastern Europe it is the custom that the agricultural holding is divided on the death of the owner between all his sons. Twenty years of this practice has caused a subdivision of the original holdings of the land reforms into a much greater number of tiny plots of land. If a holding consisted of land of different qualities, devoted to different kinds of production, then each son must have a piece of each type. It is arguable that even the original holdings were too small for rational cultivation, but there is no doubt at all of the hopelessly uneconomic nature of the dwarf properties into which they have since been divided. A holding of a few acres may consist of as many as forty small strips, separated from each other by several miles. Large areas of cultivated land were wasted in the form of paths enabling owners to walk from one strip to another.[7]

The tendency for land to be transformed into dwarf holdings made the use of modern agricultural techniques, which required both training and the resources to invest in machinery and chemical fertilizers, a simple impossibility. One can view the distribution of land to the peasants as a sort of creeping paralysis which immobilized the productive potential of the countryside. From this perspective land reform was a failure, since

it shifted land away from large-scale production that, however incom-
petently organized it might be, was still at least potentially more efficient
than the intensively worked dwarf plots.

The landholding patterns would not have been nearly so serious
had not the demographic dynamics of the peasantry changed so dramatically and so rapidly. For centuries the equal share inheritance system
had produced a redistribution that, although it inevitably tended to decrease the size of individual holdings, did so very slowly. This was because
it was rare for more than one or two sons to live long enough to inherit
and to start families of their own. People had many children, but since
most died in infancy the actual population growth was quite slow and
was often halted or even temporarily reduced in times of famine or war.
But advances in sanitation and medical care changed this almost totally;
the high rate of infant mortality was the first major problem to yield to
the accomplishments of Western science.

This change affected Western Europe first, but when it hit Eastern
Europe the growth in population that followed was spectacular. For
example, in the period 1750–1800 Poland had only a slightly higher rate
of increase in population than France, a country in which a considerable
saturation of population (at that time 22 million vs. 7 million in Poland)
had much earlier caused people to limit the number of children conceived.
But in 1800–1850 the French rate increased only slightly while the Polish
increased nearly 50 percent. In the period 1850–1900 the French rate
fell by nearly half, while the Polish rate nearly doubled. The Polish rate
fell sharply after 1900, but even comparatively small percentage increases
were now producing a lot of people: the 1925 population of Poland was
28 million; this was 74 percent of the population of France as opposed
to 33 percent in 1750.[8] And in Poland, unlike France, nearly all of the
added population was rural. This demographic shift goes a long way
toward explaining the stagnation of agriculture and hence of the overall
economy in Poland and in the rest of Eastern Europe.

This bleak picture of agriculture in Poland is also generally accurate
for Eastern Europe as a whole and helps to explain the pervasive economic
malaise that inevitably constrained the potential for social and economic
development. Certainly, the status of agriculture had a direct and overwhelmingly negative effect on the growth of industry. The classical model
of industrial development is one which relies on the agricultural sector
to produce the surplus of capital and labor necessary to construct and
maintain factories and mines, to build communications and transport
facilities, and to provide technical training. Once the process had begun,
it is theoretically possible that the surplus needed for further development

can be provided from the industrial base (although agriculture must continue to become more efficient in order to feed a continually larger nonagricultural population). But if the process of industrialization is to be rapid, so must be the transformation in the countryside. In Poland there was very little change in the villages, and what did occur came only very gradually. Industrial growth was consequently very slow as well.

Polish industry faced three major problems: the need for reconstruction of war-related damage; the necessity of finding new markets; and a shortage of capital. Reconstruction was perhaps the easiest of the difficulties with which to deal. The government recognized the need to replace and rebuild destroyed bridges and rail lines, and even provided assistance to reconstruct privately owned factories. But beyond assistance in recreating the basic structure, little was done. The government was essentially helpless in making it possible for industry to find new markets. The case of the Polish textile industry, centered around the eastern city of Łódź, is a classic example. The mills of Łódź were built to serve the needs of the Russian Empire and shipped virtually all of their production eastward. But the political situation between Poland and the Soviet Union made the old markets almost completely inaccesible—less than one percent of Poland's interwar trade was with the Soviet Union. The replacement of Russian with other markets was an extraordinarily difficult and ultimately never totally successful struggle for the manufactures of Łódź. It was even difficult to distribute goods within Poland, since Łódź's water, road, and rail connections with the rest of the country were at worst non-existent, and at best poor. Export to western Europe or to the rest of Eastern Europe was also hampered by difficult transportation as well as competition with technologically more advanced mills. Also these new markets had far more sophisticated consumers than was the case in Russia. As Poland became independent, Łódź changed from a boomtown to one of perpetual economic stagnation.

Another example of Poland's industrial problems was to be found in the coal mines of the southwest, the region known as Upper Silesia. Here, mines in the vicinity of the city of Katowice produced coal, which everyone wanted. Even so, the situation was not so very different from that of Łódź. The mines were developed under Prussian (later German) rule, and the communications and technical support, not to mention the markets, were in Germany. The Poles could not use all of the production themselves (even with the acquisition of the steel mills and associated industries of the area) and consequently sought to market the surplus in return for much-needed foreign exchange. That proved very difficult. The Katowice region did not have good rail connections with the rest of Poland. To ship coal to the Baltic port of Danzig required traversing first a German, then an Austrian, then a Russian, then again a German-built rail network, none of which was oriented in the proper direction or designed to handle coal (nor for that matter were the port facilities). To redo all of this required an enormous amount of investment, as did efforts to expand production in the mines. Finally, expansion also required large quantities of skilled and semi-skilled labor which were in as short supply in Poland as was investment capital. That the government in Warsaw nonetheless succeeded in exporting a significant amount of coal throughout the interwar period is a tribute to the kind of determination that comes from the need to survive. Such an achievement should not suggest that the process was efficient or that coal production ever came close to reaching its potential contribution to the Polish economy. Far more advanced societies would have found it very difficult to resolve complex economic problems such as those presented by Poland's textile and coal mining industries; Poland herself, dragged down by agricultural backwardness, could do little more than attempt to cope.

A final note on the status of industry in interwar Poland: the country was distinguished on the one hand by the lowest level of foreign investment in any East European country and on the other by the highest level of direct state participation in the economy. Both of these factors reflected the region's history. The new state confiscated the property of the three former imperial powers and thus acquired a great deal of land and many industrial, commercial, and financial enterprises (this was particularly the case in the Russian areas—the tsar, tsarist officials, and the imperial government had together owned most of the wealth). It was difficult for the Polish government to divest itself of these holdings—in large part because there was insufficient domestic capital to purchase them, but also because it was politically easier to hold on than to risk conflict over who should get what. State monopolies on salt, alcohol, and tobacco were continued. Finally, as the depression and the general stagnation of industry threatened economic collapse, the government often intervened to assist faltering companies which then fell under the ownership of state-owned banks.

The relative lack of foreign capital reflected principally the very low participation of private foreign investors in the Russian and Austrian empires. Foreign ownership that remained after 1918 was primarily that of Austrian and German individuals and corporations which held a strong position in the heavy industry of the south. But the weakness of the economy and the government's discouragement of a foreign role in Poland's economy effectively prevented further infusions of outside capital.[9]

The net result was to maintain Polish economic sovereignty but also to keep that economy relatively anemic.

Polish society in the interwar period was divided into essentially three classes. First, of course, came the peasantry. Next were the remnants of the aristocracy. The spectacular wealth and prestige of some of this group was in sharp contrast to the drab misery of the peasantry. Scions of great families, such as the Prince Radziwiłł, could still control estates larger than 50,000 acres. But such dramatic examples were rare and can easily lead one to overstate the importance of the nobility. The traditional position of national leadership held by the nobility had been badly shaken by the failure of the national revolts of 1830 and 1863. This, together with the erosion of economic strength that followed the emancipation of the peasants in Russia in 1864, and the gradual shift of economic life from agriculture to industry, left the nobility only a small place in interwar political life. There had been no serious thought of reviving the monarchy in 1918 and though the names of the great families were often to be found in the Warsaw press, their place was most often in the society pages.

The most important social class in Poland was what Americans call the "middle class" but East Europeans call the "intelligentsia." The translation is in fact far from accurate. When Americans think of the middle class, they think primarily of an economic group marked by prosperity and an association with business. An East European, on the other hand, would describe a member of the intelligentsia first of all as someone with a higher education performing "mental" work—more precisely someone who does not perform physical labor. To Americans, who place far more esteem on financial than educational achievement and who have no particular prejudice against working with one's hands, these criteria are very surprising.

In the 1920s and 1930s the typical representative of the American middle class would have been a small businessman, someone with at best a high school education but making a good income. In contrast, the typical member of the Polish (or East European) intelligentsia would have been a government employee, probably no more than a glorified clerk, possessed of a university education and perhaps an advanced degree, but making a very small salary and with little hope of ever having any financial independence.

These contrasting descriptions of a "middle" class tell us a great deal about Polish society both in an economic and a political sense. The former reflects what should by now be obvious—Poland had very little participation in its economy by small or medium private commercial

ventures. More important, perhaps, this sort of occupation had comparatively little social prestige and consequently a very small reservoir of
potential recruits. Industrial and to a very large extent commercial un-
dertakings are logically associated with manual labor, financial risk-taking, and a high degree of individualism. These elements were rare in
Polish (or East European) society. Since most industry grows from small
assembly operations in which the key figure is a direct participant (Henry
Ford was a mechanic first), it is logically tied up with physical labor or
at the very least with an intimate understanding of the manual process.
That factor alone made industry unappealing to the children of both
nobles and peasants (who aspired to remain aloof from or escape from
physical labor). The concept of risk-taking, though not unknown to gentry
with their well-established passion for gambling, was foreign to the peasantry; indeed as noted earlier, the peasant mentality did not countenance
even minimal short-term risk-taking. Finally, neither peasant nor nobles
in the traditional East European societies placed high value on personal
independence as compared to their counterparts in Western Europe or
the United States. At both social extremes in Poland a "corporate" view
of society—one which stressed interrelationships and interdependence—
was predominant.

Taken together these factors help to explain not only the comparative backwardness of Polish society but also the relatively slow rate of
change that occurred in the interwar period. It should be emphasized, at
this point, however, that comparison here means in contrast to the Soviet
Union at the same time or to post–World War II Eastern Europe. In
actual numbers some fairly significant changes did occur over two decades. In 1920, about 75 percent of the Polish population was engaged
in agriculture (i.e., peasants), but twenty years later that percentage had
declined to about 60 percent. This means that there were well over five
million fewer people in agriculture in 1940 than would have been the
case if the rate had not changed. Certainly this statistic demonstrates that
significant development was taking place.

The social stratification was not only economic—equally if not more
important was the difference among nationalities. Only about 66 percent
of the population was Polish. East Slavs made up nearly 19 percent
(Ukrainians, 14 percent; Belorussians, 4 percent; Russians, 0.5 percent).
Germans comprised some 4 percent and Jews, most of whom were speakers of Yiddish or German, were more than 10 percent. The breakdown
by religion mirrored the nationality statistics fairly closely: Poles were
almost universally Roman Catholic; Germans were Protestant; and Jews
(obviously) Jewish. Only the East Slavs were sharply divided: about half

were Orthodox and half Uniate (those from Austro-Hungarian territory). The minorities were also fairly homogenous in their economic status: Belorussians and Ukrainians were overwhelmingly peasants, while Jews and (to a lesser extent) Germans were urban dwellers involved in commerce, industry, and government or other service.

The minority problem added an element of great complexity to an otherwise uncomplicated socioeconomic picture. Moreover, it was a significant factor both in numbers and in distribution. Minorities that comprise one-third of the population become a factor in all political calculations no matter how divided they are. They assume an even greater importance when some of them are concentrated in the sector of the economy, commerce and industry, whose greatest priority is development—nearly 80 percent of Jews were employed in these two sectors.[10] The geographic distribution of the minorities was also a critical concern: Belorussians and Ukrainians were compactly settled on the eastern borderlands, next to the Soviet Union where most of their brethren resided. Similarly, Germans were overwhelmingly in the west next to Germany.

The educational system of interwar Poland had little effect on social stratification. The new state mandated seven years of compulsory schooling, and this ambitious goal (there were only the rudiments of a school system in the formerly Russian areas) was eventually achieved. After elementary school, however, education became distinctly elitist. Though secondary and higher education were theoretically free and accessible only on the basis of talent, little effort was made to compensate for the weaker background of children from poorer families in order to improve their competitive position: only 7 percent of students in higher education were the offspring of peasants or workers.[11] Further, the educational system was rigorously Polish. The minorities did not have the opportunity to study in their own language in state schools. There were Jewish and German schools, but these were supported by private funds. The bright spot of the educational system was clearly the great Jagellonian University in Kraków, which continued to be among Europe's finest, while the University at Warsaw was revived and also acquired great prestige.

The early political life of Poland was formed by the constitution of 1921. Curiously, in view of Polish history, this document gave virtually all power to the legislature (the Sejm) and left the executive (the presidency) extremely weak. It is generally considered that this approach reflected a fear that Piłsudski, who acted as president while the constitution was being draw up, would become a dictator if given more than a token amount of power. This was particularly a concern of conservatives who were only too aware of Piłsudski's association with the Socialist party. In any case, it soon became apparent that the constitutional system tended to magnify divisions within the country. Since proportional representation gave just about any political group a good chance of winning a seat in the Sejm, the number of parties multiplied without restraint; a vast number of separate organizations contested the election of 1922.[12] Since the largest group (the National Democrats) could capture at best only 28 percent of the seats, coalition government became a necessity. Though it is impossible in this text to dissect the relationship of the factions and fractions, a brief description of the principal parties and their leaders is essential.

The National Democrats have been mentioned previously. They owed their strength to several factors, not the least of which was the energy and determination of their leader, Dmowski. The National Democrats were the leaders of the right wing; they advocated a highly centralized state, were opposed to minority rights, and were particularly hostile to the Jews. The National Democrats favored the rapid development of industry under exclusively Polish ownership and rejected significant land reform. The party drew its strength from the commercial classes, from bureaucrats, from Poles living in minority areas, from elements of the Catholic hierarchy, and from the formerly Prussian areas (where the party was first organized).

In the center, the principal party was the peasant party known as "Piast." Capably led by Witos, this party was not nearly so national as even the National Democrats. Its fundamental base was the comparatively prosperous Polish peasantry of the formerly Austro-Hungarian areas. It never developed strong support elsewhere, and it actively opposed the interests of the non-Polish peasant parties. This nationalistic attitude, together with the Piasts' strong affiliation with the Roman Catholic Church and hence with the Right, made even a coalition of peasant parties impossible. The Piast captured only 18 percent of the Sejm seats in the 1922 election.

On the left there were two parties. The Wyzwolenie (Liberation) party was essentially a peasant party with radical land reform as its principal goal. Since its leaders (mostly from Central Poland) were willing to appeal to peasants of all nationalities, a strictly class analysis would suggest that Wyzwolenie should win 50 percent or more of the vote. Instead, it garnered less than 13 percent. The reasons are obvious and numerous: many Polish peasants objected to the association with the minorities; many non-Polish peasants distrusted an appeal from Poles; many Polish peasants were unhappy with the anticlericalism of the party leadership; and last but not least, many peasants were too poor and too uneducated and hence too isolated to have any interest in or understanding of politics.

The Polish Socialist Party (usually known by its initials, PPS) has also been mentioned previously. Though it was the largest working class party by far (roughly ten times the size of the communists), it was still quite weak. In 1922, the PPS had only 10 percent of the vote and 9 percent of the seats in the Sejm. This was respectable given the number of industrial workers in Poland, but the PPS was in fact fading. It was important primarily because of Piłsudski's leadership, and when he abandoned it in the first years of the interwar period, the impact of the socialists declined significantly.

These four parties, all of them quite different from each other in philosophy and constituency, won about two-thirds of the votes for the 1922 Sejm. The remainder went to a plethora of parties representing nearly every conceivable interest.

Parliamentary government under the new constitution began inauspiciously. Piłsudski, disgusted with the weak status of the executive, refused to be nominated for president and withdrew from political life. However, a friend of his, Gabriel Narutowicz, ran with the Marshal's tacit support. He was elected, primarily because Piłsudski and his allies were known to be sympathetic to the minorities but were nonetheless of unquestioned patriotism. But Narutowicz was assassinated a few days after taking office, and the ensuing political situation never rose much above chaos. Given the strength of the National Democrats, the tendency of coalitions on the Sejm was right of center. But given the radical differences within even the strongest coalitions, neither comprehensive legislation nor effective leadership was possible.

The principal issues confronting Poland after the end of the war with the Soviet Union (1920) and prior to the end of free parliamentary government (1926) were: foreign affairs and particularly relations with Germany; land reform; and the organization of the new administration (including the status of the minorities). Only in the latter area was much achieved. Here the centralizing, Polonizing, philosophy of the National Democrats carried the day. The central administration in Warsaw was given responsibility for economic affairs, and for the administration of justice, education, and even culture and the arts. Warsaw's power in all cases superseded the very minimal rule of local authorities. The minorities, denied power in their own areas and with scarcely any representation in the central government and bureaucracy, had as a result almost no voice in public affairs.

The issue of land reform was complex, but the result (described above) is hardly surprising. The peasants had no single strong party representing them, and indeed many peasant parties had deeply conflicting views. Consequently, given the strong opposition of the right, only modest compromises could be expected out of coalition agreements. The Piast under Witos was in fact not at all dismayed with a result that improved the situation of peasants only in some geographical areas (i.e., where their party was strong) and which prevented reform almost entirely in others (where the peasants were not Polish).

Foreign policy was by far the least controversial area. There was a general consensus (in this case that means at least a rough majority) for a close (but not a dependent) relationship with France. This was effected fairly easily. Following the defeat of the Soviet Union the principal threat to Poland's national interests was from Germany. Most Poles favored a hard line on issues between the two nations: the rights of Germans residing in Poland; the rights of German nationals owning property in Poland; the level and nature of trade; and especially on the status of communications through the Polish corridor and the port of Danzig. Since the Germans, temporarily without hope of redressing their territorial grievances in the west, thought it likely they could regain land to the east from Poland, relations between the two countries were very bad. When the German government formally guaranteed its western but not its eastern boundaries in the Locarno treaties of 1925, the Poles were outraged. A bitter Polish-German tariff war ensued. Overall, the whole question of relations with Germany was one of the few unifying factors in Polish politics.

Polish parliamentary government was eventually brought down by two problems: one, endemic political hostility, was fairly obvious; the other, a chronic inability to manage state finances and the economy, was not perceived as a serious problem until it had become all but uncontrollable. The inflation that devastated most of postwar Europe was especially severe in Poland. A unit of Polish currency, exchanged at about 10 to the dollar in the months following the armistice, fell to an incredible six million to one dollar five years later.[13] Most of this decline came during 1923 and naturally led to a change in government—one of fourteen such turnovers in the eight years from 1918–1926. It would be easy to ascribe the Polish fiscal mismanagement to untrained bureaucrats, inexperienced and even obtuse politicians, and to general backwardness. These factors certainly contributed, but one should remember that most of Europe was similarly afflicted and that the Americans, who tended to be arrogantly amused by Europe's troubles in the early twenties, found the fatal flaws in their own system in 1929.

Although misery loves company, it cannot be said that an awareness of others' fiscal dilemmas eased the domestic political situation in Poland. Factionalism was rapidly giving way to a sense of bitter frustration. The final straw was the tariff war with Germany at the end of 1925. Though this struggle, like any with Germany, was immensely popular with every important element of Polish politics, the short-term effect was a dramatic worsening of the economic situation. This in turn resulted in a significant darkening of the political outlook—more than ever people felt that the existing political structure was incapable of resolving the serious problems that confronted the nation.

The stage was set for the return of Piłsudski. Though the Marshal had not been a direct participant in politics, he had not been far away. If anything, the end of his affiliation with the PPS had enhanced his popularity; certainly the ambient chaos made the idea of a strong ruler attractive to many people. Piłsudski's supporters had urged him to carry out a coup d'etat on several occasions, but the soldier's fear of excessive bloodshed brought refusals. By the spring of 1926, however, it was apparent to Piłsudski that the potential opposition was at an extreme of weakness and division. Calling on old friends in the army, the Marshal launched a coup and was able to take power after only a few days of fighting in Warsaw (May 22).

A characteristic of the authoritarian movements that spread across Europe in the interwar period was a claim to be "above politics." Piłsudski carried this to something of an extreme: although he was the decisive force in government from 1926 until his death in 1935, he was never formally head of state and only briefly head of government—he was content to be the minister of defense and pull strings from the shadows. Less unusual was Piłsudski's method of structuring the state. The old constitution was left in place, but important modifications in favor of the executive were made. The Sejm continued to be a fractious body including numerous opponents of the government—but except on trivial issues antigovernment legislation was not passed.

Control was indirect: a coalition of individuals called the "Non-Party Bloc" was put together to support Piłsudski; opponents were kept in check for the most part through bureaucratic measures (including electoral fraud as needed), although some coercion in the form of arrest and imprisonment was employed as well. Freedom of speech and of the press were maintained, but critics had to realize, for example, that especially flagrant opposition might bring an action for libel that was sure to be endorsed by the government-appointed judiciary.

Beyond a determination to keep the domestic lid on and to maintain a fierce defense of Poland's national security, it is difficult to discern the guiding philosophy of Piłsudski and his successors. The Marshal was more open to the problems of the minorities, but aside from a diminution of bureaucratic hostility to the Jews, little change occurred. The Ukrainians, for example, did not get their own schools or a strong voice in local government, and when some of their leaders pressed too hard, they were imprisoned. No further land reform was effected. Government participation in the economy increased, particularly through improved transport and communication facilities (notably the port of Gdynia and new railroads), but Poland continued to ride the west's economic roller coaster. The situation improved in the late twenties until the effects of the great depression hit. Poland, like all predominantly agricultural countries, was hurt especially badly by the depression, and its government was able to do little to alleviate the damage.[14] Further, Piłsudski did not make significant gestures toward improving social mobility through improved access to education, nor did he make a real effort toward improving the lot of the working man. Overall, Piłsudski's domestic policies can be described as conservative and improvisational.

Though not an innovator in foreign policy any more than in domestic affairs, Piłsudski showed a flexibility in this arena that went beyond improvisation. Relations with the USSR were bad, but Piłsudski was willing to negotiate and to establish normal diplomatic relations. The strong relationship with France continued, but it was far from untroubled. Poland would not join the Little Entente because of strong hostility to its leading member, Czechoslovakia. An agreement with this nation could have been a breakthrough for Polish security, but Piłsudski would not consider it and this inevitably strained relations with France. Relations with Paris went downhill after 1933 when Piłsudski put them to a stringent test. Showing a burst of the prescience that guided him through wartime politics, Piłsudski saw the danger of Hitler with absolute clarity. Shortly after the Nazi seizure of power, Piłsudski proposed that France and Poland intervene directly to keep Germany under control.[15] The French refused, and relations wavered as the Poles perceived a serious weakening of their ally's self-confidence and sense of purpose. Shortly afterward, in January of 1934, Poland signed a treaty of friendship and nonaggression with Germany. This was far from an alliance, since it intended to do no more than lessen tension for a while, but it nonetheless symbolized Poland's defensiveness and fear of isolation.

Piłsudski's death in May of 1935 did not result in important change.

His personal friends and allies, most of them army colonels, collectively asserted full authority over a government over which they had had day-to-day control for many years.

Domestically there was a gradual shift toward more authoritarian rule. Increasingly, critics of the regime were harassed and imprisoned rather than ignored. More than anything, however, this pressure was a reaction to deeper fears about national security. The spectacular success of Nazi Germany, and the seemingly concomitant enfeeblement of France and disinterest of Britain, left Poland in an ever more isolated position. The most prominent man in the "government of colonels," Foreign Minister Joseph Beck, tried again to interest the French and the British in some sort of preemptive action against Germany, but he was rejected and commanded less and less attention from the confused leaders in Paris.[16]

Poland ended her two decades of freedom with essentially the same set of problems with which she started them. It would be unfair to say that her significant concerns had been untouched, but it would be an exaggeration to claim any important progress. In her inertia, of course, Poland was far from alone.

9

Interwar Czechoslovakia

THE BIRTH OF CZECHOSLOVAKIA was quite different from that of Poland. It was more difficult in that Czechoslovakia was truly born, not reborn as was Poland. But it was also easier, for the lands of the new nation had been almost entirely spared the destruction of war. The transition, though difficult, proceeded in a far more favorable environment than elsewhere in Eastern Europe.

Since the agreements for uniting the Czechs and Slovaks had taken place in a foreign country and were unknown to most of the people (see above), making them known and having them accepted at home became the most pressing task after the armistice. This was remarkably easy, for although Habsburg military authority disappeared as did that of the imperial offices in Vienna, a full panoply of regional and local administrative structures remained and could be influenced in favor of Masaryk and his ideas by representatives of the Allies. It was not difficult to find support for the new leadership, since Masaryk was clearly the most popular man amongst Czechs and Slovaks, and his word was readily accepted. The Czechoslovak National Council sitting in Paris declared itself the provisional government of Czechoslovakia in October of 1918, with Masaryk as its head. All of the Allies recognized the new regime, and when its leader came home to Prague two months later, he was given a hero's welcome.

The provisional government resigned in favor of an elected one after only eight months. After less than two years of independence a new constitution had been drawn up and ratified and a regular parliamentary democracy had begun to function. That Czechoslovakia remained a democracy throughout the interwar period is one of the few widely known facts of East European history. But the economic and social structure upon which this success was built is rarely understood, and the serious political fissures which kept the foundation always shaky just below the surface are rarely perceived.

Economically Czechoslovakia was a very strong state. There had been virtually no wartime damage, and the effects of overstrained and distorted production were quickly remedied. Communications were generally excellent. The Czech lands had superb roads and railroads, and although the Slovak equivalents were generally poor, they were at least linked up and part of a standard system—a far cry from the problem faced by the Poles. Czechoslovakia is a landlocked country, but there are good maritime connections through the Danube river ports and to the river and canal network of the Oder.

By 1918 Czechoslovakia was already a predominantly industrial country: nearly 45 percent of the population of 13 million was engaged in or dependent upon industry, commerce, or communications, and only 40 percent in agriculture.[1] By the end of the period only 30 percent of about 15.5 million people were in agriculture. Industry was concentrated in the Czech provinces of Bohemia and Moravia (Slovakia and Carpatho-Ruthenia were as overwhelmingly agrarian as Poland). Czechoslovakia had had more than half of the industrial production of the Austro-Hungarian Empire.

Industry in interwar Czechoslovakia was reasonably well diversified. There had been a solid base of heavy industry in Bohemia and Moravia thanks to relatively abundant coal and iron ore, and the new state was given even more strength in this sphere by the acquisition of part of Teschen Silesia. Manufacturing ranged from machine tools of very high quality—generally equivalent to that of Western Europe—to Pilsner beer. Czech-made machinery had an excellent reputation in export markets. Unfortunately, perhaps the best known Czechoslovakian products were those turned about by the Škoda works—one of the world's foremost armaments manufacturers (everything from hand weapons to cannon). In addition to heavy and medium industry, the Czech lands also had an important light industrial complement. Ample water power had fostered a textile industry in the early nineteenth century; the Bat'a shoe factory was one of Europe's largest and its products among the best.

The most serious problem faced by Czechoslovak industry was that of finding replacement markets for those parts of the old empire no longer able or willing to buy Czech manufactures. Although this dislocation was a continuing concern, it was never crippling; the comparative competitive ability of Czech industrial goods meant that markets could always be found. Capital was something of a problem also, since Austria-Hungary's banking had been concentrated in Vienna, as had been much of the ownership of both banks and industry itself. However, the Czechs soon organized an adequate banking system, and their enterprises drew considerable foreign investment. A significant portion of invested funds came from France, whose government was interested in supporting Czech industry in general and the Czech armaments industry in particular. But funds also came from Austria, where many had former connections with or knowledge of Czech enterprises. This influx of foreign capital, together with the fact that prewar foreign ownership had not been systematically forced out (as had been the case in Poland) meant that foreign participation in the economy was significant. But it was far from dominant: foreigners tended to be shareholders in large and well-known corporations; the small and medium units comprised the bulk of production and were overwhelmingly locally owned.[2] The direct role of the Czech government in industry was comparatively small.

One should not have the impression that the strength and quality of Czech industry left the nation economically untroubled. On the contrary, Czechoslovakia was vulnerable to the vicissitudes of the world economy. Industrial production dipped below prewar levels during the depression, and recovery was slow in all areas. But in contrast to the rest of Eastern Europe, the situation in Czechoslovakia was quite good. The export market for machinery (and armaments) slumped but it never collapsed, as was the case for the agricultural and consumer products upon which other East European nations were dependent for foreign exchange.

Czechoslovakia possessed within its borders the entire spectrum of East European agricultural systems. There were large estate owners—indeed among the largest anywhere: an American diplomatic report of 1921 noted that six noble families held estates averaging well over 100,000 hectares.[3] There were also many medium-size farms, held largely by Czechs and Germans in Bohemia who operated also as small businessmen. And there were peasants: landless workers on the estates which were to be found in both the Czech and Slovak lands, and dwarf holders, found everywhere but especially numerous in Slovakia. There was also a fourth category of landownership that was much stronger than anywhere else in Eastern Europe: lands held by the Roman Catholic Church.

The provisional government was determined to effect a substantial land reform and cleared the way early in 1919 by declaring a freeze on transactions involving large estates. This action had both the effect of halting unhealthy land speculation and of providing a promise of change that would be all but impossible to retract. In fact, opposition to a serious land reform was scattered and weak. Estate owners were overwhelmingly

Germans or Hungarians (in Slovakia) whose voices scarcely were heeded by the Czech and Slovak deputies in the National Assembly. The resistance of the Church was more formidable, but not as significant as statistics on religious belief (76 percent Roman Catholic) would suggest. In the prewar Czech lands the Church had long been associated with the interests of the German-dominated government and society; moreover, Czech history and hence national feeling was closely tied to Jan Hus and the Protestant movement. Though all but a handful of Czechs were at least nominal Catholics, many felt that their persuasion was the result of force (the defeat at White Mountain in 1618 and the weight of subsequent Habsburg rule), and anticlericalism was consequently very strong. This situation was somewhat reversed in Slovakia, where many peasants had considered the Church a shield and balm from Hungarian oppression. Even so, feeling was sufficiently strong that the Church's defense of its own and the nobility's landed interests was brushed aside.

The land reform that was enacted in 1919 and put into effect over the subsequent decade was not the largest in numerical terms in Eastern Europe (that of Romania was), but it was the most effective in achieving its goal. The amount of land redistributed reached only 14 percent, but it was selected and parcelled out with such care that comparatively few new dwarf holdings were created and a number of the preexisting ones were eliminated. The process of subdivision of land into strips was stopped and in part reversed, and peasant access to forest land was provided for in most cases. By 1930 the percentage of dwarf holdings in Czechoslovakia was only 28 percent (the second lowest in Eastern Europe—after Bulgaria); this figure is in itself deceptive, however, for most of the dwarf holdings were in Slovakia and Carpatho-Ruthenia where the quality of the land and the distribution of the population made better solutions impossible.[4] Though large estates continued to exist, Czechoslovakia became a country characterized by comparatively prosperous peasants and farmers. Czechoslovakia had the lowest percent of population dependent on agriculture in Eastern Europe (40 percent), but it also had the lowest number of people per standard unit of land and livestock and the highest yields of wheat and potatoes per hectare. Where Poland was considered to have 30 percent of its agricultural population as surplus to its needs, Czechoslovakia was calculated to have only 12 percent.[5] These data, taken together with those for industry, describe by far the strongest economy in Eastern Europe.

Czechoslovak society, like the economy, was comparatively well balanced. In addition to peasants and large landowners, there were important numbers of farmers and a strong middle class. There was also a real working class.

The peasantry in Czechoslovakia was quite diverse. In Bohemia and Moravia, peasants were few in number and comparatively prosperous. Even Czech dwarfholders had the economic advantage of easy access to supplementary employment in the small and medium industry of the numerous towns. Moreover, the Czech peasantry as a whole had accepted change and was clearly evolving into a new economic and social group. Such an enormous number of Czech peasants had left the land to become workers, artisans, or members of the middle class that the remainder could not be unaware of the possibilities open to them. Land reform and government assistance with training and capital also demonstrated that peasants could become farmers. Communications to the villages were generally good, and most Czech peasants could read and had a sense of the importance of education.

The favorable situation of the peasantry in the Czech lands was in sharp contrast with the status of their brethren in Slovakia and Carpatho-Ruthenia. In these formerly Hungarian provinces the peasants were among the most backward in East Europe. The holdings were small and the land was poor. Emigration from the villages had been strong but mostly to the United States rather than to regional towns and cities. A traditionally high birth rate, combined with recent advances in sanitation and medical care, quickly replaced the emigres and worsened overcrowding. Population growth in Slovakia was half again as high as in Bohemia; in Carpatho-Ruthenia it was more than twice as high. Per capita agricultural production in the two poorer regions was only 36 percent of that in the Czech lands.[6] Literacy in these provinces was initially very low and was usually to be found in "outsiders"—Czechs, Hungarians, Germans, and Jews. Though many contemporaries considered interwar Czechoslovakia to be really West European, few noticed that, if so, this "new Switzerland" had, in Slovakia and Carpatho-Ruthenia, its own internal Eastern Europe.

Farmers in Czechoslovakia were to be found principally in Bohemia and Moravia and were overwhelmingly Czech or German nationals. They generally had some education and some knowledge of modern agricultural techniques. Their land was of only average fertility, but good roads leading to strong markets in the surrounding towns made it possible for them to sell both their crops (usually wheat, potatoes, and sugar beets) and their livestock at a profit. Though badly hurt by the depression, the farmers continued to have access to markets, and most survived although their expansion as an economic group was halted.

The nobility of Czechoslovakia was seriously weakened by the creation of the new state. Only a handful of the aristocrats were Czech nationals: the vast majority were German or if they had Czech names long since Germanized (or Magyarized in Slovakia); their principal residence had been Vienna (or Budapest). The land reform did not break them as a class, since large estates were still permitted and since some compensation was paid. But wealth was not power. The aristocrats, long associated with the worst aspects of Habsburg rule, could not command any support among Czechs or Slovaks. Even the German population found few compatible interests with the old aristocracy. Schwarzenbergs, Liechtensteins, Coburgs, etc. were mainly curiosities (albeit rich ones).

The Czech middle class was also a regional phenomenon—found almost exclusively in the Czech lands and comprised almost entirely of Czechs, Germans, and Jews. The middle class in Czechoslovakia was more like that of America than of Poland, but it also contained elements of the East European concept of "intelligentsia." The capitalist or commercial bourgeois was both respected and common in the Czech lands. A high level of education and a long commercial history provided for the acceptance of an industrial society and prevented social prejudice against business. Residents of the Czech lands were not embarrassed by an association with manual labor. In other respects Czechoslovakia closely resembled the rest of Eastern Europe; thus, education, particularly higher education, had enormous status. University professors and writers were accorded great respect but so were government officials down to and including clerks. The idea that working with paper (even just shuffling it) constituted a high calling was strong in this society. The bureaucracy had considerable prestige, decent pay, and unparalleled security. Consequently, it was much larger than it needed to be.

Industrial workers in Czechoslovakia comprised some 40 percent of the employed—by far the highest percentage in Eastern Europe. Concentrated in the larger towns and in the cities of Bohemia and Moravia, the workers were principally Czech and German by nationality. Ties to the villages were still strong, since most workers were only a few generations removed from the land, but the links were more familial than economic or cultural. The Czechoslovak workers were class-conscious, unionized, and politically aware. There were very few industrial workers in Slovakia and virtually none in Carpatho-Ruthenia.

Social stratification in Czechoslovakia was national and religious as well as economic. Official censuses listed Czechoslovak as a single nationality, but reliable estimates are that Czechs were about 5 percent of the population and Slovaks about 15 percent.[7] The history of the peoples and the economic analysis of the country make it obvious that the Czechs were the more advanced as well as the more numerous group. The Czechs were middle-class, workers, farmers, and peasants and the Slovaks just the latter. Even as peasants the Czechs were more prosperous. In addition to economic strength, the Czechs had a high level of literacy and education, a strong and established literary language, a proud national history and culture written in that language, and an important sense of national self-confidence. The Slovaks had none of these.

Emerging from the Magyar shadow, the Slovaks were many generations behind the Czechs. Few Slovaks were literate in their own language—a new and not entirely accepted construct. The history of one thousand years of Magyar rule was not a happy tale and provided few sources of inspiration; Slovak culture was essentially folklore. Most of all, the potential for economic development was not good. Given the fact that Slovak is similar to Czech and provides for a degree of mutual intelligibility, the Slovak nationality would seem to have been primed for early evaporation. That this did not occur was a testament to the strength, endurance, and above all the fierce nationalism of the thousand or so members of the Slovak intelligentsia.

Only slightly less numerous than the Slovaks were the Germans (23 percent). In education, social and economic status, and in national consciousness, the Germans were very similar to the Czechs—a fact that seemed to exacerbate rather than to lessen hostility between the two. Germans and Czechs were frequently in direct competition: as farmers, as merchants and entrepreneurs, and perhaps most important as rivals for training in higher education and for slots in the bureaucracy. Germans were distributed in the same area as Czechs (Bohemia and Moravia), but while mixed in towns and cities they were more often separated by village. Even so, the only large part of the country that was predominantly German was the Sudeten fringe to the west, adjacent to Germany proper.

Hungarians made up some five percent of the population and were primarily peasants living in Slovakia. Nearly all of the population of Carpatho-Ruthenia was Ukrainian, but this was only about 3.5–4 percent of the total. Carpatho-Ruthenia was solidly peasant and totally backward; one historian described the area as a former "Magyar deer park."

Jews were only about 2.5 percent of the population, were primarily resident in the urban areas of Bohemia and Moravia, and were more often speakers of German and Yiddish than of Czech. The Jews had been highly assimilated into prewar Habsburg society and as such tended to adhere more closely to German than to Czech cultural, social, and (inevitably) political views. Even so, anti-Semitism was not strong among either

Czechs or Germans. The Jews were not particularly numerous, were not better educated, and although there were some wealthy Jews, were not perceived as having predominant or exploitative economic power. Again, the situation was different in Slovakia and Carpatho-Ruthenia, where middle class intellectual jealousy and rivalry was reinforced by peasant superstition. But even in those regions, the comparatively small number and lack of prominence of the Jewish communities made anti-Semitism less of a concern than elsewhere.

Aside from the Jews, the only religiously homogenous group was the Ukrainians, who were solidly Uniate. All of the other nationalities of Czechoslovakia were predominantly Catholic, but some Czechs and Slovaks and quite a few Germans were Protestant. The Slovaks were notably devout members of the Roman Catholic fold, the Germans moderately so, and the Czechs known for a skepticism that was often translated into a hostile view of Church participation in educational, cultural, and political affairs. Generally speaking, governments of the interwar period reflected this Czech approach.

Education was both a strength and a weakness of Czechoslovakia. Education was controlled directly by the state through the ministry of education, which set standards and policy for all levels of institutions (including private ones). Eight years of schooling was made compulsory by law and was put into effect everywhere without difficulty. Secondary education had a technical and a college preparatory track, and was open to talent. Four universities and seven higher technical institutes were also open to everyone on a competitive basis. Though data on the social origins of university students are not available, it is generally agreed that the educational system was highly accessible and did promote social mobility. There was a general consensus that the overall quality of education was on a par with that of Western Europe and that the Charles University in Prague was one of Europe's finest institutions.

The flaw in all this was that the system was organized on national lines. The law provided for education in the native language when a minimal concentration of students was found. This meant that Slovaks and Ukrainians had their own schools (Czech language was required, however). But it also meant that Czechs and Germans went to separate elementary and secondary schools and different universities and technical institutes. The intent of this system was a good one—the Czechs did not want to deny to the others the cultural opportunities that they themselves had had to struggle for. But the nobility of purpose was lost in execution. Germans were unappeased, and Czechs and Germans were segregated in a way that exacerbated nationalistic tensions.

The Czech constitution of 1920, like the Polish constitution, provided for proportional representation in the national assembly. The result
was a plethora of parties and a continuum of coalitions. But the Czechs,
unlike the Poles, opted for a strong executive. The president (elected by
the assembly for seven years) was the real head of government. He appointed the ministers (including the prime minister), and although the
cabinet could not function without support in the assembly, the balance
of power was clearly on the side of the executive. It is significant that
the president was also commander-in-chief of the army and that, in
addition to the ministers, he appointed the top army officers, civil servants,
judges, and even university professors. The framers of the constitution
were wise to provide this authority and hence stability, for without it the
extraordinarily complex party system would have kept government on
the edge of chaos.

As in Poland, there was a large number of political parties, most
of them so small and evanescent that a precise count is hard to establish.
Typically, however, there were between fifty and sixty parties of which
about thirty contested elections and about fifteen achieved parliamentary
representation. The strongest party never won as much as 30 percent of
the vote; typically the largest party had less than 20 percent. In practical
terms a coalition of at least five parties was needed for a majority.

Initially, the strongest single party was the Czechoslovak Social
Democratic Party, which won just over 25 percent of the vote in the
elections of 1920—more than twice the total of the next largest single
party.[8] Since the SDs were an old party with established leaders and
parliamentary experience from the Austrian days, the success of 1920
could logically have been seen as a giant step toward a socialist Czechoslovakia. But disaster struck before the leaders had finished toasting
their success. The Comintern's Twenty-One conditions forced a split in
the Social Democratic Party that was more severe than that faced by its
major European counterparts. The new Communist party that appeared
as a result of the fissure took nearly all of the organizational structure
and most of the Social Democratic voters (on the split see below). In
1925, the Czechoslovak SDs had only 9 percent of the vote and the
Communists just over 13 percent. Perhaps more serious in the long run
than the split with the communists was the Czech Social Democrats'
failure to unite with the German Social Democrats. This latter party was
the ideological mirror image of the Czech version. In 1920 it had 11
percent of the vote and in 1925 just under 6 percent (this party also split
with the communists). If the Czech and German parties had united, they
would still have had the largest party in 1925. Moreover, a single party

would have been more effective in drawing votes away from the communists when that party produced first mystification and then disillusionment in its blind pursuit of the Comintern's line. The fact remains, however, that in a country with strong, politically active trade unions, and in which as much as 40 percent of the electorate voted socialist, at least half and typically two-thirds of the workers voted only for the socialist party that identified with their nationality. This propensity increased rather than decreased over time. Never has the fundamental Marxist tenet of the primacy of class consciousness been so clearly and directly refuted.

After the Social Democrats, the most important continuing political party was the National Democratic. This group was similar to its Polish equivalent in that it was supported by merchants and industrialists of the predominant ethnic group (Czechs, obviously) and because it had an established, popular leader—Karel Kramář. But the parties revealed the differences as well as the similarities of the two nations. The Czech version was as anticlerical as the Polish was linked to the Catholic hierarchy; the Czechs were panslavist, interested in Russian culture, and inclined to listen sympathetically to Soviet overtures, while the Polish party reflected a popular hostility to everything in the past and present of Poland's neighbor to the east. Most important of all, Czechoslovakia was ethnically and socially less homogenous than Poland, and the Czech National Democrats could not draw more than 10 percent of the vote. Nevertheless, that party had strength in politics out of proportion to its support. This power resulted in part from skilled leadership, which in turn was a reflection of the fact that the National Democrats were entrenched in the upper levels of the state bureaucracy.

Of the newer parties, the most important was the Czechoslovakian Agrarian Party. United in national affairs but with separate Czech and Slovak organizations, this party drew balanced 70 percent Czech/30 percent Slovak electoral support. Together the Agrarians had some 14 percent of the vote in the first election and grew steadily, if not spectacularly, throughout the period. The Agrarians' strength lay in skilled leadership and a broad appeal. The party was deeply involved in the problems of peasants and small farmers: its leaders were instrumental in drawing up and carrying out the land reform and followed it with measures, such as improved transportation and access to credit, that were popular in the countryside. But the Agrarians also pushed the interests of, and consequently drew the support of, small traders and businessmen, workers in smaller nonunionized enterprises, and, as the party became more prominent, civil servants. The Agrarians managed to steer a fairly neutral course in the struggle between clericals and anticlericals.

The remaining parties must be described briefly. There were separate Czech and Slovak Populist parties: these were both clerical and peasant oriented, but the Slovak version, led by Msgr. Hlinka, was anti-Czech and in favor of a restructuring of the state. There was a Czech National Socialist Party which differed from the Social Democrats largely in its strong Czech nationalism. There were many German parties in addition to the German SDs; these included the German Farmer, the German Christian Social, and the German National Democrat (the Nazis—strong as early as 1920). There were also Magyar parties and even an array of Ruthenian (Ukrainian) parties. Though there was a clear line between the larger and the smaller parties, one should not underestimate the importance of the latter: what they lacked in size they compensated for in numbers; and since the larger parties were too hostile to form coalitions together, a number of the smaller parties always took part in government.

The principal issues confronting the governments of interwar Czechoslovakia can be put into the following categories: land reform; foreign policy; church-state relations; social security; financial-economic policy; nationality policies and state organization. Although all of these problems were difficult ones, particularly for a new state, most were dealt with in a remarkably efficient and expeditious manner. The land reform, though hardly perfect, was nonetheless effected quickly and was removed as a major bone of political contention after just a few years. The entire question of foreign policy was equally simple and straightforward. By the end of 1921, Czechoslovakia had sealed an alliance with France and had joined the Little Entente; this strategy effectively neutralized one enemy (Hungary) and restrained another (Poland). The former was simply outgunned, while the latter was prevented from upsetting the status quo by the French who, if they could not bring their allies together, could at least keep them apart. The French alliance system was anti-Soviet, but even though the border province of Ruthenia was disputed between Prague and Moscow, emotions did not run high on either side; Czechoslovakia and the USSR got along reasonably well. The remaining frontiers were with a weak neutral (Austria) and a distracted Great Power (Germany). The governments in Berlin, though they did not accept in any way Czechoslovak sovereignty over the Sudetenland, considered it an issue of secondary importance until well into the Nazi period, when Hitler suddenly saw the issue as a logical *point d'appui.*

Church-state relations were an emotional issue, but were nonetheless resolved sensibly. The key word was compromise. The state asserted secular authority in important areas such as marriage, education, and selection of higher clergy. But once ultimate power was defined, the state then consented to recognize religious marriage as legal, agreed to permit church-run (albeit state-regulated) schools, and refrained from opposition to most appointments in the hierarchy. Not infrequently, compromise was forced on the more secular Czech groups by their more pious co-nationals in coalition with traditionally proclerical Germans and Slovaks. Some of the emotionalism was evidenced in Czech nationalism, as when Masaryk's participation in the unveiling of a monument to Hus caused the Vatican to sever relations with Czechoslovakia.[9]

Social legislation also moved through the Czech parliamentary process far more easily than elsewhere in Eastern Europe. The eight-hour day was adopted, as were provisions for unemployment compensation and a comprehensive pension system. Trade unions were regulated in a manner favorable to their further development, and there was much effort to protect the interests of the working classes whether unionized or not. This outpouring of benevolence was directly related to the initially very favorable economic and financial situation of the country. The lack of war damage, the availability of natural resources, traditionally high productivity, and continued access to export markets kept the Czech economy stable through the first tumultuous years of the 1920s. This stability in turn strengthened the national currency and, together with very conservative fiscal policies, sheltered Czechoslovakia from the inflationary winds which flattened the economies of neighboring Germany, Austria, and Poland in the middle part of the decade. Foreign investment was consequently drawn to this haven, and the overall economy remained strong several years into the depression.

The Czech engine eventually lost its head of steam, however. The depression was too comprehensive an economic phenomenon to allow any industrial nation to remain aloof. The Czech system did not collapse, but a sharp downturn occurred which no amount of technical expertise could reverse. Czechoslovakia was still deep in the depression when the state ceased to exist.

The problems that were not solved were those relating to the relative status of the various nationalities. The new state was conceived by Czechs, and because they were strongest in numbers and most loyal to the Czechoslovak concept, they also tended to dominate politics and the bureaucracy. On the other hand the Czechs had themselves recently suffered oppression, and they displayed tolerance and flexibility that went beyond that shown by the other nationalities of Eastern Europe. Unfortunately, good intentions were not enough, for there was present from the very birth of the nation a climate of tension and distrust which prevented the development of harmonious relations.

In theory, it should have been easy to forge strong links between Czechs and Slovaks. Both were slavic, both had suffered centuries of foreign domination, both were anxious for a fresh start, and both had a sense of needing the other. During the war these positive factors outweighed the more numerous negative ones: different attitudes toward religion, different levels of cultural development, and different social and economic environments. It was the positive side that led to the famous Pittsburgh Agreement (see above), which in turn created the atmosphere in which the western allies chose to accept and then support the concept of a Czechoslovak state (the idea was mentioned for example, in Woodrow Wilson's Fourteen Points of January, 1918).

Unfortunately, the Pittsburgh Agreement, far from being a point of unity and cohesion between Czechs and Slovaks, rapidly became the focal point of struggle between them. This was because, although the agreement specifically stated that Slovakia would have autonomy within Czechoslovakia, the Czechs were unwilling to implement it. There were many reasons cited for the Czechs' abandonment of their promise, but these all came down ultimately to one fact: the Czechs did not believe that the Slovaks were sufficiently mature in politics and culture to be masters of their own affairs. Autonomy for the Slovaks, the Czechs believed, would only create confusion and weaken the state. Those Czechs who were willing to accept the idea that Slovak autonomy would eventually become a reality, were nonetheless generally skeptical to the point of refusing to name a date for it.

Whatever the validity of Czech fears that autonomy would lead to weakness, it is incontestable that failure to grant autonomy also led to weakness. The Hungarian invasion of Slovakia created sufficient dislocation that Slovak protests about failure to implement the Pittsburgh Agreement were at first quite muted. But as time passed and the direction of events became clear, Slovak hostility mounted rapidly.

The governments in Prague were able to do little to improve the situation—often they seemed to have no choice but to make it worse. This was particularly the case in education: Czech leaders worked hard to promote the rapid growth of literacy in the Slovak language, and their efforts were overwhelmingly successful. But the teachers necessary to make this possible were inevitably Czechs, as were the bureaucrats needed to manage this and other governmental programs. The large influx of well-paid foreigners into Slovak towns and villages caused much tension and resentment.

An equally serious problem was the tendency of the leaders in Prague to call upon the minority Slovak Protestants for assistance in governments. The unsurprising quid pro quo was the offer of administrative positions in Slovakia proper. Though this approach had a certain logic, since the Protestants tended to be better educated and above all more supportive of the Czechoslovak concept, it angered most Slovaks and thus exacerbated relations within Slovakia itself as well as between Czechs and Slovaks.

Economic differences were also important. The Slovaks were as preoccupied with agrarian concerns as the Czechs were with industrial problems. Slovakia suffered far more from war damage and disruption of communications and lost access to markets than did the Czech lands. The questions of trade union rights, the number of hours in the working day, and social security, which consumed the time of legislators in Prague, were of little or no interest to peasants in the Slovakian hills. In good times and bad, Czechs were far better off than Slovaks.

The end result of these tensions was a pattern of political hostility that escalated throughout the interwar period. Although some Slovaks, mostly bourgeois and Protestants, supported the Agrarian Party, the vast majority voted either for Msgr. Hlinka's Slovak People's Party or for the communists. This seems a strange dichotomy, but in fact both parties represented opposition to the status quo. The communists drew the votes, rather than the allegiance, of those who wished to express their protest as radically as possible; this phenomenon was quite common in interwar Eastern Europe (see below).

Relations between Czechs and Germans had different origins than those between Czechs and Slovaks, but the end result was much the same. One could say that while the latter relationship was soured by jealousy, the former was characterized by rivalry. Czech concessions in education and culture, which provided for virtual autonomy, were accepted by the Germans but not gratefully. The perspective of history is crucial to an understanding of this attitude. The Czechs, who were acutely aware of the problems of national minorities, felt that the status accorded to the Germans was uniquely generous, as indeed it was. The Czechs felt that the Germans should fall on their knees in thanks for this extraordinary benevolence. But the Germans were not an emerging minority, indeed they had no memory of ever being a minority. The Germans saw things from the standpoint of a privileged majority for whom concessions did not make things better but rather less bad.

The atmosphere was considerably worsened by growing economic disparities. The German areas had had an initially higher level of industrial development, but the Czech regions had caught up in the latter half of the nineteenth century. Thus, in the intensely competitive interwar economy, the newer, more modern Czech plant and equipment had a significant advantage. Scarce investment capital tended to flow to the strongest companies. The financial situation of the Germans was exacerbated first by losses experienced by Viennese banks associated with the old regime, and second by the tendency of Germans to keep their money in banks in Germany and Austria—where accounts were wiped out by the inflation that these countries suffered in the early and mid twenties. It was particularly galling for proud Germans to watch their holdings in marks and schillings evaporate while the crown of the despised Czechoslovak state proved to be one of the strongest currencies in Europe.

Except for the communist party, German voters supported only German parties. Since more than 20 percent of the population was German, this represented a potentially sizable bloc in the parliament. Fortunately for the state, however, the German parties never functioned as a coherent group. In the first postwar years the German Social Democrats cooperated closely with their Czech counterparts on legislation and in the government. Cooperation between the two continued, but was made much less important when the emergence of the communists shattered social democracy. The remaining parties then began to divide on the very question of their own participation in government. A sizable group of Germans was willing to participate in local government and back candidates for parliament but was determined to limit its national role to obstructionism. Some German politicians referred to treason as a duty. But other German parties, particularly those representing bourgeois interests, resisted this approach. Though they also disdained the Czech state, they feared that to remain aloof from government might seriously damage their economic interests. Accordingly some German parties participated in government coalitions from 1926 until 1938.

Despite the presence of Germans and Slovaks in various governments, it is clear that rivalry between nationalities was Czechoslovakia's most severe problem—one that became ever more serious as time passed. The image of Czechoslovakia as a bastion of the west in the east, as the one solidly democratic state in Eastern Europe, is indeed appealing. But the shallowness of this view must again be stressed: in the parliamentary elections of 1935, nearly 40 percent of the vote went to political parties which were hostile to the existence of the Czechoslovak state (communists, German parties, and Slovak parties). By 1938, 91 percent of the German vote was won by the Nazis—a figure never approached in free elections in Germany proper. That the delegates elected to parliament in 1935 overwhelmingly voted two years later to reelect Masaryk as president should not be construed as support for the Czech state or even for its leader. Rather, the opposition was merely biding its time until a better opportunity presented itself.

The crisis was not long in coming: the interwar period was one year shorter in Czechoslovakia than in the rest of Eastern Europe. The Munich capitulation is generally ascribed to the failure of British and French nerve, but the leadership of Czechoslovakia is often blamed as well. Many believe that if Beneš had been determined to fight (Masaryk died in 1937 and Beneš, his protégé, succeeded him as president), that there would have been a different outcome, perhaps a German capitulation at the conference table or perhaps even a Czechoslovak military victory. These views are either in error (Hitler was fully prepared to fight) or are overly sanguine: the Czech army would have been fighting in large part in hostile territory (the Sudetenland), would have faced possible attacks from both Poland and Hungary, and would probably have experienced a lack of enthusiasm if not outright resistance from many Slovaks. On the other hand, the Czech army had excellent training, superb equipment, and a vastly superior tactical position. German casualties would have been very high, particularly if Hitler had pressed for a rapid victory as he undoubtedly would have.

From the perspective of history we certainly know that Czech resistance to Hitler would have speeded the rearmament of Britain, France, and the United States, and would probably have stiffened their resolve. Moreover, the Nazis would have found Czech military stores mostly exhausted, destroyed, or damaged, and Czech industrial capacity mostly under rubble. Instead, of course, they took both intact. Finally, the momentum of one easy victory after another, which took German troops to the gates of Moscow four years later, would have been lost or at least dissipated before the real struggle began. Whether Beneš could have or should have seen this is doubtful. It is ironic that only one year later the Poles had no difficulty in recognizing the danger and did not hesitate to sacrifice, but were helpless in the face of a juggernaut.

10

Interwar Hungary

THE WAR AND ITS AFTERMATH were very different for Hungary than for the other nations of Eastern Europe. The Hungarians had not only been belligerents, they had been actively and enthusiastically involved on the losing side. As a consequence, defeat for Hungary did not mean the opportunity to create or renew but was instead the occasion for a thorough reexamination of the past: it was a time to find the explanation for errors and perhaps to find scapegoats as well. Where others were infused with the hope of a bright new future, the Magyars were plunged into gloom, rejecting their defeat and the subsequent losses, but with no clear idea of alternatives.

Hungary had a brief transitional government. Count Mihály Károlyi, a politician who favored independence and significant concessions to the minorities, was appointed head of government by the Habsburg emperor before the armistice. Károlyi's authority did not extend far, however. The non-Magyar regions—Slovakia, Transylvania and Croatia—had already all gone their own way or were in the process of doing so. In Hungary proper, the discontented masses inevitably tended to associate the new government with the old system which spawned it. Károlyi's regime proclaimed a series of democratic reforms, including such routine measures as freedom of press and assembly, but it was unable to carry out the more important changes such as a significant broadening of the franchise and a major land reform. The failure of the new leadership to take hold and set the country firmly in a new direction was rooted in a number of problems: the weak political tradition inherited from the prewar period; the difficulty of restoring economic health to a war-torn land (something which would have challenged any government); and most of all the nationalities question, or as it now manifested itself, the question of the integrity of "Great Hungary."

205

The Hungarians might have been able to hold on to the non-Magyar provinces, perhaps by negotiating a *modus vivendi* with their peoples, had not these lands been quickly incorporated into òther nations. Defeated and exhausted, the Hungarians were in no position to stifle the rebellion of Slovaks, Croats, and Romanians and at the same time take on the military forces of Czechoslovakia, Yugoslavia, and Romania. Moreover, these "successor states" had the strong support of the victorious allies, whose armies in the field would certainly have come to their aid if the Hungarians showed signs of military success.

In this unhappy situation the Károlyi government did the only thing it could do—it accepted the reality of the moment and moved militarily only to resist the encroachment of the Romanian forces which were pushing westward into Hungary proper. The problem with this strategy was that Hungarian public opinion was not about to accept reality. The desire for action quickly became paramount, as traditional Magyar nationalism transcended the fatigue and despair of war. It was in this atmosphere that the communist party led by Béla Kun was able to seize control of the country.

The story of Béla Kun and the Communist Party of Hungary (CPH) is described in some detail in a later section. At this point it is sufficient to note that the CPH took advantage of Magyar discontent and the disorganization of Károlyi's government to seize power in a revolutionary *putsch* in March of 1919. The consequences of this event were far-reaching. Kun realized that he owed his victory to popular rejection of the dismemberment of "Greater Hungary" and that if he was to stay in power, he must make at least some progress toward a restoration. He had some initial success when the Hungarian army rallied to check the advance of the Romanians in the east. This was highly popular, but it was not enough: the Romanians yielded some territory, but Transylvania proper was still firmly in their hands when the Magyar counteroffensive ran out of steam. Kun was forced to find a new diversion quickly.

The idea of moving on Croatia was never seriously considered. The Croats were hostile and militarily experienced; many Croatian divisions (led by Croat officers) had participated on both sides in the recent war. Moreover, no one could forget the role, often thought to be decisive, which the Croatian military had played in crushing the Hungarian revolt of 1848–49. Finally, Croatia was now a part of Yugoslavia, and the Serbs also had battle-hardened troops to throw into the fray. The loss of Croatia by "Great Hungary" was not accepted in principle, but it was understood that progress toward a restoration could not be expected in the near future.

The obvious choice for action was, therefore, Slovakia. The area was not well integrated either geographically or administratively into Czechoslovakia, a country which had not yet organized an army. Moreover, the Slovaks, though also hostile to Magyar rule, had no separate military tradition (thanks to the Magyars) and could not be expected to mount a very powerful resistance. Accordingly, a second front (fighting with the Romanians continued) was opened and Slovakia was quickly occupied. Though rapid and complete, Kun's victory was a hollow one. It outraged the French, British, and Americans, who, aroused by Czechoslovak complaints, threatened to send an Allied army against Hungary. A more immediate concern was the fact that the Romanians, noting that troops had been withdrawn from the forces facing them in order to invade and occupy Slovakia, launched a quick counter-counteroffensive. In this situation Kun found himself facing the worst possible consequences. He had to withdraw from Slovakia to face the new threat from the east, but the transfer of forces was too slow to prevent a Romanian breakthrough. Finally, the withdrawal, together with subsequent military reverses, eroded support for Kun to the point that his government crumbled and he was forced to flee.

The Hungarian occupation of Slovakia, brief though it was, served Hungary's neighbors as a symbol of Magyar intransigence and rejection of the Treaty of Trianon. It was the pretext for the establishment of the Little Entente and the diplomacy of confrontation that characterized Hungary's relations with her neighbors in the interwar period. It could easily be argued, however, that a similar climate of hostility would have obtained whether Kun had won power or not. Certainly it is obvious that the policy of expansion was not so much initiated by the communists as it was forced on them, and that other political groups were far more committed to the "Great Hungary" program.

The domestic policy of Béla Kun's regime is less well known than its approach to foreign affairs, but the former probably had a greater and more enduring impact on Hungary. The communist government proclaimed many radical reforms, including redistribution of land and expropriation of large holdings of capital, but it was impossible to implement them while the nation was engaged in struggle on two nearby fronts. Also, there was fierce opposition to change on the part of the landowners and the middle classes, backed by the churches and most of the bureaucracy. Since many workers and peasants were away at the front and the remainder was not generally a militant and revolutionary lot, the communist government soon found that its authority had no meaning unless accompanied by liberal use of force. Kun did not shrink from this, since he had the success story of Lenin and the Cheka as a guidebook (see below).

The communist use of terror had two immediate results. First, it served as a pretext for an even more violent counter campaign, the "White Terror," which followed immediately on the collapse of the Kun regime. The political docility which characterized interwar Hungary can be traced in large part to the numbing brutality of the right wing reaction. Prospective opponents of the authoritarian government that followed could not help but be deterred by a recollection of the horrible violence that was unleashed on everyone who was a real or fancied "red." Second, the fact that Kun and many of his aides were of Jewish origin provided an opportunity for Hungarian anti-Semites, until then a relatively unimportant group, to seize a prominence which they never fully relinquished. The tragedy for Hungarian Jews was greater than the violence of the months of "White Terror": the blood lust nurtured in that period animated a Hungarian fascist movement that ultimately had a significant role in the Holocaust.

The government that replaced the communists was composed of former Habsburg military officers, who constituted a civil authority partly because of the lingering prestige of the aristocratic officer class but mostly because there was hardly anyone to oppose them. They selected as their leader an Admiral by the name of Miklós Horthy and, in a gesture toward continuity with the Hungarian past, called him regent for the king of Hungary. Horthy's supporters were responsible for the rightist terror. A key question was "Regent for whom?" Was it for the Habsburg emperor, Charles, who called himself king of Hungary but who was living in exile and who was barred (by the peace treaties) from returning to any of his former dominions? If not Charles, who else? These were the subjects of continual, bitter debate. But despite the occasional crisis, Horthy, an admiral without a fleet and a regent without a king, retained the ultimate executive authority throughout the interwar period.

The economic landscape over which Horthy and his allies held sway was perhaps the bleakest in Eastern Europe. Where others had suffered from the war, Hungary had been devastated by the peace. The statistics alone tell much of the story. Trianon Hungary was smaller than "Great Hungary" by the following amounts: railroads, 58 percent; timber, 60 percent; arable land, 43 percent; iron ore, 83 percent; lignite, 29 percent; and coal, 27 percent.[1] The loss of these resources and attendant communications was crippling. Budapest, which had been built over the years into a great center of trade and manufacturing, was now an industrial island in an agrarian sea. And bridge building was exceptionally difficult.

Of Hungary's four neighbors, three (Czechoslovakia, Romania, and Yugoslavia) would sooner trade with the devil, and the fourth, Austria, was in straits similar to those of Hungary and in many ways more of a natural economic rival than an ally.

In addition to the lack of resources, Hungarian industry suffered a severe lack of capital. In this Hungary was similar to the other states of Eastern Europe, but where most of the others could draw on the West (France especially) for help, such assistance was rarely extended to former "enemy" states. The geographical and consequently economic reorientation of Hungary made exports far more important than had been the case previously, but ironically it was also far more difficult than before. Indeed, a vicious circle quickly developed: Hungarian manufactured products could not be exported because of technological backwardness; to reverse this deficiency it was necessary to invest in new plant and equipment; but investment required capital which was available in sufficient quantities only from foreign sources. And, of course, to obtain foreign capital it was necessary to export. Back to square one.

In fact, there are several ways to escape from this rather common economic dilemma. One is to squeeze the required capital out of the domestic economy. This is the approach pioneered by the Soviet Union (see below), but even the Soviets had not thought of it in the early 1920s, and in any case it is a strategy that requires a totalitarian government. A second and rather obvious option is to export agricultural goods. This had strong appeal for the Hungarians, who could easily produce more food than they consumed. Unfortunately, the practice did not fulfill the theory. Trade in agricultural products is always unstable, in part because weather cycles always create unpredictable changes, but also because importers tend to shut off demand in hard times. Even more important in the present case were tariff barriers. Protectionism was the vogue throughout the world in the 1920s, and Hungary was no exception: tariffs were set especially high to protect developing industry. But these tariffs in turn invited retaliation against Hungarian agricultural exports. The situation was exacerbated by the fact that exports had to traverse at least one frontier before reaching their destination. And the odds were three to one that the frontier was a hostile one.

Despite all these difficulties, some agricultural products were exported and these did help the economy. But far more was needed. The government in Budapest tried to cope for a while by speeding up the printing presses in the ministry of the treasury. As is usually the case with inflation, this was helpful in the beginning. Production soared as prices rose faster than wages. Indebtedness disappeared as people eliminated obligations in currency worth a fraction of the value of the original loan; funds thus freed could be invested in corporate stocks and bonds. But as with any narcotic, the delirium is all too short and the hangover excessively long. If wages do not keep pace with prices, demand will soon fall sharply; products will not sell, and production will also decline rapidly. People will lose their jobs and have less money to spend on products. Equally bad, in such a situation no one wants to be a creditor. Bank deposits become worthless, and bank loans cease to exist. Stocks and bonds are similarly unattractive. Those who have capital seek to shelter it in various nonproductive ways such as the holding of gold and precious gems and accounts held in stable foreign currencies. All of these factors together are the classic components of the equation for a depression.

Hungary avoided a depression in 1924 (when the inflation hit its peak) by trying the third principal option for developing its type of economy: the foreign loan. This is essentially the same as exporting in return for capital, except that instead of a balanced current account, it assumes that capital received now will be paid for in exports sent in the future. Build now, pay later (but don't forget the interest). Hungary received a massive international loan (through the League of Nations) in late 1923. Its origin was largely political: first, the British had had a change of heart and now considered that the peace settlement had been too hard on the defeated nations (similar assistance was undertaken for Germany and Austria); second, the United States had an interest in international financial stability; and finally, Italy, now under Mussolini and the fascists, was interested in currying favor with the revisionist states. These three nations led the way in overcoming the objections of France and her East European allies.

The influx of foreign money effectively halted the inflation, and although the Hungarian economy did not prosper, it ceased to deteriorate. Interestingly, the League protected its investment by effectively placing Hungary in receivership. An American banker from Boston, Jeremiah Smith, Jr., was sent to Budapest to oversee the country's finances and had ultimate responsibility for balancing the budget.[2] For several years the situation was stable or improving and there was much optimism. Yet little thought was given to the question of repayment. For a loan to be effective, the funds must be invested in such a way as to facilitate its liquidation—including, of course, the accumulating interest. In the case of Hungary, this meant that funds should be funneled into enterprises that would become efficient, effective exporters. Unfortunately, it is estimated that only about 20 percent of the funds from foreign loans went directly for this purpose.[3] Some expenditures helped indirectly (e.g., paying off other debts), but much went for totally unproductive purposes such as public works, expanding bureaucracy, and graft. When the economy of the west as a whole went sour and foreign bankers began calling in old loans instead of issuing new ones, the situation of the Hungarian economy was desperate.

Before discussing the depression, however, a brief survey of Hungarian agriculture is essential. Hungary was and remained a nation of large estates: more than 47 percent of the land was in holdings in excess of 100 hectares. Land reform had virtually no effect on this. The reform of 1922 distributed only 5 percent of arable land, by far the lowest percentage in Eastern Europe. Hungarian agriculture was a curious mixture of backwardness and efficiency. On the one hand, the system suffered from the low productivity that typically results from a semifeudal organization. On the other hand, the size of the estates and the nature of the land made modern farming techniques possible. The use of machinery was not uncommon in the interwar Hungarian countryside and the use of chemical fertilizers was widespread. In this respect, farming was advanced by East European standards (though backward by comparison to Western Europe or the United States). The net result was that average yields of wheat per hectare in Hungary were higher than all other East European countries except Czechoslovakia, and on a par with France. But for more labor-intensive crops, such as potatoes, for which flat land and the occasional harvester had little impact, Hungarian yields were about average for Eastern Europe and only about half those of France.[4]

Demographically, the Hungarian situation was also mixed. Just over 50 percent of the population was dependent on agriculture, and only 11 percent of the agricultural population was calculated to be "surplus" (see above); in Eastern Europe only the Czech lands of Czechoslovakia had lower numbers.[5] These figures suggest that the transformation from an agricultural to an industrial society was well underway, but as such they are somewhat deceptive. This process had indeed begun but had lost most of its momentum as a consequence of the disruption and recurring economic crises that followed the war. The situation might even have begun to reverse if the rate of population increase had not remained fairly low. Most nations of Europe had begun to experience a decline in the birthrate in the early twentieth century, and in the Hungarian case the decline came relatively soon and the rate remained comparatively low. The reason for this is unclear, but the fact is that Hungary did not suffer as much from the extreme rural overpopulation that plagued most of the rest of Eastern Europe.

The Hungarian peasantry was nonetheless quite poor. Though food was relatively more accessible than in much of Eastern Europe, very few peasants were close enough to an urban area to make it possible for them to market produce or to seek occasional or part-time employment. Peasants owning land suffered from the lack of capital and access to technical education that would make it possible for them to move up the economic ladder. There were, in fact, few farmers in Hungary. The agricultural class structure went from one extreme to the other.

At the extreme opposite pole from the peasantry the situation was certainly very different. The Hungarian nobility still included great magnates whose estates encompassed villages and towns and upon whom thousands of people were economically dependent. The members of the elite suffered some economic hardship (at least by comparison to earlier days) but still managed to remain wealthy and politically powerful throughout the interwar period. Below them, however, were many others who had the mentality of magnates but the holdings of farmers. These fared badly, particularly in the early days of the depression as food prices fell to a level that permitted the subsistence of those who worked the land but could not provide the surplus needed to maintain the expensive lifestyle of absentee landlords. Penniless people of distinguished lineage were quite common in interwar Hungary.

The Hungarian middle class was comparatively small. The Magyars had never been a trading people, and manufacturing enterprises tended to be few and large. Individuals belonging to the middle class were typically bureaucrats of one type or another. The question of the "wealthy foreigner," a lively issue in all of Eastern Europe, was also a factor in Hungary. As elsewhere, Jews were largely concentrated in the commercial classes. Even though the Jewish population was small and better assimilated than in Poland or Romania, the traditional anti-Semitism of the villages had been heightened by the Béla Kun affair and became even more acute in the depression.

The Hungarian working class was comparable in size to that of Poland, but it was potentially much more powerful since it was so heavily concentrated in Budapest (nearly 60 percent of the national total was there). At any given time, however, a large number of these were unemployed, a situation made worse by the continual influx into the urban areas of starving peasants who were willing to work for the lowest wages that would permit survival. Despite the rapid industrialization of the latter part of the nineteenth century, the Hungarian half of the Austro-Hungarian Empire had never accepted the development of the trade union movement as had the Austrians. This weak tradition, coupled with right-wing reaction to the Bela Kun revolution, left the working class in a very poor situation. The government resisted both unionization and social reform. Only at the very end of the interwar period were laws requiring an eight-hour day and a minimum wage enacted. The impact of these was slight, however. Generally the standard of living of workers (and of peasants) in the interwar period never attained the prewar level.[6]

The advent of the depression threatened to knock the Hungarian economy flat. When foreign banks began calling in their loans in the summer of 1931, the entire Hungarian National Bank's reserve of cash and precious metals disappeared within a few weeks. In order to avoid national bankruptcy the government in Budapest was again forced to submit to foreign supervision of national finances. A period of severe austerity and declining economic activity followed. It was only the economic links forged by the Nazis (the clearing agreements; see above) that served to effect a revival of the economy.

Hungarian politics were far more placid than one would expect after reading this survey of economic problems. There were far fewer changes of leadership in Hungary than in any other East European country. The reason for this is to be found in the unwaveringly authoritarian character of Horthy's regime. Since Hungary was a defeated nation subject to the authority of the former allies, Horthy, as commander of the only military force in the nation, was initially under intense pressure to sanction a broadly democratic governmental structure. It was impossible for him to ignore these demands entirely, but he could and did take advantage of the fact that the Allies were both physically remote and unsophisticated in their knowledge of Hungarian political dynamics. It was clear to Horthy that he need only pretend to comply until the leaders in Paris, London, and Washington lost interest and turned their attention to competing problems that were closer to home.

Horthy and his backers agreed to appoint a provisional government that included representatives of peasant and socialist parties and to hold free and open elections (i.e., with a secret ballot and a broad suffrage). This was done in January of 1920. The result was a victory for the agrarians, known as the Smallholders Party, who took some 44 percent of the seats in parliament and had the possibility of combining with left-wing parties to form a majority. In fact, however, the Smallholders were like most peasant parties in that they were radical only on the issue of land reform and related agrarian problems, and were inclined to be very conservative on most other matters. Further, a coalition with even the tamest element of the left was unattractive so soon after the Béla Kun affair.

The elections of 1920 thus produced a conservative result. Though the right wing was itself split badly between the traditionalists (in turn sharply divided on the issue of whether the Habsburgs were still the royal family) and the proto-fascist right radicals, it was easy to produce agreement on some key matters. All legal actions taken by the Károlyi and Kun governments were revoked (this had the emotional advantage of disavowing, albeit symbolically, the armistice which was signed by Károlyi), and Horthy was elected as regent with essentially all of the powers of the king. The problem of who was king was put aside for the moment. Hungary thus finally entered the interwar period.

The first government leader of interwar Hungary was Count Bethlen, a Transylvanian nobleman. Bethlen was an exceptionally shrewd politician who was able to weave the threads of Hungary's political history with those of its economic present to form a mildly authoritarian and totally conservative regime. Indeed, Bethlen's only serious challenges came from fellow members of the right. Hungary had no broadly democratic tradition. In 1910 only 8 percent of the population could vote. Illiteracy, particularly among the agricultural population, was still widespread. To the extent that there was a real public opinion, it was focused on the "national" question (i.e., revision of the frontiers). Finally, the great mass of the people still retained a tradition of obeisance to their social superiors—the aristocrats.

In July of 1920, Bethlen merged the Smallholders with the Christian Union Party (a rightist coalition) to form the Government Party. The two parties compromised by agreeing to put aside key interests: the Smallholders agreed to postpone the question of land reform and the Christian Union shelved a Habsburg restoration. This exchange cheated the Smallholders since the Allies would not in any case have permitted the heir apparent, Charles of Habsburg, to return to the country (he actually tried to retake the throne twice in 1921, but was repulsed by the combined hostility of Horthy and the Allies). The final step in preventing political change in Hungary occurred in March of 1922, when Bethlen issued a decree abolishing the secret ballot in the countryside (it continued to exist in the larger towns) and ending the experiment in a broad (in Hungarian terms at least) suffrage. Though the Smallholders Party did not represent the poorer peasants, it was the only party that contemplated significant alterations in landholding and consequently in the social, economic, and political structure of the country. Open voting made it impossible for radicals within the party to develop a power base and thus to force a reopening of the issue of land reform.

With the agrarians under control and the socialists legally crippled

and physically afraid, the only political contests that remained were between factions of the right. Though these struggles were remarkably
incoherent and frequently pointless (Horthy became ever more powerful
and was ultimately always successful about having his own way), they
do reveal some interesting facets of Hungarian and East European society.

The radical right in Hungary was defined by ultranationalism, rejection of the tradition of aristocratic stewardship of the affairs of state,
and anti-Semitism. The ultranationalism was hardly unusual, but the
radical right manifested a particularly implacable attitude to Trianon
Hungary. The cry of "Nem, nem, soha!" ("No, no, never!"—will we
recognize the loss of our territory), was above all that of the radical right.
This might have been relatively harmless, except that it soon found an
outlet in foreign affairs. The old-line conservatives, who were no less
revisionist than the radicals, found themselves impelled to jettison their
cautious approach to foreign involvement in favor of such radical policies
as close ties to fascist Italy and, later, economic and then political involvement with Nazi Germany.

The radical right, whose leaders were largely lesser (i.e., poor) gentry
or members of the middle class (including especially current or former
military officers) felt that the old-line aristocrats should take the blame
for the sorry state of contemporary Hungary. Their attacks were motivated by a blend of genuine criticism, economic and social jealousy, and
political ambition. The rejection of the noble tradition had heavy going
at first, but it had roots stretching back to the time of Kossuth and
developed broad appeal as the nation's economic situation took its final
turn for the worse.

The role of anti-Semitism and particularly the underlying reasons
for it is a complex and controversial issue.[7] As stated earlier, anti-Semitism
in Eastern Europe cannot be dismissed as either the outgrowth of peasant
superstition or the desire to find scapegoats for social, political, and
economic difficulties. These factors were present, of course, but taken
alone cannot explain the ferocious hatred of Jews. Especially important
in viewing anti-Semitism at this time was its middle-class component.
Hungarian aristocrats and peasants were largely indifferent to the role
of the Jews, most of whom were well assimilated culturally and no less
genuine patriots than other Hungarians with whom they came into daily
contact (here there is a contrast with Poland and Romania). The Béla
Kun affair did tend to equate the Jews with Soviet Communism in the
public mind, but this was not a universally damaging phenomenon: the
aristocrats knew that the Jewish merchants and industrialists were not

communists, and the peasants, at the other extreme, had a lingering sympathy for those who had promised to break up the large estates and give them land.

What then was the concern of the middle classes? Essentially it was competition. Hungary started the interwar period with a greater number of highly educated people than it needed, and in the course of two decades, both the absolute number of such people, and the rate at which they were unemployed, grew rapidly. Industrial and commercial development was very slow, and in any case employed relatively few of the people graduating from secondary and higher educational institutions. This might have been different if more graduates had been trained in scientific, technical, and managerial programs. But in Hungary, as in most of Eastern Europe, higher education was heavily oriented toward the humanities and law (more in the philosophical than the applied sense).[8] Everyone aspired to a cultured, genteel way of life (aping the aristocracy, of course); it was not fashionable to think of education as something acquired for practical reasons. When a university graduate went to a business to look for a job, he usually found that if there were openings, he was either not trained for them or not willing to accept them for fear of loss of prestige. What he really wanted to be was a leisured executive, burdened more with social obligation than business decisions. When such positions were unavailable, the frustrated applicant was likely to blame his unemployment on the discriminatory attitude of a Jewish owner.

A similar scenario obtained in the case of the civil service. Government bureaucracies were a popular refuge for highly educated people who wished employment but not work. Hungarian university graduates often submitted applications only to find the ranks of officialdom so hopelessly overinflated as to permit no increase, and found it convenient to blame their failure on those Jews (relatively few in number) who, owing to a traditional belief in the value of education, had gotten there first. The frustrated Hungarian aspirants, who would rather live in Budapest on handouts from friends and relatives than take a job in the provinces or learn a practical, perhaps even a manual, profession, formed the core of right wing anti-Semitic thinking. It is a tragic irony that the most educated sector of the population was most inclined to find emotional hatred the best substitute for logic and reason.

Right radical thinking grew in strength throughout the 1920s, but it did not reach the stage of challenging for political control until the worst effects of the depression began to be felt in 1930–31. Until then, Horthy, Bethlen, and the old-line aristocratic elite had had little difficulty in controlling affairs. But Bethlen resigned in the teeth of the economic storm (August, 1931), and his aristocratic successor could not bring calm. The right radicals strengthened their bid for power by adopting the cause of land reform as their own; this was a potentially powerful weapon, which at the very least terrorized the great landowners. In this charged atmosphere Horthy yielded and appointed the most prominent right radical leader, Gyula Gömbös, as head of government (October, 1932).

Gömbös' background can be summarized by pointing out that he was an early associate of Hitler. But where Hitler had a powerful, spell-binding personality and a methodically constructed organization, Gömbös was merely the best known leader of a rabble of highly emotional but incoherent and loosely allied movements. Moreover, Horthy, both in his office and in his person, was a far more formidable rival than Hitler ever faced. Gömbös drew much popular support (he led the government party to a solid electoral victory in 1935, carrying even those areas where there was a secret ballot), but he also was forced by Horthy to drop his plans for anti-Semitic legislation and for land reform. When Gömbös died in 1936, Horthy was sufficiently frightened by the experiment in fascism to return to aristocratic leadership.

The trend to the radical right was not reversed, however. The new aristocratic leaders were not strong, but even if they had been, it seems most unlikely that they could have arrested the trend. Indeed, it is probable that Gömbös' government itself was relatively unimportant in Hungary's slide toward fascism. By 1936, Hungary was snared in the economic and diplomatic traps set by Nazi Germany. Though the actual capture began late and took time, the social and economic precondition for Hungary's path had been set a decade and a half earlier. Hungary's freedom to choose a new direction was in doubt as early as 1930.

Thus, although Gömbös' successors were all conservative aristocrats who were fundamentally hostile to the right radicals and the gangs who supported them, it was during their governments that serious anti-Semitic legislation was passed and put into effect.[9] Although the attack on the Jews was essentially non-violent, it is significant that the concerns of the educated radicals were addressed first and most thoroughly. Consequently, the number of positions in universities open to Jews—either as students or faculty—was severely limited. Similar restrictions were placed on Jews in the civil service, though this was more of a gesture to the right radicals who worked there than it was a genuine blow: since the white terror of 1920, few Jews had wished to take the risk of public service. By 1938 and 1939, far more serious measures were adopted. These new laws mandated a sharp cutback in the number of Jews who could legally practice the "free professions," such as law, medicine, architecture, and engineering. Finally, the number of businesses that could be owned by Jews as well as the number of Jews who could be employed in business was set at an extremely low figure. Jews were also effectively barred from all areas of actual or potential cultural and political influence such as book publishing, the communications media and the theatre.

Far more significant than the anti-Semitic laws was the manner in which they were enforced. Traditionally, Hungarians had always discriminated against those whose language and culture was not exclusively Magyar; thus a Yiddish-speaking Jew, whose orthodox beliefs demanded an orientation toward Hebrew religious culture, could expect trouble (so, of course, could a Romanian, a Slovak, or even a German whose allegiance was elsewhere). On the other hand, a culturally assimilated Jew, who spoke fluent Hungarian and who was schooled in Magyar history, philosophy, and literature could expect to lead a normal life if he did not flaunt his religion (to attend synagogue would not be a problem: to leave work or close a business on a religious holiday would). Since the great majority of Hungarian Jews were in this latter category, they had long been able to escape the more routine elements of anti-Semitism (they were affected, of course, by outbursts such as the white terror). This tolerance was ended by 1939. In the laws of that year Jewishness was defined as the religion of a person's grandparents, and even conversions to Christianity dating from as long as two decades earlier were declared invalid. At the onset of the war, Hungarian Jewry was limited and watched. Though Jews were not yet the victims of mass imprisonment, it goes without saying that Hungarian Jews could not expect justice in their native land.

Although the origins of Magyar anti-Semitism are native to the Hungarian soil, the rapid progress of legal anti-Semitism in the late 1930s is testimony to the enormous power of Nazi Germany at that time. In the space of a few years Hitler was able to synchronize Hungary's domestic as well as her foreign policies with those of his regime. The explanation of Nazi influence is far less complicated than an understanding of a phenomenon such as anti-Semitism. Hungary's attitude toward the peace settlement of 1919 prepared her for entanglement in the arms of the swastika.

11

Interwar Romania

THE CASUAL OBSERVER of the East European situation in 1919 would doubtless have thought Romania the most fortunate of the states of the region. This was a nation with both tradition and a continuing governmental structure (one of only three in the region), and most important of all, it was the only state that was territorially satiated. "Greater Romania" was more than double the size of its predecessor of 1914; it had no serious claim on any of its neighbors' territory. This was also a land known to be well endowed in natural resources. In addition to the traditional mineral reserves of the Carpathians and of the Western Mountains of Transylvania, two elements of obvious importance for the future were present in abundance: oil, and water power for the making of electricity. Finally, the lowlands had a history of producing grain for export. To our casual observer, Romania's most serious problem would have been the considerable war damage.

This superficial picture is an extremely inaccurate one. Upon close analysis, most of the things that appeared to be Romania's greatest benefits were at the same time the sources of potentially fatal weaknesses. The territorial settlement was the most obvious case. Though Romania did not claim any of her neighbors' land, three of the five did not return the favor—Bulgaria, Hungary and the Soviet Union; indeed the latter two were unrelentingly hostile and strove ceaselessly to chop Romania down by at least half. Thus, a "have" nation was no more secure than a "have not"; the issue of maintaining national integrity was for Romania every bit as crucial a concern as was irredentism for Hungary or Bulgaria. And, just as in the revisionist states, the issue of national frontiers had sufficient power to warp the entire fabric of domestic political, social, and economic life.

Romania's territorial success had another dark side. The prewar nation was relatively homogenous ethnically, but "Greater Romania" was a state with large, vocal, and powerful minorities. Before 1914, Romania had had only one minority, the Jews, and a comparatively small one at that. Even so, the government had not coped well; no mutually acceptable resolution has been achieved. The new situation, however, was far more serious. Not only had the number of non–Romanian-speaking Jews increased dramatically, but also an enormous number of extremely hostile Hungarians and Germans were now forcibly given the status of Romanian citizens. The problem of the minorities contributed to the seemingly permanent enervation of the country's many interwar governments.

Romania even had great difficulty in assimilating the millions of ethnic Romanians residing in the newly acquired territories. The problems were many, but different cultural backgrounds contributed to what emerged as a rather bitter power struggle. Essentially, the "new" Romanians demanded significant political, social, and economic changes from a governing elite which was drawn from the oligarchy of the Regat (the term for the lands of prewar Romania). The conflict of "old" and "new" Romanians helped to render the already fragmented political system into something that frequently resembled dust. Finally, the economic picture was rosy only in potential; in actual achievement both the international situation and the continuing domestic disagreements served to prevent significant progress. Again, since an understanding of the economy is fundamental to the overall picture, it is in this area that the first detailed discussion is made.

Romania was the East European leader in many areas of economic backwardness. At the beginning of the interwar period some 72 percent of the population was dependent on agriculture. Of the entire population, nearly one-quarter was considered to be "surplus"—that is, unnecessary if reasonable levels of productivity could be achieved (see above).[1] This meant that some three million people were economically redundant. At the same time, the Romanian birth-rate was close to the highest in Europe—more than 50 percent higher than that of even an undeveloped country such as Greece. Another statistic also provides insight into agriculture: at the beginning of the interwar period there was only one tractor (or other mechanical tilling or harvesting device) for every 2,500 Romanians employed in agriculture.[2] A comparable figure for the United States was fifty times greater.

Land distribution—better, lack of distribution—was an especially serious problem in Romania. The Regat had a tradition of large estates worked by landless or dwarfholding peasants. The situation in the newly acquired provinces of Transylvania and Bessarabia was similar but worse. The words "land reform" were shouted rather than whispered by the angry peasants, and even the old guard politicians in Bucharest, remembering the rebellion of 1907, knew that something had to be done. After much political maneuvering (see below) a land reform law was passed in July of 1921. In terms of both total land distributed and percentage of land distributed, this was the largest reform in Eastern Europe (nearly 30 percent of agricultural land was distributed in Romania—the next highest, Czechoslovakia, was 14 percent).

The net result was a political rather than an economic victory, however. Slaking the peasants' thirst for land calmed the domestic political environment, which had been increasingly explosive and in which communist agitators had begun to have some success. But the increased incentives to labor were offset by decreased efficiency. After reform, 75 percent of the holdings were less than five hectares. In most of Romania this was too little to feed the peasant proprietors. And in the more fertile regions, tradition diminished potential: the peasants planted the same cereal crops that they had grown for their landlords. Though logically suited for large-scale cultivation (even when poorly managed) cereals do not benefit even in theory from intensive agriculture; in practice, the fact that most peasants had only occasional access to draught animals (much less to machinery) meant that actual productivity was much lower than it had been before. The Romanian peasants also suffered from the typical problems of East European peasants: poor access to markets, scarce credit, and limited technical training and advice.

Romania did have some farms of medium size, principally in the fertile Banat, which were highly efficient and productive. But, as elsewhere in Eastern Europe, these farmers' numbers were few and their influence was quite limited. Large estates were not eliminated by the land reform. Particularly in the Regat, the great families held on to the rest of their lands. Even after reform, some 28 percent of the land was held by only four-tenths of one percent of the landowners. That only half of this land was cultivated indicates that the *boiars* (noblemen) held on to much of the forest land and continued to control the supply of firewood desperately needed by the peasants. Overall, agriculture, which should have been a strength of the Romanian economy, was even weaker than before. The export of some of the principal products, corn and wheat, was still possible, but even in the best of times vastly more efficient producers as far away as the United States undercut the price. The further relative decline in the value of agricultural products brought about by the depression made the produce of the Danubian plains all but worthless for export.

Romanian industry was comparatively strong because of the country's natural resource base. Oil was the most important of these resources, but one must remember that its value as measured against that of other products was much lower in 1920–1940 than has been the case since 1973. Even so, the price of oil, and even more its strategic value, increased sharply during the two decades of the interwar period. By 1940, Romania was far and away Europe's leading oil producer (excluding the USSR), and that factor alone made her an important part of the world economy.

Much Romanian industry centered on the production of raw materials (timber, coal, various metals and minerals) which, like oil, were mainly exported. Foreign investment in industry was very heavy both in direct ownership and in ownership of banks that in turn controlled industries. In addition, Romanian-owned corporations were often dependent on foreign corporations which controlled world markets in the relevant areas. Overall, the participation of foreigners in the domestic economy was higher in Romania than anywhere else in Eastern Europe; just before World War I it was estimated that some 80 percent of Romanian industry was owned by foreigners, and this incredible figure is thought to be significantly lower than that of a decade earlier.[3]

Particularly in the 1920s and early 1930s, Romanian governments strove to limit direct foreign participation in industry, emphasizing instead the use of foreign loans to the government as a source of capital. There was some limited success from this strategy, particularly in the highly visible and strategic oil industry, where the role of American, British, French, and Dutch corporations, though still dominant, was reduced somewhat. Even so, in 1931 it is estimated that 80 percent of industrial stocks were still held by foreigners and that per capita foreign debt was among the highest in Eastern Europe; 28 percent of exports at that time were needed just to pay off the interest on the debt.[4] Romania had used the foreign loans in part to stabilize the inflation which, as elsewhere in Eastern Europe, hit the country in waves in the 1920s.

Despite all of this, the Romanian economy did grow throughout the interwar period. The index of manufacturing output in 1938 was nearly 80 percent greater than that of 1913.[5] But also by 1938 Germany supplied 56 percent of Romania's imports and took 43 percent of her exports.[6] Though Germany did not have the leverage in Romania that she had in Bulgaria, Hungary, and Yugoslovia, her position in the economy was very strong, and some of Romania's overall economic recovery must be attributed to the artificial stimulation of Nazi rearmament.

In social structure Romania was very similar to Poland and Hungary, but more like the latter in that aristocrats had a key political role;

large landowners were still very wealthy even after land reform. There were some important regional differences in class structure in that the landowners and aristocrats in Transylvania and Bessarabia had been almost entirely non-Romanian and had either been dispossessed or fled the country or most likely both. Thus, the aristocratic, large landowner perspective was essentially only that of the Regat.

The middle class was quite small. The entire nation had a thin veneer of intelligentsia, which, if Romanian, was generally oriented toward things French (and if Magyar or German toward the respective national cultures). Merchants and small businessmen were overwhelmingly foreign—Jews (Yiddish or Ukrainian speakers), Hungarians, Germans, Greeks, and Bulgarians. Because of the Ottoman system, trade in the Regat had been largely dominated by foreigners for centuries, while in the newly acquired provinces Romanians had previously suffered official discrimination to the point of exclusion. There was very little in the way of a rural middle class; as in most modern societies, professionals preferred the cities.[7]

The peasants, who comprised at least three-quarters of the population, were extremely poor. Most worked entirely for their own subsistence; there was very little in the way of market production from peasant holdings. The diet of the peasants was generally insufficient, lacking especially in protein. The relatively high concentration of industry in Bucharest and a few other cities meant that peasants looking for supplemental income generally had to leave the land entirely rather than commute. Most did this only from necessity, for the ties to the land, not least the newly acquired parcels, were extremely strong. The relatively large distribution of land in Romania seems to have hurt in another way: although Romania's birthrate in the interwar period declined by about 18 percent, this decrease was less significant than that of nearly all other East European countries (Poland, 29 percent; Czechoslovakia, 40 percent; Hungary, 32 percent; Bulgaria, 38 percent). On the eve of the war, only Albania in Eastern Europe had a higher birth rate than Romania.[8]

The Romanian working class was small but obviously growing. The concentration of industry in Bucharest gave that city a relatively large worker population and made it the center of class-related social, economic, and political activity.

The composition of Romania's population was complex. Official statistics, which were probably skewed but not grossly so, claimed as Romanian only 71 percent of the population. The largest minority (and probably the most undercounted) was the Hungarian at 9 percent, followed by Ukrainians and Russians at 6 percent combined, Germans at

4 percent, Jews also at 4 percent, and Bulgarians and Gypsies each at 2 percent (leaving 2 percent of "other"). The Hungarians and Germans were very hostile to Romanian rule. Both had a tradition of arrogant behavior toward the Romanians and, naturally, conceit was complemented by a real fear of what might happen when the oppressed had the chance to become the oppressors. In practical terms, of course, the superior economic and hence educational position of the Hungarians and Germans made them different in nearly every way from their largely peasant Romanian neighbors in Transylvania (there were many Hungarian and some German peasants, however).

Romanian behavior toward these two minorities was mixed. The land reform discriminated directly against foreign owners and, as stated earlier, dispossessed most of them almost entirely and with comparatively trivial compensation. Much of this was in violation of the clauses in the peace treaties that protected minorities, and the Romanian laws led to endless wrangling in the World Court and a campaign of academic polemics between Hungary and Romania that had the interesting side effect of providing public libraries in many western countries with their first volumes on Transylvania—provided free by the respective governments. Though the plight of the cultured count who had lost his ancestral estate had a certain romantic appeal, especially in Britain and France, the practical effect of all the legal, diplomatic, and propagandistic excitement was almost nil. The Romanians had the land, they believed they had a right to it, and they refused to yield it or to pay what they considered exorbitant compensation (in western currency) to people they saw as particularly flagrant former oppressors of the Romanian nationality.

The Romanians were also quite aggressive in eliminating any Magyar-German role in state administration. The new Romania, like the old, was a highly centralized state with virtually all power flowing from Bucharest. Local officials were all thus centrally appointed, and through the simple and not unreasonable policy that such people should be fluent in the Romanian language, the bureaucracy was quickly purged of Magyar and German incumbents. Even if these or others of their nationalities were to acquire the necessary linguistic skills, it was most unlikely that they would also have the influential friends in Bucharest necessary to secure any government appointment. This factor, together with the political dynamics discussed below, meant that Magyars and Germans (indeed all minorities) had little or no voice in local, regional, or national affairs.

The Romanian policy in cultural affairs was very different. Where the Hungarian governments had acted consistently and aggressively to suppress minority culture, and the Romanian especially, the Romanians (like the Czechs) chose to turn the other cheek and permit the broad linguistic and cultural rights which they themselves had sought earlier. Thus, a minority school system was established to the extent that only where Hungarians and Germans were a small minority were they constrained to attend Romanian schools. Broad educational rights were implemented by the freedom to speak, publish, or perform in any language. Specified minority languages could be used in a wide range of governmental business, including judicial proceedings. Though it would be foolish to suggest that the laws were uniformly applied with no prejudice, the fact is that the Hungarians, in pressing for a greater political role, took for granted the exercise of an educational and cultural license which they had never allowed the Romanians.

Minorities other than Hungarians and Germans were less well treated, in part because of their smaller numbers and in part because they had little or no support from outside Romania. The status of the Jews was a special concern. Though only 4 percent of the overall population, they were 15–20 percent in the eastern part of the country and more than 50 percent of many large towns including the provincial capitals of Iaşi and Chişinău. Nationally, Jews owned some 20 percent of all factories and comprised a similar percentage of traders. Nearly three-fourths of all artisans—watchmakers, bookbinders, and tinsmiths—were Jews, and, most important, most of the small moneylenders and tavernkeepers of the eastern countryside were Jews.[9] Romanian Jews were nearly all refugees from Russia who settled in compact groups. Consequently, few spoke more than rudimentary Romanian or had any knowledge of or interest in Romanian history or culture. The situation was similar to that of Poland, except that Polish Jewry included a larger number of individuals who could function in both societies and who could thus hlep to improve communications. Given these facts about Romanian Jewry, it is not surprising that interwar Romania was plagued with virulent anti-Semitism. It was an important factor, though not necessarily a decisive one, in the rise of Romanian fascism.

Education in interwar Romania provided an accurate reflection of the chaos of the nation's society and economy. The educational system of Greater Romania developed from a weak and uneven base. In the Regat the educational heritage was both brilliant and dismal. It was brilliant because the Romanians had a century-old tradition of sending young men to the finest universities of Europe; as a consequence, the leaders of Romanian society were very much in the mainstream of European intellectual life. But the inheritance was also dismal because the educated were a tiny elite. The great mass of the peasantry was practically untouched by even the most basic training. The situation in Transylvania was significantly better, for there the national struggle had developed widespread literacy; secondary and higher education, though more difficult of access because of Magyar discrimination, was nevertheless achieved by a surprisingly large number. Bessarabia was at the other extreme. The miserable educational system of the tsarist empire, coupled with the province's physical remoteness from the cities of Russia, left the Romanian villagers in an isolation broken only by the direct or indirect consequences of war.

Officially, illiteracy at the beginning of the interwar period stood at 45 percent; the actual figure was probably much higher. Four years of elementary school were mandated by law, but it is estimated that fewer than three-quarters of the children actually went to school. The system, like those in most of Europe, was designed to make a very early selection between those children who would go beyond the minimum and those who would not. A special preparatory school for secondary education took children at about the age of seven (typically in their second year of school). Though perhaps more efficient given the limited resources available, such a strategy effectively blocked the way for the children of peasants, who had virtually no opportunity to overcome the lack of parental reinforcement. In fact, only about 6 percent of elementary school students continued their education.

The secondary schools of Romania were organized on the prevailing French pattern. The emphasis was on the liberal arts, the curriculum was rigorous and inflexible, and those who actually earned the baccalaureate degree were very well educated. The quality of the training would compare far more directly with a bachelor's degree from a typical contemporary American university than to an American high school degree. Higher education was also of good quality. There were four universities, two polytechnical institutes, and a number of small, highly specialized institutes. Access to post-secondary education was also comparatively high. The number of Romanian students in higher education as a percentage of the population was greater than that of Czechoslovakia and approximated that of Germany.[10] Unfortunately, as in Hungary, most university students studied abstract subjects and saw their learning as a vehicle to remaining aloof from the problems of society. Romania's intellectual tradition flourished even as her political, social, and economic fabric disintegrated.

Even by East European measures, interwar Romanian politics were tumultuous and chaotic. This seems somewhat surprising in view of the fact that the essential political structure of the nation was unaltered by the war or its aftermath, and that the long-dominant Liberal Party continued in power. Yet the appearance of stability was an illusion. The prewar Romanian constitution gave power to the king and to the propertied classes; the situation was further limited by the fact that the same dynamic individual was king from 1866 to 1916, and that the two political parties (Liberals and Conservatives), each of which had few strong leaders of its own, could deal on a fairly personal level with the monarch. Prewar Romania was an oligarchy.

The structure survived the war, but the personalities either did not or disappeared soon after. And with firm hands gone from the rudder, the ever stronger currents from below suddenly made themselves felt. The ship of state was never really fully stable until it succumbed to the distant but nonetheless overwhelming power first of Hitler and then of Stalin.

Carol I died in 1916 after a half century of stewardship. That his legacy was one of improvisation rather than stability was quickly apparent. His successor, Ferdinand, was much less able to deal effectively with the strong political personalities around him. He was also quickly constrained to compromises and concessions that had been repeatedly rejected during his uncle's lifetime. In April of 1917, Ferdinand told the peasants of the Romanian army, reeling from German blows from the west and dangerously infected with the virus of Bolshevism from the east, that victory would make them owners of the soil they tilled. A few months after this, the king proclaimed that universal male suffrage would replace the old, property-based electoral system.

The immediate consequence of these measures was to eliminate the Conservative Party as an important factor in politics. The demise of the Conservatives did not mean that the great landowners who formed its core were suddenly impoverished or without sufficient support to secure election to parliament. In fact, they retained much of their wealth and, since election results were still easily manipulated, they could continue to have access to power. Rather, the disappearance of the Conservatives was a consequence of the disappearance of their political raison d'être. Once the two major principles against which the Conservatives had struggled with such longstanding passion had been cemented into the political edifice, the Conservatives lacked the great issues upon which political parties are usually based.

If the Conservatives had faded into a merger with the Liberals, a fairly strong coalition might have resulted. In the postwar political spectrum, the Liberals were clearly the conservatives. But three-quarters of a century of political struggle, which had on occasion resulted in the (brief) imprisonment of losers and even included a mysterious assassination, made reconciliation impossible. The Liberals had to face the new challenges without allies. Although they staggered on for a decade, they too were unable to cope with the new situation.

The Romanian Liberal Party (also called the National-Liberal) was born in the crisis of 1848, and its entire history bore the stamp of that tumultuous year. The party had three pillars: radical nationalism; brilliant, charismatic leaders; and an interest in commercial-industrial development that in the nineteenth century defined the word "liberal." The radical nationalism of Romanian public opinion had always been useful to the party, though it must be added that the Liberals were largely responsible for creating this feeling in the first place. The brilliance of the leaders, particularly the famous Brătianu family, was double-edged. On the one hand they were skilled, passionate orators who could raise the Bucharest mob to support them in a crisis; on the other hand, they were sophisticated, western-trained intellectuals who captivated the king. The final interest of the Liberals, that of economic modernization, was ironic in that the sons of aristocratic landowners formed a party to support the interests of a bourgeoisie which did not exist, but which they wished to create.

By the end of World War I there was, of course, a Romanian middle class, and the Liberals now had a real constituency in the merchants and industrialists whose prosperity they had fostered. But even as this political pillar grew strong, the Liberals, like the Conservatives, lost two others in the postwar years. First, the nationalism of the past, though not exactly passé, was no longer the same. The crowning success of Ionel Brătianu in making possible the birth of Greater Romania was also a defeat because irredentism, long the rallying cry of the Liberals, was now no longer an issue. And finally, Ionel Brătinau, though he lived until 1927, was a weaker figure because he dealt with a weaker king. Ferdinand was manipulable but not masterful. A bargain struck with him could be quickly undone by even a minor crisis; in this he was utterly unlike the tenacious Carol.

Two new parties rushed into the void created by the collapse of the Conservatives and the weakening of the Liberals. One was the Peasant Party—the first of that type to be successful in Romania after many false starts. Led by Ion Mihalache, the Peasant Party was organized on the single issue of land reform, and was based overwhelmingly in the Regat. The king's two major wartime decrees helped and hurt this party. The declaration of universal manhood suffrage gave the masses a real vote for the first time and was essential to the political viability of the Peasant

Party. But the king's declaration of land reform deprived the peasant leaders of the opportunity to claim credit for forcing the great change. Mihalache was thus forced to assume the role of administrator rather than revolutionary. The astute agrarian specialist was well suited for this role, but the diminished passion of his political mission also diminished the importance of his party.

The peasants of the Regat were not the only unhappy people in Greater Romania. The peasants of the newly acquired provinces of Bessarabia and Transylvania were equally concerned about land reform. They did not join the Peasant Party, however, because they naturally followed the lead of intellectuals from their own regions who, in addition to the land reform issue, were also struggling for a measure of local autonomy. Both Bessarabia and Transylvania had been outlying provinces of great empires, and the Romanian leaders in these provinces had developed, in addition to a fierce nationalism, a hostility to the inefficiency and insensitivity of the remote central administration which always seems to characterize provincial politiccs. The shifting of political boundaries resolved the nationality problem, but it in many ways exacerbated the administrative one. A number of factors came together in this case. One was certainly the fact that the Romanian administration, though less remote and obviously more sensitive to linguistic-national issues, was, in the case of Transylvania, even less efficient and far more corrupt. While the overwhelmingly peasant society of Bessarabia accepted the transition with the passive, minimal cooperation accorded the oppressors of the past, the reaction in Transylvania was a very different matter.

The Romanians of Transylvania had developed, during centuries of struggle with Hungarian and German oppressors, an accomplished intelligentsia of their own. These men were educated in the finest universities of Western Europe and had been trained in one of the toughest political schools in history: imperial Hungary. The fact that they had not been able to establish political parties in the usual way but had been forced instead to work partly underground meant that their organizational and tactical skills were finely honed. When they began to operate in the unstable climate of Greater Romania, they were formidable competitors to the existing power structure. Their party, which was organized in Transylvania and which quickly spread to Bessarabia, was called the National Party (a name obviously drawn from prewar experiences). Its leaders were Iuliu Maniu and Alexandru Vaida-Voievod, both veterans of the long struggle with the Hungarians.

The principal issues that confronted postwar Romania were very similar to those confronting the other nations of Eastern Europe. First, of course, was land reform. It was one thing to declare that it would be done ("reform" had been proclaimed on at least one occasion in the past), it was quite another to carry it out in a way that would assauage the anger of the peasantry. Linked to land reform was the overall question of economic strategy: should an overwhelmingly peasant, agrarian country pursue an approach that maximized the improvement of agriculture and thus at least in the short run the lives of most of its people? Or should it move aggressively to transform the country into a modern industrial state, even if that meant considerable suffering in the short term? And then there was the question, vital in all East European countries except Hungary, of where the locus of power should be: should decisions be made by bureaucrats in the capital or by their analogs in the provinces? Finally, the issue of national security loomed as large as elsewhere; Romania lived in a hostile geographic environment.

Romania got off to a strange start in her interwar political development. Ionel Brătianu, who like his father had a penchant for strategic retreat, resigned the premiership immediately after the negotiation of the peace treaties. He did this partly to maximize his glory and partly to shift the burden for determining the nature of the land reform to someone else. Clearly, he hoped that he could return as a hero untouched by the mud that was about to be slung in all directions. But the strategy backfired. The unthinkable occurred when the caretaker government appointed by Ferdinand conducted elections (1919) that were actually honest. The result was a sweeping victory for the Peasant and National parties who promptly formed a coalition and forced Ferdinand to name Vaida-Voievod as premier.

The new government was in an awkward position. Though it had the support of the country, it faced the implacable opposition of the king and the bureaucuracy (overwhelmingly composed of Liberal appointees). Moreover, the two parties had little experience in working with each other, and the Peasant Party in particular lacked the infrastructure necessary for effective manipulation of their constituency (more simply put: they were not yet able to produce an army of angry peasants when needed on crucial occasions). Nevertheless, the National-Peasant coalition made preparations to make dramatic changes, particularly in effecting a truly radical land reform. This was too much for Ferdinand, who dismissesd the government and parliament and appointed a caretaker government to hold new elections. Since in Romania holding an election could and usually did mean managing one, the results in 1920 completely reversed those of 1919. The Liberals dominated, but Brătianu was content to let the caretaker premier, the popular General Averescu, remain in office.

Thus it was Averescu's government which was charged with making land reform a reality. The inevitable compromise (1921) fell far short of the peasant's expectations but was still more thorough than many of the conservative elements had wished. However, Brătianu's hopes that by standing aside he could escape blame for the land reform and the suppression of the inevitable peasant protests (there was also a brief general strike in October of 1920) were dashed. The National-Peasant leaders made a point of identifying him as the *éminence grise*, the evil genius who was principally responsible for their troubles. Ferdinand remained personally popular, but when Brătianu stepped back into the driver's seat in 1922, he operated from a power base which rested precariously on the shoulders of the king and the bureaucracy.

Despite the lack of mass support, Brătianu and the Liberals moved aggressively to cast Greater Romania irretrievably into the Liberal mold. Economic policy was clear cut. High tariffs were made even higher to protect native industry, even though this meant that the peasants paid more for manufactured goods. Those who produced agricultural products for export were hit doubly hard: retaliatory tariffs barred access to many markets and, even more damaging, the government took the highly unusual step of levying export taxes as a means of generating revenue. The squeeze in the countryside forced many peasants to abandon the land and move to the cities where they supplied cheap labor for industry. The government also made every effort to expand the availability of capital for the manufacturing sector. The effort to limit the direct participation of foreign capital by channeling it through loans to the government rather than to individual banks or corporations was, as noted above, only partially successful in reducing the very large amount of foreign economic control. The Liberal slogan "Prin noi înşine" (by ourselves alone) was not really achievable in its fullest meaning. Romania also had to follow the East European pattern of floating loans to stabilize the currency.

One area in which the Liberals took no chances was in the question of centralization. Taking full advantage of their influence on the king and the electoral machinery, the Liberals rammed through a new constitution in March of 1923. This document was constituted with the primary objective of reinforcing the already highly centralized governmental structure, and the principle was followed to the point of eliminating even the potential for local decision-making and authority. Not coincidentally, this move also served to hamstring the National and Peasant parties. These organizations were denied access to the local electoral victories that had the potential to develop patronage—always a crucial element for the long-term success of political parties. In fact, the attack was so blatant and so direct that it led to the merger of the opposition into a single National-Peasant Party (1926).

The diplomacy of the Liberals was what would be expected. The party's leadership, which was in any case traditionally Francophile, accepted the direct alliance with France with great enthusiasm. Similarly, the anti-Hungarian collective security of the Little Entente and the anti-Bulgarian Balkan entente were speedily negotiated. Hostility to the Soviet Union was also maintained at a fever pitch. In part this reflected the bitter debate over Bessarabia, the loss of which was never accepted by the Soviet government. But the antagonism also had a quite natural ideological foundation; the Soviet regime championed the proletariat, the Liberals the Romanian bourgeoisie. If there was a weakness to Liberal foreign policy at this time, it was that the drive to curb the power of foreign capital necessarily irritated many large and powerful western corporations, which in turn did not hesitate to communicate their displeasure to their respective governments. Since, for example, the Romanians needed the French more than the French needed them (Poland, with its frontier on Germany, was far more important to Paris), this was potentially a very serious problem.

The Liberal era of interwar Romanian history collapsed when both King Ferdinand and Ionel Brătianu died unexpectedly and within a few months of each other in 1927. Brătianu's successor was his brother, Vintilă, an accomplished and competent man who nevertheless lacked the flare for political infighting that had characterized both his father and his brother. Far more important, however, was the succession to the throne. The heir apparent, Carol, had been forced some years earlier to renounce his title and live in exile because of his decision to live openly with his mistress, Magda Lupescu, instead of his wife, Princess Helen of Greece. Accordingly, upon Ferdinand's death a Regency Council of three members was set up to exercise royal authority until Carol's son, Michael, reached the age of majority (since Michael was only six in 1927, the wait would be a long one).

The Liberals had the ear of two of the three members of the Regency Council, and if it had been the aggressive Ionel instead of the restrained Vintila Brătianu giving orders, their party might have controlled the transition. But the National-Peasants, sensing the lack of resolve at the top, organized enormous peasant demonstrations throughout the country and especially in Bucharest. Such barely controlled demonstrations provoked great fear amongst the bureaucratic elite, who realized that between them and the peasant mob there stood only a peasant army. To the pressure of the masses was added that of the Western powers, who saw

an opportunity to repay the Liberals for their hostility to foreign investment by ostentatiously refusing a large loan needed to stabilize the Romanian currency. The crisis thus became too deep for Brătianu and he
was forced to resign. The Regency Council did not have the nerve to rig
the subsequent elections in December, 1928, in which the National-
Peasants won 78 percent of the vote (a year earlier, the Liberals had won
79 percent).

The new National-Peasant government was headed by Iuliu Maniu.
It enhanced its prestige by securing the foreign loan that had eluded the
Liberals, and thus buttressed by domestic and foreign votes of confidence,
it began to dismantle the structure set up in the previous decade. Tariffs
were lowered and export taxes on agricultural products were dropped;
the restrictions on foreign investment were relaxed if not eliminated
entirely. Various steps, such as greater availability of credit and improved
access to technical training, were taken to aid the peasants. But, despite
the passionate determination of many National-Peasant representatives,
no effort was made to effect a second radical land reform. The leaders
of the party, however much they sympathized, had come to the conclusion
that a simple redistribution of land into ever smaller plots was of little
value in the short run and probably very harmful in the long run. The
government also made little progress toward decentralization. Partly this
was because the Liberals had embedded centralization into the constitution, but it also doubtless reflected a human tendency to yield authority
slowly and with great reluctance.

Maniu's government was a competent one, but it quickly ran into
serious problems. The first was the advent of the world depression—in
nearly every European country the party in power in 1929–30 was fixed
with the blame for this cataclysm. The National-Peasant leaders were
often powerless in dealing with the economy and other problems by the
fact that their party was in fact a coalition with little tradition and with
few experienced people below the very top. And while the leadership had
to cope with significant disagreements on policy (e.g., land reform) it also
had to deal with a bureaucracy (including the military elite) which ranged
from openly hostile to quietly obstructionist.

The issue that brought the National-Peasants down was not, however, any of the significant social, economic, or foreign policy issues which
they faced. Instead, it was their inability to deal with the continuing soap
opera of Carol and Magda that lost them control of the country. Carol,
bored with life in Paris, returned to Romania (in violation of his solemmn
oath) in June of 1930. Maniu, cognizant of Carol's popularity and mindful
of a public need to perceive strong leadership in times that were becoming

progressively more chaotic (fascist groups were now very much in evidence), did not resist. Carol was named king and the Regency Council abolished. But monarch and minister quickly fell into bitter conflict over Magda Lupescu. Maniu was determined that she should remain in Paris and Carol (now Carol II) as equally determined that she should be at his side. When Magda returned in October, despite Maniu's explicit and public orders, the prime minister felt he had no choice but to resign. This was a mistake, for as the historian Hugh Seton-Watson noted in a now famous comment, "Bourgeois sexual morality is probably less esteemed in Romania than anywhere else on the continent."[11]

Maniu's resignation forced new elections which were manipulated by the king's appointees. Carol was not able to build a genuinely popular political party with him as its leader, but he did have the power to prevent the growth of a united, electorally successful opposition. The National-Peasants, for example, were vulnerable because of severe internal policy differences, but their problems were exacerbated by Carol's ability to split them by appointing as ministers leaders of only certain factions or to weaken other factions by preventing their candidates from being elected. The Liberals, who had developed internal quarrels that reflected primarily differences of personality rather than policy, were similarly easy prey to the destructive power of the throne.

Thus, in the early thirties Romanian politics came to resemble those of Poland in the early twenties. Political parties proliferated, and even the smaller units were further broken down into splinters and factions. At the center of the storm stood the king, who was not strong enough to bring calm, but who was for the moment powerful enough to prevent the buffeting winds from acquiring hurricane force. In such an environment, fascist parties grew rapidly. In the 1920s the fascists had been able to draw upon only two sources of support: virulent nationalism and an unvanquished national enemy (the Jews). But the 1930s added two new elements: economic depression (which was everywhere a catalyst for radical groups), and a popular feeling that government was out of control— that a firm hand was needed. Carol, of course, aspired to be the great leader himself, and there is some evidence that he fostered political chaos in order to make direct royal authority seem the most desirable alternative.[12]

But Carol II and the fascists were not natural allies. The fascists were from petit bourgeois or peasant background and, even though many of their leaders were well educated, shared little in the way of social values with the aristocratic-bureaucratic elite of which the king was inevitably a part. Certainly, anti-Semitism was not a feeling the two groups had in common. Just as in Hungary, the elite could hardly be called pro-Jewish, and many were not above using anti-Semitism as a lesser political weapon, but they did not feel at all the sense of competition that animated so much of the intellectual anti-Semitism and they were utterly unable to comprehend the mystical prejudice that sprang from the peasantry. In the case of Carol II, the distance between king and fascists was greatly increased by the fact that Magda Lupescu was herself of partly Jewish origin.

The strongest fascist group was the Iron Guard (also known for a time as the League of the Archangel Michael), which had its origin in Moldavia where the number of Jews and the level of anti-Semitism were highest. The Iron Guard's leader was a fanatical nationalist with the almost too perfect Romanian name of Corneliu Codreanu (in fact, one of his parents was German, the other Ukrainian).[13] By the time that the Iron Guard began to push toward a national role in the early 30s, its leader had literally gotten away with murder. The success of Hitler was an important factor in enhancing public recognition of the Guard as a political force (there were at first no direct ties to the Nazis, however). A fairly unique aspect of the Iron Guard was its extreme cult of violence. In one much-publicized case, a defector from the Guard was killed in what can only be termed a ritual murder. A number of scholars believe that the Iron Guard's fascination with violence can be traced to the Russian pogroms—incidences of brutal anti-Jewish mob violence which had occurred especially frequently in that part of Russia which was now a part of Romania (Bessarabia).

Like Horthy in Hungary, Carol II chose to make a gesture toward fascism by co-opting one of their tamer sects. The Romanian version of Gömbös was Octavian Goga, a noted poet and a leader of the National Christian Party, who was named premier in December of 1937 (five years after Gömbös). Goga was not a skilled leader and his party had polled less than 10 percent in the most recent elections. Further, although the National Christians shared a position on the radical right with the Iron Guard, the two parties were more often enemies than allies. Thus, Goga, incompetent and without support, discovered too late that Carol's gesture to the fascists was to give them the rope with which to hang themselves. In February of 1938, with the nation in a state of chaos remarkable even for a people who had seen very little stability, Carol suspended the constitution and made himself dictator.

One of Carol's first moves was to suppress the Iron Guard. Though he had often provided Codreanu with covert support in the past (with the objective of using his party against other, temporarily more dangerous rivals), the king no longer intended to tolerate this frantic rabble. In a rapid stroke the party was outlawed and its leaders arrested. Codreanu was "shot while trying to escape." Carol formed a new political party, the Front of National Renaissance, which rapidly became the only vehicle for the small amount of political expression that occurred in the nation. Carol was not genuinely popular, however, and the elimination of the superstructure of the Iron Guard hardly affected the right radical sentiment of which it was the fruit.

Interwar Romania was different from nearly all of her East European neighbors in that she pursued, for nearly half of the period, a fairly coherent program designed to effect both rapid modernization and economic independence. The significant economic growth of the country in that very difficult time suggests that this strategy was not without some success. But in the long run the approach failed because the power base of its proponents, the Liberals, was far too fragile to survive Romania's economic and social turbulence. Their successors lacked clear goals of their own, but even if they had had coherent objectives, it seems unlikely that they could have gathered the strength to achieve them.

In the final analysis, however, it is doubtful that Romania's internal weaknesses, despite their occasionally spectacular nature, were the cause of her ultimate collapse. The sequence of events that caused Carol and Magda to flee Bucharest (September, 1940) would probably have followed just as inevitably on a well-governed Romania as they did a well-governed Czechoslovakia. Romania's failure in falling prey to the Nazi plan was not her failure alone, it was a part of the general weakness of both east and west. Even so, one finds little to praise in the history of interwar Romania.

12

Interwar Yugoslavia

WAS THE YUGOSLAVIA OF 1919 a new state or an old one? Certainly it was a new state in that no nation with that name or territory had existed prior to the war (actually Yugoslavia was known as the Kingdom of Serbs, Croats, and Slovenes until 1929). But it was also an old state in that its government, including the royal family, was the same as that of prewar Serbia. Even the capital remained at Belgrade. The fundamental problem of interwar Yugoslavia was that the question of old versus new was never really settled. At the beginning of the period the people were split roughly fifty-fifty on this key issue; at the end of the two decades the percentages were about the same, but the emotional temperature was much higher. Such is the stuff of failure.

Yugoslavia was really created by the Corfu Agreement of 1917 (see above). In essence, this document did little more than call for the establishment of a state comprising traditional Serbia, Croatia, and Slovenia (as well as Bosnia-Hercegovina and Macedonia). It specified that the Serbian Karageorgeovich dynasty would continue and serve for the nation as a whole, but this was about the extent to which the structure of the new state was spelled out. The vagueness favored the Serbs, who, after all and despite their battered condition in 1917, had not only a dynasty but also a government, a bureaucracy, a body of law, an army, and a police force. The representatives of the Croats and Slovenes had nothing comparable, indeed they lacked a clear mandate from their own people (even before the war, genuine referendums on subjects such as this had, of course, been impossible). The Croat and Slovene deputies from the Habsburg lands later endorsed the Corfu agreement as well, but their authority and credibility was scarcely greater than that of their self-appointed colleagues and did not alter the fundamental balance. The new state would resemble Serbia, albeit not without a struggle.

Yugoslavia and Bulgaria were the only states of Eastern Europe in which economic affairs were comparatively less important. This is not to say that there were not problems or that they were not serious, but rather that they did not provide as much steam for the political engine as in most other states. Nevertheless, it is still true of Yugoslavia, as of the other nations of Eastern Europe, that an understanding of the economic framework is essential to any real comprehension of its political counterpart.

To a certain extent the economy of Yugoslavia will seem familiar to the student of interwar Eastern Europe. A single statistic, that 76 percent of the population was dependent on agriculture, seems alone sufficient to place a new piece into the puzzle. But there are some differences as well. As our survey moves south of the Danube, we find not only less industry and more agriculture; we also find a different kind of agriculture. Yugoslavia was a land of small proprietors. The only large estates to be found in 1918 were in Croatia and in other sections of prewar Habsburg territory. But the owners of the large holdings had for the most part been made foreigners by the Paris Peace Conference, and though Yugoslav politicians could not agree on many things, absolute harmony prevailed on the principle of dispossessing Magyar or other foreign landlords. The vast majority of the estates were swept away by a land reform of 1919.

The agricultural landscape that remained was only partly typical of Eastern Europe. There were dwarf holdings: 68 percent of the owners (but only 28 percent of the land) fell into this category. But there was also a very important group of medium-size farms: some 11 percent of these owners had holdings in the 10–50 hectare range, and these accounted for nearly 35 percent of all arable land. Of those states studied so far, only in Czechoslovakia do we find farmers in comparable numbers and with equivalent economic strength.[1] It is important to note that these farmers were fairly evenly divided between Serbs and Croats: the terrain of the core regions inhabited by these two peoples is roughly similar.

The existence of an important group of comparatively prosperous farmers did not mean, of course, that Yugoslav agriculture as a whole was successful. This was still an overwhelmingly peasant nation: the surplus population formula cited earlier yields a figure of 39 percent for Yugoslavia.[2] Moreover, the Yugoslav climate, while warmer than that north of the Danube, is also somewhat drier. Internal communications, particularly roads and railroads, were much less well developed than elsewhere. This was the combined result of difficult terrain, comparatively late efforts at development, and war damage that was probably greater than that suffered by any other state of Eastern Europe.

In addition to its special problems, Yugoslavia also experienced all of the standard problems of Eastern Europe. The system of inheritance tended to increase the number of dwarf plots. Both peasants and farmers suffered from a chronic lack of the capital needed to invest in seed, livestock, and implements. Few people in the entire country had any scientific or technical training in agriculture. It is safe to say that very few farmers, and practically no peasants, ever received the sort of advice on crop rotation, plowing techniques, or use of fertilizer that was now routinely given to their counterparts in much of Western Europe and in the United States. Another single statistic is striking: there was only one tractor for every 5,300 people living on the land.[3]

Industrial development in Yugoslavia was focused heavily on the extractive industries. Yugoslav mines produced copper, chromium, bauxite, silver, and other ores. Overall, Yugoslavia was one of Europe's richest sources of metals. But foreign corporations played a dominant role in these enterprises, and most of the production was exported. There were few manufacturing facilities on Yugoslav soil, and even these tended to be relatively unsophisticated with their output aimed entirely at the domestic market. Further, these small industries were clustered in only a few areas: the central part of Slovenia, and the cities of Zagreb and Belgrade. The potential for maritime industry, which was considerable, was largely unrealized owing to competition, lack of capital, and insufficient technical expertise. Overall, in the interwar period only Bulgaria and Albania had a lower level of industrial development than Yugoslavia.

The only positive aspect to Yugoslavia's lack of industrialization was that it was spared the violent financial ups and downs that plagued its more developed neighbors to the north. The economy even experienced a steady albeit modest boom in the 1920s. But this strength was attributable primarily to agricultural exports and collapsed with the advent of the depression. This unexpected turn of events proved a disaster for the government, which had borrowed heavily in the West during the 1920s. These loans were not intended, for example, to stabilize the currency, as had been the case in Poland and Hungary, but were meant essentially to accelerate development (of course, a not insignificant proportion of these funds found its way into the pockets of government officials and their friends). However noble the purpose of the loans, the fact was that the drastic decline in agricultural exports made it very hard for the government to meet its payments. By 1932, Yugoslavia's debt service ratio (the portion of exports needed to pay off the interest on foreign debts) had reached 29 percent—the second highest in Eastern Europe.[4]

The Yugoslav economy was also greatly affected by the shifting diplomatic winds. In the 1920s Yugoslavia was firmly tied to France and her eastern alliance system. Initially, this was helpful in that it assured her some trading partners, but not harmful because the alliance's enemies were more potential than actual political and economic factors. In this climate Yugoslavia even got along reasonably well with Italy, a neighbor with whom she had important territorial disputes. In fact, in the becalmed diplomatic atmosphere of the 1920s, economic logic was allowed to have its way, and Italy took as much as 25 percent of Yugoslavia's exports. But when the depression threatened trade everywhere, Mussolini allowed his economic relations with Yugoslavia to collapse. Italy was by then committed to an actively revisionist policy, and this made her an enemy of status quo Yugoslavia. The latter, of course, suffered most of the economic damage caused by the rupture.

The Yugoslav economy limped along on the brink of disaster in the mid 1930s. While it is true that subsistence peasants were relatively unaffected by such a crisis, virtually everyone else was hurt and hurt badly. In particular, many farmers had borrowed money to make improvements to increase production, and they now found themselves unable to market their goods even at the old level. Their consequent inability to pay off the loans threatened them with loss of their land. In this extremely grim economic atmosphere it is not surprising that Herr Schacht and his band of trade experts appeared to be good knights riding their white chargers to the rescue. The clearing agreements (see above) were gratefully accepted in Belgrade, and as early as 1936 Germany had asserted a measure of control over the Yugoslav economy; by 1938, Berlin was clearly calling the tune—music which inevitably had an effect on diplomatic affairs.[5]

The social structure of Yugoslavia was remarkably homogenous. There was no real aristocracy outside of the Moslem areas of Bosnia. The middle class was very small, congregated in the comparatively few cities and towns, but was mostly native. The great bulk of the population was composed of peasants in the classic sense. The only important internal difference was that the peasants in the south tended to be much poorer because of the rocky, arid, and isolated land upon which they lived.

The social homogeneity of Yugoslavia was in sharp contrast to the nation's ethnic and religious makeup. Estimates suggest that the nationality composition of Yugoslavia was 43 percent Serb, 23 percent Croat, 8.5 percent Slovene, 5 percent Macedonian, 6 percent Bosniak, 4 percent

Albanian, and 10 percent "other." The ethnic diversity was complemented by (and was a function of) religious diversity. Approximately 49 percent of the population was Orthodox, 38 percent Catholic, and 11 percent Moslem. Tensions between these groups were many and varied, but the most important conflict was between the Orthodox Serbs and the Catholic Croats, both of whom, of course, spoke essentially the same language. Although religion effectively defines the difference between Serbs and Croats, it would not be accurate to say that religion alone was the source of conflict. It is certainly true that in traditional societies, in which the village church is often the center of political as well as social activity, that religious affiliation can be the source of rivalry and in some situations hostility. But the same can be said of rival schools with their athletic contests, and that analogy is, in this case, not such a bad one.

The fact is that history does not reveal a record of bitter conflict, let alone protracted religious wars, between Orthodox and Catholic. There were significant doctrinal differences, but, by comparison to those between Protestants and Catholics, these were ancient history. And where the latter two religions had recently taken opposite sides in such enormously bloody struggles as the Thirty Years War, the average Serb or Croat would certainly not be able to describe anything remotely similar between Orthodox and Catholic. On the contrary, the two Christian peoples of the Balkans had struggled together for centuries in a common effort to drive the Moslem Turks from their lands. One could argue that, at least in the context of Southeastern Europe, the recent history of Orthodox and Catholic was more one of cooperation than of conflict.

Why then did Serbs and Croats disagree so violently? The answer seems to lie primarily in cultural differences which were tied somewhat to religion but in fact were principally a reflection of whether an area had or had not suffered long-term occupation by the Turks. The problem of education will provide a good example of the differences.

The Roman Catholic Church was highly centralized and hierarchical in structure; it depended on literacy, and hence education, to carry messages to its far-flung outposts. In an environment of literate people it is not surprising that a love of learning developed and that Catholics founded schools and universities which dealt with many secular subjects as well as religion. By contrast, the situation was very different in Orthodox areas, although there is nothing in Orthodox doctrine that makes its attitude to education any different from Catholicism. Indeed, Byzantium was the world's leading cultural center when Rome was a provincial backwater. But Byzantium fell to the Turks.

Again, there is no reason to believe that Islam is inherently hostile to education; in fact, we know that Moslem scholars preserved and transmitted classical knowledge during dark times in Europe and that they also added many new insights. The Ottoman system was, however, a vast war machine. Education was not a state priority for Moslems and certainly therefore not for Christians. The Turks were tolerant of Christians (and Jews and others) but were not about to support the development of the infidels through the establishment of schools other than those for narrow religious training. Further, although Orthodoxy was centralized in the Patriarchate in Istanbul, the Turks did not allow this to become a strong, independent authority (like the Vatican), and in later times even assisted in the splitting off of separate Serbian and Bulgarian patriarchates.

The net result of all this was that the Croats had, by comparison to the Serbs, a very large cadre of educated (in the western sense) men. While it is possible to make too much of the difference in educational levels between Serbs and Croats, it requires little insight to appreciate that there were some reasons entirely apart from religion that Croats would resent being governed by Serbs.

Another factor often cited as an explanation for hostility between Croats and Serbs is that the latter, having lived under Ottoman jurisdiction when that empire was in decay, had acquired habits of administration that were hopelessly corrupt. Though there may be an element of truth in this, one should remember that first the Austrian Empire and later the Austro-Hungarian Empire were notoriously corrupt as well. The methods by which officials received payoffs may have been somewhat more subtle in the west, but the practice was nonetheless prevalent. It seems likely that people did not resent the corruption so much as they did having to pay it to "foreigners," and that the opportunity to complain out loud was much greater in Yugoslavia than it had been under Hungarian or Austrian rule.

A complicating factor in the Serb-Croat quarrel was the settlement pattern of the two peoples. Although both had distinct core areas in which they formed nearly 100 percent of the population, there were important areas of overlap. There were, for example, quite a few Serbs in areas traditionally part of Croatia: particularly in the northwest and in Dalmatia. More important, the very large area of Bosnia-Hercegovina had a population roughly balanced between Serbs, Croats, and Bosniaks. Though there was some tendency for the Serbs to reside in the northeast, the Croats in the northwest, and the Bosniaks in the south of this province, the villages were sufficiently intermixed that nothing resembling a line of separation could be drawn. Thus, even if Serbs and Croats had agreed to go their separate ways, a struggle over frontiers would have become an immediate problem of enormous propositions.

Yugoslavia also experienced significant tensions between peoples of the same religious and historical background: in this case Serbs and Macedonians. As described above, the official Serbian view was that the Macedonian Slavs were "south Serbs." This argument had very little historical and no linguistic validity, but that did not diminish the tenacity with which it was maintained. The argument provided a rationale for Serbia when she was attempting to gain control of Macedonia, and it served equally well when she was trying to hold on to it. A full description of the Macedonian problem in the interwar period belongs in the section on Bulgaria, but it is important to note the continued existence of Serb-Macedonian tension within Yugoslavia.

Except for the Macedonians, the smaller nationalities of Yugoslavia prospered somewhat by being off the main axis of Serb-Croat hostility. The Slovenes, who had a natural religious and historical affinity for the Croats, nevertheless lacked their neighbors' violent opposition to things Serbian. In part this was because the Slovenes were intelligent enough to realize that their small numbers would be insufficient to form a successful independent nation. Also, they had reason to fear that, in a union with just the Croats, Slovene cultural and political interests might fare no better than they did in Yugoslavia. As a consequence, the Slovene politicians showed a tendency to straddle political fences in order to win as much local freedom as possible when the inevitable bargaining for votes occurred. The Slovenes were quite successful in this, and Slovene grievances were not a principal problem in interwar Yugoslavia.

To a certain extent, the Moslem peoples, the Bosniaks and nearly all of the Albanians, were also able to win concessions through strategic alliances made and unmade in the struggle between Serbs and Croats. But the Moslems, still known to the Christians as "Turks" no matter what language they spoke, were yet the objects of a fierce hatred, particularly from Serbs. Promises to them often remained just that and, once real party government was suppressed by the royal dictatorship of 1929, many earlier agreements were revoked in practice if not in law. The situation was somewhat worse for the Albanians, who could not speak the official language, but all Moslems suffered intense discrimination in interwar Yugoslavia.

Other important minorities in interwar Yugoslavia were Hungarians, Italians, Greeks, Bulgarians, and Romanians. With the usual exception of the latter, all of these were poorly treated in the sense that little or no attention was given to the maintenance of their linguistic and cultural heritage, and no concessions whatever were made in the direction of local political autonomy. Since all of these people were tied to nations which contested Yugoslavia's frontiers, Belgrade's lack of solicitude was hardly surprising. Yugoslavia's Jewish population was very small and quite well assimilated; anti-semitism was not a major problem.

Primary education in interwar Yugoslavia was free and compulsory but was in fact largely unavailable to peasants. Nationally, illiteracy was only 50 percent, but regional variations were significant. In Slovenia, less than 9 percent of the population was illiterate; in Croatia, the figure was about 32 percent and in Serbia, a little more than 65 percent.[6] In the very backward southern part of the nation (Macedonia and Bosnia-Hercegovina) fewer than 20 percent of the people could read. The ineffectiveness of education as a vehicle for social mobility and change is illustrated by the fact that only one of nine students was in secondary school—a percentage that tells us that no more than a handful of peasants or urban poor had such schooling.[7] The university system was nonetheless comparatively large and quite good. There were comprehensive universities at Belgrade, Zagreb, and Ljubljana. As elsewhere in Eastern Europe, however, the focus was on the liberal arts with scant attention paid to scientific and technical training. The cities were pools for spawning the bureaucratic elite (but also, as will be seen later, for developing the leaders of the radical left).

The early phase of domestic politics in Yugoslavia rivaled in complexity and turmoil that of the analogous stage in Poland. The primary dispute, of course, was over the nature of the constitution that would be created for the new state and which would obviously determine the framework for all future political maneuvering. Elections for a constituent assembly were not held until November of 1920; the long delay of two years from the end of the war resulted largely from the protracted diplomatic wrangling over frontiers. The interval gave Croat, Slovene, and other minority group politicians time to organize, but on balance it seems to have favored the Serbs, who inevitably had assumed primary responsibility for running the state. The Serbs also had another advantage: although they were themselves solidly behind politicians who favored a centralized state based in Belgrade, there were among the Croats and Slovenes a significant number of "Yugoslav" types who were willing to accept the general principle of a unitary state (with modifications, of course) in order to preserve national unity. The result was that the constituent assembly had a clear, albeit slender majority of those who favored a centralized Yugoslavia.

The initial political dynamics of the assembly had unfortunate consequences. Those Croats and others who favored a federated or even a confederated state descended into a mood of violent despair, which soon led them to the invariably foolish tactic of resignation in protest. Their opponents, consequently deprived of the need for significant compromise, voted into existence a constitution (the "Vidovdan Constitution," after the Serbian national holiday of June 28 on which it was proclaimed) which was highly centralized. There was a single assembly in Belgrade (to be called the *Skupština* as in old Serbia) which elected the government. Members were selected by proportional representation for four years by a direct, secret ballot based on universal male suffrage. But the king had the power to dismiss the assembly and appoint interim governments, and he quickly demonstrated greater authority over the ministers than that wielded by the majority in the assembly. The king also controlled the military, had a direct voice in foreign affairs, and, most important of all in the Yugoslav context, effectively controlled local government down to the village level.

In failing to address the problem of nationalities, the Vidovdan Constitution ensured that the political parties of Yugoslavia would be based largely on ethnic lines. The most important group was the Serbian Radical-Democratic. This was a coalition of two parties, the oldest and most important of which was the Radical, whose leader, Nikola Pašić, had been the most powerful man of prewar Serbia. The Radicals were consequently well entrenched in the bureaucracy and had power beyond their numbers; they were almost totally Serbian, strongly monarchist, and fierce defenders of the centralized state. The Democrats were more liberal, drawing support from Serbs who had been in the Habsburg lands prior to the war, but were much less well organized and led. Both parties styled themselves as "peasant" parties, but both were in fact dominated by farmers. While they were in coalition, the Radicals dominated.

The Croatian Peasant Party was the second or third largest party, depending on whether the Radicals and Democrats are counted as one. This group was, in fact, very similar in its economic and social objectives to the Radicals and Democrats. It expressed great concern for the status of the peasantry, but its leadership tended to be composed of farmers with a sprinkling of Zagreb intellectuals. It was, however, strongly in favor of a federalist structure, and its delegates had refused to vote on the Vidovdan Constitution. As time passed, elements favoring an independent Croatia became more and more powerful. The Croatian Peasants had a strong, capable leader in Stjepan Radić.

The Slovenes also had a separate party, known as the Slovene People's Party. It was led by the rather significant Solvene intelligentsia and was more a regional than a class party, drawing support from Slovenes of nearly all backgrounds and closely tied to the Catholic Church.

The only truly national party was the Communist (as in Czechoslovakia) which was initially very strong, winning more than 12 percent of the votes for the constituent assembly. The Communists were led by students, intellectuals, and a few workers, drew their financial support from trade unions, but found most of their electorate among the poorest peasants. Their auspicious start was quickly ended, however, as the provisional government moved to suppress them even before the vote on the Vidovdan Constitution (which they opposed). The story of the Yugoslav Communist Party is told below.

Interwar Yugoslavia also had many smaller parties. There were several Moslem political groups, there was an Agrarian Party (which was essentially an anti-establishment Serbian party), there were Social Democrats and numerous splinter and single-issue parties. As in Poland and Czechoslovakia, the system of proportional representation encouraged constant political mutation. Once the Vidovdan Constitution was put into effect, the key political issue in Yugoslavia was whether or not it could be destroyed.

The struggle over the constitutional structure was, as noted earlier, essentially a quarrel between Serbs and Croats, although the other nationalities were also involved and there were ramifications of many kinds and levels: partly cultural and religious, partly economic; partly a direct battle over the perquisites and benefits that flow from access to political power. Overall, it was a question of nationalism and one that transcended all others.

Economic questions were perhaps the next most important political issue: there was general agreement that something had to be done to improve the lot of the peasants and farmers. But even when there was a consensus on how this could be accomplished, which was by no means always the case, the lack of resources available to provide support often made debate moot and legislation irrelevant. The leaders of the various peasant parties also realized, in a vague and general sense, that something should be done to promote industrialization. But there was nothing that resembled a unified approach, largely because the internal quarrel sapped the energies and the wills of those who would be charged with creating a coherent program.

Yugoslavia's foreign policy, like that of Romania, was essentially defensive but also nonetheless a great concern. Yugoslavia was surrounded by predatory neighbors, nearly all of whom were awaiting the proper moment to gobble up vast chunks of territory. As a result, Yugoslavia was an ardent member of the Little Entente, the Balkan Entente, and the French alliance system. These moves were generally popular—even the Croats were no less anxious than the Serbs to see Hungary closely fettered—but as time wore on and the conflict over internal structure remained unresolved, some Croats and Macedonians were moving in directions that Belgrade considered to be treasonous.

Yugoslavia was governed by the Radical-Democrat coalition for a year and a half after the new constitution was put into effect. The Radical leader, Pašić, served as prime minister and governed with the support of King Alexander. But the constitution did require elections, and, when these were held in March of 1923, the opposition groups emerged much stronger. A crisis would have followed immediately except that Radić and the Croatian Peasants again realized that they could not form a coalition sufficiently strong to take power and again refused to take their seats. Instead, they negotiated from afar, and after just a year of effort put together enough votes to bring down Pašić and his Radical-Democrat coalition. New elections were then called for in February of 1925. King Alexander, recognizing that a new government would mean a new and radically different constitution (Radić had even argued that Croatia should have her own, separate army), conspired with Pašić. Taking advantage of the fact that Radić had visited Moscow and that he and his party had endorsed certain policies also advocated by the Comintern, the government declared the Croatian Peasant Party subversive and had it dissolved. Radić was imprisoned.

The government coalition controlled the elections of 1925, but the victory was obviously an artificial one. Pašić, always a flamboyant operator, sought to resolve the situation by direct negotiations with Radić. The result was a brief spectacle; Radić was a prisoner one day and minister of education the next. The principal issues were shoved aside in order to consummate the deal, however, and after a few months Radić was again in opposition, albeit no longer in prison.

At this point developments in Yugoslavia begin to show a remarkable parallel with those in Romania. There were some differences of sequence and chronology, but the overall thrust is amazingly similar. Pašić died in December of 1926, and with him went much of the energy and skill that kept the Serbian Radicals on top. His government did not immediately disintegrate, indeed it appeared to have won a major victory just a few months later when the Slovene People's Party joined the ruling coalition. This was a far more significant move than Radić's fling at harmony: the Slovenes formally accepted the Vidovdan Constitution in return for a high degree of local autonomy. But instead of making the Croats feel weaker and hence more malleable, this defeat for the principle if not the practice of decentralization angered and further radicalized the Croatian Peasant Party and its leaders. The heightened intransigence of Croatian rhetoric was the backdrop for an incident in the parliament in which a Radical deputy, inflamed by Croat "treason," shot and killed three Croatians, including Radić, and wounded several others.[8]

The bloodbath provided King Alexander with the pretext he needed to take a more direct role. When the Croats, now more hostile than ever, refused to recognize the constitution, the king abolished it and ruled by decree. From January of 1929 until September of 1931, there was no legal party activity in Yugoslavia. But Alexander experienced the same problems as Carol of Romania, as he was unable to build a coalition of genuine supporters of his regime. The king was easily able to persuade the bureaucracy, the army, and the police to remain loyal, but it was a giant step from turning the wheels of government to getting a significant portion of the people to help push. The strength of the regime was further weakened by the depression and particularly the collapse of the market for Yugoslav agricultural exports.

Italy's role in the latter blow to Yugoslavia was obvious as was her covert but nonetheless clear part in the assassination of King Alexander, which took place during an official visit to France in the autumn of 1934. The killers were Yugoslavs from Macedonia, and there was a clear tie to IMRO and probably therefore also to some official Bulgarian circles. But there was another trail as well. The terrorists were also linked to a Croatian fascist party, known as Ustaša, which in turn had support from Italy and Hungary.[9] That a radical Croat organization would want to murder a Serb king was hardly surprising. But that in so doing they would cooperate with the authorities of Italy and Hungary, two nations whose well-known designs on Yugoslav territory were focused almost entirely on Croatia, reveals the depth of hatred which had developed between the two largest nationalities in Yugoslavia.

King Alexander's son was too young to take the throne, leaving Yugoslavia with a regency. Unlike the case of Romania, this phase followed rather than preceded the period of royal dictatorship. Indeed, in Yugoslavia the period of regency was largely a continuation of the dictatorship. But if the order of events was different, the effect was much the same. The ability of the government, now headed by the dead king's cousin, Prince Paul, to garner widespread public support declined with each passing day. The economic crisis deepened and nothing was done to ameliorate much less resolve the conflict of nationalities. The nation's security declined, and her enemies' power waxed while her allies' authority waned. In such an atmosphere fascist parties flourished.

Yugoslav fascism differed from that of its sister parties elsewhere in Europe in that it was not markedly anti-Semitic. This was, however, simply a consequence of the fact that there were virtually no Jews upon whom to blame the people's misfortunes. Consequently, the parties were intensely nationalistic, and since religion rather than language distinguished Serbs from Croats, party ritual gave a central place to religion. The Ustaša were not endorsed by the Vatican or the Croat church leaders, even though the party's leader, Ante Pavelić, did win the open support of some members of the clergy. On the other hand, the Serb counterpart, the Yugoslav National Union, reached its peak strength in a successful effort to reject a *concordat* between the Vatican and the Yugoslav government. The *concordat* was an attempt on the part of Belgrade to appease the Croats by regularizing the status of the Catholic Church. It failed not only because of Serbian opposition but also because it was clearly too little too late as far as most Croats were concerned. It is an interesting reflection of history that the Ustaša were willing to cooperate with Moslem groups but the Serbian fascists were not.

Prince Paul was able to find a competent politician to stand at the helm during interwar Yugoslavia's stormy last years. Milan Stoyadinović (who held the title of premier under a new constitution mandated by Alexander in 1931) was a Serb and a centralist, but he was willing to make many concessions in the everyday running of the state. Stoyadinović was also, however, a realist in foreign affairs who sought to improve relations with resurgent Germany and continually hostile Italy. He was successful in this, but it was a hollow achievement. Germany's aims were to neutralize Yugoslavia while Austria and Czechoslovakia were swallowed up, and at the same time to exploit Yugoslavia's natural resources. In both cases the Nazis got what they wanted. Italy took advantage of the *rapprochement* to take control of Albania. The Yugoslavs were asked to view this as a gesture of friendship: as an alternative, Italy could have taken large chunks of Istria and Dalmatia.

Prince Paul finally became concerned that Yugoslavia was getting progressively weaker, and in early 1939 he dismissed Stoyadinović and charged a new government with negotiating a deal with the Croat Peasant Party (then led by Vladimir Maček). An arrangement known as the *sporazum* (accord) was worked out which provided for an autonomous Croatia within Yugoslavia. This state within a state had her own parliament and a government that handled all local administration with some power to tax. The central government retained all other powers although Maček became vice premier. In many ways the *sporazum* made things worse rather than better. Moslems, Macedonians, and quite a few Slovenes now demanded the same deal. Radical Serbs were bitterly opposed. The Radical Croats of the Ustaša were unappeased (they were particularly incensed at the small size of *sporazum* Croatia) yet found their activities somewhat facilitated by the shelter of the new substate.

Prince Paul's failures as leader became apparent when the coup of March 27, 1941, removed him from power (see above). But it would be inaccurate to blame Yugoslavia's fateful disunity on a single man or even on the dozen most important leaders of the period. In restrospect, it seems unlikely that any but a powerful dictator could have harnessed the historical forces which pulled the hybrid state of Yugoslavia in different directions.

13

Interwar Bulgaria

BULGARIA WAS ONE of interwar Eastern Europe's two defeated nations, and like the other vanquished power, Hungary, the peace treaties severed from Bulgaria lands that all Bulgarians considered to be not merely physical parts of the country but also central components of the national cultural heritage. Bulgarians could no more accept the Treaty of Neuilly than Hungarians the Treaty of Trianon. But the similarities of these two revisionist states did not go much beyond irredentism. Bulgaria continued with the same constitution, governmental structure, and leaders that she had had before the war; she was the only country of Eastern Europe that had no need for major internal struggles over land reform or the status of minorities. Yet, despite this good fortune, Bulgarians found plenty of things to worry and quarrel about: the bureaucracy was corrupt to the point of provoking rebellion; the country lacked an economic raison d'être; and the problem of the "lost provinces" distorted debate on every issue and in the end was instrumental in causing the nation to fall prey to the Nazis.

Bulgaria was a thoroughly peasant country: some 75 percent of the population was dependent on agriculture.[1] But it was also very different from all of the other agrarian countries (with the partial exception of Yugoslavia) in that it was a land of peasant proprietors, a very large proportion of whom had the potential to produce for the market. Bulgaria did have a land reform after the war, but it was a comparatively minor affair which served to reduce the holdings of the state, the church, and a very few wealthy farmers rather than to break up great estates. The process of land distribution had actually been completed a generation earlier when the newly liberated Bulgarians dispossessed the Turkish landlords. There had been no opportunity for a class of native nobility to take the place of the Turks.

The nature of land holding in Bulgaria was thus remarkably homogenous. At the two extremes, only one-tenth of 1 percent of holdings were more than 50 hectares, and only 57 percent were 5 hectares and under; some 30 percent of holdings were in the 6–10 range and the remainder clustered in the lower end of the 11–49 range. Even the percent of dwarf holders (using the standard definition of 5 hectares or less) is deceptive. In many parts of Bulgaria, peasants holding 3–5 hectares could and did produce for the market.[2] In part this reflected relatively favorable climate and soils, but it also was a consequence of a tradition of hard work that served the peasants well in times of trouble. The Turkish landlords for whom the peasants' fathers had worked had often been cruel and were noted for their corruption and rapaciousness. But they were equally famous for their absentee, inefficent stewardship and this, combined with the prevalent Turkish practice of requiring payments in cash or produce rather than in labor had left the Bulgarian peasants with more incentive to work hard and efficiently than was the case for their counterparts in, for example, Poland, Hungary, or Romania.

This tradition of independent hard work was invaluable to the Bulgarians when they discovered that the cereals traditionally produced on their farms could not be marketed effectively in the postwar world. As noted earlier, the advent of the steamship had made it possible for large-scale producers as far away as the United States to undersell the peasant proprietors in any market to which they could gain access— including the peasants' home country (in the unlikely event that the local government would permit this). While peasants elsewhere had no alternative in this case but to suffer even more, the Bulgarians were able to switch with considerable success to the production of climate-dependent, labor-intensive cash crops such as fruits, vegetables, and, particularly important, tobacco.

However, Bulgarian agriculture was by no means an overwhelming success. The "surplus population" calculation for Bulgaria yields a staggering 36 percent, which, even though it may be distorted by the unusual composition of the produce of Bulgarian farms, suggests a comparatively high rate of rural overpopulation.[3] And the shift to more productive crops was largely offset by two other dynammic factors: first, the Bulgarians were particularly fond of absolutely equal distribution of land to all surviving sons and daughters. Bulgaria thus had an especially serious problem with the proliferation of scattered strips of land. Second, the Bulgarian population was growing at one of the highest rates in Europe. Finally, of course, one must remember that all nations which relied on agricultural exports to earn foreign exchange were hurt badly by the change in the terms of trade that followed the great depression of 1929.

Bulgaria had virtually no manufacturing industry at the beginning of the interwar period. The land lacked the natural resources essential for basic heavy industry. Further, communications, both internally and with the west, were so poor that there was little effort to exploit the more specialized natural resources that were known to exist. Bulgarian industry was thus essentially oriented toward the production of light consumer goods, principally textiles, and toward handicrafts. In fact, both sectors required significant tariff protection in order to survive. As a result, Bulgaria relied on imports for virtually all manufactured goods, including agricultural implements for which the peasants could pay only by exporting food. Needless to say, they were largely unsuccessful in this—particularly after 1929. The ratio of tractors or other mechanical tilling or harvesting machines in Bulgaria was only one to every one thousand persons employed in agriculture.[4]

The fact that Bulgaria's economy was comparatively primitive did have its bright side, however. Inflation in the 1920s, though it existed, was relatively manageable, and borrowing in international markets produced a debt service ratio of only 16 percent in 1931. This was the second lowest in Eastern Europe (after Czechoslovakia's 5 percent) and much lower than the average of some 30 percent for the remaining countries; it is also impressive in that Bulgaria was exporting very little by 1931.[5] At the same time, foreign ownership of Bulgarian industry was just under half of the available stock; this is a high figure but nonetheless stands out in sharp contrast to the 80 percent rate of foreign ownership obtaining in industrially more advanced Romania.

Bulgarian society was as homogenous as the statistics on agriculture would lead one to expect. To the extent that there were social classes in Bulgaria, it was essentially a consequence of the difference between rich and poor peasants. Of the very small proportion of the population that lived in the towns or the single city (Sofia), most were still closely tied to the peasant lifestyle both culturally and through relatives. One would think that such a society would have few reasons for social tension, and at least in a comparative sense that is so. Yet people always seem to find a reason for strife, and the Bulgarians were no exception. The burning social issue that developed in early interwar Bulgaria was a conflict of rural versus urban, which, in practical terms, meant all of the country against Sofia. To some extent the differences were the rather artificial construct of shrewd political manipulation of the peasants' traditional

distrust of the "city slicker." Fundamentally, however, the struggle of the
rural against the urban was a simple revolt of the governed against the
governors. This topic will be discussed in more detail in the section on
Alexander Stambuliski.

Bulgaria did have national minorities: Turks comprised some 11
percent of the population and Bulgarian-speaking Moslems perhaps another 3 percent (these people, the equivalents of the Bosniaks in Yugoslavia, were known as Pomaks). Orthodox Bulgarians were about 84
percent of the total. Overall, in Eastern Europe only Albania was more
homogenous linguistically, and no other country was nearly so unified
in religion. In such an environment minority affairs were not a major
concern, and gestures toward the Moslems were few. The Moslems were
in any case alienated from the state for religious and social reasons (they
included the remnants of the Ottoman landowning class) and not because
of a conflicting nationaliam. The Turks and Bulgarian Moslems did not
struggle for minority rights. They refused to send their children to the
schools, which naturally stressed Bulgarian language and culture as well
as the established Orthodox religion, but they did not at the same time
press for state-funded schools of their own. The Moslems wished simply
to withdraw from society as much as possible. This was fine with the
government, which intruded in their lives principally to offer them assistance in emigrating.

Bulgaria's educational system did not reflect her economic backwardness. As mentioned earlier, the Bulgarian nationalist leaders of the
nineteenth century, like their counterparts in the Czech lands, stressed
the importance of literacy as a vehicle for national unity. This was also
true in Poland, Hungary, and Romania, but in those countries class
differences were a formidable barrier between theory and practice. Such
could not be the case in Bulgaria, which in the middle of the interwar
period had an illiteracy rate of only about 45 percent. Even this figure
is deceptively high, for only 30 percent of the school-age population
(children 7–14 in this case) was illiterate—a figure which in turn is
artificially inflated by the nonparticipation of the Moslems. When it is
considered that the Bulgarian literacy rate was attained with very little
outside help in a land that was by comparison quite remote from the
west, the achievement must be considered to be remarkable.

Primary education of eight years was compulsory in interwar Bulgaria, and even more important some 83 percent of the school-age population actually went to school. In many areas free kindergartens were
also available. The percent proceeding to secondary education was high
by comparative if not absolute standards: some 8 percent were in regular

secondary schools (modeled on the German *gymnasium*) and another 5 percent were in technical schools. Higher education was accessible through competitive examinations; the participation rate was about the same as that for Hungary, but lower than that in Poland, Czechoslovakia, and Romania. Even this statistic may be deceptive, however, since many Bulgarians went abroad to study (primarily to Germany and Austria; ties with Russian universities were ended by the Bolshevik revolution). There was, in fact, only one university in Bulgaria—a quite good one at Sofia. This was complemented by a number of specialized academies and institutes located both in Sofia and in some of the major towns.

The overall picture of education in Bulgaria is a very positive one. Education could be and was a means by which the children of peasants could improve their status. To be sure, the sons of urban dwellers and rich peasants advanced in disproportionate numbers, but nowhere else in Eastern Europe did eduation radiate so directly into the villages. There was a darker side, however. As elsewhere, secondary and especially higher education was oriented toward the arts and humanities to the department of scientific and technical training. This meant that Sofia was as cursed as any other East European capital with unemployed intellectuals who sought jobs nowhere but in the bureaucracy and whose goals seemed to be to receive salaries for not working. These people formed part of the nucleus of the remarkably strong Bulgarian Communist Party.

The constitutional structure of Bulgaria incorporated the deadly ambiguity which plagued most constitutional monarchies: control over the government ("ministerial responsibility" in the terminology of political science) was not clearly given to either king or parliament (called the *Sobranie* in Bulgaria). The framers of the Tirnovo Constitution clearly intended for ultimate power to remain with the assembly, but they had given the king enough authority that, if he were strong and a clever politician, he could use the tactics of divide and conquer to effectively control government. This had been the case with Tsar Ferdinand from 1894 until he abdicated in 1918. Ferdinand might have continued for the rest of his life to win at this slick game had he not been a big loser in more important contests. Bulgaria's position as a defeated nation in World War I, coming close on the heels of her crushing losses in the Second Balkan War, made the tsar's position untenable. Ferdinand left his throne to his son, Boris III (the number was intended to tie the present dynasty to the Bulgarian empire of a thousand years earlier), who was twenty-four in 1918.

Ferdinand could not leave Boris much more than the throne, however. The royal power which the father wielded had been built on decades

of intrigue and crumbled like a house of cards when its architect's hand
was removed. Thus, the pendulum swung toward genuine parliamentary
government when Boris appointed Alexander Stambuliski, head of the
Agrarian Party, as premier in late 1918. The new head of government
had as one of his first duties the requirement of signing the Treaty of
Neuilly. The provisions of this document were, of course, highly unpopular, but since Stambuliski had no association with the series of diplomatic
blunders that had paved the way to defeat, popular sentiment was not
against him for what was generally construed as a simple acceptance of
the inevitable.

Stambuliski and the agrarians were, in fact, extremely popular. In
the reasonably honest election of 1920 the prototypically peasant Agrarian Party won some 48 percent of the seats in the parliament. For a party
that was less than twenty-five years old (founded in 1899) and which
had been forced to operate for most of that time in a climate of official
hostility and occasional oppression, this was an auspicious beginning.
The Agrarians' ideology was based essentially on the desire of the peasants
to be left alone. The hostility of the villagers to the city was, as noted
above, primarily a reaction to bureaucratic exploitation. Under Ferdinand's exceedingly corrupt system, the government had taken not only
the peasants' money but also their sons. The people supported the claim
to Macedonia, but there was much bitterness about the apparently futile
bloodshed. Stambuliski's wartime criticism of the government was sufficiently outspoken that he had spent three years in jail.

Strangely, the next largest party and indeed the only other one of
consequence was the Bulgarian Communist Party (BCP) which had 22
percent of the seats. The history of the BCP is discussed in some detail
below, but it should be noted at this point that it drew its considerable
strength from widely disparate sources: its leaders were workers and
members of the disillusioned intelligentsia, but its voters were drawn
largely from the poorest peasants and from minority groups. The tight
organization of the party also magnified its strength. Aside from Agrarians
and Communists, there were seven other parties which were important
enough to win seats, but these smaller groups had by comparison little
actual or potential influence over the electorate.

The leadership of the Agrarian Party came, as one would expect,
from the more prosperous peasants. But Stambuliski was also very concerned about the poorer peasants, not least because so many of them had
supported the communists. One of his first acts, therefore, was to effect
the land reform mentioned earlier. The consequences were not drastic,

but the expropriation of the holdings of a few rich men, together with the parcelling out of some state and church lands, was politically very popular. The Agrarians were able to move expeditiously in this matter because they quickly forged an electoral alliance with the communists. The latter joined with the Agrarians only because they hoped to make use of the power that they expected would flow to them as members of a government coalition.

Whatever dreams the communists may have had about walking the corridors of power were quickly shattered by Stambuliski. The Agrarian leader was enough of a pragmatist to see the need for a parliamentary alliance, but he was in all of his views a convinced anticommunist. Stambuliski aspired, in fact, to be the creator of an organization that would directly challenge the spread of world communism. As a counter to the "Red International" of the Marxists he advocated the establishment of a "Green International" of the peasants. Stambuliski traveled throughout Eastern Europe speaking on this subject and lobbying with other politicians and leaders. He even succeeded in setting up a skeleton organization with its headquarters in Prague. But the beginning of Stambuliski's downfall came when he extended his peasant alliance network to Yugoslavia. This was certainly a logical thing for him to do, since Yugoslavia was the nation which most closely shared Bulgaria's social and economic concerns: it too was an agrarian state without much industry but with a communist problem. Moreover, Stambuliski was a logical person to approach Belgrade; he had been openly opposed to the attempts to solve the Macedonian problem through the force of arms, and he was known to favor the creation of a genuine "Yugoslavia" which would include Bulgaria. The only problem was that IMRO strongly opposed such a solution, and IMRO, as it turned out, could be a decisive factor in Bulgarian politics.

The period of the early 1920s was an especially bad time to antagonize IMRO. As noted earlier, Sofia had become the haven for many of Macedonia's leaders after the failure of the 1903 revolt against the Turks. This group was now enlarged by the addition of a new stream of refugees from the resolutely "anti-Macedonian" (in the sense of denying that Macedonians were separate from Serbs) Yugoslav administration. In addition to its strong power base in Sofia proper, the IMRO chieftains took advantage of the small size of the Bulgarian army as mandated by the Treaty of Neuilly to assert control over much of the area along the Bulgarian-Yugoslav border, in particular the large area in Bulgaria known as "Pirin Macedonia" (because it was in an extension of the Bulgarian

Pirin Mountains). Stambuliski challenged IMRO directly when he negotiated an agreement with Yugoslavia to maintain the tranquility of the
frontier.

Stamuliski's party appeared to be in complete control when they
won 87 percent of the seats in the elections of 1923 (the communists fell
to 7 percent). But the Agrarians' victory solidified the opposition. IMRO,
which showed more internal unity in the face of this crisis than it had
displayed for some time, was able to work with the largely disaffected
leaders of the army and the bureaucracy to execute a coup on June 9 of
the same year. The insurgents' plan was a good one, and the legitimate
government was hardly able to muster any armed forces to defend its
cause. The "Orange Guards," a sort of peasant militia organized by
Stambuliski, had only scythes and hoes for weapons. Even so, the affair
was extremely bloody. IMRO regarded the members of the Agrarian
leadership as more than political enemies—to the Macedonians they were
also traitors. This is the best explanation for the widespread violence
against helpless peasants and for the particularly brutal murder of Stambuliski. This affair, like the savage killing of Stambulov less than two
decades earlier, seriously blackened the image of the Bulgarians in western
public opinion.

The coalition that overthrew the Agararians fell apart once it had
achieved its goal. Ostensibly led by the inevitable colonel (a certain Damian Velchev in this case), it was in fact leaderless. Parliamentary government was allowed to continue, but it only occasionally had much
relationship to public opinion and didn't always reflect who was in power.
The main contenders for authority were IMRO, the army, an organization
of bureaucrats and intellectuals known as Zveno, and Tsar Boris. This
was complicated further by the fact that the three groups were each usually
split into at least two factions, and Boris himself was not famous for his
decisiveness.

The government was still in flux when it weathered a communist
coup attempt in September. This event was important primarily for its
internal effect on the BCP (see below), but it also had the effect of removing
one at least potentially important factor from the political equation.
IMRO now stepped to the fore, but once the crisis period was past the
leaders of this organization resumed their internal quarrels. The principal
issue at dispute within IMRO was whether Macedonia should become
a part of Bulgaria or whether it should become independent. A disinter-
ested observer would have said the issue was moot since much of the
area was at the time a part of Yugoslavia, but facts did not bother the
IMRO activists, who frequently exchanged their views in gun battles

fought on the streets of Sofia. The Bulgarian authorities obviously favored the pro-Bulgarian faction, but they were unable to intervene effectively, primarily because of the safe havens available to IMRO in the Pirin region.

Bulgarian foreign policy shifted rapidly after the coup of 1923. The rapprochement with Yugoslavia was ended quickly, not least because the number of IMRO raids into that country increased dramatically. Concomitantly, revisionist Bulgaria drew closer to the first interwar champion of irredentist causes, Mussolini's Italy. The latter defended the governments in Sofia when the Yugoslavs complained to international bodies about IMRO raids. A number of economic agreements were signed, and Bulgaria gave Italy what amounted to a naval base on the Black Sea.

In 1930 Tsar Boris even married an Italian princess. However, it would be a mistake to characterize Bulgarian foreign policy as implacable and challenging. The Bulgarians were not so emotional as the Hungarians, and quite a few leaders in Sofia were sufficiently concerned about the dangers of their country's isolation that they signalled a willingness to negotiate. But at the same time no Bulgarian government was able to flatly endorse the Treaty of Neuilly. This attitude was largely responsible for the formal creation of the Balkan Entente by Greece, Romania, Yugoslavia, and Turkey (February, 1934; in fact, the former three had been cooperating on Balkan, and particularly Bulgarian, matters since the early 1920s).

The shadow of the Balkan Entente, combined with a resurgence of communist popularity as expressed by votes for the BCP's front party, led elements within Bulgaria to believe that a change was needed. In May of 1934, a new coup led by Colonel (still) Velchev and Zveno took power and abolished parliamentary government. Unlike many such movements, the leaders did not announce that they were suspending parliament "until new elections can be held in a peaceful atmosphere"; instead, they proclaimed traditional parliamentary democracy to be an evil and made no pretense of restoring it. The new government carried its philosophy to the logical end by attacking IMRO which, weakened by a decade of internal strife and frequent albeit futile attacks on Yugoslavia, succumbed with remarkable ease. IMRO was declared to be illegal, its autonomy in the Pirin region was ended, and its leadership either went into exile or was imprisoned.

These dramatic events did not yet bring stability, however. Velchev and his associates were antimonarchist as well as anti-democratic, and they had launched their coup quickly in order to forestall one by the king. But the latter had a great deal of support in the army, and in April of 1935, Velchev was removed from power.[6] From that point forward,

Bulgaria was governed by direct royal authority in which Boris had the largest role, although he always had to rely to a very great extent on senior army officers. The new government experimented with a unique structure: a nonparty parliament. This was an essentially powerless body, weakened even further by the fact that its delegates were legally forbidden to form political alliances with each other. There were at this time some attempts at creating fascist organizations in Bulgaria, but these were quickly suppressed, not least because much of their ideology and methodology (as well as some of their leaders) were drawn from IMRO.

Boris did not wish to limit Bulgaria's foreign policy options, and he did maintain much better relations with Yugoslavia. The elimination of IMRO was very helpful in this. Following the Munich agreements of 1938, Boris actually negotiated a treaty with the Balkan Entente: in return for Bulgarian renunciation of force in settling border disputes the Entente members agreed to allow Bulgaria to expand its military. Boris did not, however, recognize the Treaty of Neuilly.

Though Bulgaria's action in negotiating with the Balkan Entente is viewed by some as a gesture toward the status quo powers, a more realistic assessment is that it was a clever use of Hitler's success to wring heretofore unavailable concessions from Bulgaria's neighbors. Subsequently, Boris flirted with Britain and France and was even able to secure some financing and arms from them.

But whatever may have appeared on the diplomatic stage, the truth is that by 1938 Bulgaria was no longer a free agent. Her economy at that point was controlled in Berlin: Nazi planners were now telling the ministers in Sofia what crops should be planted and which rail lines should be improved. It would have been extraordinarily difficult for any Bulgarian government to break these ties, despite the fact that in the long run they did not benefit Bulgaria. In any case the diplomatic climate was not supportive of change. Both Yugoslavia and Romania had moved to accommodate Germany, while Italian ground forces were based in Albania, only a hundred miles from the Bulgarian frontier. Boris did not seem to mind the changes that were occurring in Europe, and the prevailing mood among the Bulgarian leaders on the eve of war was one of optimism that Greater Bulgaria would soon become a reality. Their hopes were rewarded, but victory was to be bitter and briefly held. Bulgaria was once again rushing toward defeat.

14

Interwar Albania

THE HISTORY OF INTERWAR ALBANIA is the least known of the interwar East European states. Its diminutive size does not make its history any easier to describe, however. Politically, Albania's story is complex and even mysterious. The hint of secrecy even extends to the social and economic spheres, where the lack of data is such an overwhelming problem that Albania is rarely included in studies of interwar Eastern Europe. The very fact that Albania continued to exist seems to have amazed scholars as much as it did the statesmen who rarely gave it a place in the diplomatic equations with which they struggled daily. Albania was a curiosity and in a very real sense a negative entity: it existed only because the great powers wanted it to, but they favored an independent Albania only because they could not agree upon the manner in which to divide it. Albania's existence could quickly cease upon the striking of a bargain by strangers in a far-off city, or, as actually occurred in the end, because a similar group was too preoccupied elsewhere to care.

As was noted earlier, Albania did cease to function as a political entity during World War I. There was no Albanian national government during this period; governmental affairs above the village level were in the hands of the occupying armies (which changed frequently). Further, since Prince William had fled the country before achieving even a superficial control, there was no government in exile (the prince's brief appearance as a European monarch was quickly forgotten by all concerned). At the end of hostilities in November of 1918, most of Albania was controlled by Italian forces. Since Italy at that time was hoping to annex most of the country, its military government was working to establish an administrative network that would link the villages to the central command and thus bind the Albanians to Italy.

Italian attempts to annex Albania ran into two major obstacles.

261

THE OTHER EUROPE

The first, and probably the most important, was the tenacious resistance of Woodrow Wilson (see above). Wilson was opposed not only to the secret treaties of the wartime years (made before the United States joined the struggle), but he also favored (usually) the principle of national self-determination. Since the Italians couldn't make even a weak claim on this latter point, they were vulnerable to the attacks of the idealistic and powerful American. Given that Greece and Yugoslavia were prepared to cooperate with Italy in making Albania disappear, Wilson should be given most of the credit for the fact that there was an interwar Albania at all. But the Albanians did the best they could to help their own cause. Despite enormous wartime destruction and the nearly complete breakdown of the already weak communications system, Albanians from all over rallied to challenge the Italians. The implacable resistance of the rugged mountaineers opened a second front and certainly helped convince the Italians that their struggle to retain Albania was not worth the price.

The Albanians convened a national congress at Lushnjë in January of 1920, and this body established a provisional government which in turn was recognized by the Italians in late summer of the same year. Since the Italian theory was that if they could not have Albania, no one else should either, Rome became a backer of the new government in the ongoing diplomatic battle over the state's frontier. Albania was admitted to the League of Nations in December of 1920, and the wrangling over the frontiers continued for just less than a year. Finally, as noted earlier, she emerged with the prewar boundaries essentially intact.

In Albania, as elsewhere, political structures were in large part a reflection of economic patterns. Since some 80 percent of the population was dependent on agriculture, and since there was no industry to mention until the very end of the period, the story of the economy must be told in agrarian terms.[1] But, because the pattern of landholding was still a direct consequence of earlier political realities, the status of agriculture cannot be separated from the prevailing social class system. Only some 20 percent of Albania's land in the interwar period could be used for agriculture, and of that more than half was nonarable. Nearly 65 percent of arable land was in the central lowlands—a region in which the descendants of Ottoman nobility owned nearly all of the land and rented it to tenants whose condition was little better than that of serfs. Elsewhere most of the tilled land was owned by the peasants who worked it, but since the plots were small and the terrain rugged, the peasants were not likely to be in a better economic situation than their servile peers.

Statistics on the interwar Albanian economy are generally not available. Although this makes analysis more difficult, it does make one fact clear—Albania had only a very small part in international trade; her exports and imports were minimal. Indeed, the type of exchange that did occur sounds very much like that of a colony: hides and pelts, wool and woolen goods, dairy products, and fish were exchanged for petroleum products and light manufactured goods (e.g., iron plows). The balance of trade was in a chronic deficit (exports on the average paid for only 28 percent of imports), and the balance of payments, though helped by funds sent by emigrants abroad to their families at home, was also consistently in the red.[2] Albania received a loan of some 10 million dollars from Italy in 1925; there were no repayment problems, however, since the Italians made it contingent upon direct access to the nation's customs receipts.[3] It is easy to see how a country with an economy like Albania's could become a financial captive of another. On the other hand, such a backward system can remain stable with virtually no imports since these have essentially no effect on the subsistence farmer. Albania's captivity was, therefore, not entirely dictated by economic need.

The economic survey suggests that Albania had two social classes— landowners and peasants—which is indeed true. The peasants of the mountains and the peasants of the plain, however, were very different. The former were freeholders with a tradition of independence—or at least a struggle for it. The clan was a principal form of economic as well as social organization in the mountains, where the men would often pool their herds for transportation to summer pasture. Consequently, the women had to do nearly all of the farming themselves, and they often cooperated out of necessity. Joint ventures included the occasional marketing of livestock or crops, although the primary purpose of the clan was, of course, defense. In the lowlands clan and cooperative associations were not unknown, but the principal tie of the villagers was to the estate owner, who took 40–50 percent of the crop as rent. Livestock was pastured in the same place all year round, and security was provided by the landlord (a necessity in prewar Albania, since possession alone amounted to legal ownership of land).

The landlords should not be thought of as estate owners in the Polish or Hungarian sense. Very few had holdings large enough to permit them to settle outside of the villages. Their income was sporadic (dependent on weather and war) and mostly in kind; they were typically much too poor to afford estate managers, and by the same token their mentality was little different than that of the peasants themselves. The landlords did not, for example, show much interest in investment in new equipment or in learning about and experimenting with new techniques of cultivation. There were, of course, some who had managed to put together comparatively large estates, and these men played a very large role in national as well as local politics.

Interwar Albania had very few minorities: estimates are that 92 percent of the population was Albanian. The principal minority group was the Greek (the settlement pattern in the south made it physically impossible to draw a clear line between the two nationalities). There were also some Slavic peoples in the border areas to the north and east, a sprinkling of Vlachs in the mountains, and a few Italians in the coastal towns. The two dialects of Albanian split the country roughly in half, but, although they appear quite different to the outsider, communication between educated native speakers was not a serious problem.

The ethnic homogeneity of the nation was not paralleled in religion. Statistics are again not available, but reliable estimates suggest that 70 percent of the population was Moslem, 20 percent Orthodox, and 10 percent Roman Catholic. All of the latter were Ghegs and lived in a fairly compact region of the mountains of the far north. The Orthodox, on the other hand, were mostly Tosks and lived mostly in the south and south central part of the country. The Moslems were both Gheg and Tosk and concentrated in the central area, although Moslems could be found in all parts of the country. Moslems were themselves subdivided into two groups, Sunni (equivalent in meaning to "orthodox") and Bektashi. The latter is a mystic offshoot of the Shiite branch of Islam, and Bektashis are known for a broad, humanistic approach to religion which is highly tolerant of divergent views. Since Islam was a conqueror's religion in Albania (where it was not uncommon for a husband to be a Moslem and a wife a Christian), the Bektashi philosophy had broad appeal. Some 20 percent of Albanians belonged to this sect and, when it was suppressed by Attaturk in 1929, its world headquarters moved from Turkey to Albania.

Despite the divergence of faiths, religion was not a source of great conflict in interwar Albania—there were no attempts legally to establish any faith. Sunni as well as Bektashi Moslems are tolerant of other religions, and the Christian groups had had little opportunity for conflict with each other or for organized opposition to Islam. The fact that the Moslems and Christians were often mixed together and participated in daily life side by side contributed to the atmosphere of tolerance. The overwhelmingly Moslem character of the landlord class might have been a source of tension were it not for the fact that most of the peasants who suffered under them were of the same religion.

More than 80 percent of the population of interwar Albania was illiterate, a statistic which changed little over the two decades of independence. The law made education obligatory from age four to age thirteen if a kindergarten were available; otherwise, education began at age seven. In practice, only an unknown but certainly small percentage of children actually attended for the entire period or even for long enough to learn to read. Even if the state had been able to force the children to attend, there were not nearly enough teachers available since there had been no Albanian public schools under the Turks. Few students went on to the secondary schools, the number of which was not great in any case. The schools were nationalized in 1933, and only one private school, the American-Albanian Agricultural School, was allowed to continue a separate existence. There were no universities or higher technical institutes in Albania; those students who chose to go on for a higher education went principally to Vienna, Paris, Berlin, and (especially later) to Rome.

Before the Congress of Lushnjë finished its work, it established a new constitution for the country. The form of a constitutional monarchy was retained, but no thought was given to finding a new occupant for the throne. Instead, a regency council including one Sunni, one Bektashi, one Orthodox, and one Catholic was established. Needless to say, this stratagem avoided many problems. Elections were then held in April of 1921, for seats in the national parliament, which in turn selected the first regularly constituted government.

Albania never had any political parties in the organized western sense of the word. Rather, it was possible to identify broad factions whose interests were similar and whose actions were usually taken in concert. The most important faction, of course, was that of the large landowners. Their principal objective was defense: they wished to hold on to their land and to the political authority which they considered their birthright. Their power was sufficient to impel most of the villagers of their home regions to support them in the elections. Indeed, in the environment of interwar central Albania it is difficult to see how elections could be really free.

Curiously, the second most important faction was not even based in Albania. Instead, it derived its energy from Albanian-Americans and was led by Bishop Fan Noli of Boston. These Albanians had played a crucial role in the development of Albanian nationalism and were consequently given the right to elect a representative to parliament. The Americans' choice, Noli, was not only a bishop of the Orthodox Church but also the publisher of their newspaper, *Dielli* (The Sun), a founder of their cultural organization, *Vatra* (The Hearth), and a Harvard graduate. Noli's group was oriented toward Western-style parliamentary democracy and had grand designs for modernizing the country. In addition to the emigrants (many of whom returned with Noli), this faction appealed to other western-educated Albanians and to those of the nationalists whose primary allegiance was not to the landlords.

The third faction was that of the mountaineers, who had virtually no organization beyond the local or regional level, but who had a tradition of resisting central authority. They remained a fairly passive force until affected by an issue that threatened their autonomy (e.g., the imposition of taxes, or attempts to take away their arms). As in Ottoman times, central government control over the mountain villages was sporadic at best.

The government that followed the elections of 1921 was dominated by the landowners, but since this group lacked a central organization and leadership or sense of party politics, several of the reformers also won enough support to participate in the cabinet. Noli was one of the latter, taking the post of foreign minister. The most important minister as it turned out, however, was Ahmet Zog, a nominal reformer but actual aficionado of the art of *realpolitik*, who served as minister of the interior.[4] When a revolt occurred against the government in 1922, Zog (whose policies were largely responsible for the crisis) gained fame as the only leader to stand his ground. When the rebellion folded, he was, therefore, both very popular and very powerful. When Zog moved to reinforce his position with a political (and marital) alliance with one of the most important landowners, he found himself in nearly total control of the government.

Zog was not yet a dictator, however, and he lost the elections of January, 1924. He resigned but was replaced by a landowner who was a close associate. The opposition was unappeased, and when one of their young leaders was murdered, they agitated violently for change. Zog then fled the country and his cabinet resigned. Noli became prime minister in June of 1924, but his government lasted just less than six months. Noli drove the landowners to a new level of unity by pressing for radical land reform, and he alienated the army and bureaucracy with pressure for an end to endemic corruption. The mountaineers, who helped Noli win power, did not help him hang on to it. In mid-December, Zog invaded Albania with the asistance of Yugoslav troops (and some die-hard remnants of General Wrangel's White Russian forces). Noli was unable to organize any real opposition and was forced to return to Boston, this time for good.

In January of 1925, Albania became a republic with Zog as its nominal president but in fact its dictator. He was not without opponents, however, for he had to contend not only with the remnants of Noli's party but also with the mountaineers who were particularly hostile to the tax system. Taxation was essentially the same as it had been under the Turks: the farmers owed one-tenth of their crops to the state, but since the government lacked the resources to collect the produce directly, it in effect franchised the right to gather the taxes by selling it to private entrepreneurs. This system was inevitably open to corruption, but even if it had not been, the mere fact that the government was making a concerted effort to collect taxes would have caused trouble in the mountains.

Given the enormous potential resistance to his rule, Zog chose to seek outside help. He disdained his recent allies, the Yugoslavs, because he rightly feared the consequences of dependence on a close neighbor who claimed much of his territory. Instead, he chose as his patron the more distant Italian state. Zog knew that this option was not without considerable risk of its own, but the strength of the opposition, together with the weakness of the economy, impelled him to take the chance. The president's first move toward Italy was the 10-million-dollar loan of 1925 described earlier, and this was quickly followed, in November of 1926, with a formal treaty of mutual support and collaboration (Treaty of Tiranä). Zog next permitted heavy Italian investments and brought in Italian officers to reorganize the army. Albania then got in deeper when Yugoslavia officially joined the Little Entente; the Italians used this as a lever to get Zog to sign a full military alliance (November, 1927). Rome also now began to be more generous with the terms of her loans; it was clear that she expected a more comprehensive return than principal and interest.

On September 1, 1928, Zog decided to dispense with the trappings of democracy and had himself proclaimed King Zog I (Zog means ɒird" in Albanian). The Italian connection, now more a prop than a link, made it possible for Zog to seize power in this way. It did not, however, ensure that he would be popular. The regime's enemies multiplied rapidly. Zog was ruthless in suppressing the guerilla bands in the mountains, but his success in scattering them also increased the number of those who were sworn to see him dead. The extreme corruption of the royal court (which now had not only an overnight king, but also a queen mother and numerous princesses) outraged even those reformers who had thought an authoritarian government would be the most effective vehicle for modernization. And, finally, the proliferation of arrogant Italian businessmen, bureaucrats, and officers fed the fires of nascent Albanian nationalism.

A British journalist by the name of J. Swire, who spent a number of years in Albania, has described Zog's closest personal brush with his enemies: "The King left Albania on January 25 [1932] in great secrecy, sailing from Durrës on an Italian cruiser and traveling to Vienna to consult a specialist, for it was thought he was suffering from tuberculosis. . . . Three weeks later came the startling news. The attempt was made as the King was leaving the Opera House. Three men rushed up and opened fire. The King was already in his lighted car and his *aide de camp*, Topalloj, was getting in. The first shot killed Topalloj, who fell on the King and probably saved him by stopping another bullet; and Libohova [another aide] was struck down by a bullet in the leg but drew his revolver and opened fire from the ground. The King also emptied his own revolver, then called to Topalloj for his, not knowing Topalloj was already dead. . . . The police rushed up and the two most determined assailants—Albanians—were overpowered."[5] At their trial it was determined that the assassins were based in Yugoslavia, but no proof of official involvement in that country was found.

Shortly thereafter, Zog made an effort to free himself of Italian control. He closed Italian schools (actually all foreign schools were closed), and when Rome reacted by cutting off financial aid, Zog ordered Italian police and military advisers to leave the country. The Italians then tried various other forms of pressure, including a naval demonstration, but Zog continued to resist. After nearly two years of confrontation, however, the Albanians were forced to give in. The country was on the verge of bankruptcy, and the king's domestic enemies were growing bolder. Gradually at first, but then with greater momentum than before, Italian economic, military, and political influence in Albania increased.

In the last five years of Zog's rule (1934–1939) Albania was clearly an Italian client state. For example, the government in Tiranä was virtually the sole international supporter of the Italian invasion of Ethiopia. Mussolini wanted an empire not an alliance, however, and in April of 1939 the Italian army, with the assistance of the many Italian advisers in the Albanian military and police forces, overthrew the government and declared Albania to be a part of Italy. The Italian king became the Albanian king in a meaningless charade. Zog, together with his American wife, fled abroad. There were few international protests since the great powers were preoccupied with the growing crisis over Poland. This quiet collapse suggests that Albania had never had a real chance at independence. Faced with enormous internal problems and surrounded by avaricious neighbors, she could have succeeded only with sustained economic and diplomatic assistance from Britain, France, and the United States. But the idealism of Wilson at Paris in 1919 was merely a brief curiosity, and the cynical practitioners of *realpolitik* who followed were unconcerned about Albania's fate. The memory of this interwar experience was a principal factor in the foreign policy of postwar Albania.

15

Eastern Europe in World War II

*I*T IS DIFFICULT to generalize about the experience of East Europeans during the war. For the Czechs, war, in the sense of occupation, began in 1938; for the Poles, war, in every possible meaning of the word, began in 1939. Albania succumbed to foreign troops in 1939. Romanians and Hungarians saw their sons march off to the Eastern Front in 1941, but did not directly experience warfare and occupation until 1944. Yugoslavia was shattered in 1941, and its territories were occupied by the armies of four nations. Bulgaria, never controlled from the outside and only briefly a battleground in 1944, suffered least. To a very great extent, the peoples of Eastern Europe experienced what we in the West call the Second World War in very different ways.

Yet there are some general statements about the war that can be made. Certainly, the peoples of Eastern Europe died in far greater numbers than those of Western Europe.[1] This is true even if Germany is considered as part of Western Europe and whether one counts absolute figures or a percentage of the population. The same would be true of physical destruction: the type of fighting was very different from west to east. In France, Scandinavia, the low countries, Italy, and of course Britain, cities were not the focal point of battle; this was true even in Germany (with the exception of Berlin). The cities of the west did suffer from bombing, but as battered as London was, it would have seemed untouched to the residents of Warsaw. This was so because most of the cities of Eastern Europe suffered not only bombing but also the effects of artillery, street fighting, and from the work of the ubiquitous Nazi demolitions experts who destroyed, among other monuments, all of the bridges of Budapest.

The nature of human suffering was also different in Eastern Europe, for here it was primarily the civilians who died. The armed forces of Poland, Hugngary, Romania, and Yugoslavia took a dreadful beating, as did all the resistance groups, but in absolute terms their losses were dwarfed by those of the noncombatants. Foremost among the sufferers were the Jews, of whose six milion dead more than half were East European, principally Polish, Hungarian, and Romanian. The Holocaust forever altered the structure of society in much of the area and particularly in Poland, the Czech lands, and Hungary, where the Jews had played an important cultural as well as an economic role. At the other end of society the Gypsies were equally savaged by the Nazi death machine. The campaign of mass murder also touched the Poles and lay in wait for the Czechs and others. And finally, the East Europeans still suffered from each other: the Hungarian occupation of parts of Transylvania, Croatia, the Banat, and Carpatho-Ruthenia was frequently brutal, as was the Bulgarian occupation in Macedonia and parts of Serbia, and the Croatian fascist administration in Serb areas.

The story of the war years is recounted below. The detail is inadequate for a subject that encompasses such great human tragedy. But it is to be hoped that the reader will nevertheless glean from this chapter some sense of the mental and physical legacy that still very much affects Eastern Europe over a generation later.

Poland—Government and Military

The Blitzkrieg of 1939 was everything that the name implies, but important elements of the Polish government managed to escape via Romania. These reassembled in Paris where a new government, a coalition of all of the major Polish political parties then extant, was formed. The prime minister was General Sikorski, who also was head of the remaining Polish military forces. The new government was immediately recognized as legitimate by the British, French, and Americans; the Soviet Union withheld recognition (of course, Moscow had not declared war in 1939 either). Sikorski and his aides again had to flee when the Germans struck into France in May of 1940; they finally took up residence in London, where they remained for the duration of the war.

The new government got a mixed reaction from the British and the Americans. There were inevitable associations with the prewar "government of colonels," which to many in London and Washington was a symbol of the degeneracy that had led to war (of course the politicians of the West had as much or more to answer to themselves, but they managed to overlook that). On the other hand, the Polish government was a broad coalition, and Poland was, if nothing else, an ally of great symbolic importance. Thus, the Poles were treated cordially, but they were not privy to the major diplomatic and military decision-making bodies, and their interests were routinely put on the back burner.[2]

The status of the Poles changed when Hitler invaded the Soviet Union. Shortly after this, British pressure achieved a resumption of diplomatic relation between Moscow and the London Poles. It was in the intrest of Winston Churchill (and soon thereafter of Franklin Roosevelt as well) that Britain's two allies should themselves become allies. But the attempt to produce a show of harmony inevitably had the effect of bringing basic differences between the two nations to the fore. The British (and subsequently the American) view was that the issue at hand was the war and that the question of the Polish-Soviet frontier should be settled later. This was acceptable to Stalin, who at this time was too busy to look ahead. The London Poles, on the other hand, found themselves in an extremely awkward position. They were in alliance with a neighbor which still claimed an enormous part of their territory and which in fact had only recently launched an undeclared war against them. In such an atmosphere Sikorski took the only road open to him: he made every effort to maintain correct relations, but he lost no opportunity, public or private, to assert the necessity of maintaining the territorial integrity of prewar Poland. Stalin's response was simply to reaffirm the Soviet Union's earlier claims.

Relations between Moscow and the London Poles were thus strained from the beginning and could only get worse as the tide turned and the approach of victory made preliminary discussions of the postwar settlement imperative. Tensions rose quickly after the victory at Stalingrad (winter 1942–1943) made Stalin bolder and more confident. Henceforth there were no indications of an inclination to negotiate, much less compromise, from Moscow. It was into this volatile atmosphere that the Nazis dropped an incendiary bomb: the Katyn Forest affair.

In their 1939 attack on Poland, the Red Army forces captured more than a quarter million Polish soldiers. This was done with very little fighting. The Poles, exhausted but retreating in remarkably good order, had no real opportunity to organize resistance on two fronts. In official parlance, these troops were "interned" in the Soviet Union. They could not be prisoners of war, since there had been no formal war between Poland and the USSR. Once hostilities on Polish soil ended, these men naturally began to send letters home. The impression of their relatives was that, although conditions in the internment camps were not good,

in the context of life in the Soviet Union their situation was not bad. At
least they were safe.

For nearly two years following the invasion of Poland, no one in
the West paid much attention to these soldiers: after a brief, heroic
appearance on center stage, they were forgotten by those watching the
equally dramatic acts that followed. This changed at least somewhat after
Operation Barbarossa led to a restoration of Polish-Soviet relations. The
London Poles asked Stalin to let them organize a Polish army based on
the interned troops. Stalin, who needed all the help he could get and who
was consequently in the most agreeable mood of his life, acquiesced.[3]
Polish officers were allowed to scour the USSR collecting their countrymen. As the effort unfolded, however, the Polish leaders noticed a disturbing fact: very few officers were among those reporting to the new
army. The Poles began to compile lists of the missing and asked the Soviet
authorities for help. The latter seemed for the most part cooperative, and
in the general chaos of war, with Nazi armor already deep in Russia and
constantly advancing, for a time it seemed plausible that the men simply
could not be found.

But by 1942 the situation changed. The front stabilized; the Soviets
seemed to have good records on most of the internees. Most ominous,
official Soviet explanations began to change and to become contradictory:
from being simply "lost," the men were now sometimes described as
"transferred to Siberia" (yet somehow "out of contact"), "never captured
at all," or most absurd of all, from Stalin's own mouth, "escaped to
Manchuria" (conveniently, a territory occupied by the Japanese).[4] The
Polish leaders now could also add some new information: relatives in
Poland, queried by the newly organized resistance forces, reported that
the men had stopped writing home in April and May of 1940—more
than a year before the Nazi attack on the Soviet Union.

The case of the missing men went unresolved. Stalin was clearly
either unable or unwilling to provide an answer. Differences between the
new Polish army and the Red Army grew, and it was decided in 1942
to withdraw the Poles to the west (see below). The issue festered in the
minds of the Poles until February of 1943, when the Nazi radio announced
the discovery of a mass grave of Polish soldiers in German-occupied Soviet
territory. A small, hitherto unremarkable area known as the Katyn Forest,
just west of Smolensk, thus made its way into history. In April, the
Germans announced that there were some eleven thousand bodies, that
the men had been murdered (shot), and accused the Soviet Union of the
deed.[5] Moscow immediately denied it, but the Nazis, sensing an issue

that could divide the Allies (by this time Germany's only hope), pushed the propaganda effort. An international group of scientists from eight nations was brought in to examine the bodies (although only one of the men, a Swiss, was from an area not controlled by the Nazis or their allies). This group quickly concluded that the men had died in April and May of 1940, that they had been bound with Soviet-made rope and shot with German manufactured bullets, which it was established had been sold in quantity to the USSR before the war. The Nazi authorities brought in as observers the Polish Red Cross (of course, also from a German-controlled area) and various allied prisoners of war, including some Americans.

In itself this was not enough. By the summer of 1943, the world was beginning to wake to the reality of the Nazi machine of mass murder. Hitler had the motive, the opportunity, and the means to rig the results of the "international investigation." There the issue might have remained except that the Poles, who knew that Stalin was no less a monster than Hitler, could not forget about the missing letters. Consequently, against the advice of the Americans and the British, the London Poles asked the International Red Cross (based in Switzerland) to investigate. Remarkably, at almost the same time, Berlin did the same. This gave Moscow the opportunity to claim that the Poles were clearly anti-Soviet and acting in collusion with the Nazis; the incident also provided Stalin with an excuse to break diplomatic relations. The International Red Cross refused to accept the invitation to investigate unless all parties involved agreed. Stalin did not agree, and there was never an impartial analysis of the evidence. When the Soviets recaptured the area in 1944, they conducted an investigation which reversed the conclusion of the Nazis.

The bodies of the Polish soldiers have lain in peace since 1944, but evidence of various kinds has continued to accumulate at the doorstep of the murderers—the Soviet NKVD (secret police, now the KGB). The story begins with the letters—there is no evidence that any of the missing men were alive from April–May 1940 until the Soviet-determined death date of July—August 1941.[6] The changing Soviet story also follows the lines of a hastily conceived series of lies: the men were first "lost," then "escaped"; but only after the German announcement of the discovery of the grave site were they "captured." The official Soviet version, which includes the specific German units and officers claimed to be responsible, is also demonstrably false based on records available in the west. There is, in fact, no Soviet case on this matter: the evidence from Moscow is at worst contradictory and at best unverifiable.

There are many small points, which taken together, reinforce the

view that Stalin and the N.K.V.D. were responsible for the Katyn massacre. These are masterfully organized in J.K. Zawodny's book, *Death
in the Forest*. However, one final argument, not emphasized by Zawodny,
is important: the entire German civilian and military archives were captured by the western allies virtually intact at the end of the war. These
documents, now mostly in Washington, have been reviewed and indexed.
Yet no researcher has uncovered evidence which suggests Nazi guilt. Quite
to the contrary, the Nazi records reflect a belief that Stalin was responsible
(and, of course, recorded the desire to pin the crime on him). After so
many years, the evidence, however circumstantial, seems nevertheless
conclusive.

Why is the story of the Katyn Forest, an episode involving the death
of some fifteen thousand men, given so much attention in a survey of
East European history? The answer is simply that there can only be one
explanation for the Katyn Forest massacre, one that makes it part of a
deliberate plan. The missing soldiers were only 6 percent of all Polish
troops interned by the Soviets, but they were 84 percent of the officers.[7]
And these, of course, were only in small part professional military men.
A great many were reservists: university professors, attorneys, doctors—
a large part of the nation's educated elite. Another significant proportion
was young officers and cadets—men drawn from the cities and institutes
to meet the crisis but who would later go on into various universities. In
sum, the men were part of the intelligentsia. The Soviets tried hard to
recruit them to communism—this is almost certainly the explanation for
the fact that their camps were run by the NKVD instead of the regular
army—but they failed. Since these men would be the leaders of postwar
Poland, Stalin's philosophy of "he who is not with us is against us,"
provided the rationale for adding another group to the murder of millions.

Katyn was not among the crimes which Nikita Krushchev later laid
at Stalin's door. At first glance the omission seems surprising. But one
should remember that the recognized victims of Stalin were either Soviet
citizens, whose relatives were still under tight control, or foreign communists, for whom mourners were few and unimportant. To admit the
massacre of fifteen thousand Polish noncombatants would have started
a conflagration in Poland. Even Krushchev, who could not see all of the
consequences of de-Stalinization, would have seen that without difficulty.
As it is, the issue is an unwavering flame in the heart of the Polish nation.
Officials are warned not to permit that references to certain dead men
list their end as 1940; the censors are instructed to change the date to
1941. Thus, as often happens in postwar Eastern Europe, the written
word says one thing, but the reader sees another.

Diplomatic relations between Moscow and the London Poles were never restored. Before the Katyn massacre came to light the Soviets had organized the remains of the Communist Party of Poland into a front organization named the Union of Polish Patriots. When the Red Army moved on to Polish territory (as defined by Moscow), this group provided the nucleus for the Lublin Committee which was established by the Soviets when that city was liberated in the summer of 1944. The Lublin Committee took over those administrative duties in the Soviet-controlled areas which the Red Army did not want. In late December of 1944, this group declared itself the provisional government of Poland and was so organized by Moscow less than a week later. As the war ended, Katyn and even the question of the eastern frontiers were fading as issues for the London Poles: they were now worried that they and other democratic forces would not be permitted any role in postwar Poland.

Before passing to the home front, it is worthy of note that the Polish government in Poland was more than a symbolic ally. The London Poles commanded not only a well-organized resistance movement at home (see below) but also a sizable force in the west. The army assembled in the USSR in 1941–1942 was withdrawn via Persia where, together with other units that had escaped to the west, it was reequipped and sent into battle. The Poles fought bravely in North Africa, but really earned their distinction in Italy. During the pivotal battle of Monte Casino, it was a Polish force which, despite enormous losses, actually succeeded in capturing the principal objective. Later, a Polish armored division played a crucial role in the Battle of Falaise, which secured the Normandy beachhead and opened the way to Paris. While these and other Polish divisions entered Germany from the west, six Polish divisions under Russian command entered from the east and took part in the battle for Berlin.

While Polish ground forces were distinguishing themselves on all fronts, the Polish air force played a key role in the Battle of Britain. The Polish fliers had had little opportunity to show their talents in 1939, since the surprise attack had destroyed most of the aircraft on the ground. But, many escaped to the West where they comprised the largest group of foreign pilots in the Royal Air Force (RAF). In fact, a Polish squadron was the most successful in the RAF in total numbers of German planes shot down, and the Polish pilots, despite casualties of more than 20 percent, were among the most highly decorated of the war. The historian M. K. Dziewanowski has noted that, if Polish forces fighting in the east and west were added to resistance fighters, Poland had the fourth largest Allied army in the war (after the USSR, the U.S., and Britain).[8] The London Polish government alone commanded more than a half million men.

Poland—The Home Front

Although the Polish military took heavy casualties in six years of fighting, their losses were no more than a small percentage of those suffered by the civilian population. In addition to the staggering population losses—about six million—Poland as a land was physically bludgeoned by warfare and terror. And once again, for the second time in less than a century, foreign conquerors sought to eliminate the very existence of Poland as a nation. Germany directly annexed Posen, Pomerania, and the remainder of Silesia, and then moved swiftly in these lands to obliterate even the most subtle vestiges of Polishness. A visitor to the area a few months after the occupation would have seen no signs in Polish, and although he might have conversed with some who spoke broken, badly accented German, he would have heard no Polish spoken in public. Even young children spoke German or remained silent.

In the in-between area of Poland (remember that the Soviet Union held the eastern part) the situation was far worse. For, while the Poles in Germany and the Soviet Union could lead reasonably normal lives if they did what they were told and kept their national feelings to themselves, the Poles in occupied Poland were subject to constant harassment and terror. The area was officially known as the General Gouvernement, and its civilian administrator, Dr. Hans Frank, was among the most vicious and insane of Nazi ideologues. And indeed ideology was supreme in this case. Berlin made no effort to win the local population over to its side; instead, the Nazis made it clear that they considered the Poles to be subhuman. Official documents seized by the Allies at the end of the war demonstrate that Hitler saw the General Gouvernement as a transitory phenomenon for the duration of the war.[9] While the struggle continued, Poland's role was to be a source of slave labor for the German war effort. The civilian population was to be kept alive during this period, albeit with minimum rations and with the frequent use of terror as an incentive to work. Once the fighting was over and the Poles' labor was no longer needed, this "liberal" treatment was to end. The documents make it quite clear that the Nazis planned to murder the entire Polish population in order to make room for German settlers. At that, ethnic Poles were comparatively lucky—the Jews of Poland were given no mercy from the start (see below).

Even before Nazi policy for Poland became clear, a resistance movement was organized by Polish patriots. Although the terrain of Poland lacks the extensive mountains which form the classic refuge of guerrilla fighters, the Poles made use of the forests to shelter what eventually became an army of 300,000 men.[10] From the beginning, this organization, known as the Home Army, was loyal to the exile government in London and was anticommunist in character. This latter attitude was partly a reflection of Polish political views dating from the war of 1919–1920, but it also reflected the fact that the Soviet Union had invaded Poland in 1939, and that Moscow had at that time ordered communists not to resist the Germans (until the summer of 1941, of course). The Home Army was extraordinarily effective in harassing German communications. Most supplies for the Eastern Front had to move across the Polish rail network, and the Home Army was able to destroy a small portion in transit and to effect serious delays and confusion in the shipment of most of the remainder. Although the Polish resistance was of great value to the Red Army, Moscow never provided that force with any significant aid or even recognition.

Indeed, in retrospect it seems clear that Stalin was more anxious to destroy the Home Army than to help it. As the Red Army approached Warsaw in midsummer of 1944, Soviet propaganda leaflets urged the Poles to rise and help clear the area of Germans. The leaders of the Home Army and the exile government in London were now in a quandary. Their policy to this point had been to avoid a major large-scale battle with the Germans in order to preserve their command structure and their key forces to assist in governing the liberated lands. On the other hand, they feared that failure to act would give Moscow the opportunity to call them cowards and traitors. Reluctantly, they chose to take an action that would have significant symbolic as well as military importance: on August 1, 1944, the Home Army captured Warsaw from the surprised Germans. The Polish strategy was to hold the city for a few days until the Red Army, only a few miles away, could push the Germans back. Unaccountably, however, the Soviet troops which had been advancing many miles a day suddenly stopped, and, in rather ostentatious resupply activities, made it clear that they would not move for some time. The Germans got the message and concentrated their efforts on retaking Warsaw. After sixty-three days of bitter fighting, in which nearly half of the Polish force of 46,000 was killed, Warsaw was recaptured and Home Army captives were led off—often to disappear for good.[11] German sappers punished Warsaw, as the Luftwaffe had done Belgrade four years earlier. The Polish capital was literally leveled.

The Red Army finally took Warsaw in January of 1945, then sped forward to capture Berlin only a few months later. Though it is true that the Red Army was in need of rest and resupply in the late summer of 1944 (American observers confirm this),[12] it was also the case that the

Germans could do the same. Moreover, it is a rare military commander who will not seize the opportunity of an attack behind enemy lines to advance at minimal cost. The Soviets even went so far as to refuse Britiah and American planes the right to land on Soviet airstrips while supplying the Warsaw fighters: the reason given was that the munitions might fall into German hands.[13] The charge that Stalin deliberately allowed the Germans to destroy the elite of the Home Army is a grave one. Yet in the light of the Katyn Forest before, and the communist takeover afterward, such an action seems highly consistent with Moscow's policy.

Poland—The Holocaust

The Nazis began immediately to apply the Final Solution to Polish Jews both in the annexed areas and in the General Gouvernement. The concentration camps at Auschwitz, Buchenwald, and elsewhere were in the business of mass murder within a year. That the process did not begin faster and end sooner appears to have been only for logistical reasons. As the fate of the Jews in the camps became known, efforts to organize a resistance mounted. Some Jews fled to the forests and many joined elements of the Home Army. But most Jews had no option but to stay in the ghettos and fight as best they could. There were many instances of small-scale resistance, but the best known is that of the Jews of the Warsaw ghetto, who, despite a lack of arms and training, held out against German armor and artillery for three weeks from April 19 to May 10, 1943. Few survived, and, as Lucy Davidowicz notes, "the Warsaw ghetto became one huge cemetery."[14] Altogether about three million Polish Jews perished in the Holocaust; this was 86 percent of the prewar Jewish population of 3.3 million. Half of all of Europe's Jewish dead were Polish.

Czechoslovakia—Government and Military

Even before the German Army entered Czechoslovakia on October 1, 1938, President Beneš had been forced to resign by Hitler. He was replaced by Emil Hácha, who headed a feeble coalition of all principal political parties except the communists. The weak condition of this government was reflected in its inability to resist Slovak demands for complete autonomy. Less than six months later, Hitler ordered the Slovaks to declare independence; under the leadership of Msgr. Joseph Tiso, they did so immediately. The forcible separation of Slovakia (which was accompanied by Hungarian occupation of Carpatho-Ruthenia) was a prelude to German occupation of the remainder of Czechoslovakia only two days later, on March 15, 1939. Although a Czech government was allowed to continue to function, the area was renamed the "Protectorate of Bohemia-Moravia," with the true authority a deputy of Hitler's, known as the "Reichsprotector."

Beneš, meanwhile, had fled abroad and had settled in London. He soon forged an organization of other emigré politicians and began to speak for Czechoslovakia. Initially, the British and the French treated him cordially but did not extend any official recognition. This changed somewhat when the war began in September of 1939, and after the fall of France, Beneš' government received provisional recognition.[15] Subsequent to the launching of *Barbarossa*, all of the Allies, including the Soviet Union, accepted Beneš and his associates as official representatives of Czechoslovakia. Although Beneš was hardly a major figure in allied war councils, his was a generally well-respected voice, and the Czechs were well treated.

Czechoslovakia did not have anything like the kind of conflict with the Soviet Union that the Poles did. Czechoslovakia had never outlawed its communist party, and Beneš was not personally stigmatized as anti-Soviet. There was a potential border conflict between the two over Carpatho-Ruthenia, but Beneš, who was far more concerned about preserving the integrity of his country's western frontier, was disposed to be reasonable about Czechoslovakia's remote and poverty-stricken "tail." On several occasions Beneš mentioned to Soviet representatives that he would not object if Carpatho-Ruthenia were annexed to the USSR; in December of 1943, Beneš even said this to Stalin personally.[16] The Soviets were coy about this unusual generosity, but in the winter of 1944–1945, when Soviet troops occupied the area, they allowed the local populace to express "freely and voluntarily" its desire to be united with its brethren in the USSR. Stalin's assumption that Beneš would not object to this proved to be correct.

The Czechoslovak government in exile did command some military forces on the Western front. Czech pilots in the RAF, like the Poles, distinguished themselves in the Battle of Britain. A Czech armored brigade took part in the Normandy landings and was involved in several major battles in the drive toward Germany. Beyond the control of Beneš in London, there were also some 60,000 Czech troops fighting with the Red Army in the east. Overall, the manner in which Czechoslovakia had collapsed made it extremely difficult for Czech soldiers to find a way to participate in the war. That so many nevertheless succeeded in gaining the front lines in the struggle against Nazi Germany is a tribute to Czech courage and tenacity.

Czechoslovakia—The Home Front

The Germans proposed to treat the Czechs essentially the same as the Poles. Some, like the Poles in the areas directly incorporated into Germany, were to be allowed to "assimilate"; they had the opportunity to become German. The rest were doomed. Even so, there was a significant difference in strategy in the Czech lands. By the capture of Bohemia and Moravia, the German military had reaped an enormous harvest of weapons of the highest quality. The Škoda works became one of the Wehrmacht's principal suppliers. And behind the Czech munitions industry there lay a mature, sophisticated industrial base. While the war continued, the Nazis had no desire to kill the geese that laid such useful golden eggs. Indeed, the attractiveness of the Czechs lands for German industrial production increased in direct proportion to the growth of British and American air power. Most of Bohemia and Moravia were on the eastern fringe of the bombers' range and were consequently rarely attacked.

The Nazi policy in the Czech lands was one of the carrot and the stick. To a very great extent the carrot was simply letting people alone— a treatment which, in view of Nazi behavior elsewhere, was clearly understood as exceptional. There were more positive incentives as well, but bonuses were of little use in wartime and awards had no interest for the Czech workers. The stick was applied to those who were foolish enough to be outspoken; from the earliest days there were Czechs who knew the horror of the concentration camps. The civil administration was run by the Czechs, although all senior officials reported to German superiors. The police, needless to say, were closely supervised by the Gestapo.

Slovakia was nominally independent, although it too was under German "protection." The history of this region during the war was, until recently, little known. The reason for the obscurity is simple: few wished to talk about a fanatically pro-Nazi regime which was led by members of the local Catholic hierarchy. Though Slovakia was not occupied by German troops until 1944, Tiso's government lent the Nazis propaganda support and provided troops to assist the Wehrmacht. Most important, the regime promulgated a full range of anti-Jewish laws which were soon rendered moot because so many Slovaks cooperated fully with Hitler's plans to remove Slovak Jewry to the concentration camps.[17] Although the Slovak peasants had a long tradition of anti-Semitism, part of their fanaticism is explained by the fact that nearly all of the Jews in the area had been assimilated into Hungarian culture. Thus, national rivalry once again had a role in producing violence in Eastern Europe.

The situation in the Czech lands was not well suited for a guerrilla movement. This was so partly in that the terrain lacked the traditional mountain hideouts, but mostly because of the distribution of the German population. Mao Ze Dong has said that a guerrilla is like a fish in water— the people being the water. The classic guerrilla bands draw food, supplies, and intelligence from villagers or (rarely) urban neighborhoods. The village will typically have only an occasional enemy presence, or at worst there will be one or two obvious enemy agents; the guerrillas can thus move in and out with very little danger. But in the Czech lands such situations were rare. Large areas, including those with terrain best suited for guerrilla operations, had a high concentration of Germans. Even in the further reaches of Moravia, there were many Germans who spoke fluent Czech and were thus not readily identifiable as enemies. The towns and cities were the most dangerous; informers were everywhere.

In this environment, it is not surprising that the Czechs did not organize an equivalent of the Polish Home Army or that the units that did exist suffered greatly at the hands of the Gestapo. Even so, the Czechs had some success. Their greatest achievement, perhaps the single best known guerrilla act of the war, was the assassination of the reichspro-tector, Reinhard Heydrich, in late 1941. The actual killing was planned in Britain and was carried out by Czech commandos parachuted in by Allied aircraft. But the deed would not have been possible without the support of the Czech underground. Certainly the SS and the Gestapo thought so, for they launched a campaign of terror in a search for the killers. Finally, as official revenge, the Nazis wiped out the Czech village of Lidice. All of the men and older boys (172 people) were executed on the spot; women and children were sent to concentration camps. Pregnant women were taken to hospitals until their children were born; the babies were then killed and the women sent to the camps. The village itself was burned and bulldozed—the only remaining sign of its existence was the charred earth. Lidice is famous because the Nazis chose to publicize it. In fact, at least one other Czech village suffered the same fate, and similar barbarism was almost commonplace in Poland and Yugoslavia.

Some twenty-three thousand people were executed in the aftermath of the Heydrich assassination.[18] The Czech resistance subsequently waned.

The Czechs had to content themselves with industrial sabotage, a practice at which, like their colleagues in France, Belgium, Holland, and Denmark, they had become quite skilled by the end of the war. Slovakia, however, was an area well suited to guerrilla warfare. At first not much occurred as Slovaks basked in the glory of their first independent state. Change came gradually, but by 1943 opposition was widespread and partisan bands were gathering strength rapidly. Two groups formed the core of the resistance. First was the intelligentsia, many of whose members were shocked at the barbarism of the regime but found that the only way to effect change was to take to the hills. Although Tiso and other regime officials were members of the Catholic hierarchy, many of the rebels were also Catholics whose views were those of most of the Slovak clergy as well as of the Vatican.

The most important element in the Slovak resistance, however, was the communist party. The communists had always had strong support among the poorest peasants, and, after the summer of 1941, many rallied to Moscow's call. The party made good use of its experience with clandestine operations, and this, coupled with the traditional communist emphasis on organization and discipline, made it easy for Moscow's representatives to take control. The efforts of the resistance, which had as its political arm the Slovak National Council, culminated in a national revolt in August of 1944. At first successful in seizing control of much of the country, the rebels came into conflict with German forces defending the eastern front (now very close to Slovakia). the Slovaks were defeated and forced back into the mountains after some four months of bloody fighting, but the affair had the twofold effect of reducing the image of Slovaks as Nazi collaborators and of enhancing the prestige of the communists.

Czechoslovakia—The Holocaust

The small Jewish population of the Czech lands never really had a chance to resist the Nazis—Von Neurath (the first reichsprotector) swiftly proclaimed the full panoply of Nazi racial laws in the protectorate and used the Gestapo to enforce them in the stead of the unwilling Czech police. Deportations and executions began almost immediately. Some Czech Jews did have the opportunity to join the resistance, however, and there they played a prominent role. In Slovakia, the picture was even bleaker. Tiso's regime cooperated with the Nazis and actively rounded up Jews for deportation. Only toward the end of the war, when pressure from the Vatican began to be felt and public opposition mounted, did the regime balk at further arrests.[19] By then, however, there were very few Jews left. Overall in Czechoslovakia, only about 10 percent of the Jewish population survived the war—and at least half of those saved were in the camps waiting to die when the war ended.[20]

Hungary—Government and Military

Hungary's status as an ally of Nazi Germany was probably opposed by a solid majority of the population, but then the Hungarian people had never really had an opportunity to be heard on major issues. On the other hand, it is certainly true that Hungary's territorial avariciousness, which commanded the support of nearly all Hungarians, and the tendency toward anti-Semitism, which was the attitude of a small but noisy minority, helped smooth the path toward the Nazi embrace. Hungary's governmental structure did not change until the very end of the war. Horthy continued as regent. He left day-to-day government to a prime minister, who was selected with an eye to the popular mood. On key issues of policy, however, Horthy made all of the final decisions.

The premier at the beginning of the war in the east was László Bárdossy—perceived to be pro-German because he replaced Teleki, whose suicide was clearly a protest against alliance with Berlin. In fact, Bárdossy had rather a neutralist background and seemed to be willing to follow the Nazi line only so far as necessary. Even so, the changes were substantial. New legislation for the first time provided a racial as opposed to a religious definition of who was a Jew. Shortly after taking this step, Bárdossy and Horthy had to deal with the prospect of war with the Soviet Union. Hitler did not at first insist on Hungarian participation, and the official line of Budapest on that fateful June 22 was one of benevolent neutrality. But by the end of the day the government changed its mind and severed diplomatic relations with Moscow, and by June 25 Hungary had declared war on the Soviet Union. A few days later Hungarian troops crossed the frontier.

The reversal of Hungarian policy was a result of several factors. Officially, it was in retaliation for a rather mysterious "Soviet air attack" on Hungary (in fact, since observers noted that planes had Axis markings, this may have been a German provocation or, according to another version, a free-lance action by Slovak or Czech pilots escaping to the

USSR).[21] Far more important, however, was the fact that Hitler changed his mind. The attack in the sector immediately opposite Hungary was going slowly, and the führer now specifically asked for Hungarian assistance. Moreover, the Magyar leaders were deeply concerned that their remaining rivals in Eastern Europe, the Slovaks and the Romanians, were already participating in the struggle—the latter with many divisions. There was a real concern in Budapest that failure to assist the Nazis would lead to a reversal of Berlin's earlier award of parts of Slovakia and Romania to Hungary. The race for Hitler's favor thus began.

The available evidence, particularly that gathered by the historian C. A. Macartney, suggests that neither Bárdossy nor Horthy wished to enter the war, but they felt that they had no choice.[22] Hungary did not declare war on Britain or the United States until forced to do so by the Germans. Nevertheless, Bárdossy was, as a result of these events, indelibly marked as pro-Axis, a view which Horthy seems not to have discouraged. By March of 1942, with Berlin pressing the Hungarians to mobilize fully in order to help bring a quick end to the war in the east, Horthy dropped Bárdossy and replaced him with Miklós Kállay, a man known for his opposition to the German alliance and to Nazism. Kállay was not able to stop the flow of Hungarian soldiers eastward, but he did alter the pro-Axis tone of domestic propaganda, and he began to explore ways of extricating Hungary from the war through secret discussions with the western allies.[23]

The Germans were well represented in the neutral capitals of Istanbul, Lisbon, and Stockholm, however, and they soon learned of Hungary's double dealing. Hitler was furious, and in April of 1943, he castigated Horthy for his government's actions, but Horthy did not alter course and did not dismiss Kállay. A year later, after Kállay had made a radio appeal which sounded suspiciously like a call for Hungarian withdrawal from the war, Hitler again commanded Horthy to a meeting. This time, Horthy was held prisoner while German forces occupied key positions in Hungary. Horthy was then forced to name a genuine pro-Nazi, Döme Sztójay, as premier; Kállay took refuge in the Turkish embassy. Two things are interesting about this Hitler-Horthy meeting. One is that Hitler, who had the power to do anything he wanted with Horthy (and with Hungary for that matter), clearly believed that Horthy's prestige would greatly ease Germany's effort to bind Hungary to its will. Horthy, by the same token, believed that he was powerless and chose to stay only with the intention of saving what he could of his countrymen's blood and favor. Interestingly (but not surprisingly), the Hungarians took as Hitler's most terrible threat the Nazi plan to use Romanian, Slovak, and Croat troops in the occupation of their country; the lack of resistance to the penetration of German troops is in large part ascribed to this (in fact, even as Hungarian and Romanian troops fought side by side in the horrible Russian winter of 1942–1943, a large part of the best Hungarian troops were guarding the frontier with Romania).[24]

Sztójay, unlike Hungarian premiers of the past, could operate fairly independently of Horthy. Given that his patron was in Berlin, not Budapest, and not Horthy but Hitler, it is unsurprising that Sztójay quickly nazified Hungary. In a matter of a few months a relatively placid society was torn apart. German advisers were ubiquitous and frequently in charge. It is incredible to think that such a dramatic change could begin and continue at a time when the Red Army was pushing inexorably forward on the fringes of Eastern Europe and when an Allied army in Italy was serving as the anvil for the successful hammer blow in Normandy. Any intelligent person could see that the Nazi system which Sztójay was aping could last a few more months but definitely not a year. Yet intelligence does not prevent insanity, and it was clearly madness that reigned in Hungary.

Horthy was not finished, however, and in August he took advantage of the ineptitude of Sztójay's management, coupled with the presence of Soviet troops on the Hungarian frontier, to name as a fait accompli a replacement premier. The new man, a general named Géza Lakatos, was a neutralist along the lines of Kállay. Although efforts were made to resume diplomatic contacts with the Allies, German troops still occupied the country, and there was little room for maneuver. This helplessness, made all the more glaring by the successful anti-German revolt in Romania, forced Horthy to gamble in order to "restore Hungary's honor": (a more cynical view is that Horthy, and other leaders in Budapest, realized that if Hungary finished the war as an ally of the Nazis, the territories gained from Romania, Czechoslovakia, and Yugoslavia would again be lost). Horthy thus resolved to have an anti-Nazi coup of his own.

On October 15, 1944, Horthy declared an armistice with the USSR. The situation, however, was far from opportune. The Hungarian Army was nearly all at the front; in Budapest itself the Germans were stronger than their allies. And even then there was disloyalty—the Hungarian chief-of-staff effectively negated the change by giving the troops orders that were taken to mean that they should continue to fight the Russians.[25] Horthy then surrendered and was taken to the reich as a prisoner (he survived and lived out his days in Portugal). The Nazis now allowed the degenerates of the anti-Semitic Arrowcross to take over. Szálasi became premier. The depravity of the Arrowcross made Sztójay's regime seem a model of sanity. Most residents of Budapest could not help but feel relief, even in the presence of a new fear, as Russian tanks fought their way into the city in January of 1945. By April 4 of that year, the Nazis, with the Arrowcross in their baggage, were gone from all of Hungary.

The Hungarian Army was badly mauled during the war. Although only a few units fought in the first campaigns in Russia, by 1942 Hungarian troops were fighting in large numbers hundreds of miles from home. The delay in Hungarian participation was a consequence of the fact that Hungary had not had a real army until the very end of the interwar period and had not made much progress in equipment and training when Barbarossa was launched. The Germans, although they pressed hard for Hungarian participation, were slow to provide the armaments needed for modern warfare. This weakness became acutely apparent in early 1943, when the Axis forces spearheading the attack on Stalingrad were outflanked and sent reeling backwards by the Red Army. The reserve troops, who in this sector were overwhelmingly Hungarian, found themselves on the front line. The results, known as the Battle of Voronezh, were disastrous.

Hitler's orders to the Hungarians were to stand and fight to the last man. That they did not do so is unsurprising: poorly equipped, unseasoned, and bewildered as to why they were there (especially when the Wehrmacht was itself in chaos), the Hungarians turned and fled. Their fate in joining the retreat was not much better than it would have been in direct battle. The roads were clogged and the fields deep with snow; aircraft and artillery harassed the roads and partisans picked off those who were lucky enough not to starve and freeze to death in the fields. The remainder was captured. Altogether, the Hungarian Army lost (killed or captured) more than 100,000 men at Voronezh.[26] By the time the front was stabilized the Hungarian Army was destroyed as an effective force. The Germans, furious at what they considered to be cowardice, allowed the Hungarian troops to be withdrawn from the fighting.

After the creation of the Sztójay government, the Hungarians again sent men to the front. Nearly all existing units were called up and, ready or not, were thrown against the Red Army. Casualties were again enormous, but this time the Hungarians, however hopeless the cause, left no doubt as to their bravery: they were now fighting on the frontiers of the homeland, and however much they despised Germans, they had every reason to want to spare their countrymen the agonies of Soviet "liberation." Hungarian troops fought together with the Germans street by street and house by house for their capital, yielding the surrounded fortress of Buda after more than three weeks of extremely bitter fighting. The

Soviets retaliated by taking very few prisoners. Hungarian troops, with little opportunity to do otherwise, struggled on to the very end. In the process they saw their country collapse into flaming rubble.

There was virtually no resistance movement in wartime Hungary. While few Hungarians were in favor of Nazi Germany, Hungarian fascism or the war, most were still loyal citizens who saw no alternative but to remain so. The allied appeals for resistance seemed, as indeed they were, wildly impractical. Those few Hungarians willing to operate against their own government could find no safe haven either in the hearts of their countrymen or in the countryside. To the extent that there was a resistance it was organized by the communists, who had a few scattered cells operating and who organized an antifascist front group in cooperation with some noncommunist politicians. There were no partisan bands to speak of, however, and even sabotage and propaganda activity were practically unknown.

Hungary—The Holocaust

Horthy apparently never knew what Hitler envisaged as the Final Solution, but while he was in control he nevertheless took precautions not to allow Hungarian Jews to fall into Nazi hands. The sole exception to this came in the early days of the fighting in the east when a Hungarian commander transferred some 17,000 Ruthenian Jews (Czechoslovak nationals) to German control. These were subsequently massacred, but there is no evidence that the Hungarians knew of their fate. Early in 1942, a similar sort of action took place when a police commander in the Hungarian-occupied Vojvodina decided on his own initiative to take reprisals against local villagers and townsmen who were thought to be supporting Yugoslav partisans. In the mass executions that followed, some 700 Jews perished (about 20 percent of the total), apparently for no other reason than to appease local anti-Semitism. Horthy ordered an investigation, but the report failed to mention the Jewish victims and the matter was dropped.[27] On the other hand, there was nothing more in the way of pogroms in Hungary until the Nazis intervened directly.

For most of the war the Jews of Hungary lived under a sword of Damocles but at least they lived. Their social and economic life was severely limited, and their political participation was nonexistent. They were not, however, subjected to physical terror, and radical Hungarian anti-Semitic groups, such as the Arrowcross, were kept in check by the authorities. The greatest initial suffering of the Jews in the early period was that men of military age, by law no longer eligible to serve in the armed forces, were nevertheless drafted into labor battalions. Together with other "untrustworthy nationalities" (principally Romanians), the Jews in the labor battalions were sent to support the troops on the Eastern Front. Though behind the frontlines, they suffered heavy losses from the cold, malnutrition, artillery and air attacks, and even partisan raids.

Hitler's pressure on Horthy and the subsequent German invasion of Hungary cut the wire and caused the long dangling sword to fall on Hungarian Jewry. Just as Horthy was forced to accept direct German activity in many areas of his government, he was told that local authorities must assist in rounding up Jews to be sent to Germany for "labor service." There is no indication that Horthy knew or suspected that more than this was intended; in fact a number of documents suggest that some German officials actually intended to use the Jews for the stated purpose (at least initially). Even so, the Sztójay government, which had introduced a law requiring that Jews wear a yellow Star of David, cooperated enthusiastically in forcing Jews into camps for delivery to Nazi authorities. When reports of miserable conditions and brutality in these camps reached Horthy, he ordered another investigation. The person selected by Sztójay to look into the matter was a fanatical anti-Semite whose incredible report included the following: "Everything was in perfect order. The provincial ghettos had the character of Sanatoria. At last the Jews had taken up an open-air life and exchanged their former mode of living for a healthier one."[28]

However this absurdity was taken, it is clear that Horthy and others soon became suspicious. A principal factor in raising doubts was the Nazi proposal that all Jews, including the very old and the very young, be deported for "labor." Concern about the fate of Hungarian Jewry reached Horthy from a number of sources, including the Catholic and Protestant churches, and seems to have been the major reason for his dismissal of Sztójay. The new government under Lakatos ordered a halt to the deportations. The Germans protested, but, probably because they urgently needed Hungarian troops to help on the shrinking Eastern Front, did not attempt to force a change.

Horthy's action saved a large part of Hungarian Jewry, principally the roughly two-hundred thousand residing in Budapest. But the respite was short-lived. The Regent's abortive coup in October removed all protection for the Jews. Although the failing communications of the collapsing Third Reich made further mass deportations infeasible, the Arrowcross subjected the Jews of Budapest to murder and torture, not to mention robbery. These final days of madness were eased somewhat by the activities of the incredible Swedish diplomat, Raul Wallenberg, who passed out thousands of Swedish passports to Jews, even pulling some off of trains under SS guard. No one can be certain as to how many people were saved by Wallenberg, but his reward is known: he was arrested by the Soviet military and turned over to the NKVD. He is presumed to have perished somewhere in the system of forced labor camps called the Gulag Archipelago. Overall, about 70 percent of Hungary's Jews, some 450,000 people, were killed during the war.[29]

Yugoslavia—Occupation and Administration

The hammer blows of the Luftwaffe's "Operation Punishment" crushed the Yugoslav government as well as its headquarters in Belgrade. The fate of the Royal Army was equally swift: within a matter of days the command structure collapsed under overwhelming force applied from nearly every possible direction. The king, the senior members of the court, and the cabinet fled to London to join the exile goverments of Poland and Czechoslovakia. But the military could not be evacuated, and both soldiers and officers were left to their fate. Some kept their units intact and retreated to the hills and mountains from which they never stopped fighting. Others melted into the countryside as the peasant soldiers went home to help with the spring planting. But both groups kept their arms, and both were heard from again.

Even before King Peter arrived in London, the Axis powers had divided up the nation over which he had ruled for such a short time. Most of the spoils went to the victors: Germany herself took a large part of Slovenia, while Italy took the rest and incorporated it, together with Dalmatia, into the Italian kingdom; Hungary took the Vojvodina, and Bulgaria was awarded Macedonia; Albania (actually, of course, a dependency of Italy) got the Kosovo region. The remainder—essentially the core of Croatia and Serbia—was then split in two. An "Independent State of Croatia" was established with its capital of Zagreb. This entity was under Italian control and was even given an Italian "king" (the duke of Spoleto, who bettered Prince William of Albania's record by never even visiting his "kingdom."[30] A Croatian fascist, Ante Pavelić, who had lived in Italy and who had been involved in the murder of King Alexander, was named leader (*poglavnik*). The Serbian state, by contrast, was under the direct authority of the German ministry, although a native civilian administration was maintained.

The Allies ignored all of these changes and continued to recognize King Peter and his exile government in London as the legitimate authority in all of Yugoslavia. It would be wrong, however, to assume that the status of Peter and his entourage was similar to that of the Poles or the Czechoslovaks. The king himself had little experience, and none of the members of the government could claim to have had a very strong following in the country as a whole before the war. The exile government's historical weakness was made even worse in the present by its lack of armed forces. The Poles had troops within and outside of Poland, and the Czechs had some on the outside, but the Yugoslavs at first had neither. Nevertheless, the United States, Britain, and the Soviet Union all gave full accreditation to Peter and his ministers. It is ironic in view of later events that the leaders in Washington and London began to back away from this alliance earlier than did those in Moscow.

The situation in the "Croatian Kingdom" was probably the worst in all of Yugoslavia. Although a political dependency of Italy and garrisoned by both Italian and German troops, Pavelić's regime was given virtually free reign in domestic affairs. The Poglavnik and his Ustaša immediately set out on a mission to "purify" their new nation. A part of this activity was directed against the Jews, despite their small numbers and relatively small role in the economic and social life of the region. A full range of anti-Jewish legislation was put into effect, and within a short time most Jews had been executed, sent into forced labor camps, or deported to Germany. Very few Croatian Jews survived the war.[31]

The Ustaša are better remembered for their anti-Serb than their anti-Jewish violence because the former was carried out on a far greater scale. Pavelić and his gang were the legacy of the hatred between Croats and Serbs that had developed during the war. It was not sufficient for them to torture, imprison, or kill everyone who had been directly or indirectly associated with the Belgrade regime. They wished instead to go much farther and eliminate any Serbian presence in the lands they controlled. Their targets included a very high percentage of the Croatian kingdom. There had always been Serb villages in Croatia proper, and perhaps two-thirds of Bosnia-Hercegovina (which was assigned to the kingdom of Croatia) was either Orthodox or Moslem. Overall, it is estimated that only about half of Pavelić's subjects were actually Croats (i.e., Serbo-Croatian speaking Roman Catholics).

The Ustaša launched an immediate wave of terror against Serbian villages in the territory they controlled. The official goal was to get as many people as possible to convert to Catholicism. Since villages typically only had one church, the emphasis was on mass conversions. That such an effort would be doomed to failure in a traditional society is hardly surprising. The few changeovers that did occur were essentially superficial; for the most part the Ustaša generated not conversions but armed resistance. The result was a sort of civil war in which one side (the Ustaša) clearly dominated in both firepower and ruthlessness.

It is estimated that the Ustaša murdered more than 350,000 Serbs during the war.[32] Although there were concentration camps whose inmates rarely emerged alive, for the most part those killed were simply the inhabitants of a recalcitrant village. The Ustaša murdered most often by shooting, but more brutal methods were frequently employed. Deeply infected by the hatred of the interwar years, Pavelić and his cohorts developed a contagious mental illness that in turn produced a blood lust unequalled beyond the realm of the Nazi SS. The Italians were contemptuous of and eventually sickened by the behavior of their creation but were powerless to control it. The Vatican, which cheered the establishment of a Catholic state, and which must share some of the guilt for Pavelić's crimes because it chose for a very long time to look the other way, also came to understand the inherent criminality of the Zagreb regime, but it too was unable to overcome the momentum.

Serbia was far more ethnically homogenous than Croatia, and the German military government had, in any case, no interest in exacerbating ethnic or religious feuds. The Serbian civil administration had a police force but not a militia, and even these units were carefully supervised by German officers. Hitler had no great aims for Serbia: the area was essentially a strategic buffer zone and as such the goal was merely to keep it quiet. There was significant economic exploration of the area, however, and this process was facilitated by the fact that many mining and industrial enterprises had been under either German ownership or management before the war. Once the fighting ceased, the initial overall German policy was fairly liberal in the Nazi context: the Serbs were allowed to live much as they had before so long as they did not challenge the system. In many ways, the early situation resembled that in the Czech lands. Tragically, the analogy also extends to the Jewish community which though small (perhaps 12,000) was nonetheless highly visible. The Nazis had murdered all but a handful after only a year of occupation.[33]

The policies of the two subsidiary Axis allies which participated in the partition of Yugoslavia were very similar. Both Hungary and Bulgaria aggressively seized the opportunity to establish not only political but also cultural and linguistic hegemony in their areas. This was most difficult for the Hungarians who lacked a plurality much less a majority in the Vojvodina. The Magyars had a long (albeit unsuccessful) tradition of forcing their culture on others, however, and their effort displayed the usual zeal as well as the usual negative results. The regime often resorted to violence to attain at least superficial acquiescence. Though there was one incident of mass executions (see above), for the most part violence was on a small scale, more akin to calculated terror than to mass reprisals such as those favored by the Ustaša.

In Bulgarian-occupied Macedonia the situation was different. Many Macedonians considered themselves to be Bulgarians and believed that they had finally achieved liberation from foreign rule and reunification with the homeland. Another group, probably somewhat smaller than the first (though no one can be really sure), considered that they had merely exchanged one foreign occupation for another. These were the descendants of IMRO (see above). Had the Bulgarian regime taken a pacific approach, granting the region a large measure of autonomy and trying to undermine the independence-minded group by winning over its more moderate members with cultural concessions and jobs in the bureaucracy, it could probably have assimilated Macedonia without great difficulty. Instead, however, Bulgaria behaved like a typical East European state. All governmental affairs remained highly centralized in Sofia, and regional bureaucrats were appointed on the basis of political cronyism rather than from the group of local leaders. The Bulgarian army and police were used vigorously against dissidents. Consequently, opposition developed and grew rapidly.[34]

In Kosovo, occupied by Italy's Albanian puppet, no attempt was made to reorient national and ethnic relationships. The administration was theoretically Albanian, and this theoretically improved the status of the Albanians vis à vis the formerly dominant Serbs. On the other hand, all important posts in the civilian government were held by Italians, and since the region quickly became a war zone, de facto rule was by Italian military authorities. The Italians, whether civilian or military, considered both Serbs and Albanians as at best culturally backward and at worst subhumans. Their rule was correspondingly unpopular.

Yugoslavia—Resistance

The history of Yugoslav resistance to Axis authority is, at least overall, a saga of incredible sacrifice and unquestioned heroism. It is also, however, a story which is exceedingly controversial from the political point of view. A generation has been born and matured since the events took place, but new evidence and new arguments still surface. A narrative such as this cannot do justice to the complexity of the subject, and its objective must necessarily be limited to acquainting the reader with the principal facts and points of view.

One fact is that of the units of the Serbian Army which retreated intact into the rugged terrain of the south, the largest and best organized was led by General Draža Mihailović. This group took the name of Četniks', which literally means "bandits" but in fact is a historical term which refers to the outlaws who attempted to protect the people during the centuries of Turkish occupation (the usual term for such groups, as noted earlier, was hajduks). Mihailović was able to carry out some harassment of German troops and communications in the first months after the occupation, and news of these activities quickly reached King Peter's government in exile. The king was delighted at the prospect of having a Yugoslav army in the field, as were Churchill and Roosevelt, and Milhailović was quickly given extensive publicity as the heroic commander of a major resistance movement.

The excitement about the Četniks occurred before anything substantive was known about their activities. In fact, even before the first British mission made its way to Mihailović's headquarters (late October, 1941), the Četniks had all but stopped offensive actions against Axis forces. The reasons for this inactivity were partly philosophical and partly pragmatic. The philosophy was simple and straightforward (albeit rarely expressed openly): the goal of the Četniks was to build a strong military-political organization which would be ready to strike a mighty blow against enemy forces at the appropriate time (e.g., in the early stages of an Allied invasion) and which would then be able to move quickly to restore the authority of the royal government when hostility ceased. In the interim, the Četniks would develop an intelligence capability, perform chores such as rescuing downed fliers, and perhaps also undertake occasional sabotage of great military significance (e.g., the destruction of a key bridge).

The pragmatic reasons for inactivity were also strong. The Četniks were poorly armed and lacking in organization. The former severely limited their potential effectiveness while the latter threatened their very existence. In the chaos of defeat the Germans had been able to gather, through blackmail and purchase, a large number of covert Serbian agents. In the fragile structure of the early Četnik movement, these men could do enormous damage. Until these traitors were isolated and eliminated, and until reasonably well armed troops could be put under at least a somewhat coherent command structure, even the limited objectives of Milhailović could not be achieved.

The Četnik philosophy was in fact consistent with that which the Anglo-Americans had adopted in other occupied countries such as France, Belgium, Denmark, and Norway and was not far from that of the Polish Home Army. Further, the material weaknesses of Milhailović's forces were soon appreciated, and it was understood by military authorities in London and Washington that without time to regroup and receive an influx of armaments, little could be expected of the Četniks. In fact, Mihailović's situation would have been reasonably strong (the Soviets also recognized and praised him) had it not been for two factors: (1) Allied commanders decided that early attacks on Axis communications in the Balkans could have an important effect on the fighting in North Africa; and (2) the Četniks were soon competing with a rival organization, the Partisans, whose activities waxed as theirs waned. The contrast between the two eventually threw Allied support to the latter.

The Partisan organization was the structural outgrowth of Tito's Communist Party of Yugoslavia (CPY), though this connection was not openly admitted until the war was over. Tito, in fact downplayed his communist past to the extent that that was possible; the Partisans did not develop an overt political arm until 1944, and even then the program was not clearly communist.[35] The Partisans do not seem to have been much hampered by the affiliation of their leadership: to the extent that it was known, which was not much, few seemed to think it important. The initial handicaps of the Partisans were in fact much less subtle: they had few arms, few officers, and no outside source of aid (the Soviets were obviously unable to help even if they had been willing).

The strengths of the Partisans soon offset their weaknesses, however. Through the CPY, the Partisans acquired an organization of brave people, long accustomed to extreme hardship, and skilled at the all-important task of working underground. This latter proved especially important, for the Četniks operated in the remote hills, but the Partisans operated everywhere. Also, the CPY had its own internal security structure complete with a ruthless set of procedures for dealing with informants. Compared to other communist parties in occupied Europe, the CPY structure also had a major advantage: the period between the Nazi attack on Yugoslavia and that on the Soviet Union was very brief and chaotic. Thus, the CPY had largely avoided the stain of collaboration that seriously weakened many other communist parties.

Of all of the advantages which the Partisans had over the Četniks, two were of paramount importance. First, the Partisans were truly Yugoslav, while the Četniks were exclusively Serb. This meant that Tito's forces could operate throughout the country while Mihailović's were limited to a smaller area, and more important, it meant that the former could draw recruits from all across the country. It is important to remember that the CPY, though its leadership was of diverse origin (e.g., Tito's Croatian-Slovenian parentage), had had its strongest base in the Serbian city of Belgrade among students and workers who were rarely more than a generation removed the countryside. It was also the case that general discontent with the old regime, of which Mihailović was the representative, had been significant in Serbia as well as in the rest of the country.

The second principal advantage of the Partisans was that they quickly developed a reputation as effective fighters, a factor which drew them first recruits and eventually significant outside assistance. Though the Partissans lacked officers in the traditional sense, they had among their ranks many veterans of the International Brigade which fought in the Spanish Civil War. These men were survivors, fearless, and experienced in dealing with an enemy possessing both superior numbers and superior arms. In Spain, they had learned how to operate with a minimum of supplies and above all how to use rugged terrain to make the enemy suffer for every village and every kilometer of road he attempted to control. Thus if the Axis occupiers chose to keep their forces out of the hills and mountains, they could expect nightly raids of increasing intensity on installations in the valleys and lowlands; if they chose to pursue the guerrillas, they would need a large force and could expect heavy casualties.

Casualties, in fact, were a principal reason for the growing contrast between Četniks and Partisans. The German commander in Yugoslavia, General Böhme, had carried Hitler's orders to the limit and had begun to execute one hundred civilians for every German soldier killed by guerrillas. Thousands were killed almost immediately in a series of massacres. Since, in the early days, both Četniks and Partisans were operating in Serbia, all of the first victims were Serbs. The prospect of an unending bloodbath in Serbia, coupled with the wholesale slaughter of Serbs by the Ustaša, caused the already cautious Mihailović to cease all offensive activity. Tito, on the other hand, saw the German policy as a means of recruitment—better for the villagers to join the Partisans than to stay behind and be murdered. His aggressive policy won many recruits, especially in Bosnia, and also brought the adherence of some of Mihailović's commanders and with them their men and arms.

Early in the war, when the Partisans and Četniks were operating in adjacent territory, the two forces cooperated in small ways—primarily in efforts to avoid transgressing on each other's theater of operations. Open conflict soon occurred, however, and the responsibility appears to belong entirely to the Četnniks who attempted to seize a Partisan headquarters.[36] Mihailović's forces were soundly defeated in this effort, and it seems to have marked the beginning of the end for the Serb commander. Jealous of the Partisans, yet sometimes unable and sometimes unwilling to follow their aggressive lead, he negotiated with the Germans. Mihailović did not actually agree to anything (the Germans wanted unconditional surrender), but a pattern of willingness to deal with the enemy was established. Shortly thereafter, Četnik organizations to the west began to cooperate with the Italians against the Partisans. This latter almost certainly occurred without Mihailović's approval but was significant in that the ostensible leader of the Četniks could not or would not prevent such collaboration.[37]

The British, who had a mission at Mihailović's headquarters, began to be concerned about their ally. They did not know about the meetings with the Germans, but they could not fail to notice that such offensive operations as did occur were directed against the Partisans and that there was evidence that some Četnik leaders were acting in concert with the enemy. There was no indication of Mihailović"s personal involvement in anything improper much less treasonous, but it was obvious that the Partisans were fighting and the Četniks were not (in fact both groups were often fighting on the defensive, but even here there was a difference: the Četniks tended to melt away as the Germans advanced; the Partisans often stood and held key objectives, retreating only after inflicting maximum casualties). Since the British and the Americans were fighting on a front not far from the Balkans—North Africa—they decided to support the more aggressive forces.

In March of 1943, as the Anglo-American forces were fighting the closing battles in North Africa and preparing to invade Italy (July of 1943), the British decided to send a mission to the Partisans. This followed a long period of bad relations with Mihailović which included several deliberate interruptions in air drops to the Četniks. A subsequent anti-British speech by Mihailović and the growing publicity in the west about Partisan activities contributed to the decision.[38] When the British officers arrived at Tito's headquarters in May, they immediately reported that the Partisans were engaging some one hundred thousand Axis troops. Supplies then began to be sent to the Partisans in large quantities. More important for Tito, however, was the surrender of the Italians on September 8, 1943. This event enabled the Partisans to seize quantities of arms sufficiently large as to transform the capabilities of their forces (a seaborne supply link was also opened by the Americans). From this point on, one can think of Tito as the commander of a real army, holding significant territory and actually maintaining a front of sorts. Tito also now won over many Četniks and was able to protect himself fairly easily from those who remained hostile. Formal contact between the British and Mihailović ended in February of 1944, although the flow of supplies had ceased much earlier.

The Partisans had a scare in May of 1944, when a German offensive almost succeeded in capturing Tito. But their recovery was quick, and they continually expanded their territory. In late summer of 1944, the Partisans began to drive up through Serbia from their strongholds in the southwest. The purpose was to link up with the Russians, but in the process many Četnik units were also defeated or dispersed. The Soviet forces entered Yugoslavia on October 1, following completion of a military agreement between the Partisans and the Red Army commanders. On October 20, the two jointly liberated Belgrade. The German forces in the center of the country, in serious danger of being outflanked, were then rapidly withdrawn northwards. The evacuated area then fell to Tito's forces who also took over the task of liberating the rest of enemy-held territory (the overwhelming bulk of the Red Army passed quickly into Hungary). On May 2, 1945, the German troops remaining in Yugoslavia surrendered to the Partisans.

Yugoslavia—Diplomacy and the Formation of a Communist State

At the beginning of the war Tito was completely unknown to the western Allies. The Soviets were not much help in all this, even though they were in contact with him (albeit sporadically) and he and his forces were officially under the command of the Comintern.[39]

Stalin, in fact, seemed anxious to downplay the significance of his agent. The Soviet press and radio also tended to give mistaken credit to the Četniks, and the Soviet diplomats dealt with the exiles in London as the de jure government of Yugoslavia. As the war progressed, Stalin demonstrated his tendency to keep Tito *sub rosa* by such actions as forcing a retraction of Tito's declaration that a liberated area of Montenegro was to become a part of the Soviet Union and even by ordering the Partisans to back off when they were on the verge of destroying the Četniks.[40]

Stalin's purpose in keeping public distance from Tito is obvious: he did not wish to draw attention to the Partisan leader's attachment to communism (in retrospect, one might also postulate that Stalin was already distrustful of his independently successful subordinate). His caution was largely unnecessary, for the Anglo-Americans were sufficiently impressed by Tito's activity (and Mihailović's lack of it) that they were willing to ignore the very clear signals that Tito was moving to secure control of Yugoslavia for the CPY. In fact, it would be more accurate to say that they were aware of the political danger but chose to discount it. This attitude changed somewhat toward the middle of the war, when Churchill began to push for an invasion of the Balkans by Anglo-American forces. The objective of such an operation would be to strike at the Axis' "soft underbelly" (a favorite phrase of Churchill's) and at the same time to serve a blocking force to the spread of the Red Army and other communist forces such as the Partisans.

The Americans paid little attention to Churchill's pleas. They considered a Balkan campaign to be militarily frivolous, and they reminded the British that the agreed-upon stratgy was to finish Germany as quickly as possible so that Japan could meet the same fate shortly afterwards; a Balkan campaign would be a diversion to the military plan and would produce at best dubious political results. During Roosevelt's time, in any case, the Americans were still inclined to believe in open and above board dealing with the Russians.

Whatever the strategy of the British and the Americans, it is doubtful that it would have prevented the establishment of a communist Yugoslavia. The policy of the Western allies allowed Tito to achieve de jure control of Yugoslavia, but that was simply the icing on the cake, as he had much earlier secured de facto authority. As the Partisans moved into an area, they established a civilian government which was responsible to the Partisan command. Even when villages were reoccupied by the Nazis, an attempt was made to leave behind an underground government. Rival authorities were dealt with harshly. Leaders who owed their allegiance to the Četniks were forced either to yield and accept the new regime, or flee in fear for their lives. Since some at least of the Četnik forces had been collaborationist, all local officials loyal to the Četniks, whether or not personally involved with the enemy, were vulnerable to charges of treason. In areas captured from the Ustaša, the Partisans did not concern themselves with anything so subtle as threats. Pro-Ustaša civilian officials were executed with at best a summary trial. Overall, the Partisans were able systematically to eliminate most actual or potential political opposition in areas as they were liberated.

The Partisans also moved quickly to build a national political framework. An important step was the creation of a Macedonian Communist Party in 1943. This further federalization of the CPY attracted more popular support in this important region and also served as a mirror image for the state structure which Tito decided to put forward.

As early as November 1942, Tito had begun the creation of a national political framework. Under the aegis of the Partisans, an Anti-Fascist Council of National Liberation of Yugoslavia (the Serbo-Croatian initials are AVNOJ) was formed in the town of Bihać. Although not a provisional government (Tito could not yet afford to ignore the exile government in London), it did have a political platform. Interestingly, the program was not radical in that it guaranteed property rights and made no mention of the need for socialist transformation. On the other hand, it did call for a federated state along the lines of the CPY.

As the partisans grew stronger and attracted more political support in London and Washington, Tito grew bolder. The second congress of AVNOJ, held in the Bosnian town of Jajce in November of 1943, went much further than its predecessor. It decreed the end of the authority of the London government and established a provisional government drawn from AVNOJ members. Tito became prime minister, defense minister, and marshal of Yugoslavia. As a signal of the future, Tito stated that the Nazi reverses were entirely a consequence of the victories won by the Soviet Union (this despite the presence of British liaison officers).[41]

A major step for Tito was taken for him by the western allies who, disgusted with Mihailović's comparative inaction and concerned about the Serbian cast of the exile government, pressured King Peter to dismiss the old ministers and appoint new, more flexible ones. Peter followed the suggestions and appointed as prime minister Ivan Šubašić, a former governor of Croatia. Shortly after his selection, Šubašić met with Tito—negotiations urged on both men by all sides including the Soviets. By this time (June of 1944), the Partisans held all the cards, and Šubašić effectively recognized AVNOJ as a parallel if not a superior authority. In return for this recognition (including an appeal to the peoples of Yugoslavia to support the Partisans), the London government got little more from Tito than a vague promise not to impose communism after the war.

There were many complicated negotiations after the first Tito-Šubašić agreement, but the ultimate outcome depended on the balance of power within the country (which totally favored Tito), and the diplomatic dynamics—in which the British and the Soviets backed Tito and the Americans showed a mild preference for the London government but refrained from taking a real stand. Stalin and Tito made a number of concessions in the negotiations, both directly with the London government and at Yalta, but the momentum in favor of Tito and AVNOJ was such that these were no more than cosmetic. Thus, although Tito agreed to a regency council to replace Peter until elections on the monarchy could be held, and also accepted nominees of the king as members of the expanded AVNOJ, these people were totally outnumbered (not to mention outgunned). By the end of the war Tito was governing as he pleased—opposition to his rule, both at home and abroad, was scattered and incoherent.

Romania—Government and Military

The Nazis sent troops into Romania "to protect the Ploieşti oil fields" just before King Carol left the country in September of 1940. The presence of these forces, coupled with the fact that Romania had been a part of the German diplomatic and economic web for more than a year, made it easy for Hitler to dictate the transfer of power. The new leader of the Iron Guard, Horia Sima, clearly expected that his ideological counterparts would give him the reigns of authority. But the Nazis knew the Iron Guard too well to give them unfettered control of such a vital country. General Antonescu, the most senior Romanian military leader, was made prime minister (with all of the powers of the King—then the twenty-year-old Michael); Sima was only vice president, but his Guardists were given key posts including control of the national police.[42]

The Iron Guard quickly showed itself to be worthy of Hitler's distrust. After a violent purge of the police (whose leaders had been responsible for Codreanu's death), Sima and his henchmen began a bloody attack on their political opponents. Within a matter of weeks assassinations were commonplace as front page news; the victims even included the great historian, Nicolae Iorga, a former tutor of Carol II and leader of a weak and incompetent political organization. Sima's power, though it appeared vast, was really quite limited; like the National peasants under Carol II, they found that without control of the bureaucracy and the army the potential for change was limited. When the Guard stepped up its recruitment within the military, Antonescu acted. The Nazis, convinced of the general's loyalty and in need of a strong Romania for the upcoming Operation Barbarossa, were easily persuaded to jettison Sima.

The Iron Guard learned, probably through connections with the Gestapo, that Antonescu had gained Hitler's favor. They attempted a preemptive strike on January 20, 1941, by means of military action in Bucharest. Although there were many casualties and much damage, the army held firm, and a few days later Antonescu, assisted by German armor, struck back.[43] The Guardists were quickly crushed: their movement was disbanded, many leaders were again imprisoned (and not a few executed), and some (including Sima) were allowed to flee to Germany. Antonescu (now a marshal) had won, but the cost had been high: he had had to pledge his nation to Germany's cause, and, most important, to participation in the war against the Soviet Union. Moreover, although Antonescu was effectively a dictator until the end of the war, he was never fully master of his nation's fate. Like Horthy, Antonescu could negotiate and occasionally disagree with Hitler; but on key matters it was clear that he would have to bind himself to the führer's will.

An early issue of Romanian-German disagreement was the war in Yugoslavia. The Romanians, who had had excellent relations with both the new and the old Yugoslav leadership, refused to take part. Hitler was angry, but not to the point of making a change; Barbarossa, after all, was only a few months away. Indeed, when the cannon fire erupted from the Baltic to the Black Sea on June 22, 1941, many of the guns aimed eastward were Romanian.

Antonescu's government declared war on the same day, and announced that, in addition to retaking Bessarabia and Bucovina, the Bucharest regime was committed to assisting Hitler in the destruction of world communism.

The Romanian Army performed well in the initial assault on the USSR. Bessarabia and Bucovina were rapidly retaken and reincorporated into Romania; some areas across the Dniester, never a part of a modern Romanian state, were conquered as well. In fact, Antonescu, seduced by the idea of annexing to his country vast areas east of the Dniester (including Odessa), sent fourteen of his best divisions to fight with the Wehrmacht. They played a key role in the capture of Odessa and then later helped to take the great Soviet fortress at Sebastopol. But despite heavy Romanian casualties and Antonescu's absolute loyalty, Hitler did not offer any territorial concessions. The area east of the Dniester (called Transnistria) was under German military occupation; Antonescu's repeated requests for a revision of the frontiers of Transylvania were ignored. Hitler offered instead a new opportunity: participation in the great offensive of 1942.

Antonescu, who clearly believed that the Romanians would eventually prove themselves so invaluable to the Reich that his territorial demands would be granted, did not flinch at Hitler's invitation. Many

Romanian politicians protested, however, for the old line liberal leadership, divided as it was by personal rivalries, was still attached to the culture of France and the political system of Britain, and did not want to follow the Germans beyond the old frontiers.[44] The voice of this group was King Michael, whose pronouncements avoided recognition of the eastward advance. But Antonescu, though angry, was unaffected; his enemies could do no more than criticize. He castigated them for their dissent, but he did not bother to imprison them. So long as Hitler reigned supreme, Antonescu had no fear of political enemies at home.

Thus, the fourteen Romanian divisions marched to their destiny at Stalingrad (Romania provided more support to Barbarossa than all other Axis allies combined). The Romanians, as recounted earlier, were largely on the flanks of the attack, although one division fought into the city center. When the Soviet counterattack came, it was the Romanians who bore the brunt. Antonescu's forces had fought well to this point, but the situation was now different. The Romanians were essentially without armor and tactical aircraft of their own, and these the Germans could no longer supply. Moreover, even basic food and ammunition stores were no longer fully provided by the German logistics services. Essentially on their own, and facing a better equipped and vastly superior enemy, the Romanian forces were shattered. Suffering enormous casualties, they were driven back as the trap closed on the German Sixth Army in Stalingrad.

After the debacle on the Volga, the Romanians, unlike the Hungarians, regrouped and remained in the line. But they were now a much weaker force, suffering not least a dramatic drop in morale. The situation of the armed forces mirrored that of their commander. Though Antonescu's prestige was gravely damaged by the massive defeat, he too was able to remain in the line. His political enemies were encouraged, however, and active plotting began. The Allied landings in Italy further weakened Antonescu's status, since newly secured air bases on the Adriatic now made large-scale bombing of Romania possible. Physical damage was comparatively small, but the psychological blow was significant: the war was coming home to the Romanians.

The advent of 1944, with the Red Army moving irresistibly westwards, accelerated the pace of domestic opposition. Various Liberal, National Peasant, and other party leaders began to meet secretly to discuss overthrow of the Antonescu regime and a shift to the Western allies. The conspirators, who were able to contact British and American officials through Romanian embassies in neutral capitals, soon learned that they could secure no deals (e.g., on the retention of Bessarabia) and that the Soviets would have a major voice in all final decisions. This information prompted the old line party leaders to seek an alliance with the Romanian Communist Party. This was obviously a gesture to Moscow, since the RCP was still extremely weak.

In fact, the RCP leadership was mostly in jail, out of contact with its counterparts in the Soviet Union, and had been unable to mount more than a token resistance.[45] Perhaps because of this, the RCP's leader, Gheorghe Gheorghiu-Dej, eagerly accepted a part in the plot; it is significant, in view of later events, that he took this action without the approval of the Soviet Party or the Moscow wing of the RCP. (Dej could and did claim, of course, that he could not make contact. Ironically, the RCP did in a sense secure Soviet government approval of the coup, simply because the other parties with which they entered into alliance were in touch with the Soviets.)

Antonescu had been doing some negotiating of his own with a view to having the Romanian forces surrender to the Soviets. When he informed the king of this, the young ruler, who was at the heart of the conspiracy, had him arrested. This was done because the conspirators felt that a break with Antonescu was essential if Romania was to be given favorable treatment after the war. The king broadcast an appeal to the people on August 23, 1944, which anounced the arrest of Antonescu. The creation of a new government (including the communist Pătrașcanu), and an end to the struggle against the Soviet Union. The Nazis resisted, but had few forces left in the area. On August 26, the new Romanian government declared war on Germany and its army was regrouped to fight under Soviet command. The losses in the war were enormous: in the Russian campaign the Romanians suffered some 270,000 casualties (including missing) and perhaps half that many taken prisoner; in the campaign against Germany, another 170,000 were killed or wounded.[46] Civilian losses in Transylvania were also heavy in the latter struggle.

When fighting in Europe ceased in May of 1945, Romania was wholly under the control of the Soviet Union. The Red Army occupied the nation, and the government, which could claim to be both non-collaborationist and yet tied to legitimate authority (and also an ally) was nonetheless treated as representative of a defeated power.

Romania—The Holocaust

In the last two years before the war, the anti-Semitic orientation of Romanian governments had subjected the nation's Jewry to a genuine reign of terror. The nightmare became far more terrible with the arrival of the Nazis. Antonescu's regime, though it stopped the random violence of the Iron Guard, initially cooperated with German requests for deportation. This was particularly true in recaptured Bessarabia and Bucovina, regions in which the percentage of Jews was high. The Romanians, like the Hungarians in Carpatho-Ruthenia, preferred to regard these Jews as "foreign" and to turn them over to the Nazis without regard to their fate. In fact, for a time the Romanians were expelling Jews so fast that the Germans could not handle the flow and requested a slowdown. There were also some pogroms in this period, but as in Hungary, these were not government policy and when reported ceased as rapidly as they began (but without an effort to punish the perpetrators).

Antonescu was probably never innocent of the Nazis' purpose in the deportations, though such a statement is impossible to prove. On the other hand, after a brief period of time he changed his policy. The reasons for the change are unclear; it occurred before the defeat at Stalingrad and does not connect clearly with any diplomatic or political event. In any case, the reversal was abrupt. The Romanians cancelled plans to deport Jews from Romania proper (those from Bessarabia and Bucovina were for the most part already gone) in the autumn of 1942.[47] After that, Antonescu refused all further requests from the Nazis, who by then had few troops in the area and who also had sharply diminished political-military leverage after the defeat at Stalingrad. In the end, the Romanians even took back as refugees some of the Jews they had deported in 1941. Yet the toll was awesome: some 300,000 of Romania's prewar Jewish population of about 600,000 perished at the hand of the Nazis.[48]

Bulgaria—Administration and Military

Bulgaria did not officially enter the war until December of 1941, when a formal declaration was entered against the United States (Germany pressured all Axis satellites, including Hungary and Romania, to do this as a part of their treaty obligations under the Tripartite Pact). In fact, however, Bulgaria had been a de facto belligerent since she took over the administration of those parts of Greek and Yugoslav Macedonia assigned to her after the German conquest. The Bulgarian army occupied these areas after the fighting was concluded, and was not, therefore, at war with Yugoslavia or Greece. The Bulgarians never declared war on the Soviet Union, a decision which is unsurprising in view of past relations between Bulgarians and Russians. What was curious, on the other hand, was that diplomatic relations were maintained. Thus, one could find a Soviet embassy in the capital of one of Germany's official allies, even as war raged between Axis and Allies.

Hitler did not have big plans for Bulgaria. The country had been fully exploited economically long before the war began and, so long as Turkey remained neutral, it had little strategic importance. The Germans did station some troops there, partly for symbolic reasons and partly to develop intelligence and prepare a logistical framework to meet any Allied challenge in the Aegean that might develop. There was never any fighting on Bulgarian soil, aside from very occasional harassment by guerrilla bands. The only damage that occurred came after mid-1943, when Allied bombers could make fairly easy attacks from Italian airfields. Nevertheless, damage was minuscule by the standards of World War II.

Although King Boris and his advisers were initially enthusiastic about the German alliance and, like nearly all of their countrymen, were overjoyed at the achievement of their principal territorial aspirations, they quickly became disillusioned as the tide turned against Hitler. Boris repeatedly tried to negotiate a withdrawal from the war after Italy's defeat and was subsequently summoned to meet Hitler. Shortly thereafter, the king died of a heart attack. Since the heir (Simeon II) was a child, a regency was formed; however, none of its members was able to carry the contacts with the Allies through to a successful conclusion.

As the Red Army approached Bulgaria from the north in the spring of 1944, the Bulgarian government tried frantically to negotiate a deal with the British and the Americans.[49] But following the decisions of Yalta, London, and Washington instructed the Bulgarians to talk to Stalin. Before they could decide how to do this, however, the USSR declared war on Bulgaria (September 5). The Soviets occupied the country without resistance and installed as the provisional government a communist-led coalition of parties known as the Fatherland Front. This group was of course anxious to cooperate with the Red Army, and the leaders in Sofia sent some two hundred thousand men to fight under Soviet command in the war against Germany.

Bulgaria—The Holocaust

The Bulgarian government reacted to Hitler's proposed Final Solution in much the same way as the Hungarians and the Romanians. Jews in the newly annexed territories taken from Yugoslavia and Greece were immediately surrendered to the Nazis; some twelve thousand of these were subsequently murdered. The excuse was that they were not Bulgarian citizens (and it is probably also the case that, as in Hungary and Romania, few suspected and even fewer knew in the early years what plans the Nazis had for the Jews). A Bulgarian official also agreed to the deportation of Jews from Bulgaria proper, but he was overruled before the orders could be carried out. The Bulgarian Orthodox Church also played a major role in stiffening the government against German pressure.[50] The Bulgarian leaders did enact a series of anti-Jewish laws, but the prewar Jewish population of about 50,000 emerged from the war physically intact.[51]

Albania—Government and Resistance

The situation of Albania did not change during World War II. The country continued to be a part of Italy and was administered from Rome. As fighting against resistance groups increased, the role of the Italian military authorities became predominant. The resistance movement closely paralleled that in Yugoslavia and is described in the section on the Communist Party of Albania. The principal difference between Yugoslavia and Albania was that the noncommunist movement, Balli Kombëtar, fought much harder than the Četniks and only collaborated when forced to do so by Albanian Partisan attacks. Both groups fought the occupiers (and each other) bravely, however, and the German Alpine division which took over after the Italian surrender just barely escaped being cut off and annihilated in 1944.[52] Since the Albanian Partisans were receiving de facto allied support via Tito, and since the noncommunist groups were disorganized and without effective representation abroad, it was easy for the communists to take control of the country at the conclusion of the fighting.

16

The Soviet Example

*I*T IS NOT POSSIBLE TO GAIN any real understanding of Eastern Europe after World War II without first acquiring at the minimum a general knowledge of the history of the Soviet Union. This is so because the original intention of Stalin was to recast the states of Eastern Europe in the Soviet mold. All of the countries, including Yugoslavia, passed through a period of at least several years in which all aspects of society—culture, education, social relationships as well as political and economic affairs— were forcibly changed to fit the pattern established by the giant power to the east. Even today, when the Soviet template has been largely abandoned in Eastern Europe, there is a logical tendency for western observers to characterize the different regimes by the degree and the direction of their variance from the Soviet model. Finally, it is essential to remember that the Soviet leaders are themselves deeply concerned about the nature and the extent of deviations in both the practical and the idealogical spheres, and that their reactions are still of crucial importance to Eastern Europe.

A really accurate description and analysis of Soviet history requires at least one volume (indeed there are many of that length and longer), so that this narrative will attempt to provide only an outline of the key principles.

Leninism

Perhaps the most important single fact to keep in mind about the Soviet experience is that of the early, fundamental changes to Marxist philosophy made by Lenin and his colleagues and successors. As is well known, Karl

Marx believed that communism would make its first appearance in one of the highly industrialized nations of the west—probably Germany, Britian, or France. This expectation on Marx's part was not a whim but a reflection of his understanding of what he considered to be laws of history. Thus, working backward, a communist revolution required an exploited class of industrial workers (the proletariat), and such a class could not exist without industrialization. Moreover, a newly industrialized society wouldn't fit the theory, since the exploitation wouldn't have lasted long enough to build the proper level of oppression and consequent revolutionary feeling.

It is true that Marx in his later years expressed some interest in Russia and the possibility of a revolution there, but this seems to have been the response of a flattered prophet whose ideas were not doing well elsewhere (i.e., Germany, Britain, and France), rather than the result of any reconsideration of the fundamental theory. The simple fact is, that when Marx died in 1889, his philosophy clearly indicated that a country like Russia could not expect to have a communist revolution until other, more industrially developed nations had shown the way. From the Russian activist's point of view, this situation was made more serious by the fact that Marxism was considered by its adherents to be a set of revealed truths, a "scientific socialism," rather than a mere philosophy. Thus, it was impossible to deny or disagree with Marx—one could not disown the laws of history.

The person who rose to—and met—this formidable ideological challenge was a young Russian revolutionary who used the code name of Lenin. In this individual, history has recorded a mind of exceptional intelligence, tireless and dedicated with a narrow fanaticism to the achievement of a single goal. Lenin's objective, of course, was a communist revolution in his native Russia. The limits of Marxism disillusioned his colleagues but not Lenin. Relatively early in his career this driving intellect found ways to circumvent the ideological dilemma and justify the possibility, indeed the probability, of an imminent Russian revolution.[1]

Lenin's first task was to explain why the representatives of the working class had failed to seize power in the industrialized west—why, in fact, they appeared to be growing weaker rather than stronger. Lenin did this by introducing the phenomenon of imperialism to the revolutionary equation. He observed that the great economic crisis, which Marx had predicted would lead to a suddenly more severe exploitation of the workers, had not materialized because imperialism had opened up new markets in the colonial areas and thus relieved pressure on the domestic economies. Lenin saw this as only a temporary respite, however; the crisis was postponed, not eliminated. When the colonial markets were saturated, the sequence of events leading to a revolution would occur.

Nevertheless, Lenin's views had the effect of diverting attention away from the west—at least for those who agreed with him. Lenin's next chore was to explain why a revolution was possible in Russia. The process by which this was done was neither simple nor short, but the final version was essentially as follows: in a country like Russia, there were large numbers of poor peasants who owned at best a tiny plot of land and usually had to sell their labor to others to survive. Lenin argued that these peasants should also be included in the proletariat.

Since there were millions of these peasants, and since they were undoubtedly severely oppressed and therefore explosive, Russia was suddenly transformed (from the point of view of communist ideology) from an agricultural backwater to a mighty powder keg of revolution, waiting for the proper fuse. Before 1917, Lenin's arguments had little impact on Marxists in the west: they cared not at all about classifications of peasants, and the imperialism theory, while certainly interesting, did not appeal for obvious reasons. Nevertheless, Lenin's "corollaries to Marxism" had a significant impact in Russia. On the one hand, they strengthened the spirit of the existing communists, on the other, they provided the rationale for a broader base of party support.

Lenin made a number of other important contributions to Marxism. He argued strongly that the communist party should be led by a small group of dedicated professionals—the "vanguard of the proletariat"— who would be responsible for planning and directing the revolution. Only after the struggle was launched would the leaders, the "cadres," move out to organize mass support. Lenin was opposed on this point by a number of other communists who argued that the party should seek a broader base at an earlier time, in order to have more effective roots in the population. This was the issue in the famous "Bolshevik" (Leninist) vs. "Menshevik" split within the party. Neither side actually won in the initial conflict (despite Lenin's assertions), but the Bolsheviks eventually dominated—in large part because of the force of their leader's personality.

Another aspect of Leninism, closely related to the vanguard theory, was the doctrine of "democratic centralism." After the Bolsheviks seized power in 1917, they were beset by a host of enemies on all sides. To survive they had to be unified and disciplined, yet there were wide divergences of opinion within the communist ranks (many essentially unrepentant Mensheviks served at all levels of the party). Lenin therefore decreed that power must flow from the center (Lenin and his closest advisers), outward and downward to the lowest levels. Discussion and disagreement was perfectly acceptable until a decision had been made, at which point unquestioning obedience was expected. Later, "factionalism" was formally banned.

The impact of democratic centralism was considerable. Although it was a rather logical and sensible approach in a crisis such as the civil war, it was never abandoned once peace was secured. The philosophy dictated a political organization that concentrated all power in the hands of a few men (later just one man), and made it virtually impossible to effect structural changes. This doctrine is, of course, all centralism and no democracy. The fact of the adoption of completely contradictory terms was one of the first examples of what has become a consistent Soviet practice; a completely inaccurate description is given a degree of acceptance by the simple expedient of persistent repetition.

The final contribution of Lenin, the concept of the "dictatorship of the proletariat," is also closely related to the two previously cited doctrines. This idea was mentioned by Marx, but not elaborated in any clear way. But for Lenin it was a logical extension of the vanguard and the democratic centralism theories. Thus, the communist party, organized on Leninist principles, could not be content with simply carrying out the revolution. Once victory had been assured, it would be necessary to take steps to prevent a counterrevolution. The new state would be "democratic" in form, but a dictatorship of the proletariat (represented by the communist party) would have to oversee the political process to stop remnants of the "enemies of the working class," (former landowners and capitalists), from using the democratic system to subvert the revolution.

A dictatorship of the proletariat, like a democratic centralist party structure, necessarily acquires an inertia of its own: those in power are reluctant to relinquish their positions. If they are reasonably skilled politicians, there is, in fact, no other group with the power to force them to do so. Moreover, the system is open-ended. The pretext of the existence of class enemies is hard to deny when the party leadership has all the power and can create examples of opposition at will—a favorite practice of Stalin. In addition, by defining the class enemies as those outside the country as well as those within, it is possible to rationalize a dictatorship of the proletariat until the achievement of total world communism and beyond.

After this rather cursory treatment of the Leninist additions to Marxism—doctrines which one could argue reflected to a considerable extent Russian nationalism on Lenin's part—it is appropriate to pause and take a look at developments in West European Marxism. There, too, we find that the movement had been split, although much earlier and mostly during Marx's lifetime (Lenin had the good fortune to present his "corollaries" when Marx and his acerbic tongue were safely in the grave). The major issue in the west had concerned the necessity of violent revolution to achieve socialism.

Many followers of Marxist theory, most importantly the German, Edward Bernstein, had come to believe that socialism could be achieved by peaceful, parliamentary means. Like Lenin, Bernstein believed in adapting Marx to fit the national situation; unlike Lenin, he was willing to admit that that was his goal. The workers of Western Europe in fact showed little inclination to revolt. Despite their usually miserable living conditions, they seemed to feel that systems of representative government could be used to secure the reforms in pay, hours, and conditions that were their primary objectives. Their hopes were fueled by early important successes in Britain.

Since the West European Marxist parties were fundamentally democratic in character, the feelings of the rank-and-file were transmitted to the party leaders who responded accordingly. Marx objected strongly to these ideas, and the socialist movement therefore split into factions. The loyalists retained the primary emphasis on revolution but won over only a very small number of the workers; indeed these strict Marxist groups seemed to be overwhelmingly led by intellectuals. The larger, controlling factions, branded as "revisionist" by Marx, were more representative of the workers in their leaderships and took the names of Labor in Britain, Socialist in France, and Social Democrat in Germany and most of Eastern Europe. In some cases the revolutionists set up formal parties of their own; in others they remained as dissident factions.

To illustrate the rapidly growing difference between Russia and the west in Marxist theory, it is sufficient to point out that none of the groups in the west showed much interest in, much less acceptance of, Lenin's contributions (though the theory of imperialism did have some impact). The Russian Marxists were in effect taking a third road, one that corresponded perhaps very well with the Russian reality (some would say it aped the tsarist system), but which was scarcely relevant to the situation outside their vast and chaotic country.

Civil War and Nationality Policy

Lenin and the Bolsheviks had only a partial grip on the government and had not yet settled the war with Germany and Austria-Hungary when they were faced with a new and potentially more severe crisis: civil war. The early core of the opposition to the Bolsheviks was led by remnants of the imperial army, a combination of tsarist officers and soldiers representing mostly the non-Russian peoples of the old empire. In addition, Lenin and Trotsky (who was in charge of the army) faced a three-cornered struggle against the Baltic peoples in the northwest, the Caucasian peoples in the southeast, and the Ukrainians in the south (the collapse of Germany soon led to the establishment of independent Finnish and Polish states, so that these peoples were not at the forefront—though the latter were soon at war with the Russians). The magnitude of this opposition, particularly from the Ukrainians, was such that the communist leadership knew that some compromise on nationality rights was essential to their survival.

As a consequence, Lenin proclaimed a nationality policy which was incorporated into a constitution of the Soviet Union. Eventually, this doctrine established a new form of government which, instead of being based on a Russian state, created a federation of national republics of which only one was to be Russian. In each of the republics, the local language was to be used in schools, newspapers, courts, and administration; there was to be complete cultural freedom in these languages. Russian would continue to be taught and used, since it was to be the *lingua franca* of the Soviet Union itself, but Russian culture would not be imposed. The various republics would have the right to secede from the union if they so desired. As a counter to national separatism, Lenin's policy did have some impact. The Baltic states were already lost, and the Caucasus was taken by force, but in the all-important Ukraine some divisions were created and the separatists, led by Petlura, were weakened. It is doubtful that the compromise was decisive in the Soviet victory in the civil war, but it certainly made Trotsky's job easier.

Soviet nationality policy has never lived up to the theory, but the practice is not as bad as the critics would have us believe. Russian language and culture play a very strong role, but they have not eliminated any major nationality. Those peoples that have suffered most are those whose language and culture are closely linked to religion—Jews and Moslems in particular. Even so, peoples such as the Catholic Lithuanians, the Georgian Christians, and Armenian Christians appear to be holding their own. The greatest barrier to cultural development in all areas would appear to be communist censorship rather than Great Russian chauvinism.

Lenin and Stalin versus Trotsky

The (mostly) successful conslusion of the civil war was soon followed by a new crisis—this time in the leadership itself. Once the existence of the

Soviet state was secured, a major ideological question arose. Should the Soviets concentrate on strengthening the new state to preserve the revolution? Or should the primary aim be to export the revolution as soon as possible and at nearly any risk? Both approaches could be viewed as dangerous. The first, "socialism in one country,"might fail because the capitalist states might regain their strength and crush the Soviet Union before she could build herself up. The second, "permanent revolution," might lead to an early war that could also destroy the Soviet state.

The struggle within the leadership was long and complex, but it finally came down to a conflict between Stalin's socialism in one country and Trotsky's permanent revolution. Stalin, clearly the better politician, succeeded not only in defeating Trotsky and forcing him to exile, but also in taking complete control and assuring his position as the deceased Lenin's successor.

This conflict was important not because of Stalin's ascendancy— that would doubtless have occurred anyway—but because it marked an important break between the Soviet communists and their colleagues to the west. The Soviets did not abandon them entirely, but they made it quite clear where their priorities lay. This turning inward, even though it may have been the most practical course, served to reinforce the particularist Russian (now Soviet) stamp that Lenin had earlier placed on communism. The discussion of Comintern (below) will explore this matter further.

Stalin and the Party

By the time of Stalin's assumption of sole power in the late 1920s, the general pattern of communist party organization and its relation to the state structure had taken shape.[2] Both party and state were heirarchical with classic pyramid shapes. At the very bottom are found primary party organizations, almost always based on a place of work. Thus, a factory, a collective farm, or even a university or a government department will have one or more party units, depending on size. Officers of these will then represent their groups at higher levels, proceeding on a territorial basis from the regional, to the provincial, then the republic, and finally the Union (national) level.

The top level of the party has four major units: the Party Congress, the Central Committee, the Secretariat, and the Politburo. The Party Congress, which is supposed to meet at least every four years, is composed of representatives from all over the country and is theoretically the supreme power in the party. In fact, however, it is large (nearly 5,000 delegates) and cumbersome. The policies it proclaims and the officers it elects are determined for it in advance by the central party bureaucracy. The Party Congress functions essentially as a rubber stamp of blind approval.

The Central Committee is elected by the Party Congress (from a slate of candidates provided by the Central Committee itself) to supervise party affairs in the interval between congresses. However, the Central Committee is itself large: some 200 full (voting) and 150 candidate (nonvoting) members in the contemporary USSR. Partly because of this unwieldy size and also because many of the members cannot be in Moscow all of the time (regional party chiefs, military leaders, ambassadors, etc.), the Central Committee cannot meet to decide on day-to-day problems, and it in turn elects organizations to fulfill this role: the Secretariat and the Politburo.

Of these two highest bodies, the Politburo is the more important. It is the supreme body of the party. Its small membership (roughly ten full and five candidate members) allows it to meet on a regular basis—daily if necessary. The Politburo is the place where democratic centralism begins: its decisions are not to be questioned, and it maintains its control by providing the single list of candidates for all important party positions, including both the Central Committee and the Secretariat.

The Secretariat, which always has some overlapping membership with the Politburo, is entrusted with overseeing the smooth functioning of both party and state bureaucracies. As such, it has tremendous power. The Secretariat is organized along lines that mirror government functions, for example, education and foreign affairs, and it can effect immediate changes in state policy and personnel whenever it desires. In fact, the party has secretariats at all important lower levels, republic, provincial, and regional, and these have the same supervisory function with respect to the governmental organizations at those levels. There is a significant overlap of secretariat and governmental personnel at all levels.

The Mechanisms of Control

Given the extreme centralization of the party, and its absolute authority over the government, it is not difficult to understand how Stalin was able to seize control of the apparatus. The means by which he maintained and even enhanced this power (to a level never equalled before or since in history) requires some additional explanation. To make certain of his grasp on the party, Stalin developed to the ultimate Lenin's idea of a periodic purge of the membership. To ensure loyalty in the most powerful part of the state apparatus, the military, Stalin enhanced and entrenched Trotsky's system of political commissars. To be absolutely positive that none of these controls could ever fail, Stalin created a secret police network with power that had no precedent in Russia or elsewhere.

The concept of party purges was at first a relatively innocent one, elaborated by Lenin as a vehicle to cleanse the party of "careerists" and "opportunists" who were not truly dedicated communists. The procedure was simple: all party members turned in their membership cards while their records were examined by a Party Control Committee responsible to the Secretariat. Those who passed this scrutiny received new cards; those found wanting did not. This "exchange of party cards" was soon perverted by Stalin to include the purge of good communists whom he distrusted. At first the penalty for those expelled was nothing more than the loss of prestige and the public opprobrium that could be expected in a society in which party membership was a high achievement. Later, when Stalin made the word "purge" synonymous with unrestrained terror, the consequences were more serious.

Since the Soviets had had to rely from the beginning on former tsarist officers to staff their armies, Trotsky had established a system of political commissars to spy on the officers and also to maintain a constant stream of communist propaganda directed toward the troops. The commissars were party members and reported directly to the party, not to the military units to which they were assigned. This system of political control over the military, reinforced and strengthened by Stalin, has achieved its purpose. There has never been anything even mildly significant in the way of a military coup against the party.

The first Soviet secret police organization, known as the Cheka and headed by Feliz Dzerzhinsky, was formed in the early days of the revolution and functioned throughout the civil war period. Lenin believed that in a situation of such extreme danger, in which the Soviet regime was constantly imperiled, the niceties of rule by law could not be maintained. Thus, the Cheka had the right to arrest, try, imprison, and (not infrequently) execute, those that it considered to be enemies of the Soviet Union. Even more important, however, Lenin also condoned at least the limited use of terror. This meant, in effect, that the Cheka was not always careful to distinguish between friends and enemies in its killings and destruction. The purpose of the terror was to instill fear and therefore respect for authority in the population.

There was considerable revulsion in the Soviet Union and abroad at the activities of the Cheka—the "Red Terror." Lenin finally abolished the Cheka but only after the threat to the regime had been eliminated. The succeeding secret police apparatus played a limited role in the relatively placid period of the mid-twenties. Stalin's accession to power, and the launching of the first Five-Year Plan and the collectivization drive, quickly changed this, however. Under a variety of names and organizational patterns (GPU, OGPU, NKVD, and now KGB) the secret police system became the instrument for an incredible reign of terror visited on all segments of the Soviet population.

Industrialization

Stalin was firmly in control when the first Five-Year Plan was launched in 1928. The essential purpose of the plan was one that could be accepted by a broad spectrum of economists, noncommunist as well as communist. The Soviet Union was rich in natural resources of virtually all kinds, but it lacked the extractive and processing enterprises necessary to make these resources available for productive industry. It was therefore essential to first create a heavy industrial base: mines to provide ores and energy, dams to generate electricity, roads and railroads for transportation, steel and other kinds of mills for processing, and machine tool (machines that make other machines) factories. Only in this fashion could one expect to achieve Marx's goal of a society that could satisfy all of man's material needs.

The Five-Year Plan had other characteristics as well. They stipulated that the industrial base must be built very quickly, that it must be done almost entirely with internal resources, and that it must proceed according to guidelines (the plan itself) which were articulated in extreme detail by a central group in Moscow. The first two of these tenets reflected a legitimate concern for security. Western intervention on the side of the anticommunists during the civil war had made it clear to Stalin and his associates that the Soviet Union was surrounded by hostile forces. Rapid industrialization was necessary to build the military: tanks and armor cannot be made without steel, and they cannot be available for battle without roads and railroads. Any attempt to import raw materials or finished goods in significant quantities would make the Soviets extremely vulnerable in the not unlikely event that a break in relations cut off supplies.

Many economists would also agree that the idea of central planning made good sense—at least at first. The magnitude of the tasks envisioned in the first (and subsequent) Five-Year Plans was staggering. Vast quantities of widely scattered resources would have to be produced and delivered within tight time frames. It would be disastrous, for example, if a railroad needed to transport coal from mines in the Ukraine to a new steel mill in the Urals was not finished until a year after the mill was built. The tsarist government had had no apparatus even remotely capable of such coordination.

Equally important as a reason for highly centralized planning was the critical lack of trained engineers and managers. By exercising careful control it was assumed that the planners in Moscow could make the most efficient possible use of those specialists that were available, while at the same time providing for the training of new specialists for the most important areas. As it happened, incredible and costly blunders were made, and enormous human and material resources were wasted. Nevertheless, the work was completed, and it was completed quickly.

Where did the Soviet state get the resources to effect this gigantic transformation? First, the regime confiscated virtually all nonagricultural property. Not only large factories, but also small enterprises even down to the level of handicrafts were taken over by state organizations. All private holdings of capital, including bank accounts above a certain minimal level, were nationalized. Personal private property was not usually taken, although most wealthy individuals lost everything following an arrest for "crimes against the state" (which might, in fact, simply mean being wealthy). Houses and even apartments were requisitioned by the state and divided for use by the peasants flooding into the cities.

Capital, however, is only one of the inputs needed for industrialization; it is also necessary to have labor and technology. The latter was scarce in the Soviet lands, although the new educational system was dedicated to closing the gap with the same reckless energy that characterized the Five-Year Plans. Labor, on the other hand, existed in abundance in the countryside. The only problem was how to get the peasants to the factories. The solution, collectivization, will be discussed shortly. The industrialization drive thus depended on massive inputs of cheap labor to overcome the shortage of technology.

The Soviet leaders strove to make labor even cheaper, and thus more available, by sharply increasing productivity. The means of doing this could not be the carrot and the stick, since the regime was determined to produce the absolute minimum of consumer goods—even though these might provide incentives for harder work. Consumer products could not be manufactured in quantity until after the heavy industrial base was completed. The stick was used, however, for the workers were by no means immune to the secret police terror.

The Soviets developed instead an alternative to the carrot and the stick, one that could be described as the "slogan and the stick." Workers were constantly blitzed with propaganda exhorting them to produce even more than the established norms—to "overfulfill their quotas." The peak of this mania came with the advent of "Stakhanovism" in the 1930s, when workers were urged to follow the example of a coal miner who had exceeded his norm by 1,400 percent. Soon even entire factories and farms were trying to outstrip others in an insane competition. The pressure abated somewhat when the authorities realized that the Stakhanovites were more likely to be strangled than applauded by their weary comrades. Even so, the concept of overfulfilling a quota remains an integral part of the Soviet system.

Agriculture and Collectivization

As mentioned earlier, it is clear to everyone that the extremely inefficient agricultural system inherited from tsarist Russia contained an enormous surplus of labor that could be used to build industry. The only way to free these workers, however, was to make the system more efficient— not a simple problem. The solution arrived at by the communist leaders, collectivization, appealed to them more for ideological than pragmatic reasons. The collective, in which private land is pooled to form a large farm that can be operated cooperatively, is a socialist form of organization. It is not the ultimate goal of communists, since it retains some symbolic vestiges of private ownership, but as a transitional system it is most appropriate. The final objective, of course, is the state farm—the equivalent of an agricultural factory.

The communist leadership expected opposition to collectivization from the more prosperous peasants, the kulaks, but the communists appeared genuinely to believe that this would be offset by support from the far more numerous poorer peasants. As many observers have pointed out, this belief is convincing evidence that Stalin, Lenin, Marx, and virtually all other communist ideologists, were "city boys." Contrary to

Marxist-Leninist theory, what almost every peasant wanted most was more land of his own; only an insignificant minority displayed an interest in communal ownership.

Consequently, collectivization, which was supposed to be voluntary, had to be forced on the countryside. The resistance of the kulaks was naturally fiercest, and many slaughtered their animals and destroyed their tools rather than turn them over to the hated collective farms or *kolk-hozes*—Soviet livestock counts did not return to the 1928 level until a few years ago. This opposition, together with the intransigence of the rest of the peasantry, caused the government to send the army and the secret police into the villages. Collectives were organized by decree, and their obedience to the production quotas set in Moscow was ensured by forced deliveries taken by the army.

The secret police ran amuck, murdering at will and sending those who escaped execution to labor camps in the north and east where many soon died anyway. This terrible man-made disaster was exacerbated by a famine of a severity that would have killed many in even normal conditions. The final death toll will never be known with any accuracy, but the best estimates suggest that as many as four and a half million perished.

Hardly anyone in the west accepts the human cost of collectivization as effected by Stalin, but there is some disagreement as to the economic costs. Those who believe that the economic benefits were significant argue that the goal was achieved, that the necessary labor was provided for industrialization, and that food supplies were in any case adequate. Their opponents cannot, of course, deny these facts, but they argue that a more flexible approach would have achieved the same goals at a far smaller human and economic cost. They cite the continuing weakness of Soviet agriculture as a consequence of Stalin's errors. Whatever the historical judgment, there is general agreement that agriculture is still the Achilles heel of the Soviet economy.

The Purges

With industry and agriculture under control by the mid-1930s, Stalin turned his eye toward the two elements of society that had so far escaped his vigilance: the military and the party itself. The purge of the party started at a modest pace: the first victims were the last of the old Bolsheviks who had been close to Lenin and at one time or another opponents of

Stalin; in truth something of this sort had long been expected by the most perceptive Stalin-watchers.

The next phase, however, was an unrestrained madness, terror for the sole purpose of creating fear. The historian Robert Conquest describes the first stage of the preparations as follows:

> ... first the instrument of terror needed retuning. The old NKVD of Yagoda's [the secret police's recently purged leader] time was technically efficient, but in certain respects it lacked the true Stalinist spirit. In any case, its new master Yezhov could not trust his predecessor's men.
>
> In March 1937, Yezhov ordered the departmental chiefs of the NKVD to proceed to various parts of the country on a massive inspection. ... they were then arrested at the first stations out of Moscow and brought back to prison. Two days later the same trick was played on the deputy heads of the departments.[3]

With the secret police thus prepared, the army took the full force of the renewed terror. In 1937–38, some 35,000 army officers were eliminated. Included were three of five marshals, 90 percent of the generals, 80 percent of the colonels, all regional commanders, and all members of the political directorate. It is not known how many were imprisoned and how many were executed; it is to be presumed that very few escaped some punishment. Aside from a few of the most prominent leaders, there appears to have been no logical pattern for the purge. Frequently, wives, children, and other relatives were imprisoned and executed as well.

By 1937, the *Yezhovshchina*, the "reign of Yezhov" was in full swing. The secret police, like their predecessors in the Cheka, now had the right to hold their own trials and to carry out summary executions. Unlike the Cheka, however, they did not have the excuse of a wartime situation. The final great purge of the party began shortly after the attack on the military. Here too, the statistical evidence is staggering: all of the members of the Politburo (except Stalin, of course), and 70 percent of the Central Committee were purged. And, should anyone need convincing that it was only the Moscow elite that was in trouble, 98 percent of the five thousand or so delegates to the Seventeenth Party Congress of 1934 were missing from the Eighteenth Congress held in 1939.

The purge also affected those who had no party, military, or government connections. The secret police were ordered to arrest a set percentage of the population of each region. For the whole *Yezhovshchina*, Conquest estimates that, by 1939, one million had been executed, two million had died in captivity, one million were in prison, and eight million were in forced labor camps—the Gulag Archipelago described so chillingly by Alexander Solzhenitsyn. When these statistics are added to the casualties that attended the first Five-Year Plans and the collectivization drive, one can see that the decade 1928–38, in which no major war was fought, was one of the bloodiest in history.

International Communism

Even while the civil war raged, while the fate of the Soviet Union was still unclear, Lenin expended much of his energy in an effort to capture the world Marxist movement and subordiante it to the control of the Soviet party. The first step in this struggle was the convening of a conference of world Marxist parties. The fact that the chaotic conditions in Russia in 1919 prevented the leaders of all of the strongest parties from getting to Moscow was probably just what Lenin had in mind. The delegates, all but two of whom were Soviets or Soviet dependents, thus followed Lenin's lead and voted to create a Third International—usually known as the Comintern (Communist International).

The purpose of setting up a new international was to supersede the Second International, a loose confederation dominated by nonrevolutionary parties. This objective was finally achieved after the Second Conference of the Comintern, in 1921, which issued the "Twenty-One Conditions" that all member parties had to accept. The most important of these points were those that stipulated a commitment to revolution and an acceptance of the Leninist principle of democratic centralism. The latter point, of course, meant that all decisions would be made at the center, in this case the permanent bureaucracy of the Comintern. If that group could in turn be controlled by the Soviet party, as it soon was, the Politburo in Moscow would have direct control of the entire movement.

None of the large Marxist parties of Western Europe went over to the Comintern *en masse*. In most part they refused to accept the Twenty One Conditions, so that their revolutionary factions split off and formed new parties which then joined the Comintern. In some cases, preexisting revolutionary parties joined with the splinter groups. At this point, one can begin to talk about a clear difference between communist and socialist parties. The former were revolutionary (at least in theory) and therefore opposed to collaboration with bourgeois parties, and were soon to be subservient to Moscow. The latter were independent, reformist, and participated in parliamentary government. Both groups saw themselves as Marxist, although the communists usually deny this honor (as well as the right to use the word "socialism") to the socialists. Some of the communist parties were quite large (Germany, France, Italy), but in nearly every case they were smaller than their socialist counterparts.

Foreign Policy

Once the Soviet party had succeeded in making the Comintern into an extension of its own organization,[4] the domestic policies of the various communist parties reflected the foreign policy of the Soviet Union. Thus, in the early twenties, when Lenin still hoped for a world revolution, the Comintern was the voice and the coordinator of the effort. Later, however, when radical victories seemed remote, Comintern policy was aimed at helping Stalin build socialism in one country. The classic case of this transition appeared in Germany, where the Soviet government found it expedient to form an alliance first with the Weimar Republic and then with the Nazis. For a time, before the policies of foreign ministry and Comintern could be synchronized, communist German strikers were repressed by police armed with Soviet-supplied weapons. Needless to say, conflicts between Soviet interests and local communist interests damaged many parties—not least in Eastern Europe.

Soviet foreign policy as a whole could be construed as defensive. At first going it alone in a hostile world, the Soviets soon began to cooperate with their fellow outcasts, the Germans. This arrangement continued for a time after Hitler came to power, but even Stalin could see that the Nazis were strange bedfellows, and the alliance was broken. Then, after a fruitless search for an alternative, while Germany grew stronger, Stalin finally decided again to cast his lot with Hitler. The objective was to sit by while Germany bled herself to death in a struggle with Britain and France. The German-Soviet (Hitler-Stalin) alliance was thus signed in 1939.

The War

Stalin was stunned by the lightning Nazi victories in 1940, but then so was the rest of the world. What is truly amazing is that the "Generalissimo" was even more surprised by the German attack on Russia, Operation Barbarossa, in the summer of 1941. Whatever claims the Soviets may make, the final defeat of the Nazis was a consequence of Hitler's poor planning and an early winter, rather than the resistance of the unprepared and disorganized Red army; no amount of heroism or military genius could have stopped the Germans without the help of these factors.

The Second World War, known in the Soviet Union as the "Great Patriotic War," brought about destruction and bloodshed on a scale that almost defies human understanding. Nearly every city and village in the enormous area of struggle was destroyed; bridges, buildings, factories that had survived the fighting were usually blown up by the retreating Germans. In all, more than seven million military personnel and ten million civilians were killed; there are no estimates of the number of physically and mentally wounded. A final grim note: since a small but appreciable percent of the captured Soviet soldiers cooperated with the Nazis (this was particularly true of non-Russians—for example Ukrainians), the secret police routinely treated liberated prisoners of war as traitors. Millions of bewildered Soviets were thus freed from German prison camps only to be transferred to Soviet ones.

Summary

In summing up this brief and partial history of the Soviet Union from 1917 to 1945, it is essential to stress one crucial fact: in the Soviet system, the state, and through it the Communist Party, is everything. All aspects of society—education, the arts and culture, even family life and religion— fall within the purview of the state. One of Marx's severest contemporary critics, the anarchist Mikhail Bakunin, argued that Marx's reliance on the state as the vehicle for social change would inevitably lead to the complete usurpation of all individual freedom. Whether or not "inevitable" and "complete" are accurate is arguable. What is difficult to deny is the fact that Stalin was thoroughly inhumane in the name of humanity, and that the structure that made his actions possible still exists in the Soviet Union today.

17

The East European
Communist Parties to 1945

THE COMMUNIST PARTIES that came to power to Eastern Europe in the period 1944–48 owed their status to the overwhelming presence of the Red Army (the Yugoslav and Albanian cases are possible exceptions). All of these parties were very small in 1945; none could conceivably have won a free election. Since the communist parties were weak almost to the point of insignificance in the interwar period, they have been largely ignored in previous chapters. Yet they did exist and they did have histories; their pasts are in fact quite important in explaining their postwar characteristics.

The parties will be dealt with separately on a national basis. Even though all (except the Albanian) were attached to the Comintern and for the most part followed the Soviet line, their experiences, quality of leadership, and type and number of supporters, varied enormously. On the other hand, there are a number of general statements that can be made about their histories. It seems most appropriate, however, to leave the conclusions until the end and to proceed to discuss the individual parties.

Hungary

The experience of the Communist Party of Hungary represented both the peak and the nadir of communist achievement in interwar Eastern Europe. The Hungarian Soviet Republic established under the leadership of Béla Kun in 1919 was certainly the peak—the only communist state outside of the Soviet Union in the period 1917–1945. On the other hand, the defeat of the communists was so complete, the strength and vengefulness of the reaction so great, that Hungarian communism was an insignificant factor from the end of 1919 until the Red Army arrived in late 1944.

The origins of social democracy in the Hungarian Kingdom were similar to those in the Austrian half of Austria-Hungary, with one important exception. In the lands governed from Budapest, trade unions were not allowed to participate directly in politics. Although some cooperation was still achieved, this restriction certainly inhibited the growth of social democracy. Since there were few workers anyway, the memberships of both the Hungarian and the German social democratic parties were overwhelmingly comprised of intellectuals, most of whom were of Jewish origin.

The Hungarian social democrats, like their brethren throughout Europe, voted in favor of war in 1914. Contrary to the outcomes elsewhere, however, the schism in Hungary was very sharp, and the radicals were close to a majority. As the war continued and the defeat of Austria-Hungary showed itself to be inevitable, the antiwar left gained control of the party. The social democrats then played an important role in a wave of strikes that swept the country in 1918. In an atmosphere of disintegration and chaos, the socialists were able to gain popularity in competition with the traditional parties.

The strength of the left was reinforced by the arrival, after the end of the war, of a large number of radical prisoners of war from Russia. The relative success of the Bolsheviks in winning over Hungarian prisoners is difficult to explain. It has been speculated that the Hungarians, unlike captured Poles, Czechs, or Romanians, were more open to revolutionary solutions since they knew they would be returning to a defeated nation. Yet this factor would be equally important for Germans and Austrians, and it ignores the traditional animosity of Hungarians to things Russian. The real reason may be that most were not Bolshevized at all but saw the Soviet model and Lenin's approach to the national problem as possible rationales for the revival of a Greater Hungary.[1]

The external impact of the Soviet period in Hungary has been discussed earlier. At this point it is most appropriate to examine the internal dynamics of Hungarian communism in 1919. This is necessary in part because the regime of Béla Kun is of particular importance both in the history of Hungarian and East European communism and in part because the brief episode illustrates perhaps more than any other the crucial role of nationalism in eastern European history.

The Communist Party of Hungary (CPH) was actually formed in Moscow in early November of 1918. Béla Kun, its first leader, was the son of a Jewish official but had been educated in a Calvinist school.

Although a socialist from the age of sixteen (he was thirty-two in 1918), he had not been an important leader before the war. Kun owed his prominence to his aggressive leadership of Hungarian troops on the Bolshevik side during the Russian civil war. Frequently used as assault forces, the Hungarian volunteers took heavy casualties and earned much praise from Lenin and Trotsky. Many were selected to attend communist training schools.

Twenty days after the CPH was formed in Moscow, Kun presided over its first meeting on Hungarian soil. The new party's first task was to take control of the social democratic-led Worker's Councils which had come to be the most important force in the almost ungoverned country. There was considerable resistance, but Kun's party prevailed because of the force of its leader's personality, the military and propaganda experience of its cadres, the assistance provided by Soviet arms and intelligence, its superior organization in the face of unstructured opposition parties, and because the depressed and disillusioned population was unwilling to struggle further.

But the communists were almost destroyed before they could win control of the Workers Councils. In February of 1919, a demonstration in Budapest inadvertently led to violence, and the police arrested all of the top communist leadership, including Kun. The CPH survived only because its careful organization permitted a second level of cadres to move forward to replace those arrested, and these were able to win over the socialists—who had been shocked by the brutality of the police—to a united antigovernment effort. A communist-led revolt in March freed Kun and put him and his party at the head of the new Hungarian Soviet Republic.[2]

The new government faced an immediate crisis. All of the western powers were hostile to the regime, and the large Romanian army occupying Hungarian soil to the east appeared to be ready to move forward to occupy Budapest and put down the revolution. Kun, like Kossuth seven decades earlier, was able to rally most of the public to his side by appealing for a patriotic effort to preserve the independence of Hungary. The first effort along these lines was successful, as diplomacy and improved morale in the army held the Romanians in check.

Béla Kun's next task, again remarkably similar to the sequence followed in 1848, was to tackle the state-nationality problem. His solution was part Kossuth and part Lenin. Like Kossuth, Kun appealed first and foremost for the restoration of a Hungary based on the Crownlands of St. Stephen. Unlike the forty-eighters, however, he stipulated that the minorities would have full rights to their own language and culture in a federated state. Interestingly, Kun's nationality policy was only partly Leninist, as he did not accept the right of the minorities to secede, even in theory. In a more practical vein he refused to agree to any rights at all for the Romanians—at that time his deadliest enemies.[3]

The parallel between 1848 and 1919 was at best only partial. The call for the support of "Great Hungary" did rally the Magyars (indeed it is unlikely that Kun would have lasted a week if he had attempted to defend the status quo). But the effort to win the support of the non-Magyars was a total failure. Most of Slovakia was occupied by the Hungarians, and a Slovak Soviet Republic was established. But this was a puppet regime that had few ethnic Slovak supporters, and it collapsed immediately upon the departure of the Hungarian army. The reaction of all but a handful of Slovaks was either passive resistance or participation in anti-Hungarian guerrilla activity.

There is not the slightest evidence of any favorable reaction on the part of the Croats; no part of Croatia was ever occupied by Kun's forces. There was nothing to be gained or lost by offering concessions in this direction. On the other hand, the omission of the Romanians from the Soviet Hungarian plan is less surprising than it first appears. While the slight of these long-time enemies of the Magyars may reflect the prejudices of the Transylvanian-born Kun,, it is more probably a reaction to hard realities. Since Kun's authority did not cover eastern Hungary, let alone Transylvania, there was little practical purpose in embracing the Romanians. On the contrary, even a symbolic gesture in that direction would have alienated badly needed noncommunist support within Hungary itself.

In fact, a careful analysis of the Hungarian Soviet Republic shows that communist control was always precarious. The social democrats early showed their strength by forcing Kun to disband his version of the Cheka (a group known as "Lenin's Boys"), which had outraged the nation by its random use of terror.[4] The socialists were too divided amongst themselves to take over from the communists, but when united on an important issue such as terrorism, they could act as a brake. Kun's party also suffered from internal divisions on ideology as well as from a constant clash of personalities. Had the revolution survived, it seems certain that it would not have remained communist without outside (i.e., Soviet) assistance.

The final defeat of the Hungarian Soviet Republic was hastened by disagreements on the nationality problem. Kun's decision to withdraw from Slovakia, though tactically the only rational move, crystallized the opposition of noncommunist nationalists who did not want to give an inch. Their dream of a resurgent Great Hungary shattered, they abandoned the communists to an inevitable defeat.

The reaction to Kun's reign, known as the "White Terror," obliterated not only active communists but also the bulk of the sympathizers: in addition to 5,000 executed and 75,000 jailed, more than 100,000 people fled the country. The CPH existed only in exile until the final stages of World War II. But, as for many other communist parties, Soviet exile proved to be just as deadly as white terror at home.

In the Leninist system there is no greater sin than failure. Kun and his lieutenants had no sooner arrived in Moscow than they were thrust into an extensive post mortem on the defeat in Hungary. The analysis continued for years, and eventually culminated in the liquidation of Kun and the CPH's old guard in the Soviet purges. One lesson was quickly seized upon by Lenin, however. The great wizard of Bolshevism divined that the pivotal error had been the communist alliance with the socialists. The latter, Lenin decided, had betrayed the revolution from the beginning and should never have been trusted at all.

Kun and his fellow exiles might well have argued that there would have been no revolution at all without the socialists, and that the crucial failure was the inability of the Red Army to come to the aid of the Hungarian communists. But the climate in Moscow did not favor those who disagreed with Lenin, and the Hungarians reacted to criticism with self-criticism—a rapidly developing Bolshevik tradition. Lenin applied his view of the lessons of the Soviet Hungarian experience to the formation of the Comintern. The uncompromising tone of the Twenty-One Conditions, and the consequent necessity of not only splitting communism from socialism but also of totally alienating the two, owes much to Lenin's reaction to the events of 1919 in Hungary.[5]

The only important long-term survivors of the Hungarian revolution were an ideologist, György Lukács, and an *apparatchik,* Mátyás Rákosi. The former soon won an important place as a leading theoretician writing from exile in the west. The latter had a harder road to fame and power. In 1925, the Comintern decided to revive an illegal party in Hungary, and sent Rákosi back to do the organizing. He was promptly arrested and spent the next fourteen years in prison. In view of the thoroughness of the subsequent purges of the Soviet-based remnants of the CPH, however, this may have been the safest place to be.

Stalin, who was apparently convinced that the original CPH was hopelessly Trotskyite, destroyed most of the leadership of the party in exile, leaving only a small and impotent group attached to the Comintern. A favorite means of liquidating members of the CPH was to send them home on missions of terror or sabotage and then denounce them to the Hungarian police. This tactic had the double advantage of economy in the carrying out of executions while at the same time giving the impression of a determined and important communist resistance to the right-wing regime in Hungary.[6]

Rákosi was freed and allowed to go to Moscow during the period of the Nazi-Soviet alliance. During the war he rebuilt the CPH, making use of younger men who had developed communist convictions as students or in reaction to fascist oppression, and who had then escaped or had been taken prisoner while fighting with Hungarian units allied with the Germans. There was only a very small resistance movement on Hungarian soil during the war, and those communists who took part were careful not to describe themselves as such.

Poland

No communist party has a more complicated history than the Polish. In large part this is a consequence of the fact that Poland had strong socialist movements while it was still divided among three empires, and that these groups were separate. Further, conflicting parties emerged even within the framework of one political system.[7]

The most important split was logically in the most populous area: Russian Poland. From a historical perspective it is clear that the nature of the division—disagreement over the national question—prophesied what was later to become a critical problem for socialists and communists everywhere. To put the latter simply, one faction took Marx's words about the international character of the worker's objectives and the class struggle seriously and argued that Polish socialism should be a part of the greater Russian whole. The other group was not opposed to cooperation with the Russian comrades but insisted on a separate Polish party that would eventually function in an independent Polish nation.

The internationalist party was led by the brilliant Rosa Luxemburg and took the same Social Democratic Party of Poland and Lithuania (SDKPL in Polish). Besides arguing against nationalism and in favor of internationalism, the SDKPL leaders emphasized the economic advantages to Poland of continued integration in the Russian Empire. This point of view had considerable merit, since the vast market to the east had helped to create a large and prosperous industrial base in the Polish lands. Even so, these relatively abstract arguments were unsuccessful in overcoming the hatred of Russia and Russians felt by nearly everyone in Poland—including the workers.

The original SDKPL was primarily a party of intellectuals, many of them (including Rosa Luxemburg) of Jewish origin. In a country that was intensely nationalistic, devoutly Roman Catholic, and never free from strains of anti-Semitism, the SDKPL did not appear to be destined for great things. In fact, it was not. After the Bolshevik Revolution it merged with the left wing of the other socialist party to form the Communist Party of Poland (CPP) and for a few years played a minor role in national affairs. The Polish-Soviet War of 1920–21 obviously made things more than uncomfortable for the new party, however, and it all but disappeared afterwards.

The nationalist socialist party (Polish Socialist Party—PPS in Polish) at first fared much better than its rival. The PPS was led by Joseph Piłsudski, a leader who hadn't an intellect that approached Rosa Luxemburg's but who had a good deal more charisma and common sense. In fact, Piłsudski's party seemed to be far more interested in achieving a Polish state than in working toward the goals of socialism. As mentioned earlier, Piłsudski's involvement in politics turned out to be inversely proportional to his commitment to socialism, and he left the PPS during the war.

The interwar political atmosphere was not conducive to any form of socialism, much less to a communist party that followed the Soviet line. The Polish people were preoccupied with the questions of national security, the role and status of the minorities, agrarian reform, and the economy. Only the latter was in the typical domain of socialism, and even there, the Marxist approach of class struggle did not seem to appeal to more than a few people. The PPS did have considerable influence in the largest of the trade union organizations, but the workers were still a relatively weak factor in the political equation.

If the situation of the socialists was bad, that of the communists was far worse. After scarcely two years of existence, the CPP had chosen to go illegal rather than register with the state to whose very existence it passionately objected. After the Polish-Soviet war, in which the communists earned a nearly universal reputation as traitors, the legal option was no longer available. The CPP did function through political front organizations, however, and once the Comintern had given the green light, it was able to elect two candidates to the national assembly.

The obstacles to further growth for the CPP were nonetheless formidable. In addition to part of the platform that favored returning the eastern territories to the Soviet Union, the Comintern eventually forced the CPP to support giving the western and coastal territories of Poland to Germany. Even though this policy was short-lived (reflecting the Soviet desire to strengthen the German Communist Party in the struggle against Hitler), it further befouled an already unsavory reputation.

The Piłsudski coup of 1926 was at first applauded by the CPP, which hoped that it would first break the existing parliamentary stalemate and subsequently hasten the crisis of capitalism that would lead to revolution. The first part of this analysis was correct, the second was not. As the political climate in Poland became increasingly authoritarian, the influence of the communists decreased to insignificance. Their one popular card, a call for total, radical land reform, could no longer be played. In any case, this platform had long since been all but preempted, at least in the minds of the masses, by the Peasant Party. The PPS repeatedly scorned CPP calls for a united front.

Ironically, the greatest danger to the Polish Communist Party did not come from the domestic police or fascists but emanated instead from the Soviet party under Stalin. The largest ancestor of the CPP, the SDKPL, it must be remembered, was a fiercely internationalist (or to use the pejorative communist equivalent—"cosmopolitan") party. As such, its ideological approach would logically be closest to the views of Trotsky.

In fact, a significant proportion of the CPP leadership was Trotskyite by political belief and personal friendship. Most of these were purged a few years after Trotsky's downfall—that is to say by about 1932. This first purge was relatively easy for Stalin, since the Polish party was forced to hold its larger meetings and conduct many of its activities on Soviet territory. Even so, the initial round was basically nonviolent; the victims were expelled rather than executed, and many later turned up in the west. The best known of the refugees was Isaac Deutscher, who became a prominent historian and philosopher in Britain.

Despite the successful elimination of the Polish Trotskyites, Stalin appears to have retained a deep distrust of the newly cleansed CPP. This suspicion became even more acute as a consequence of the CPP's enthusiastic participation on the loyalist side in the Spanish Civil War. Even though Stalin's own Comintern was directing the effort in Spain, and even though the Polish communists did as they were told, Stalin was made more than usually nervous by reports of Poles fighting under such potentially internationalist (read cosmopolitan and thus Trotskyite) slogans as "for your freedom and ours."

For Stalin, suspicion was enough. All of the parties belonging to the Comintern suffered from the *Yezhovshchina,* but the Poles suffered the most. Close at hand, with a Trotskyite past, and with little importance and few sympathizers in Poland, there was no reason to spare the CPP from the worst that the NKVD could produce. The Polish Communist Party was physically destroyed in 1937–1938. The leadership and the rank and file on Soviet territory, as well as all those who could be enticed into leaving Poland, were imprisoned or executed.[8] The liquidation was so thorough that the party had to be dissolved in the summer of 1938. There weren't enough people left to staff the organization.

There was no Polish Communist Party from 1938 to 1942. The new party that appeared in January of that year did not take the name "communist" (that would have been a foolish provocation of the West so soon after Stalin's cooperation with Germany and the Soviet invasion of Poland), but took instead the name Polish Worker's Party (PWP). This new group was extremely small and was in reality the nucleus for a Soviet-supported resistance movement in the Polish territories. The PWP was soon paralleled by a similar organization based in Russia, this one known as the Union of Polish Patriots.

The guerilla activities organized against the Germans by the PWP were on a far smaller scale than those mounted by the noncommunist forces, yet they still manifested bravery and determination. An interesting aspect of the party's history within this period is the emergence of a faction opposed to complete subservience to the Soviets. The brief existence of this group was ended when most of its leaders fell victim to the Gestapo. Although nothing can be proved, such a coincidence must necessarily arouse suspicion—the tactic of informing on opponents within the party seems to have been a favorite of Stalin from the days of his youth. This cruel trick is also known to have been used by other communist parties.[9]

The leadership of the PWP that moved to meet the advancing Red Army in 1944 was thus primarily a small group of Poles who had survived both purges and battle, together with a number of hastily Polonized Soviets who had been parachuted in during the war. The leader of the PWP, Władisław Gomułka, owed his status not least to the good fortune of having sat out the *Yezhovshchina* in a Polish jail. Gomułka was not yet forty in 1944, extremely young for the secretary general of a communist party.

Germany

Since the de facto territorial statement created at the end of World War II transferred a substantial portion of Germany to Eastern Europe, it is appropriate to consider the history of that country's communist party in this section. Even if the territorial change had not occurred, some fairly extensive mention of German socialism would be essential. This is true because Germany, if not the birthplace of modern socialism (that honor should probably go to France), was the early home of the socialist party that was at the same time the largest, the most influential, and the most Marxist.

The German Social Democratic Party (SPD) had grown and matured together with the rapid development of industry and the consequent expansion of the working class. In this sense, it differed sharply from the highly theoretical, intellectually based parties which comprised a good portion of the world socialist movement. The SDP was really proletarian, and, although it never abandoned the entire ideological arsenal of Marxism (including the idea of revolution), in fact it evolved into a party that was primarily interested in reforms that would improve the lot of the working people. From the 1890s on, the Social Democrats played an important role in the German parliamentary system.

The SPD naturally had critics to both right and left. Bernstein, mentioned earlier, advocated revision of Marx that would formally dispense with the revolutionary credo. The main line of the party was unwilling to do this, however, and continued to pay lip service to the great master while ignoring those parts of his theory considered to be inconvenient. The leftists, on the other hand, were increasingly alienated by what they considered to be a "bourgeois trend' in socialism. The decisive breaking point came over the issue of the First World War. The radicals, now grouped in the Independent Social Democratic Party, considered the conflict to be nothing more than a quarrel between capitalists and advocated a refusal to participate in any way. But the bulk of the SPD, unhappy and confused, bowed to the pressures of national patriotism and voted in the German parliament to support the war.

Political activity was limited in the first years of conflict, but the example of the Bolshevik revolution stimulated propaganda efforts on the part of radical groups who now believed that the weary and disillusioned population could be prodded into revolt.

The most important of these groups was the Spartacus League, the extreme left wing of the Independent SPD. The leaders of this faction, which became the Communist Party of Germany (KPD) in late 1918, were Karl Liebknecht and Rosa Luxemburg (also founder of the SDKPL).

The first experiences of the KPD were not happy. There was much turmoil in the recently defeated nation, with strikes affecting the military as well as industry. Such chaos and discontent were ideal for revolutionary

activity, but the KPD had neither the numbers nor the organization to take advantage of it. Only in Berlin did the communists have much influence, and it was in that city, apparently out of frustration at their impotence, that they took a foolish and quixotic stand. In early January of 1919, the Spartacists attempted a coup d'etat in Berlin. Army troops, mostly irregulars, ended the revolt after a few days, and Liebknecht and Luxemburg were shot while "trying to escape."

News of the failure of the Spartacist revolt must have been received with mixed feelings in Moscow. On the one hand, it severely damaged hopes for a successful revolution in Germany, which many if not all Bolsheviks then believed was a pre-condition for the continued survival of their own regime. On the other hand, it eliminated a dangerous rival, for Luxemburg was no admirer of Lenin, or, for that matter his revolution (the national question again). It is doubtful that the fiery Rosa would have allowed her party to accept the Twenty-one Conditions of 1920 without a fierce and demoralizing struggle.

The successors to the Spartacists as leaders of the KPD were more amenable to the Bolshevik line, and the German communists did join the Comintern without serious argument. The first years of Moscow's control were particularly important in setting the pattern for later disasters. In the early 1920s, the Soviet leaders still aspired to lead a world revolution, and they still had high hopes for Germany. The official line in this struggle was that it was necessary for the communists to go it alone. Under no circumstances should there be cooperation with the dissolute parties of the Second International. Those who refused to join the Comintern were traitors to the cause of socialism.

High on the list of traitors, of course, was the SPD. The Social Democrats were blamed for the failure of the Spartacist revolt and were considered to be the major factor in inhibiting revolutionary development. The level of rhetoric was intense, and the unrestrained invective from the communist side created an atmosphere of total hostility; the SPD and the KPD, the two "Marxist" parties of Germany, would have nothing to do with each other.

The diminishing revolutionary atmosphere in Germany and Western Europe, as well as the move within the Soviet Union toward stabilization (the NEP), prompted a change in Comintern policy. The Soviets had concluded an alliance with Germany in 1922, but, as noted earlier, the Comintern had continued to support revolutionary activities through 1923. When this conflict no longer appeared to be tenable, the two policies were synchronized and revolutionary agitation tapered off. Stalin, not yet fully in control at home, at first had some difficulty in getting rid of

Trotskyites and other critics of Comintern policy who had considerable strength in the KPD. Stalin was too shrewd to be resisted for long, however, and in 1926 the majority of the opposition was expelled. A prominent historian has described the new leader of German communism, Ernst Thälmann, as "dull and safe, just the man to suit Stalin."[10]

Despite all of its problems, the KPD did not suffer from many of the difficulties that plagued its eastern brethren. Even though Rosa Luxemburg and Lenin had clashed over the theoretical aspects of the national problem, the practical reality was that the communists were usually able to support Germany's territorial aspirations. Moreover, the Soviets had no interest in seeing Germany pay her reparations and other debts to the western capitalist countries, and thus the KPD was able to take the popular line on an important issue. Finally, the German communists were able to take advantage of their opposition status. The interwar depression hit Germany first and hardest, and the SPD, which had been a part of the government, had to take a part of the blame. The KPD, as the most radical party in a time of great misery and despair, was able to draw many disillusioned voters from other parties, and particularly from the SPD.

As the decade of the 1930s began, the communists were becoming ever more confident. The number of voters backing the KPD was growing rapidly, and a short-term statistical projection indicated a communist majority before the decade was over. In this atmosphere of euphoria, the KPD, following the Comintern line, launched its most vicious attack ever on the socialists. The SPD was now referred to as the "Social Fascist" party, the most dangerous opponent of "true socialism," and the greatest enemy of the working class.

As for the real fascists, the Nazis, Stalin and his Soviet and most of his German advisors did not think they were a real threat. Ignoring the fact that a projection of fascist voting trends was even more impressive than that of the communists, the KDP continued to focus all its efforts on the SPD. Indeed, incredible as it may seem in retrospect, the KPD even cooperated with the Nazis in some important electoral contests. Thus, the socialists stood alone against Hitler and, inevitably, failed. By the time the communists came to appreciate the true nature and strength of Nazism, it was too late.

The war on communism was Hitler's first major offensive. The burning of the national parliament building, the Reichstag, was staged by the Nazis as an excuse to destroy the KPD. The communist party itself ceased to exist within Germany in scarcely a year. A communist record was at first every bit as bad as a Jewish origin in the fascist dictatorship:

former activists were sent to concentration camps; former members were denied decent jobs and ostracized. The part of the leadership that escaped to Moscow was savaged by the *Yezhovshchina*. To Stalin, failure was disloyalty.

There was no armed resistance movement in Germany during the war, a fact that should surprise no one. Even so, the available evidence suggests that there were a good many active and effective spies and that an important number of these had communist sympathies. The only partial declassification of western archives, and the inaccessibility of Soviet documents, makes conclusions tenuous, but it appears that a large and well-placed network, known as *Die Rote Kappelle* (The Red Orchestra), fed military secrets to Stalin throughout the war. At any rate, it is certain that there were German communist survivors at home as well as in Moscow in 1945.

Romania

The history of communism in Romania is the story of a chronically weak movement, a political grouping that always suffered from both the lack of the necessary class base as well as the need to swim against a strong nationalist tide. Thus, there was only a very small industrial proletariat in Romania at the founding of the Comintern in 1919. Moreover, the early leaders and theoreticians of Marxism in Romania, C. Dobrogeanu-Gherea and C. Rakovsky, were intellectuals respectively of Russian-Jewish and Bulgarian origin. Not only did these two and most of their early colleagues have very few workers to whom they could appeal, they had the added handicap of a foreign background that evoked suspicion in a people recently steeped in nationalism.

The Romanian Social Democratic Party, in which Dobrogeanu-Gherea and Rakovsky were activists, had drawn much of its early strength from the Hungarian movement in Transylvania, and was then reinforced somewhat by those Moldavians and Wallachians who had been strongly influenced by French utopian socialism. The first communist group, led by Rakovsky, was an offshoot of the Social Democrats. As time passed, this faction tried and failed to get the parent party to join the Comintern. Having failed, it split off and became first the Romanian Section of the Soviet Communist Party and then, without dropping its affiliation with the Bolsheviks, spawned the Communist Party of Romania (CPR).

The communist movement in Romania immediately suffered a num-

ber of heavy blows to its potential development as a consequence of the
problem of national frontiers. The new Romanian state had acquired
Transylvania from Hungary, reacquired Bessarabia from Russia, and
retained a part of the Dobrogea claimed by Bulgaria. The official Comintern policy, forced on the Romanian party, was that the proper way
to resolve these conflicts was by applying the principle of "self-determination to the point of secession." However democratic this approach
might be, it caused most Romanians to associate communism with ad-
vocacy of reducing their country's size by nearly half.

Another factor that severely damaged the Romanian party was the
Béla Kun revolution in Hungary. The communist leaders in Moscow
were, of course, strongly opposed to the intervention of Romanian troops
against Kun, and urged their compatriots in Romania to organize some
kind of resistance (e.g., strikes and mutinies). The Romanian communists
failed utterly in this task, not least because the action in Hungary was
immensely popular with the Romanian public as a whole. By taking an
official stand against the intervention, but not actually doing anything,
the Romanian party earned the contempt of Moscow as well as the hatred
of the Romanian people.

To add to all of its other difficulties, the CPR was both disorganized
and disunited. Most of the organizational structure had followed the
Social Democrats, and was never rebuilt to any meaningful extent. The
factionalization was even more serious. The story is extremely complex,
and the sources are scarcely reliable, but it appears that there were four
major orientations: the "Bessarabian," the "Transylvanian," the Left,
and the Right."[11]

The Bessarabian faction was the strongest and had the largest following, primarily because it had direct connections with the Soviet party
and could rely upon support (at least in the twenties) from disaffected
members of the Russian and Ukrainian minorities in Bessarabia and
Bucovina. The Transylvanian group was also ethnically oriented, but was
not nearly so strong because of the opposition of the Hungarians to
communism. The Left faction was internationalist in outlook and intellectual in composition: its leaders, Marcel Pauker and C. Dobrogeanu-
Gherea, were tied to Rakovsky and through him to Trotsky. The Right
was at least partly ethnically Romanian and can be best defined as comprising those elements which didn't belong to one of the other groups.
All factions had a large number, perhaps a majority, of intellectuals of
Jewish origin in the leadership; none had any significant proportion of
workers.

The Comintern officials in Moscow had a very difficult time trying
to determine what to do with such a ramshackle party, and their decisions,

characteristically, were partly sensible and partly disastrous. On the intelligent side, the Bessarabians were restrained from dominating the party as they might easily have done; for this leadership could have had only ephemeral influence and would always have been viewed by even the most ardent native communists as composed of foreign elements. The Left fell along with Trotsky, but at first was merely removed from control rather than annihilated.[12] Incredibly, however, the Right was then dropped in favor of the Transylvanians.

The rationale for this was apparently punishment for the Right's failure to support Béla Kun, but the effect was catastrophic. The Transylvanians could command even less respect in the population as a whole than the Bessarabians and soon had to be dropped as well. Rebuilding the party was then impossible, particularly since the remaining cadres had been forced to go underground when the communist party was declared illegal in 1924.

After this, the original old guard went to prison or to Moscow. In the early twenties and on into the first years of the Depression, when Romanian society and politics were in chaos, the communist party was impotent, a factor of no importance. Gradually, however, after the royal dictatorship had failed to prevent the domestic situation from worsening, a small number of ethnically Romanian workers began to carry out strikes in the name of communism. Their weakness and vulnerability is demonstrated by the fact that their first postwar leader, Gheorghe Gheorghiu-Dej, was active for scarcely more than a year before he was arrested and imprisoned for twelve years. Even though their early activities are important primarily in retrospect, these workers formed the nucleus of the present-day CPR.[13]

Given the unhappy history of the Romanian Communist Party until 1940, it is hardly surprising that it was unable to lead any sort of resistance movement during the war. Doubtless, many of the small group of faithful dropped out after the CPR gave official endorsement to the Soviet seizure of Bessarabia in July of 1940. Nevertheless, a most important victory was won by Romanian communists, quietly and in unknown circumstances, when Stalin decided to annul the *Vienna Diktat* and return all of Transylvania to Romania after the war.

Yugoslavia

The history of the communist movement in Yugoslavia is quite different from what a detached observer would have predicted in 1919 when the

Communist Party of Yugoslavia (CPY) was formed and joined the Comintern. Not only did this new party lack the foundation of an industrialized state, but it also had to cope with a nearly continuous illegal status, and a nationality problem that was at least as severe as any in Eastern Europe. Even so, the CPY, despite some sharp ups and downs, was strong throughout the country, and emerged at the end of the war as the most powerful communist party in Eastern Europe, the only one with the potential of seizing power without foreign assistance.

The explanations for this paradox are incomplete and controversial. For example, the Yugoslav communists seem to have been able to attract a higher proportion of social democrats at the very beginning than was the case elsewhere; they thus avoided much of the intrasocialist bickering that hurt other parties.[14] The reason for this higher degree of unity is itself unclear, however. Another advantage of the CPY was that it was, at least for a part of the interwar period, the only truly national, or Yugoslav, political party. This enabled it to attract the support of those who disdained the petty nationalism of the national subgroups, i.e., Serbs, Croats, and Slovenes.

Perhaps the most important factor in sustaining the party in the early years was its inheritance of the fanatically revolutionary south slav tradition. Even though the prewar radical groups had ranged across the ideological spectrum, with a not inconsiderable orientation to anarchism, many individuals and groups naturally gravitated to the only political party that styled itself revolutionary. In this fashion the CPY acquired a core of activists that could survive the dark years when the leadership was hopelessly divided and the secret police seemed to have informers everywhere. Finally, it should be remembered that communists in Yugoslavia did not have to struggle against popular Russophobia.

It seemed for a time, however, that the strengths of the nascent CPY would be too few to overcome the schism produced by the nationality problem. The Comintern line of "self-determination to the point of secession" did not appeal nearly so much to Croat and Slovene communists as it offended their Serb brethren. The situation was made altogether worse by the fact that the Comintern leadership, strongly influenced by the Bulgarians (see below), took an anti-Yugoslav view of the Macedonian question.[15] In fact, the general direction of the Comintern, which formed a special Balkan Section, was to support a new Yugoslavia, based on Sofia rather than on Belgrade.

The Serbs within the CPY, who were most important both in total numbers and in leaders, reacted in three different ways to this problem:

some left the party, some adopted the official line, and some paid lip service while doing their best to avoid any actual implementation of the guidelines from Moscow. This latter group was the strongest, but one can readily observe from the topsy-turvy career of its leader, S. Marković, who was removed from the position of secretary general of the CPY on three different occasions in the party's first decade, that the Comintern was not convinced of his loyalty.

Marković's tenacity as leader was in large part a consequence of a diversion created (consciously or unconsciously is not clear) by the Serbian wing of the party which launched a wave of assassination attempts in 1920–1921. After this, the CPY, which had drawn an amazing 12.4 percent of the popular vote in the free election of 1920, was quickly driven underground and subjected to a reign of secret police terror that wiped out nearly all of the previously existing structure.[16] In this chaotic situation, Moscow was unable for many years to pull together the cadres necessary to fashion a new, loyal leadership. This was finally done in 1928, however, when Marković was dropped for the last time, and the rather comically titled "anti-faction faction" was put in charge.

The new CPY, which was slowly reformed in the late twenties and early thirties, was based to a remarkable extent on university students, particularly those in Belgrade. The fact that the party was still disorganized and often self-contradictory, and that the students had only a sketchy knowledge of Marx and Lenin, could not destroy the momentum of a movement that seemed to run on youthful enthuasiasm and daring. Rich students as well as poor fought against the oppressive royal dictatorship. An important section of the students were not from Serbia proper but were Montenegrins and Bosnians.

Josip Broz, code named Tito, assumed the leadership of the CPY in the late thirties. Aside from personal qualities of intelligence and courage, a number of environmental factors made his rapid rise possible. Of Slovene-Croatian parentage and peasant stock, but trained as a worker, Tito was captured by the Russians while serving as a soldier in the Austro-Hungarian army during World War I, and returned from the east years later as a convinced communist. During the early factional disputes in the twenties, Tito was not important enough in the party to be associated with any group. Later, when Stalin began to display displeasure with the "anti-faction faction," Tito had the good luck to be in jail.

The *Yezhovshchina* crushed the Yugoslav party nearly as thoroughly as the Polish, liquidating practically all of the leadership that had taken refuge in the Soviet Union. Tito was in Moscow during much of this time; whether he survived through mere good fortune or because he cooperated with the NKVD will probably never be known. The former is the more probable thesis, however, for when the smoke cleared and Tito was left in charge, he quickly moved his center of operations to Western Europe, primarily Paris. After 1938, Tito made only the briefest of appearances on Soviet soil.

The party that Tito built in Yugoslavia was distinct in a number of ways. First, very few of the leaders had any extensive Soviet experience (of the other parties that took control in 1945, only the Albanian had a similar background). Second, even at the time when Moscow was downplaying the rights of national minorities in order to provide unity against the Nazi menace, Tito faced the especially difficult nationality problem head-on and endorsed Lenin's concept of self-determination to the point of secession.

The CPY's sponsorship of a federal approach was obviously more popular with non-Serbs than Serbs, but the CPY had a hard core of support all over the country on the eve of World War II. Tito's party was hurt by the six months following Hitler's invasion of Yugoslavia but preceding the attack on Russia, when the Comintern forbade resistance against the Soviet Union's Nazi ally. Nevertheless, Operation Barbarossa was only a few weeks old when Tito's forces began to harass the Germans.

The resistance movement led by Tito (known as the "Partisans": see above chapter 15) was never openly described as communist. Neither Moscow nor the CPY leadership was anxious to frighten potential volunteers or scare off western support by such a needless provocation as raising the red flag. Nevertheless, Tito and his senior communist cadres were everywhere in firm control from beginning to end. The Partisans drew much of their support by default—Croats, Albanians, and Slovenes had either to go with Tito or choose to fight with the pro-Serb Chetniks, with the fascist Croatian Ustaša, by themselves, or not fight at all. Later, the exploits of the Partisans against the Germans, both in battle and by provoking Nazi atrocities, drew to them the bulk of those who wanted to fight fascism.

The fact that Tito was able to organize an extremely effective resistance movement, while at the same time broadening and deepening the strength of the communist party, was crucial to his success. it is true that the rugged terrain of Yugoslavia, as well as its position on the periphery of the main Nazi war effort, contributed to the guerrilla victories. It is also true that the mistakes of the noncommunist Yugoslavs made his task easier. Nevertheless, Tito and his comrades were shrewd and resourceful; they emerged from the war lean, tough, and unified.

Czechoslovakia

The communist movement in Czechoslovakia appeared as the strongest in Eastern Europe in numbers and in electoral strength, and, to outside observers, was one of the world's leading parties. Yet, much as was the case for the Czechoslovak state itself, appearances were deceiving. The problems and contradictions that have plagued the party since the war can be elucidated if not explained by an examination of its early history.

Social democracy had been quite strong in the Czech lands of Austria-Hungary. The base for the political movement was to be found primarily in the urban proletariat of this highly industrialized area. The social democrats were split along national lines, however, and there were entirely separate Czech and German parties. While the latter was infleunced to a considerable extent by the internationalism of the overall German movement, the Czechs had moved before the war toward direct support of Masaryk and the drive for a separate national state. Moreover, the Czech SDs were not known as radicals and had often functioned in parliamentary government.

Given the national divisions and the lack of a revolutionary orientation it would seem, in retrospect, that the Third International would not be able to attract more than a small splinter group from the Czech lands and that social democracy would continue as the dominant force on the left. In fact, contrary to the experience of all of the other industrialized countries, the reverse occurred. First the Slovaks (who had a short-lived Soviet under Béla Kun's protection in 1919), then the Germans, and finally the Czech parties voted to accept the Twenty-One Conditions and joined the Comintern in 1921. The three parties then united to form the Communist Party of Czechoslovakia (CPCS) in the same year.[17]

The transition was not without trauma. Particularly in the Czech party, there was bitter opposition and attempts to sabotage the leftward movement. The radicals were firmly entrenched in the leadership at all of the important levels, however, and the vote was not close. Overwhelmingly, en masse, the Social Democratic party organization was transformed into a communist party—the only such case in history.

The victory was not all that it seemed, however. The CPCS was clearly unable to command the rank-and-file support of its predecessor. Precise statistics are difficult to find, but it appears that party membership after the shift dropped almost immediately from about 300,000 to only 170,000.[18] This factor (not documented until much later) considerably reduced the importance of the new party, which at the time proudly announced that it was the third largest in the Comintern and the largest in relation to national population.

More important than the defection of the rank and file, from Moscow's point of view, was the weakness of the leadership of the CPCS, which quickly split into right and left factions. The right, which had engineered the changeover, was lukewarm on revolution, half-hearted on the rights of nationalities to secede from the state, and even unsure about the name "communist." Its leader, Bohumín Šmeral, was thoroughly un-Bolshevik in nearly every respect: his decision to support the change to communism is a real mystery. In later times he would have been summarily expelled from the party for being an "opportunist" and "revisionist." As it was, he was the CPCS's founder and had to be treated with more respect—at least for a time.

The Czechoslovak communists muddled through their first years. They were ineffective in promoting revolution, internally divided on most issues, and a source of exasperation, if not embarrassment to Moscow. But they were big—in 1925, the CPCS drew the second largest vote of all parties in Czechoslovakia. The Comintern was not satisfied, however, and in that year a detailed investigation of the CPCS was undertaken. The fact that Stalin (who had other worries at the time) played a prominent role is indicative of the importance of this party to the Third International. Not unexpectedly, the decision on Šmeral and his comrades was negative, and they were dropped from the leadership.

The new Left group that assumed control of the CPCS was more intellectual rather than worker in its composition and also included a sharply higher number of Slovaks. The latter had been particularly critical of the party's attitude toward their region and in many ways closely reflected within the CPCS the attitude of their noncommunist brethren within the Czechoslovak state. Even though the new leadership was clearly aware of its raison d'être, it failed to move fast enough to follow the increasingly strict ideological line emanating from the East.

In 1929, another change was decreed in Moscow. The new head of the CPCS, Klement Gottwald, was slavishly subservient to the hard line of the Comintern. His objective was to Bolshevize the party—whatever the cost. Since these were the times in which social democrats were being referred to as "social fascists," Gottwald's sudden, sharp redirection of party policy was quite consistent with the approved line. Nevertheless, the costs were high. At the polls, the CPCS slipped from second to fourth overall. More important, some 60 to 75 percent of the remaining rank and file now chose to leave the party.[19] Perhaps because of this rather drastic and unexpected drop in popularity, Gottwald's request for a purge of the entire membership as well as of the leading cadres was denied by Moscow. Those of the rank and file who left did so of their own accord. The extreme intransigence of the Gottwald-led CPCS is reflected in the deliberately provocative statements which it issued. Thus, in one presidential campaign the communist slogan was "not Masaryk but Lenin," and Czechoslovakia was referred to as "the prison of nations."[20] Gottwald's personal involvement in these policies was such that for a brief period, 1934–36, he found it more prudent to live in the Soviet Union. The popularity of the CPCS continued to plummet, but in an overall political atmosphere that was increasingly polarized and disoriented, the communists' situation was not as bad as it might have been.

The vehemence of the CPCS line was such that Gottwald, though ever Moscow's most obedient servant, found it hard to accept the Comintern's sudden switch to a united front policy in 1935, with its stress on cooperation with other socialist and democratic parties. Even so, the communists did go along, and they, as well as Moscow, were in a position to be scathingly critical of the Munich tragedy of 1938, and consequently of the domestic parties that had been pro-Western. In the atmosphere of despair that followed the Nazi invasion, the CPCS, though soon underground, picked up considerable popular support for its anti-Nazi line.

The period of the Stalin-Hitler pact, September 1939 to June 1941, arrested the growing support for the communists, but once the war began the popularity of the CPCS started to grow again. There was little opportunity for armed resistance in wartime Czechoslovakia: the Nazi presence was too strong, and the distributions of Germans throughout the population made covert operations very dangerous. The communist role in the Czech lands was mostly propagandistic, and direct actions against the Nazis were almost entirely the work of noncommunist movements.

Slovakia, however, proved to be an important exception. The terrain was extremely favorable for guerrilla operations, and the communists, backed up by Soviet agents, were able to maintain a fairly consistent albeit small-scale harassment of both the Slovak Nazi government and of the Germans themselves. This activity, although by no means decisive, had considerable psychological importance in preparing for the ultimate CPCS takeover in Czechoslovakia.

Bulgaria

The early history of communism in Bulgaria is remarkably similar to that of the Russian movement.[21] Bulgaria's Lenin, Dimiter Blagoev, forced a split within Bulgarian social democracy at about the same time (1903) and over basically the same issue as in Russia. In this case, however, the terms used for the factions are more descriptive: Blageov's victorious "narrow" group favored a small, highly disciplined party (similar to the Bolshevik view), while the opposition, the "broad" faction, wished to have a larger party that would be more directly dependent on mass support. Blageov's group was, in fact, more clear cut winners within their socialist movement than the Bolsheviks in theirs, but the overwhelmingly rural nature of the economy and the unrepresentative governmental structure long prevented them from playing a role of any significance in national affairs.

The historical strength of Bulgarian communism should not be underestimated, however. The Bulgarian radical left seems to have always had an important hold on what there was of the Sofia proletariat, as well as a not inconsiderable attraction for propertyless persons in the countryside. As will be seen shortly, the communists had many ups and downs in the first four and a half decades of the twentieth century, but the low points in Bulgaria were never so low as those reached by the Polish, Hungarian, and Romanian parties. The explanation for this surprising communist strength in a rural environment is only as complete as that for its Yugoslav counterpart, which is to say there are many theories but not much in the way of convincing evidence.

With Blagoev in control, there was little difficulty in swinging most of the socialist movement into the Communist Party of Bulgaria (CPB), which was established and joined the Comintern in 1919. The new party, even though comparatively unified, found itself unable to establish a domestic political strategy that would meet the revolutionary requirements of the Comintern on the one hand, and the practical realities of Bulgarian society on the other. The result of these contradictions was a sort of passive inertia in which the CPB talked a great deal and did very little. Blagoev's rapidly declining health exacerbated the confusion. Finally, in 1923, a crisis point was reached.

The CPB had the worst position that a communist party could have at the time of the anti-Stambuliski coup in June of 1923. The communist leaders, Georgi Dimitrov and Vasil Kolarov, certainly knew that the coalition opposed to Stambuliski was composed of the worst sort of gangsters and criminals, and that their victory would inevitably lead to much worse conditions for the Bulgarian people in general and the CPB in particular. Moreoever, they had every reason to believe that a reactionary victory would be more than a temporary blow to their own aspirations. A communist must of necessity believe in the inevitability of the world revolution, but this is not always a comfort when the hopes for one's own country appear to recede into the indefinite future; Lenin was not the only communist who was impatient for power.

But the option of cooperating with Stambuliski was not open. The Comintern was explicit on the essentially evil nature of agrarian parties; the Bolsheviks had just completed a long and arduous civil war in which their most important opponents had been the Russian version of Stambuliski's party—the Socialist Revolutionaries. Finally, the attempt to organize the Green International (an international movement of agrarian parties), however clumsy, was a direct challenge to the Comintern. Stambuliski was, therefore, an enemy who had to be eliminated as soon as possible; to help him was unthinkable.

The consequence of these contradictions was the passive stand of the CPB at the time of the anti-agrarian coup in June of 1923, followed by the obviously futile communist putsch in September of the same year. Both of these actions had considerable practical logic and a high degree of ideological imperative from the communist point of view, even though the timing was all wrong. The white terror that followed the September fiasco drove the CPB underground and its surviving leadership into exile. Worse, upon arrival in Moscow, Bulgarian communism lost its facade of unity and split into three factions.

The Right faction, which argued that the September action had been a mistake, did not survive for long in the Soviet climate. The Comintern had expressly ordered the abortive revolt and was not at this time in the habit of admitting mistakes (later, of course, errors could be charged to the records of purged leaders). The Left faction, composed mostly of younger men and relatively new party members, argued that the party had been defeated only because it had been insufficiently prepared for revolutionary activity, and that with more skilled and aggressive leadership the CPB could have defeated the agrarians directly. Such an argument obviously appealed to the Comintern, since it placed the blame on the Bulgarian party rather than on the international leadership. After five years of factional struggle, the Left took over the leadership of the party in exile.

The great personal popularity of Dimitrov and Kolarov, leaders of the Center faction, is demonstrated by the fact that, despite the unattractiveness of their position (defending failure), they were able to resist their opponents for a very long time and were given important jobs in the Comintern when they finally lost control of the CPB. Indeed, to most outside observers, it appeared that Dimitrov had been given a substantial promotion: he was sent to Berlin as operational head of communist activities in non-Soviet Europe—including the Balkan section. In effect, Dimitrov had day-to-day responsibility for all European communist parties except his own.

The decision of the Nazis to charge Dimitrov with involvement in the Reichstag fire was an important event in Bulgarian communist history. Dimitrov's brilliant and courageous defense of himself and his movement at the show trial in Germany made him a symbol of international communism, a person of enormous prestige on the political Left. Upon his return (1935) to the Soviet Union, Dimitrov was made head (secretary-general) of the Comintern, a post he held until the organization was dissolved in 1943. Although Stalin's system did not permit any independent centers of power, Dimitrov was more than a figurehead; he was a key official who had the confidence of the supreme leader.

Dimitrov's new status in Moscow made it easy for him to take revenge upon those of his Left opponents who had been running the CPB in his absence. In truth, these leaders were by then quite vulnerable, as they had failed to impose their authority on the majority of communists at home, many of whom were still critical of the Comintern line that led to the events of 1923. Beginning in 1937, the Bulgarian Left in Moscow was purged as "Trotskyite" (not its actual orientation), and Dimitrov and Kolarov regained control of the CPB.

The purge in the Soviet Union took a fearful toll of all Bulgarian communists, not just those that could be identified as Left. The exiled Bulgarians, perhaps in part because of their affinity for Russian language and culture, played an important role in Soviet affairs, and many, probably most, had joined the CPSU(B) as well as the CPB. Their very prominence made them more vulnerable to the machinery of the Yezhovshchina, and as in other parties, those who had volunteered to fight the fascists in Spain were hit particularly hard.[22] The scant evidence available suggests that Dimitrov was personally opposed to the terror but that he was powerless except in a few isolated cases.

After Dimitrov and Kolarov were restored to their positions in the CPB, they moved to reassert the influence of the Moscow leadership over the party apparatus at home. This was a difficult task in part because of the legacy of the divisions mentioned above and in part because conditions in Bulgaria were progressively less conducive to party work—particularly since the establishment of the dictatorship in 1934. Nevertheless, the party was brought back into line by the end of the 1930s. At the beginning of the war, a small hard core of activists, loyal to Moscow, existed on Bulgarian soil.

The problems of wartime resistance were especially frustrating to the Bulgarian communists. The fact that the government's ally was at war with Russia was decidedly unpopular, but the Germans were not in direct occupation or administration of Bulgaria. Thus, the population as a whole could see little point in attacking German bases or convoys, and attacks upon Bulgarian troops or militia, most of whom were draftees, led to open hostility toward those involved. The dynamics necessary for a successful guerrilla struggle were therefore lacking.

In addition to the problems of arousing the population, the CPB also had to struggle with incredible clumsiness on the part of their helpers. The Soviet leadership, possibly influenced by the CPB leadership in exile and the tradition of Russian-Bulgarian friendship, apparently decided that Bulgaria would be an excellent place for a resistance movement. Ignoring domestic realities, as well as the fact that the Soviet Union and Bulgaria were not at war, the Soviets sent a substantial number of men (both Bulgarian and Russian) into the country by parachute and by submarine. These were quickly discovered by the Bulgarian police, who were often able to use them as guides to find local communist organizations. Most of the CPB leadership was arrested in this manner by the end of 1942[23]

The impotence of the CPB resistance movement had an important effect on the Macedonian question. The leading role of Bulgarian communists in the interwar period both at home and in the Soviet Union had made it possible for the Comintern line on Macedonia strongly to favor the Bulgarians over the Yugoslavs. The Comintern formula, an independent Macedonian republic as a part of a Balkan federation, was neutral on the surface, but the importance of the Bulgarians in the international communist movement made it clear that the federation would be based on Sofia. But Tito, by organizing a Macedonian Partisan movement and declaring Macedonia a republic of the federated Yugoslavia of the future, effectively preempted the Bulgarian position at a time when the latter were helpless to oppose him.

The Nazi defeat at Stalingrad gave renewed impetus to resistance forces in Bulgaria, but the communists were not strong enough to take full advantage. The CPB could not be faulted for not trying, but the separation of the country from the fascist alliance in 1944 was entirely the work of the Red Army.

Albania

The history of communism in Albania is very short. This is in large part a consequence of the backward, semifeudal nature of Albania's interwar society, but it also reflects the extreme isolation of the country—as a factor from earliest times to the present. Protosocialism first appeared during the brief reign of Fan Noli as a number of the bishop's younger aides, frustrated by the problems of effecting a land reform (see above), admired from afar the achievements of the distant Soviet Union in this area. When Noli was deposed (1924), his supporters scattered, many going to Western Europe, where a number of them developed an interest in socialism as the answer to their country's difficulties.

Some of these individuals worked in Vienna for a group known as "Balkan Confederation" which was itself a front for the Comintern. Subsequently, there were several attempts to found an Albanian Communist Party in the 1920s and 1930s, but these were unsuccessful for lack of support. Nevertheless, Marxist ideas did penetrate parts of the country, affecting primarily those with some education, particularly school teachers. Although trade unions were not legal, a few workers' groups (actually craftsmen) were organized by the intellectuals.

The Communist Party of Albania (CPA) was founded in Tirana in November of 1941. The meeting at which this momentous event took place was called by two Yugoslav emissaries of Tito, Miladin Popović and Dušan Mugoša; it apepars that these two foreigners were better acquainted with the Albanian Left than any of the natives.[24] Enver Hoxha, a former school teacher educated in France and Belgium, was elected provisional head of the party. But Koci Xoxe, a tinsmith by trade, was the primary liaison with the Yugoslavs and became, as a consequence, the most powerful man in the party.

Since Albania had been subjected to a highly unpopular Italian occupation for two years before the beginning of the conflict between Germany and the Soviet Union, a large part of the population was already prepared to resist the fascists actively. A very strong noncommunist resistance movement, *Balli Kombëtar* (BK) (National Union) was in operation, but the Yugoslav Partisans were quickly able to organize an Albanian offshoot of their own force, making use of the scattered groups of native Marxists for the leadership. A front organization, the National Liberation Movement, was formed in an attempt to create a facade of unity, but like its Yugoslav counterpart, the soldiers were called Partisans and the front was dominated by Communists.

Unlike the Yugoslavs, the Albanian Partisans concentrated much of their early effort in a civil war against Balli Kombëtar. They were able to do this successfully because Tito supported them, and, because the Anglo-Americans in turn backed Tito, many western arms went to the communist side of the struggle. The BK had a strong nationalist argument, however, since they favored the addition of Kosovo to a future Albanian state. This obviously gave them much popular support. The communists, who were in no position to challenge the views of their all-powerful Yugoslav mentors on the Kosovo issue, were seriously hurt by the anti-annexationist stand they were forced to take.

The news of Mussolini's fall produced, in July of 1943, an agreement of cooperation between the communists and the BK. This lasted for a short time until, following a German invasion to replace the disintegrating Italian army, the communists attacked the BK. With nowhere else to turn, the latter responded by cooperating with the Germans.[25] Having in effect forced the noncommunists to ally themselves with the fascists, the Partisans were able to claim that they were the only legitimate resistance movement. Following the Germans' hurried withdrawal, the communists, well armed by the Americans and the British, were the only important military force in the country. Seizure of absolute political power was thus quite easy.

Summary

In reviewing the history of the communist parties from their origins until the seizure of power, two fundamental questions arise: Who were the communists? What were the sources of their strengths and weaknesses? No one has yet attempted a thorough scholarly comparison of the East European communist parties, so that there are no really definitive answers. Nevertheless, there are a number of solid studies of individual parties, and historians have examined various of the general phenomena of communism that apply in the East European context.

In searching for answers to the question of who comprised the communists and their supporters, the outstanding reference is the work of R. V. Burks, an American historian whose monograph, *The Dynamics of Communism in Eastern Europe*,[26] will probably continue to be the best analysis for many years to come. Since East European archival material was (and is) either unavailable or nonexistent, and since communists are unlikely to respond to questionnaires, Burks had to work with very little documentation. The two approaches which he settled on, statistical analysis of the free interwar elections and interviews with imprisoned Greek communists, are full of potential pitfalls but, when combined with common sense and intuitive analysis, have produced valuable results.

One of Burks' initial objectives was to separate and analyze the major categories of communists. He settled on two primary groups: the "hard core" which includes leading cadres and activists; and the "soft periphery" made up of voters, opportunists, fellow travelers, front members, and guerrillas. The composition of these two groups was found to be quite different, reflecting, at least in part, the roles which they were required to play. Further, national variations in social, economic, and ethnic structure seemed to have had considerable importance.

The "hard core" referred to by Burks is usually known to communists as the *apparat* (apparatus or structure): members of the *apparat* are known as *apparatchiks*. This group is then further broken down into activists (*aktiv*) at the outside and leading cadres on the inside. The latter are the cream of the crop; they control the highest level of the party and thus make decisions for everyone.

Following an assumption that communist candidates for parliamentary elections in the interwar period would correspond to the leading cadres, Burks pulled together data on the social background of candidates in all those countries in which communists were able to participate as such in elections. The results, compared to other parties, were as follows:[27]

Party	% Workers	% Peasants	% Middle Class	% Other	Total
Communist	29.4	21.4	44.8	4.4	100.0
Socialist	22.5	19.0	50.4	8.1	100.0
All other parties	7.5	40.3	44.6	7.6	100.0

These data suggest that nearly half of the leading communists were middle class and that the remainder was divided roughly evenly between workers and peasants.

One could argue, however, that even these statistics could be skewed against the middle class and in favor of the workers. It seems quite likely that leading cadres and candidates were not always identical. For example, in a country with strong elements of anti-Semitism such as Poland, middle-class Jews in the leadership might well be underrepresented in elections. Those chosen as replacements would, for obvious reasons of symbolism, be workers if at all possible. In fact, it is probable that the communists, who certainly thought that their major audience was the proletariat, would do their best to find workers to serve as their public representatives.

Another problem with the statistical approach is that by including only countries which permitted communist participation in at least one election (Poland, Czechoslovakia, Yugoslavia, and Bulgaria), the industrialized area of Eastern Europe is given far more weight than it ought to have. Adding countries with little or no industry (Hungary, Romania, Albania) would certainly diminish the number of worker candidates in favor, most probably, of the middle class. This observation is also reinforced by an analysis of the social background of the more prominent communists from those nations.

If the cadres were not primarily proletarian, what about the activists? Burks acknowledges that this is a much harder question to answer, since the group is much harder to define, and fewer data are available for correlation. But he makes a persuasive case that the sample of Greek communists he interviewed is, if not representative, at least indicative of the overall movement in Eastern Europe. The results of his analysis of the activists are the reverse of that of the previous one, workers are now roughly 40 percent, peasants 30 percent, and the middle class 20 percent of the total. Burks qualifies this, however, by pointing out that many of the communists had not really established occupations of their own, and that an analysis by father's profession (i.e., class background) changed the proportion to about 60 percent peasant, 25 percent worker, and 15 percent middle class.[28] This strong orientation toward the peasantry is manifest in the overall party membership of two of the three East European parties for which data is available:[29]

Country	Year	% Workers	% Peasant	% Middle Class	Other	Total
Czechoslovakia	1927	53.4	14.6	18.5	13.5	100.0
Poland	1932	39.0	40.5	5.5	15.0	100.0
Bulgaria	1919	10.2	46.2	43.6	.0	100.0

Thus, a first generalization about the composition of the East European communist parties would suggest that of the leading cadres, perhaps two-thirds to three-quarters were of middle-class origin. For the activists, the front-line soldiers who carried out the orders of the leading cadres and did most of the dirty work, there is considerable variation by country but overall a tendency for peasants to play a surprisingly large role. The generalization raises a number of questions, however. The tendency of the middle class to control the top leadership is not surprising; after all, these are the educated people. But what about those Polish and Bulgarian peasants—why didn't they support the agrarian parties?

The answer to this rather perplexing question is that the activists had moved up to the hard core from the soft periphery, where many voters and others were in fact peasants. The class origins of voters, guerrillas, front-members, and other supporters of communism are also not what would be expected in theory. Burks' research in this area also used interwar electoral results, but in this case fairly sophisticated statistical techniques were used to try to find a high correlation between communist votes and various social classes. In all of the East European cases, there was either no correlation or a negative correlation between communist votes and the obvious groups: workers and landless of dwarf-holding peasants. Burks therefore concludes, "communism in Eastern Europe has not been in any significant sense of the term, a proletarian movement. It has been representative of all social classes, the peasantry and the bourgeoisie as well as the working class."[30]

After concluding what the communist movement is not, Burks goes on to ask the obvious questions: which proletarians, which bourgeois, which peasants were supporters of communism? The answers reveal an interesting mixture of social, economic, and ethnic factors. The following are groups that tended, in various areas and at different times, to support communists more than any other party:

Seasonal Workers. Burks cites tobacco workers in Bulgaria and Greece as examples of proletarians who had the experience of a common workplace and thus the communication that helped to spread socialism, but who did not have steady work and often had to return to their villages. The lack of continuity on the job site hindered the development of trade unionism, which is usually associated with social democracy, and thus tended to promote a more radical, revolutionary approach to politics.

Cash Croppers. Peasants who produce crops that are sold for cash, and whose income is thus subject to the sharp swings of the world market, are the landed equivalent of the seasonal workers. They are not the rural proletariat that attracted Lenin; on the contrary, they must have an appreciable amount of land to be producing for cash. Yet the boom-and-bust cycle radicalizes many of them, and they look for what appears to be a more potent alternative than the traditional peasant parties. In Bulgaria and Slovakia, Burks found a significant correlation between communist votes and land planted in wheat, a typical cash crop.

Refugees. Persons displaced from their native area are often the most alienated people in a society. They may have been well established as professionals or landowners and then suddenly found themselves with nothing; the idea of a total rejection of the status quo may appeal to those who are more aware and therefore more resentful of their situation. Burks found a very strong correlation between communism and Greek refugees from Anatolia. In the only East European country with a large number of displaced persons, Hungary, the Béla Kun revolution and the nature of the subsequent regime made an electoral survey impossible. A subjective view of the events of 1919, however, suggests that refugees were very important among the early supporters of Kun.

Students. Quantitative evidence is not available in this case, but there is a definite relation between youth, particularly university students, and left-wing beliefs. The American sociologist, Louis Feuer, in a study of youth around the world,[31] concluded that the tendency of the young to rebel is reinforced by education, which often produces extreme frustration at the inability of society to change quickly. This is especially the case for students who return from training in an advanced area of the west to a home that is in a relatively backward society. The role of students appears to have been most important in the communist parties of Albania, Hungary, Yugoslavia, and Czechoslovakia.

National Minorities. Interwar Eastern Europe was plagued with minority problems of the sort that produced sharp and continual conflict. In some cases at least, there was a propensity for minorities to vote communist. Examples cited by Burks are Hungarians in Slovakia, and Ukrainians in Eastern Poland (although the latter turned anticommunist after the beginning of the collectivization drive in the Soviet Union). Not all minorities reacted this way, however; the Germans in Czechoslovakia, for example, never showed much interest in communism but instead fell quickly under Nazi control.

Jews. In a sense the Jews were national minorities, though in many cases they were not. Up until 1933, Germany was the cultural focus of world Jewry and particularly of the highly educated elite in Eastern Europe. Yet even that bond was not a real one; except for parts of Poland and Czechoslovakia, there was no expectation of renewed German control before the Nazi era. On the other hand, many Jews had no real ties outside their own country; poorer Hungarian Jews, for example, did not know a language other than the local one. (This did not prevent discrimination of course.) Finally, some Jews, for example the large mass of Ukrainian and/or Polish speakers in Romania, were actually double minorities. Thus, many Jews faced the problems of minorities without the possibility of irredentism as an alternative. The phenomenon of the alienation of the western-educated student also applied to many Jews. Direct observation demonstrates that a high percentage of the leading cadres and activists of all of the East European communist parties except the Bulgarian, Yugoslav, and Albanian (countries with small Jewish populations) were of Jewish origin.

Overall, as noted before, Burks' analysis is more indicative than conclusive; the weakness, however, is entirely in the lack of data rather than in the methodology or the quality of analysis. For example, it would be very valuable to know if the Magyars in Transylvania would have voted in the same way as their co-nationals in Slovakia, but the data are not available. In fact, there were so few free elections in which legal communist parties participated actively in interwar Eastern Europe that scientific confirmation of any of Burks' theses is a practical impossibility. Nevertheless, a combination of the available data and intelligent inference does provide some useful information.

To recapitulate, the role of workers in interwar communist parties was relatively small. Workers played a proportionately larger part in the more industrialized countries, although the vast majority of the proletarians in those countries were socialists rather than communists. In the less developed areas, socialism was weaker than communism, but neither was a strong factor in local politics (with the exception of Bulgaria before 1923). Looking beyond the class basis, it is possible to determine certain types of people who are most likely to support communism: seasonal workers, cash croppers, refugees, students, and some national minorities (especially Jews). Burks concludes: "In short, a proper explanation of communism in Eastern Europe would begin, not with the industrial proletariat and the class struggle, but with the reaction of economically poorer and less sophisticated cultures to the west, as that contrast affects persons and groups subjected through social disorganization to great personal insecurity."[32]

It seems appropriate at this point to emphasize the difference between the abstract and the actual in evaluating the history of East European communism before 1945. Burks' analysis is very useful, for example, in explaining the phenomenon of the very strong Bulgarian communist movement and in projecting that, in theory, it would have evolved into a powerful and menacing minority. In the real world, however, the BCP was crushed in 1923 and was never able to recover: when thrust into power at the end of the war, it was a fragile organization that survived only because of Soviet buttresses. Thus, now that we have at least a general idea of who the communists were, it is necessary to review how they coped with their environment and to evaluate the strengths and weaknesses that followed.

The first point that should be emphasized in this regard is that the East European communist parties did not react to the outside world according to their own perceptions of it. Instead, they were constrained in every area of any importance by the dictates of the Comintern and thus of the Soviet leadership—not only approaches to foreign policy and domestic political strategy but also organizational and personnel decisions down to the local level flowed from Moscow. As a consequence, there is a high degree of uniformity on the surface of the parties' history, although the domestic impact varied a great deal.

All of the communist parties of Eastern Europe, except the Czechoslovak, were illegal or quasilegal during most of the interwar period. To a very large extent this reflects the various governments' belief that the communists were agents of the USSR. The CPP, though never formally outlawed, was subject to extreme harassment by the police, especially after the Piłsudski coup of 1926; the most prominent leaders often found themselves in Polish concentration camps. In Romania, the other state sharing a border with the Soviet Union, the CPR was outlawed in late 1924. The communists in Hungary and Bulgaria were forced to go underground immediately after their participation in the revolutionary events of 1919 and 1923, respectively. The Yugoslav party met the same fate after an assassination attempt in 1921. The German communists were in constant danger of their lives after Hitler's accession to power in 1933. Even if there had been a communist party in Albania, it would have had a difficult time, since all political parties were forbidden after 1924.

The Comintern had prepared the communist parties for illegal activity; they were required to establish clandestine organizations even when still legal, and various provisions for responsibility and reporting in the illegal phase were made. Illegal status appeared to affect different parties in different ways. In Hungary and Germany, ruthless and efficient police activity effectively eliminated party life. Repression was much less effective elsewhere, and in the case of Yugoslavia, it appears to have helped the party to attract sympathizers from student groups and former revolutionary organizations. The experience of operating illegally could be valuable in other ways. Thus, the background of conspiracy made it possible for Tito to field the Partisan movement in an extremely dangerous environment. The much smaller Polish and Romanian resistance movements benefited as well (the Bulgarians might have been very effective if the Soviets had not ruined their chances).

The Comintern nationality policy was, on balance, a disaster for the East European communist parties. Only three parties, those based in the revisionist states of Germany, Hungary, and Bulgaria, were helped by Moscow's call for a reassessment of frontiers. The rest were badly damaged. In Poland and Romania, where there were at least some prospects for the growth of communism, local party members were defined as traitors by the acceptance of the Comintern line. In Czechoslovakia and Yugoslavia, the dominant Czechs and Serbs (two traditionally Russophile peoples) were alienated without any balancing appeal to the minorities: Sudeten Germans, Slovaks, and Croats veered towards fascism, the others were largely unmoved. Thus, for the most part, communism was on the wrong side of nationalism.

Soviet guidance in domestic politics was similarly obtuse. The early policy of going it alone and of refusing alliance with social democratic and peasant parties produced disaster in Bulgaria and assisted, in varying degrees, the authoritarian takeovers in Yugoslavia and Poland. The intensification of this policy, the attack on the social democrats as "social fascists," while the real fascists were ignored or even helped, exacerbated the schism within the worker's movement in Czechoslovakia and greatly assisted the victory of the Nazis in Germany. The sudden shift thereafter toward the policy of a "united front against the fascists" caught the local parties off balance and forced them into an extremely awkward position: they had just begun to hit full stride in anti-socialist invective when they were ordered to make friends with their former enemies. Needless to say, the sudden disappearance of criticism of Nazi Germany during the period of the Hitler-Stalin pact sharply weakened what little popular support was available.

Finally, from the point of view of the local communists, it is obvious that Moscow's meddling in problems of ideology and personnel drastically damaged all of the parties. Lenin's unwillingness to compromise on small matters of detail as well as on matters of general principle drove the most intelligent and creative minds out of the parties. Thus, an unimaginative plodder like Thälmann would have doubtless soon replaced Rosa Luxemburg if she had survived. Stalin's continuation of Lenin's extremely narrow view, culminating in his penchant for creating conformity through terror, led to the elimination of even the best of the plodders. The German party was emasculated; the Czechoslovak, Romanian, and Bulgarian parties were kept in confusion and despair; the Hungarian party was entrusted to a man whose knowledge of his country was restricted to prison life; the Polish and Yugoslav parties were all but destroyed. Perhaps the most instructive point about the history of the communist parties of Eastern Europe is that the only independently successful party, the Yugoslav, came to power by means of a locally achieved understanding on the national question, and that its overall success came in spite of rather than because of the Soviet Union.

Afterword
Eastern Europe on the Eve of a New Vassalage

Eastern Europe in 1945

THE END OF THE WAR was not a time of joy for the people of Eastern Europe. There was, of course, relief that the long struggle was finally over. But even this emotion was tempered by the numbness that followed the incredible bloodletting and pervasive destruction. In the best of circumstances, it would have been years before the psychological scars had healed sufficiently for society to return to normal. But, for most Eastern Europeans, the new circumstances were not in fact good ones; the prospects seemed perhaps better than war, but scarcely more than that.

As we have seen, only a very small percentage of the population welcomed the advent of communism. The hostility of the majority was based on a number of factors. One, certainly, was the idea of communism as a social and economic system. But it would be a mistake to assume that this was a widespread reaction. The members of the bourgeoisie and the remnants of the aristocracy were adamant in their opposition to Marx and his ideas, but representatives of these classes were comparatively few in number and had suffered particularly severe loss of life and property in the war. Moreover, as the group from which the leadership of the interwar period had been with few exceptions drawn, their credibility was not particularly high. Cynicism about the old order was widespread.

If the hostility to communism on the part of the bourgeois and the nobles was not of paramount importance, who were the opponents, and why? The answer is that the communists met with enormous resistance from workers and peasants—those to whom they directed their most ardent appeals—and that the sources of these people's ill will were a direct reflection of the history of Eastern Europe.

Peasant hostility to communism was to some extent socioeconomic, in the sense that for those peasants who knew enough about communism to appreciate that it had as a goal the socialization of the land (or who knew about the collectivization drives in the Soviet Union in the 1930s), it was in direct opposition to their fundamental beliefs about landholding. Marxist doctrine does not usually appeal to peasants, not even to poor or landless ones; the latter may support radical philosophies but typically only with the objectives of securing more land for themselves. Peasant anxiety on the issue of land ownership meant a considerable amount of worker anxiety as well, since many workers were only a generation removed from the land and still had strong ties to the villages. Though the workers were obviously alert to issues affecting their new economic status, their land-oriented value systems were still very much alive.

This kind of ideological opposition to communism was considerably muted by the fact that the communists, especially in the decade prior to their advent to power, did everything possible to deny that there would be anything other than land reform in the countryside. If the communists would acknowledge the concept of socialization of the countryside at all, it was in the context of a distant, rather vague goal, something that would occur only when everyone genuinely wanted it to happen. There was a small element of truth in this argument, as serious collectivization did not in fact begin in most of Eastern Europe until 1948, and even then it appears to have been pushed forward by an unanticipated string of events. Peasant hostility to communism on ideological grounds appears to have been strongest in the regions bordering on the Soviet Union, especially in eastern Poland and in the northern and eastern parts of Romania, where there were many residents with direct knowledge of Moscow's agrarian policies, both past and present.

The strongest opposition to communism came, however, on religious and especially on national grounds. The Marxists' disdain for religion was well and widely known, and even the most flexible communists could not deny it. The communist ideal of a godless political system provoked the most visibly negative reaction in the Catholic lands, where the superior organization of that church sharpened awareness and strengthened voices, but it would be a mistake to think that the popular reaction in the villages of the equally pious Orthodox was not essentially the same. Even among the workers, religious beliefs were still quite strong, a fact that is clearly revealed by the decision of many workers in the interwar period to cast their votes for parties with a religious orientation.

In the final analysis, however, it was nationalism that was the most prominent and most powerful factor in the opposition to communism. This was true in part, of course, because nationalism usually encompasses to some extent the previously mentioned factors: the tradition (even if a new one) of peasant landholding and the national religion. Culture was certainly an important factor as well. The peoples of Eastern Europe, as described in chapter 5, considered themselves to be a part of the culture of Western Europe, a status that most would not have accorded to the Russians. The fact that there is considerable irony in this attitude (East Europeans overlooked the enormous contributions of Russia to western culture even as they protested the denigration of their own role) does not make it less real. The Czechs are generally considered to be very sympathetic to the Russians, owing in large part to the influence of T. G. Masaryk and his marvelous scholarship. But aside from some noisy panslav congresses and a ripple of reaction in intellectual circles, there is no evidence that this attitude penetrated much of the public mind: a Czech-born scholar once told a group of the author's students that, "As a young man my father walked from Prague to Paris. It would never have occurred to him to make the trip to Moscow; in that direction there were only wolves, bears, and Orthodoxy."

The nationalism of Eastern Europe was primarily reactive rather than active; that is to say that it was to a very large extent the fruit of pressure from some outside force, from another nation or nationality. In many cases that enemy nation was Russia: Poles, Hungarians, and to a lesser extent Romanians had a tradition of Russophobia. For other peoples, whose national development was the story of struggle against oppression not by Russians but by Germans, Turks, or an East European neighbor, there was no difficulty in transferring enmity to the monster state in the east. The peoples of Eastern Europe had been schooled for a century or more in the psychology of all-out active and passive resistance as a means of ensuring national survival. In such an atmosphere the grandiose promises of Soviet Communism provoked little appeal and much anger, even before the reality of Stalin's nightmarish version of Marxism was experienced directly.

Eastern Europe: Dependent or Independent?

To many, both within the region and especially outside of it, the tragic experience of interwar Eastern Europe called into question the very viability of independent nations in the region. The passing of the empires that had dominated Eastern Europe, especially Austria-Hungary, was frequently lamented by scholars and diplomats. And, even for those who did not openly yearn for the old system, there was little positive to be said for the new situation. Writing on the eve of World War II, the respected American historian Walter C. Langsam in his 1940 book, *The World Since 1914*, was referring to Eastern Europe when he remarked that, "The great emphasis on nationality during the war and the diffusion of the idea of national self-determination made political and economic international relations after the war more difficult than ever. Diplomatic intrigues, economic rivalries, jealous quarrels, and new oppressions fanned the flames of old hatreds and overwhelmed Europe with another dangerous hysteria" (p. 133). British Prime Minister Neville Chamberlain's reference, after the Munich Conference, to Czechoslovakia as "a far away country about which he knew little" fairly summarizes the exasperated, even exhausted, pre–World War II attitude of western political leaders. President Roosevelt's near total lack of interest in anything Eastern European (with the partial and cyclical exception of Poland when motivated by domestic political issues) speaks to the wartime perspective.

Yet these suggestions that independent Eastern Europe was something of a failed experiment, a bad idea that had little real chance of success, seem unfair. It is true that the nations of Eastern Europe made little progress in solving their social and economic problems in the roughly two decades available to them. And there can be no denying that the area as a whole drifted from democracy to authoritarianism and that the nations' many internal and external quarrels contributed to the world's cataclysmic slide into a new war. But it would be difficult to make the case that, absent these problems in Eastern Europe, peace would have been assured or even much more likely. There were tensions that turned into crises in Western Europe proper as well as in Asia and Africa. Moreover, there is the fact that a *dependent* Eastern Europe had already been the focal point of war: independence could hardly be worse.

But the easy task of absolving the Eastern Europeans of responsibility for the new war does not complete the argument for the viability of independent states in this region. Even in the unlikely event that harmony within the area could be guaranteed, the presence of extraordinarily powerful neighbors to the east and west makes the prospects for true Eastern European independence in the contemporary world precarious at best. The fact that the eastern neighbor is in fact now dominant, and has been so for four decades, makes the argument for potential independence hard to sustain. Still, despite the odds, there is abundant evidence that the Eastern Europeans themselves have not given up on the struggle. Resistance to outside control even appears to be growing as it takes on new forms. It took scarcely a century for the modern concept of independent nation-states to pass from theory to reality in Eastern Europe. It is too soon to accept that it has disappeared from the horizon.

Appendix
Maps

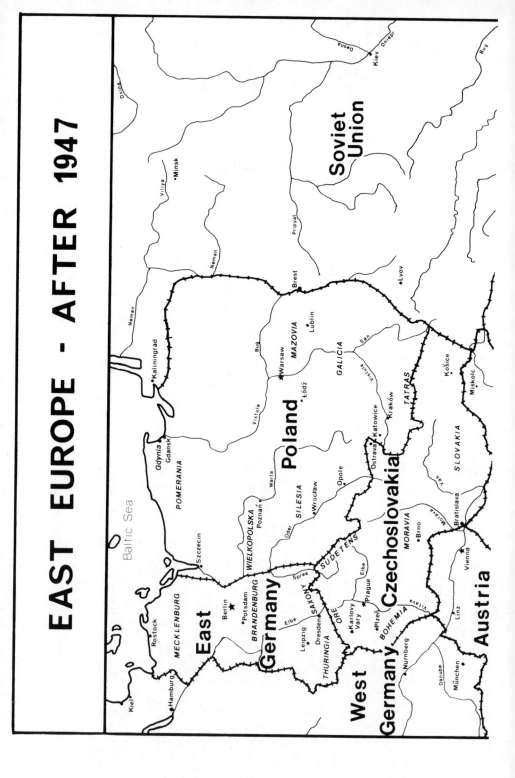

EAST EUROPE - AFTER 1947

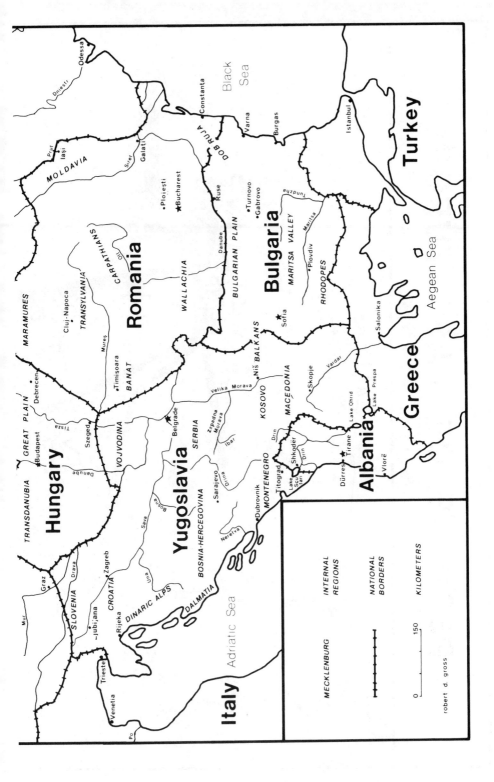

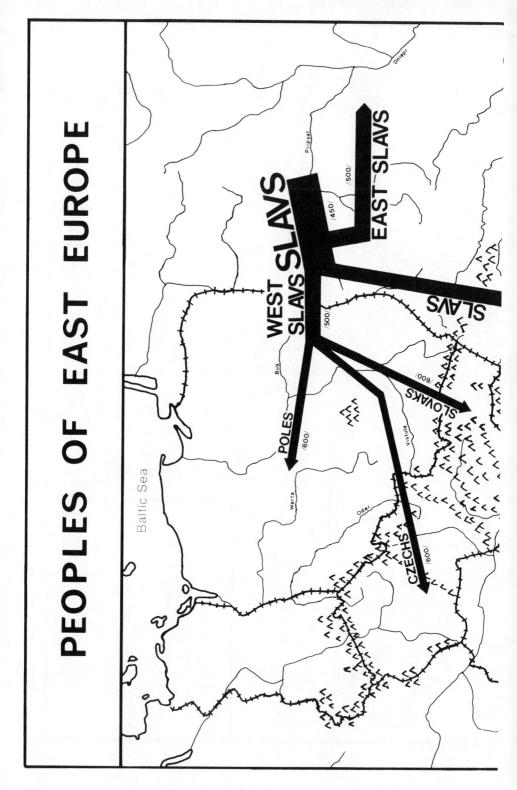

PEOPLES OF EAST EUROPE

Baltic Sea

Dniepr

Pripyat

EAST SLAVS

/500/

WEST SLAVS

/450/

SLAVS

/500/

Bug

SLOVAKS

/600/

POLES

/600/

Vistula

Warta

Oder

CZECHS

/600/

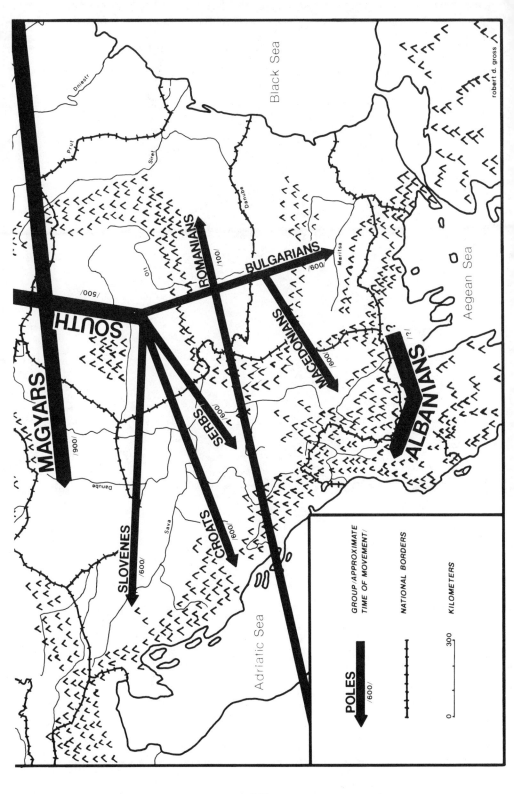

369

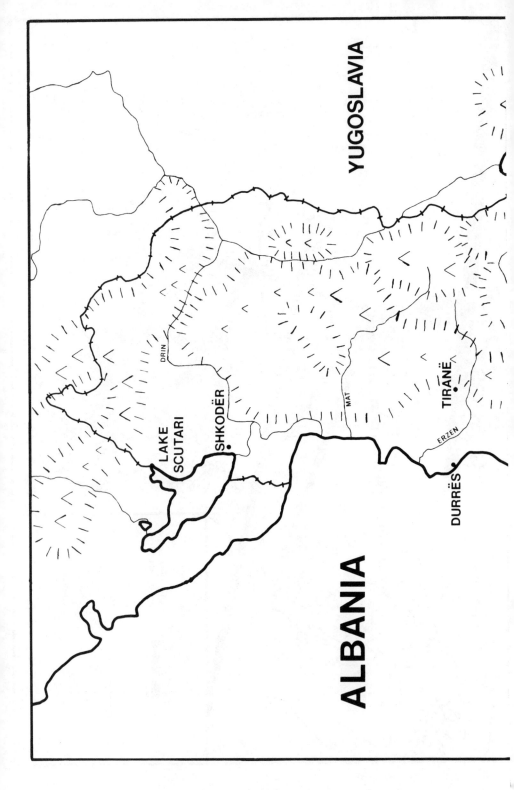

YUGOSLAVIA

DRIN

LAKE
SCUTARI

SHKODËR

MAT

TIRANË

ERZEN

DURRËS

ALBANIA

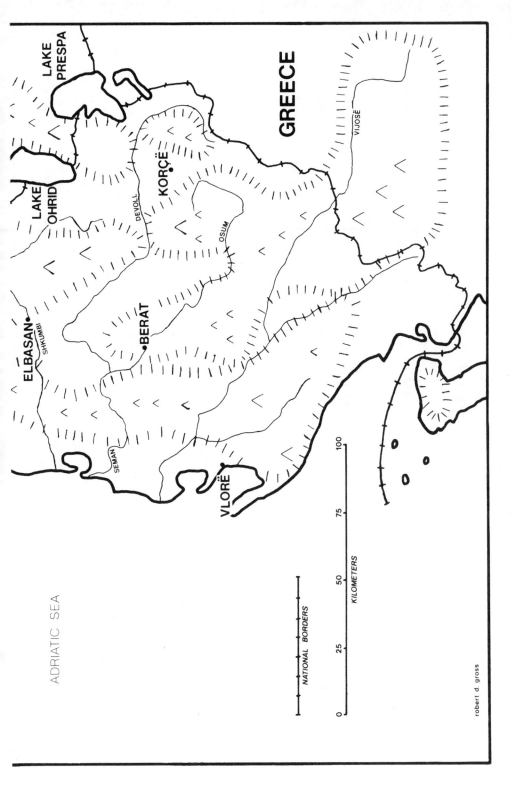

LAKE PRESPA

LAKE OHRID

GREECE

KORÇË

DEVOLL

OSUM

VIJOSË

ELBASAN

SHKUMBI

BERAT

SEMAN

VLORË

ADRIATIC SEA

NATIONAL BORDERS

0   25   50   75   100

KILOMETERS

robert d. gross

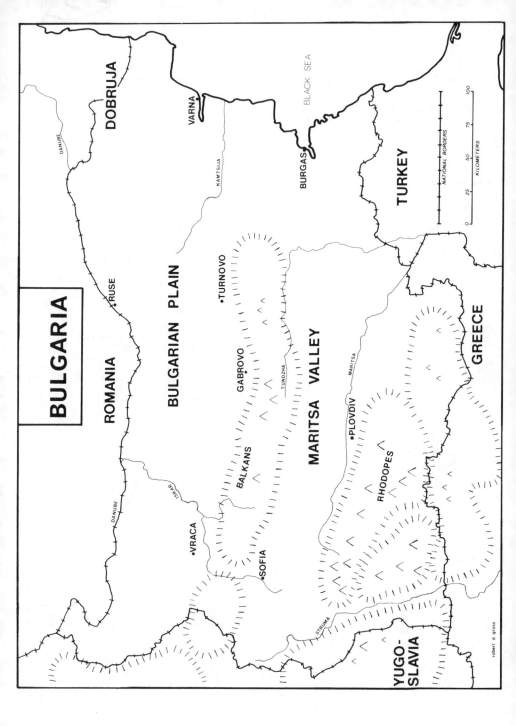

BULGARIA

ROMANIA

DOBRUJA

DANUBE

BLACK SEA

VARNA

KAMTSIJA

BURGAS

TURKEY

NATIONAL BORDERS

KILOMETERS

0   25   50   75   100

•RUSE

BULGARIAN PLAIN

•TURNOVO

GABROVO
•

BALKANS

TUNDZHA

MARITSA VALLEY

•PLOVDIV

MARITSA

GREECE

ISKAR

DANUBE

•VRACA

•SOFIA

RHODOPES

STRUMA

YUGO-
SLAVIA

robert d. gross

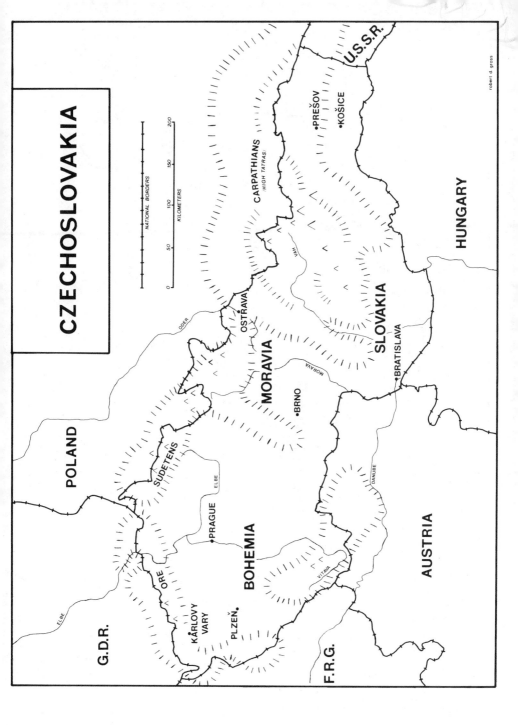

CZECHOSLOVAKIA

NATIONAL BORDERS

KILOMETERS

0 50 100 150 200

robert d. gross

U.S.S.R.

•PREŠOV •KOŠICE

HUNGARY

CARPATHIANS
(HIGH TATRAS)

ODER

OSTRAVA

SLOVAKIA

VAH

MORAVIA

MORAVA

•BRNO

•BRATISLAVA

POLAND

SUDETENS

ELBE

PRAGUE

DANUBE

ORE

BOHEMIA

•KARLOVY
VARY

PLZEŇ•

VLTAVA

ELBE

G.D.R.

F.R.G.

AUSTRIA

373

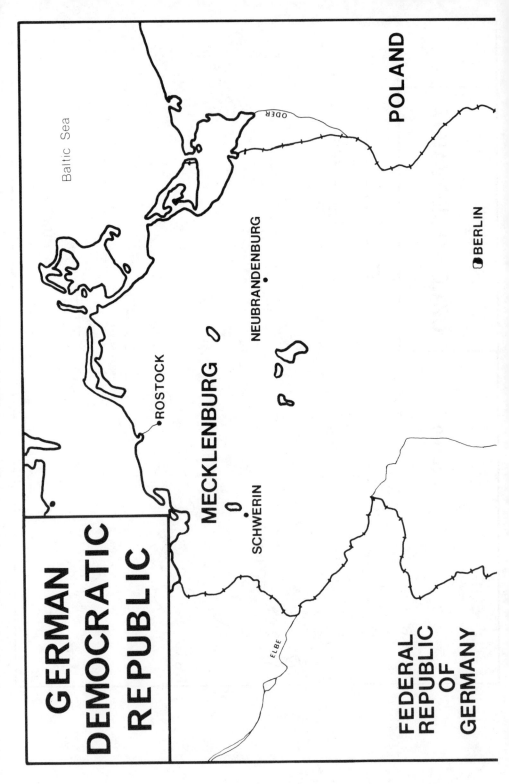

GERMAN DEMOCRATIC REPUBLIC

Baltic Sea

POLAND

ODER

BERLIN

MECKLENBURG

NEUBRANDENBURG

ROSTOCK

SCHWERIN

ELBE

FEDERAL REPUBLIC OF GERMANY

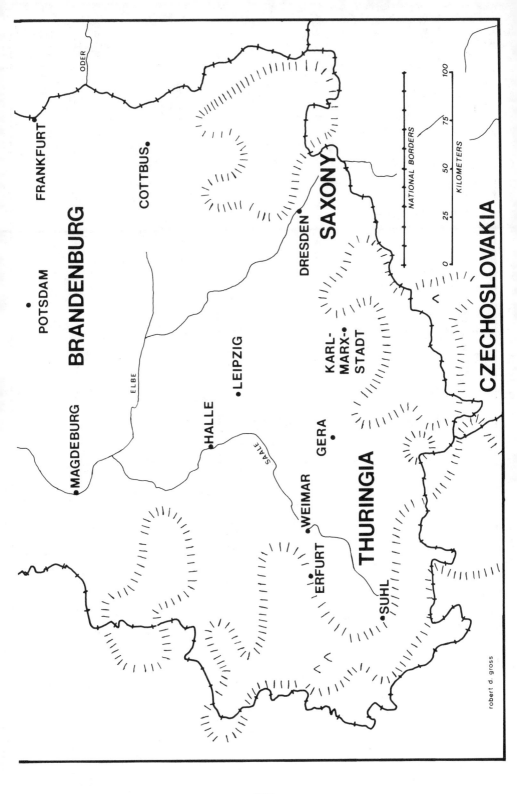

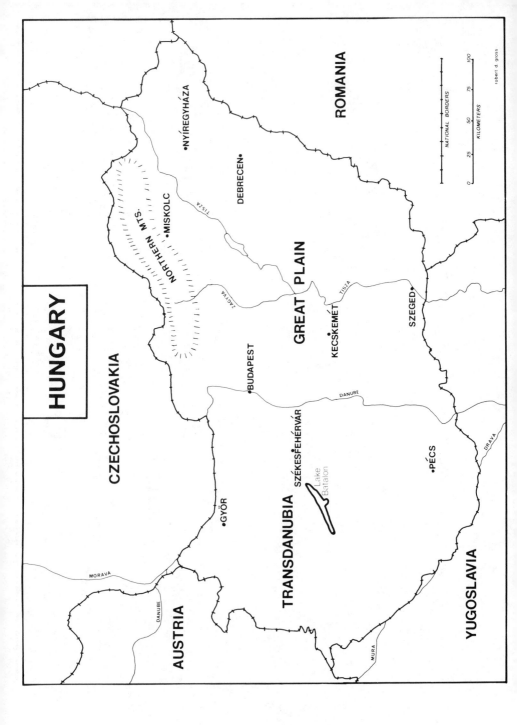

HUNGARY

AUSTRIA

CZECHOSLOVAKIA

ROMANIA

YUGOSLAVIA

•NYÍREGYHÁZA

DEBRECEN•

•MISKOLC

NORTHERN MTS.

TISZA

ZAGYVA

TISZA

GREAT PLAIN

KECSKEMÉT

SZEGED•

•BUDAPEST

DANUBE

SZÉKESFEHÉRVÁR

Lake
Balaton

TRANSDANUBIA

•PÉCS

DRAVA

•GYÖR

MORAVA

DANUBE

MURA

NATIONAL BORDERS

KILOMETERS

0   25   50   75   100

robert d. gross

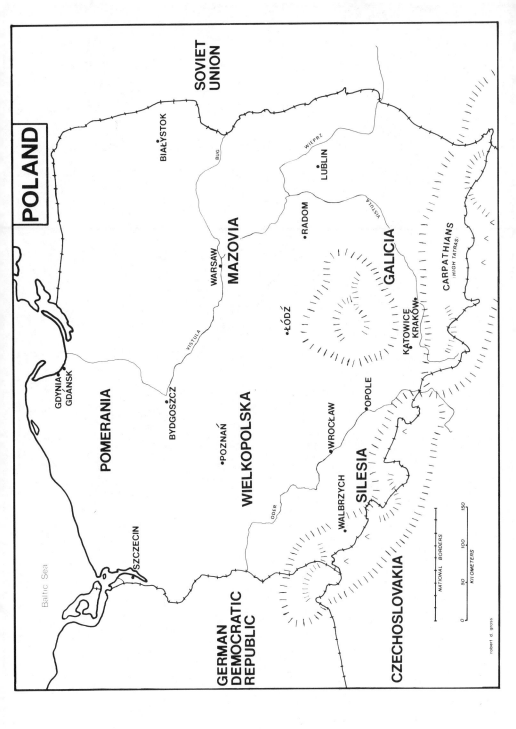

POLAND

SOVIET UNION

BIAŁYSTOK

BUG

WIEPRZ

LUBLIN

MAZOVIA

RADOM

WARSAW

VISTULA

GALICIA

VISTULA

ŁÓDŹ

KATOWICE
KRAKÓW

CARPATHIANS
(HIGH TATRAS)

GDYNIA
GDAŃSK

POMERANIA

BYDGOSZCZ

POZNAŃ

WIELKOPOLSKA

OPOLE

WROCŁAW

SILESIA

WAŁBRZYCH

ODER

SZCZECIN

Baltic Sea

GERMAN
DEMOCRATIC
REPUBLIC

CZECHOSLOVAKIA

NATIONAL BORDERS

KILOMETERS

0   50   100   150

robert d. gross

377

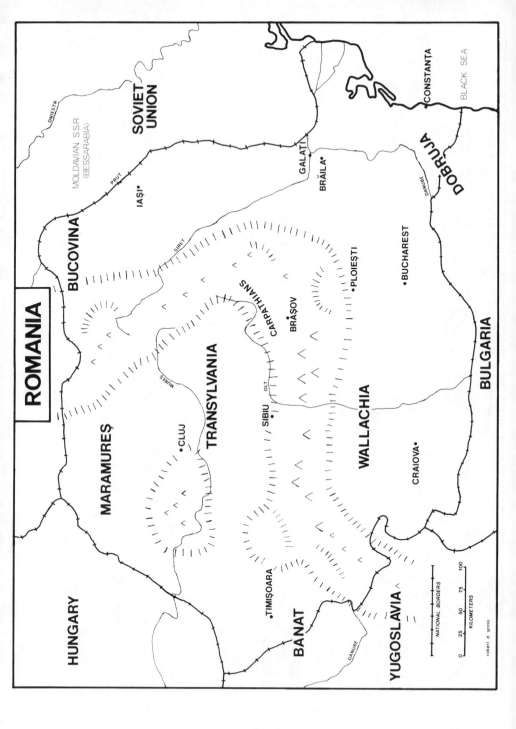

ROMANIA

BLACK SEA

CONSTANTA

DOBRUJA

SOVIET UNION

MOLDAVIAN S.S.R. (BESSARABIA)

DNIESTR

PRUT

IAŞI•

BUCOVINA

GALAŢI

BRĂILA•

DANUBE

SIRET

PLOIEŞTI•

•BUCHAREST

CARPATHIANS

BRAŞOV•

MUREŞ

TRANSYLVANIA

SIBIU•

OLT

WALLACHIA

MARAMUREŞ

•CLUJ

CRAIOVA•

BULGARIA

HUNGARY

•TIMIŞOARA

BANAT

DANUBE

YUGOSLAVIA

NATIONAL BORDERS

0   25   50   75   100
KILOMETERS

robert d. gross

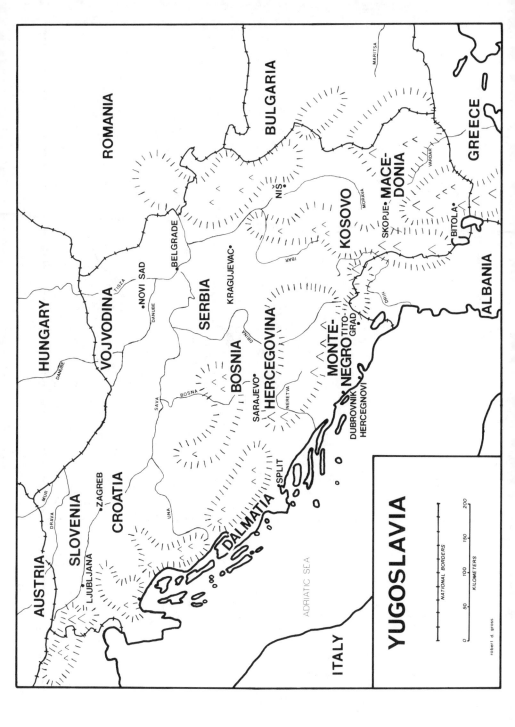

AUSTRIA
HUNGARY
ROMANIA
BULGARIA
GREECE
ALBANIA
ITALY

SLOVENIA
LJUBLJANA
ZAGREB
CROATIA
VOJVODINA
NOVI SAD
BELGRADE
SERBIA
KRAGUJEVAC
NIS
KOSOVO
SKOPJE
MACE-DONIA
BITOLA

BOSNIA
SARAJEVO
HERCEGOVINA
MONTE-NEGRO
TITO-GRAD
DUBROVNIK
HERCEGNOVI

DALMATIA
SPLIT

ADRIATIC SEA

MUR
DRAVA
DANUBE
TISZA
DANUBE
SAVA
UNA
BOSNA
ORINA
DRINA
NERETVA
IBAR
MORAVA
DRIN
VARDAR
MARITSA

YUGOSLAVIA

NATIONAL BORDERS

0   50   100   150   200
KILOMETERS

robert d. gross

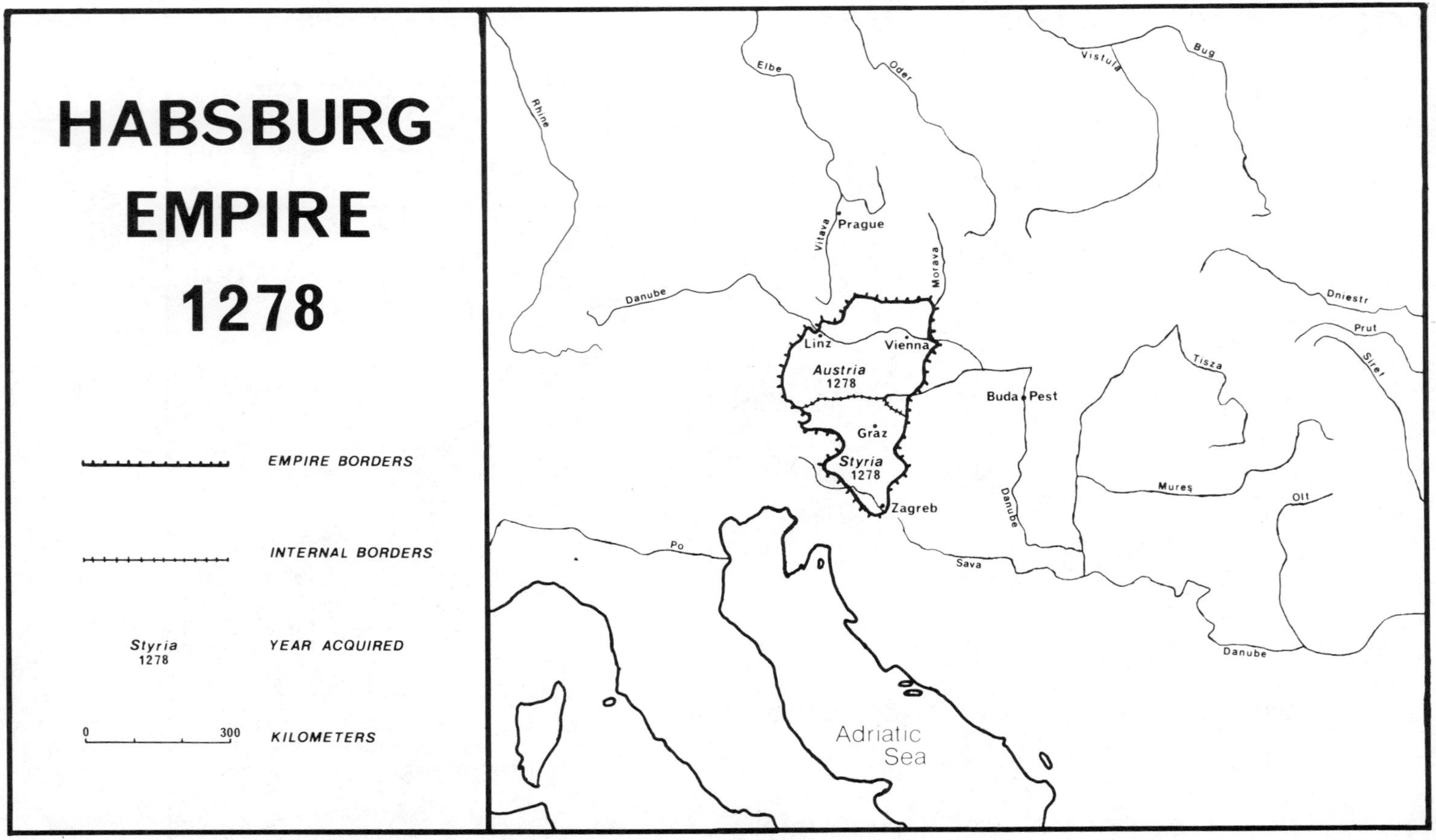

HABSBURG EMPIRE 1278

EMPIRE BORDERS

INTERNAL BORDERS

Styria
1278   YEAR ACQUIRED

0   300   KILOMETERS

Austria
1278

Styria
1278

Vienna

Graz

Linz

Zagreb

Buda Pest

Prague

Adriatic
Sea

Bug

Vistula

Oder

Elbe

Vltava

Morava

Danube

Rhine

Tisza

Dniestr

Prut

Siret

Mures

Olt

Danube

Sava

Danube

Po

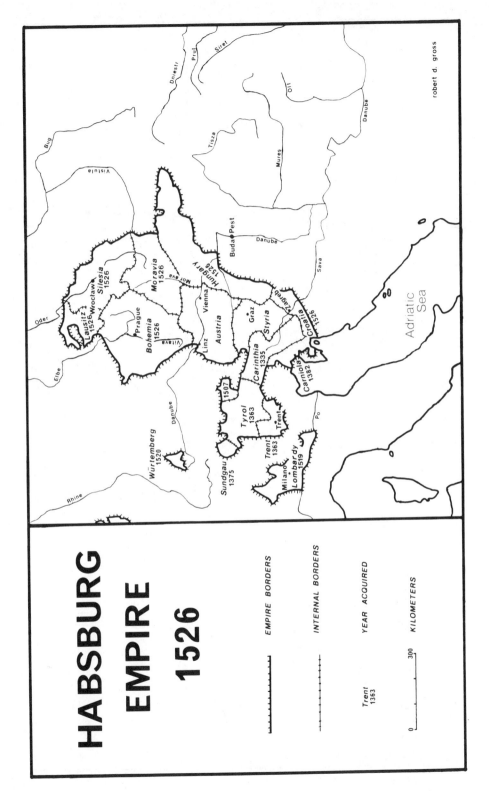

HABSBURG EMPIRE 1526

├─────┤	EMPIRE BORDERS
┼┼┼┼┼┼	INTERNAL BORDERS
Trent 1363	YEAR ACQUIRED
0 ├──┤ 300	KILOMETERS

robert d. gross

Lausitz 1526
Wrocław
Silesia 1526
Moravia 1526
Prague
Bohemia 1526
Mor ava
Vltava
Linz
Vienna
Austria
Hungary 1526
Buda Pest
Graz
Styria
Croatia 1526
Szeged
Carinthia 1335
Carniola 1382
Würtemberg 1520
1507
Tyrol 1363
Sundgau 1375
Trent 1363
Trent 1363
Milano
Lombardy 1519

Adriatic Sea

Bug
Vistula
Dniestr
Prut
Siret
Oder
Elbe
Rhine
Danube
Tisza
Mures
Danube
Olt
Sava
Po

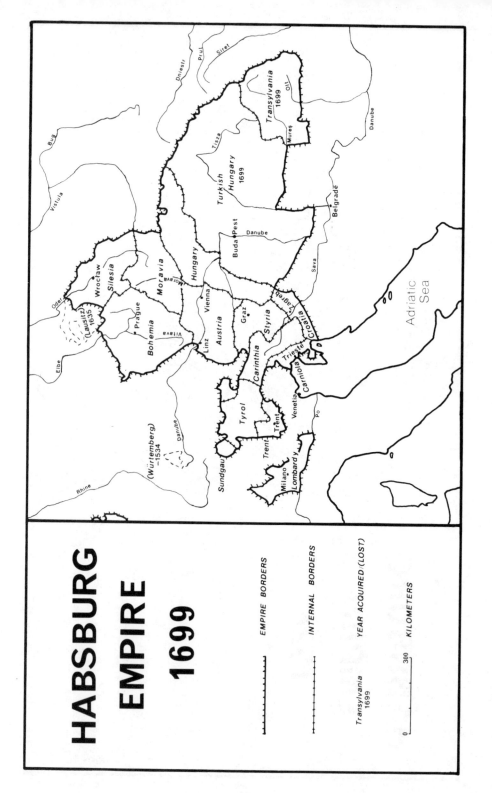

HABSBURG EMPIRE 1699

EMPIRE BORDERS

INTERNAL BORDERS

YEAR ACQUIRED (LOST)

Transylvania
1699

0   300   KILOMETERS

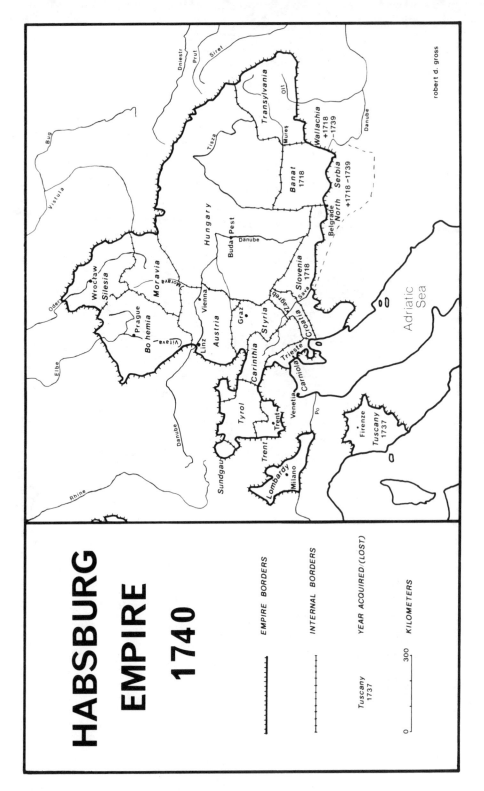

HABSBURG EMPIRE 1740

EMPIRE BORDERS

INTERNAL BORDERS

Tuscany
1737   YEAR ACQUIRED/(LOST)

KILOMETERS

0   300

Bug

Vistula

Dniestr

Prut

Siret

Oder

Elbe

Rhine

Danube

Tisza

Morava

Vltava

Danube

Mureş

Olt

Danube

Po

Wrocław
Silesia

Prague
Bohemia

Moravia

Buda Pest

Hungary

Transylvania

Banat
1718

Wallachia
+1718
–1739

Serbia
+1718–1739

Belgrade
North

Vienna

Austria

Linz

Graz

Styria

Carinthia

Tyrol

Trent

Trent

Sundgau

Venetia

Lombardy

Milano

Zagreb

Slovenia 1718

Croatia

Sava

Carniola

Trieste

Firenze

Tuscany
1737

Adriatic
Sea

robert d. gross

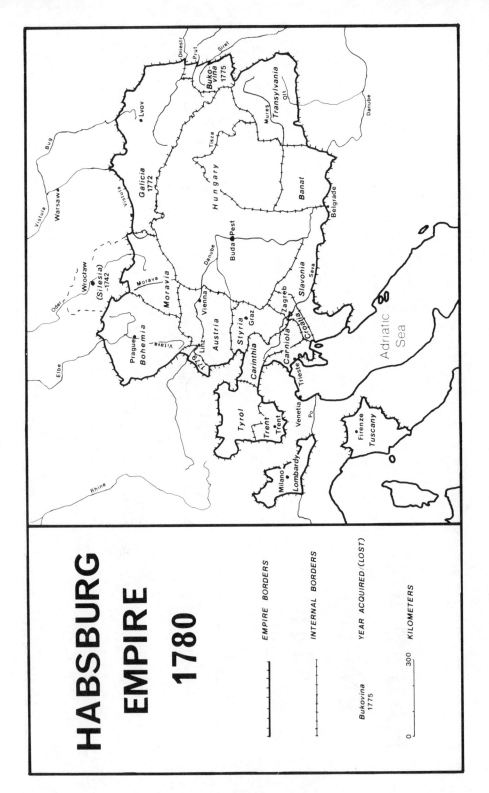

HABSBURG EMPIRE 1780

EMPIRE BORDERS

INTERNAL BORDERS

Bukovina
1775   YEAR ACQUIRED/(LOST)

0   300   KILOMETERS

Dniestr
Prut
Siret
Buko-vina 1775
Transylvania
Olt
Danube
Lvov
Mures
Tisza
Galicia 1772
Hungary
Banat
Belgrade
Bug
Vistula
Warsaw
Vistula
Buda ● Pest
Danube
Zagreb
Sava
Wrocław
(Silesia) -1742
Morava
Moravia
Slavonia
Adriatic Sea
Oder
Prague ●
Bohemia
Vltava
Linz
Vienna
Austria
Styria
Graz
Carniola
Croatia
Trieste
Elbe
Carinthia
Tyrol
Trent
Trent
Venetia
Po
Firenze
Tuscany
Rhine
Milano ●
Lombardy

384

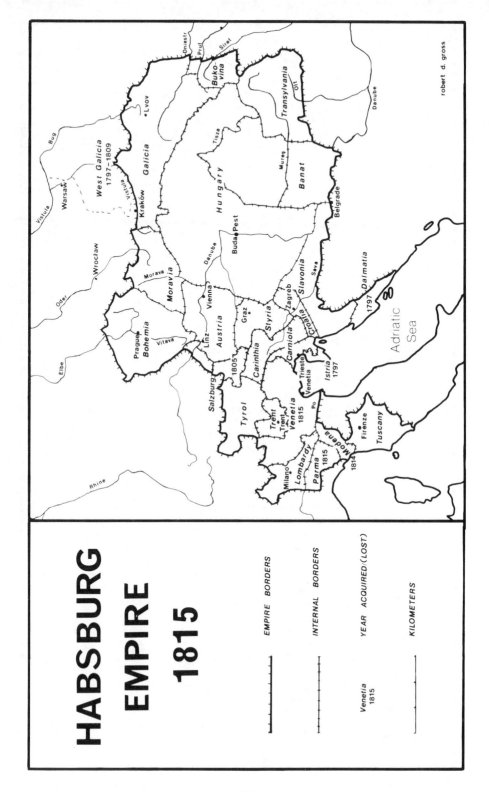

HABSBURG EMPIRE 1815

EMPIRE BORDERS

INTERNAL BORDERS

YEAR ACQUIRED/(LOST)

Venetia
1815

KILOMETERS

robert d. gross

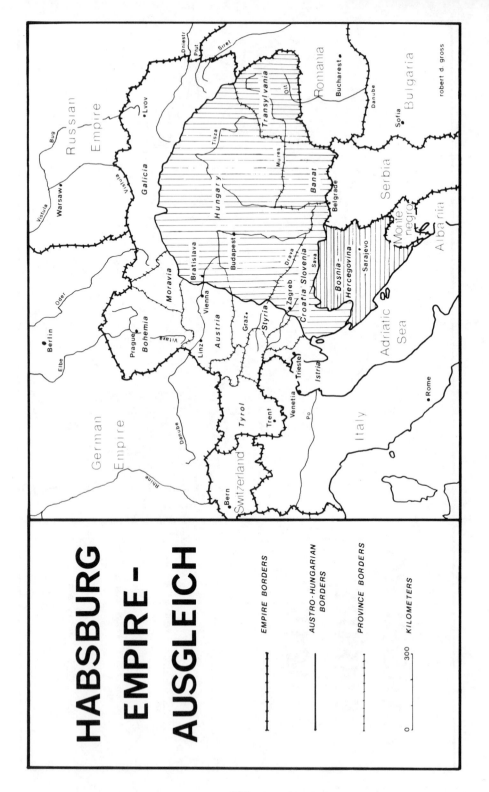

HABSBURG EMPIRE – AUSGLEICH

EMPIRE BORDERS

AUSTRO-HUNGARIAN BORDERS

PROVINCE BORDERS

KILOMETERS

0   300

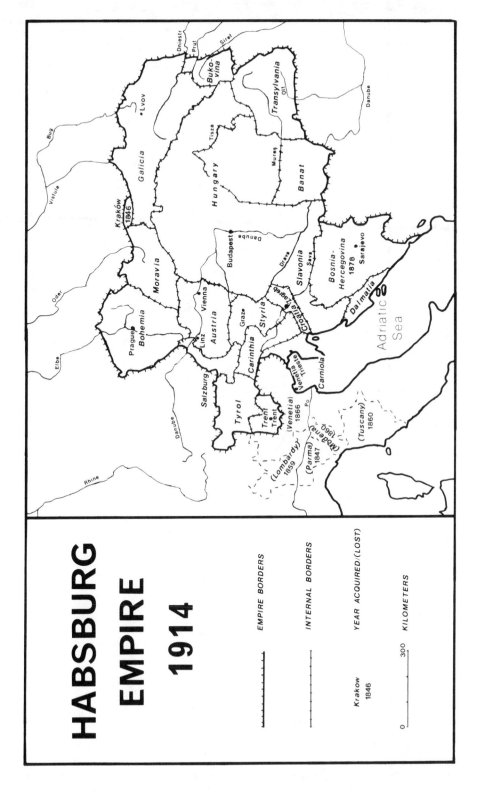

HABSBURG EMPIRE 1914

EMPIRE BORDERS

INTERNAL BORDERS

YEAR ACQUIRED/(LOST)

Krakow
1846

0   300   KILOMETERS

Dniestr
Prut
Siret
Buko-vina
Transylvania
Olt
Bug
Lvov
Galicia
Tisza
Vistula
Kraków
1846
Hungary
Mureş
Banat
Moravia
Danube
Budapest
Drava
Sava
Bosnia-Hercegovina
1878
Sarajevo
Oder
Zagreb
Slavonia
Vienna
Prague
Bohemia
Linz
Austria
Graz
Styria
Croatia
Dalmatia
Adriatic Sea
Elbe
Salzburg
Carinthia
Carniola
Venetia
Trieste
Tyrol
Trent
Trent
(Venetia)
1866
Po
(Lombardy)
1859
(Parma)
1847
(Modena)
1860
(Tuscany)
1860
Danube
Rhine
Danube

EAST EUROPE - 1914

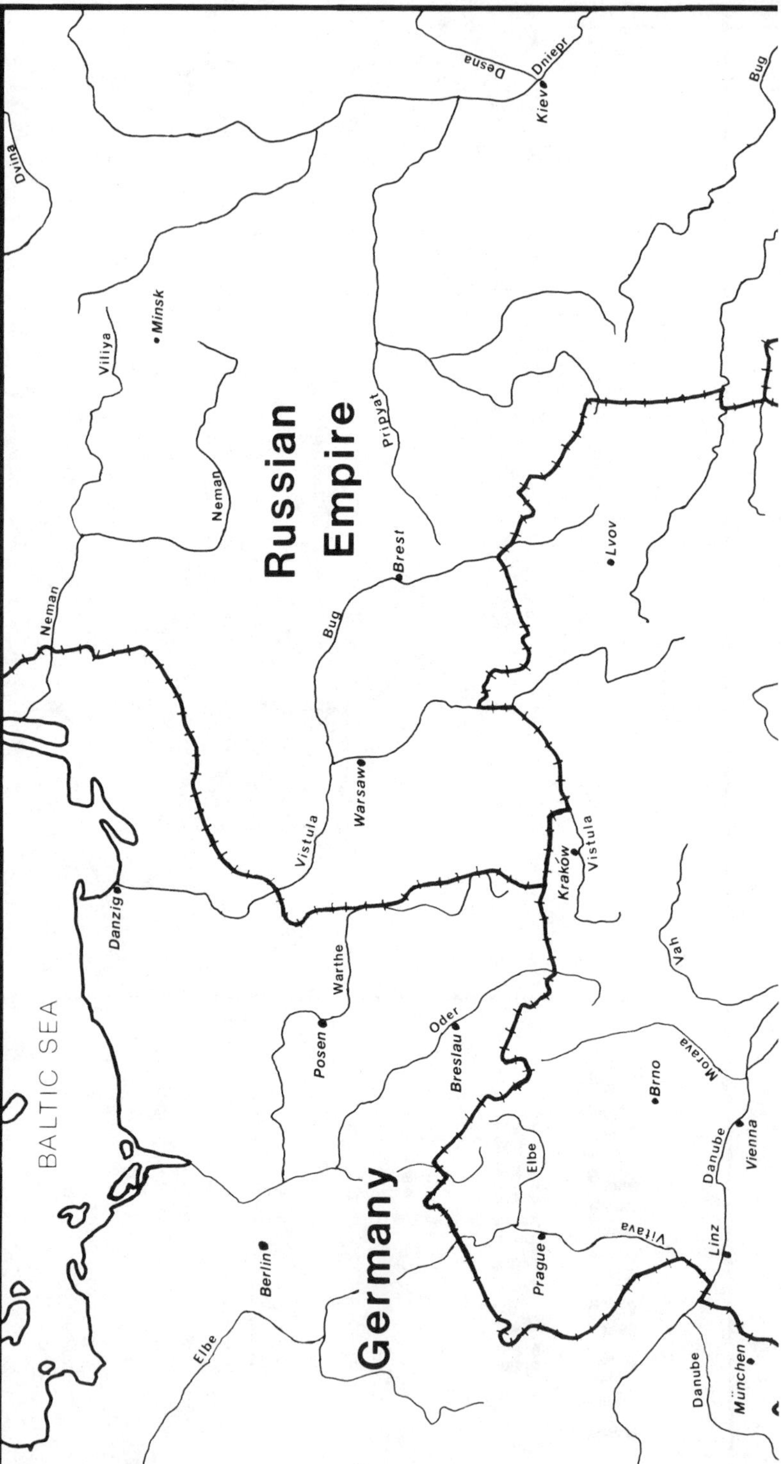

Dvina

Desna

Dniepr

Kiev

Bug

Minsk

Viliya

Neman

Pripyat

Russian

Empire

Lvov

Neman

Bug

Brest

BALTIC SEA

Vistula

Warsaw

Kraków

Vistula

Danzig

Warthe

Posen

Oder

Breslau

Vistula

Vah

Morava

Brno

Vienna

Germany

Elbe

Berlin

Prague

Elbe

Danube

Vltava

Linz

Danube

München

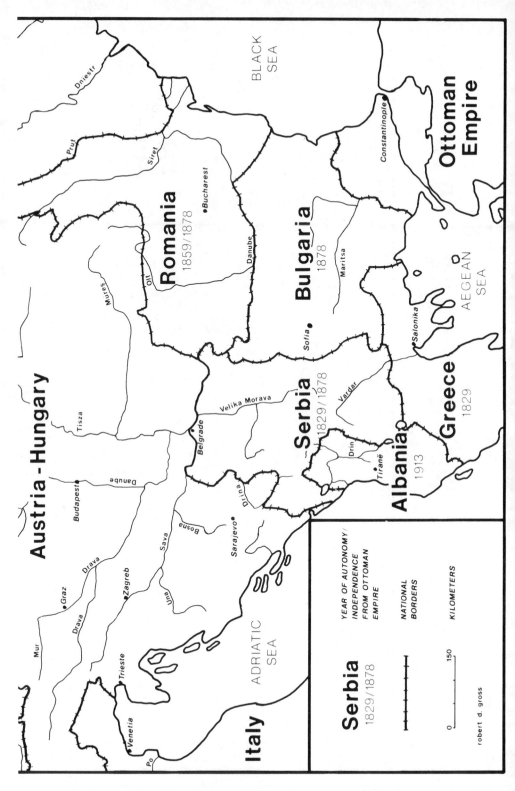

389

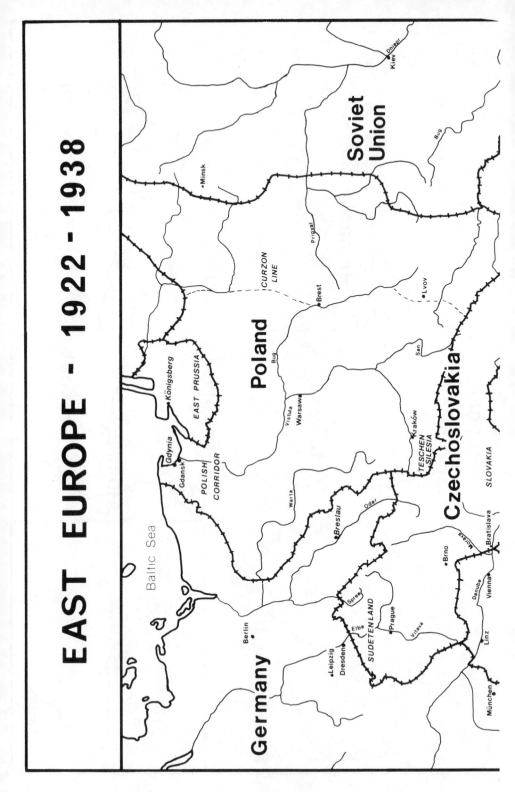

EAST EUROPE - 1922 - 1938

Soviet Union

Dnepr
•Kiev
Bug
•Minsk
Pripyat
CURZON LINE
•Brest
•Lvov

Poland

Bug
San
Vistula
Warsaw•
Kraków•
TESCHEN SILESIA
SLOVAKIA

EAST PRUSSIA
Königsberg
Gdynia
Gdansk
POLISH CORRIDOR
Warta
Breslau•
Oder
Czechoslovakia
Morava
Bratislava•
•Brno

Baltic Sea

Berlin
Leipzig•
Dresden•
Spree
SUDETENLAND
Elbe
•Prague
Vltava
Danube
Vienna•
Linz
München•

Germany

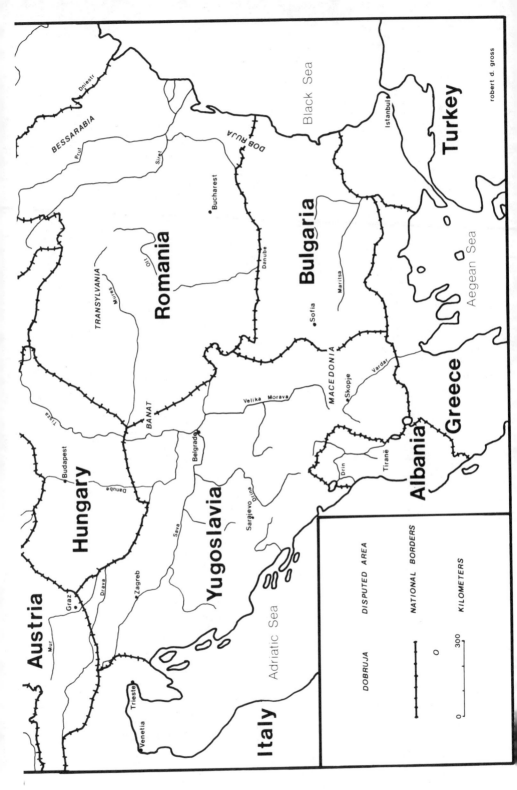

391

Notes

Chapter 1—The Lands of Eastern Europe

1. A good summary of the regionalization of Eastern Europe is provided in George W. Hoffman, "Regional Synthesis: An Introduction," in George W. Hoffman, ed., *Eastern Europe: Essays in Geographical Problems* (New York: Praeger Publishers, 1970), pp. 1–31.

Chapter 2—History to 1800

1. Francis Dvornik, *The Slavs: Their Early History and Civilization* (Boston: American Academy of Arts and Sciences, 1956), pp. 13–14.

2. This interpretation of Ottoman rule in the Balkans is controversial; many, especially Greeks, Bulgarians, Serbs, and Macedonians, have a harsher view. For an excellent analysis of the structure and operation of the Ottoman state in Southeast Europe see Peter F. Sugar, *Southeastern Europe under Ottoman Rule, 1354–1804* (Seattle: University of Washington Press, 1977), pp. 31–59.

3. For a summary of the reasons for the decline of the Ottoman economy, see John R. Lampe and Marvin R. Jackson, *Balkan Economic History, 1550–1950* (Bloomington: Indiana University Press, 1982), pp. 21–49.

Chapter 3—History, 1800–1848

1. For an excellent discussion of both the influence of France and the role of the Polish emigres, see John C. Campbell, *French Influence and the Rise of Roumanian Nationalism* (New York: Arno Press & the New York Times, 1971).

2. Norman Davies remarks that the Poles "belong to a community which has acquired its modern sense of nationality in active opposition to the policies of the states in which they lived." *God's Playground: A History of Poland* (New York: Columbia University Press, 1984), 2, p. 11.

3. The Habsburg Emperor Joseph II attempted to Germanize the Jews as a part of his overall effort at centralization; this effort met with considerable success, with some effect even in the Polish areas where the Jews had lived quite apart from the rest of society.

393

See Piotr S. Wandycz, *The Lands of Partitioned Poland* (Seattle: University of Washington Press, 1974), pp. 13–14.

4. Though the nobility had been restructured in the seventeenth century to be loyal to the Habsburgs, Vienna's aggressive policy of taxation in the rich lands of Bohemia and Moravia eventually led to a significant opposition to central authority from that quarter which, though opposed to the ethnic Czech movement, had the effect of strengthening it. Robert J. Kerner, "The Czechoslovaks from the Battle of White Mountain to the World War," in Robert J. Kerner, ed., *Czechoslovakia* (Berkeley: University of California Press, 1949), p. 34.

5. The Hungarians actively opposed Slovak cultural development even before 1848. See Vaclav L. Benes, "The Slovaks in the Habsburg Empire: A Struggle for Existence," *Austrian History Yearbook* 3, Pt. 2 (1967), pp. 342–43.

6. The Hungarians had, however, laid the foundations for movement away from control by Vienna through a series of measures that culminated in 1790 with the end of attempts by the Habsburgs to complete the centralization of the government. See Bela K. Kiraly, *Hungary in the Late Eighteenth Century* (New York: Columbia University Press, 1969).

7. Hungarian nationalism before 1848 is discussed in George Barany, "The Awakening of Hungarian nationalism before 1848," in *Austrian History Yearbook* 2 (1966), pp. 19–54.

8. Fran Zwitter, "The Slovenes and the Habsburg Monarchy," *Austrian History Yearbook* 3, Pt. 2 (1967), p. 162.

9. A major issue was the use of Hungarian instead of Latin as the official language of the Hungarian kingdom; the Croats were able to block the change when first proposed in 1790, but in return conceded the perhaps more important change of requiring Hungarian as a required subject in Croatian schools (1827). See Elinor Murray Despalatovic, "The Illyrian Solution to the Problem of Modern National Identity for the Croats," *Balkanistica* 1 (1974), p. 77. The Croats led in the formation of an anti-Magyar political party, the Illyrian Party (later the National Party) in 1840. See Charles Jelavich, "The Croatian Problem in the Habsburg Empire in the Nineteenth Century," *Austrian History Yearbook* 3, Pt. 2 (1967), p. 90.

10. Michael B. Petrovich, *History of Serbia* (New York: Harcourt, Brace, Jovanovich, 1976), 1, pp. 42–43.

11. Stavro Skendi, *The Albanian National Awakening, 1878–1912* (Princeton: Princeton University Press, 1967), p. 18.

12. Thomas A. Meininger, "Teachers and School Boards in the Late Bulgarian Renaissance," in Thomas Butler, ed., *Bulgaria: Past and Present* (Columbus, Ohio: American Association for the Advancement of Slavic Studies, 1976), pp. 31–35.

13. Cornelia Bodea, *The Romanian's Struggle for Unification* (Bucharest: Publishing House of the Academy of the Socialist Republic of Romania, 1970), pp. 111–29.

14. Istvan Deak, *The Lawful Revolution: Louis Kossuth and the Hungarians, 1848–49* (New York: Columbia University Press, 1979), p. 122.

Chapter 4—History, 1848–1914

1. Wandycz, *The Lands,* p. 196.
2. On the effects of the land reform see ibid., pp. 197–200.

3. Dmowski's views are summarized in R. F. Leslie, ed. *The History of Poland since 1863* (Cambridge: Cambridge University Press, 1980), pp. 71–73.

4. M. K. Dziewanowski, *Poland in the Twentieth Century* (New York: Columbia University Press, 1977), pp. 80–81.

5. Robert A. Kann, *The Multinational Empire: Nationalism and National Reform in the Habsburg Monarchy, 1848–1918*, 2 vols. (New York: Columbia University Press, 1950), 2:332n.

6. For a discussion of different views of the nature of the constitutional situation see Peter Hanak, "Hungary in the Austro-Hungarian Monarchy," *Austrian History Yearbook* 3, Pt. 1 (1967): 260–65.

7. The Hungarian and Croatian language versions of the treaty even differed on the key question of the administrative location of the port city of Rijeka (Fiume) Arthur J. May, *The Habsburg Monarchy* (New York: W. W. Norton & Company, 1968), p. 74.

8. Victor L. Tapie, *The Habsburg Monarchy*, trans. Stephen Hardman (New York: Praeger, 1969), p. 342.

9. Peter F. Sugar, "An Underrated Event: The Hungarian Constitutional Crisis of 1905–06," *East European Quarterly* 15, No. 3 (Fall 1981):302–4.

10. The Taafe family emigrated from Ireland in 1690. William A. Jenks, *Austria Under the Iron Ring, 1879–1893* (Charlottesville: The University Press of Virginia, 1965), p. 29.

11. May, *Habsburg Monarchy*, p. 25.

12. For a discussion of the Czech reaction to the Ausgleich see William V. Wallace, *Czechoslovakia* (Boulder, Colorado: Westview Press, 1976), pp. 27–30.

13. The most significant action was the often-used tactic of parliamentary boycott. See Robert A. Kann and Zdenek A. David, *The Peoples of the Eastern Habsburg Lands, 1526–1918* (Seattle: University of Washington Press, 1984), pp. 303–4.

14. In a celebrated incident in 1906, Czech recruits answered roll call in Czech rather than German. This small gesture resulted in a series of court martials. See Gunther Rothenberg, "The Habsburg Army," *Austrian History Yearbook* 3, Pt. 1 (1967):83.

15. Oscar Jaszi, *The Dissolution of the Habsburg Monarchy* (Chicago: University of Chicago Press, 1929), p. 310.

16. In 1867 only 5 percent of Slovaks were industrial laborers. Wallace, *Czechoslovakia*, p. 66.

17. The period of Magyarization in fact coincides with the flowering of Romanian culture in Transylvania. See Constantin Daicoviciu and Miron Constantinescu, eds., *Brève histoire de la Transylvanie* (Bucharest: Editions de l'Academie de la Republique Socialist de la Roumanie, 1965), pp. 326–58.

18. Carole Rogel, *The Slovenes and Cultural Yugoslavism* (New York: East European Quarterly, 1977), pp. 94–95.

19. A number of young Croats studied at the University of Prague, where they were influenced by the growing revolutionary radicalism then affecting the Czechs. Stanku Goldescu, "Croatian Political History: 1526–1918," in Francis H. Eterovich, ed., *Croatia: Land, People Culture.* (Toronto, University of Toronto Press, 1964–1970),1:49–50. By the 1890s there was a convergence toward Yugoslavism in Croatian politics. Mirjana Gross, "Croatian National-Integrative ideologies from the End of Illyrism to the Creation of Yugoslavia," *Austrian History Yearbook* 15–16 (1979–1980): 29.

20. With the annexation of Bosnia-Hercegovina by the Dual Monarchy in 1878, the dominant sentiment of the Habsburg Serbs became opposition. Dimitrie Djordjevic,

"The Serbs as an Integrating and Disintegrating Factor," *Austrian History Yearbook* 3, Pt. 2 (1967): 70.

21. Conflicting views of the nature of the Galician revolt of 1846 are discussed in Piotr S. Wandycz, "The Poles in the Habsburg Monarchy," *Austrian History Yearbook* 3, Pt. 2 (1967):268–70.

22. Although outsiders encouraged resistance to the Turks in a general sense, it does not appear that the actual revolt was planned by any nation or group. David MacKenzie, *The Serbs and Russian Panslavism, 1875–1878* (Ithaca, New York: Cornell University Press, 1967), p. 31.

23. On the first currents surrounding the concept of a separate Macedoninan language, see: Stoyan Pribichevich, *Macedonia: Its People and History* (University Park, Pennsylvania: The Pennsylvania State University Press, 1982), pp. 106–14.

24. The formation of IMRO is discussed in ibid., pp. 119–23.

25. On the role of Karadžic see Duncan Wilson, *The Life and Times of Vuk Stefanović Karadzić* (Oxford: The Clarendon Press, 1974), pp. 312–13.

26. Serbia already had begun to take seriously its role of unifier of the south Slavs in 1844. Petrovich, *Serbia*, 1:232–33.

27. The crisis was actually the result of a ripple effect: when Germany put a high tariff on Hungarian hogs, producers in that country used their political muscle to eliminate Serbian competition from the domestic market. See: Lampe and Jackson, *Balkan Economic History*, pp. 175–76.

28. Despite the problems caused by these changes, the Bulgarian village economy continued to grow in many respects. See ibid., pp. 133–34, 151–53.

29. On Levsky, Karavelov, and Botev see Mercia Macdermott, *A History of Bulgaria* (London: Allen & Unwin, 1962), pp. 201–35.

30. The extremely complex Russian-Bulgarian relationship is described in Charles Jelavich, *Tsarist Russia and Balkan Nationalism* (Berkeley: University of California Press, 1962).

31. R. W. Seton-Watson, *A History of the Roumanians from Roman Times to the Completion of Unity* (Cambridge: Cambridge University Press, 1934), pp. 377–80.

32. On the organization of the League of Prizren see Skendi, *Albanian Awakening*, p. 36.

Chapter 5—Why Is There an Eastern Europe?

1. William H. McNeill, *The Shape of European History* (New York: Oxford University Press, 1974). For a different approach to the history of Eastern Europe see Oscar Halecki, *The Limits and Divisions of European History* (South Bend, Indiana: University of Notre Dame Press, 1962).

2. See Jagellonian University, *An Outline History of Polish Culture* (Warsaw: Interpress, 1984), p. 73.

3. See Keith L. Hitchins, *The Rumanian National Movement in Transylvania, 1780–1849* (Cambridge: Harvard University Press, 1969).

4. On the early problems of education in Albania see Skendi, *Albanian Awakening*, pp. 129–39.

5. Robert Auty, "Czech," in Alexander M. Schenker and Edward Stankewicz, eds.,

The Slavic Literary Languages: Formation and Development (New Haven: Yale Concilium on International and Area Studies, 1980), pp. 167–68.

6. The impact of Palacký's ideas on the national movement is discussed in Arne Novak, *Czech Literature*, trans. Peter Kussi (Anne Arbor: Michigan Slavic Publications, 1976), pp. 137–40.

7. On the impact of Protestanism on Polish literature see Czeslaw Miłosz, *The History of Polish Literature* (Berkeley: University of California Press, 1983), pp. 28–35.

8. For discussions of these writers, see ibid., pp. 60–79, 56–59, 90–95.

9. Mickiewicz and his work are described in ibid., pp. 208–31.

10. Juraj Slavik, "One Hundred and Twenty Years of Slovak Literary Language," in Miloslav Rechcigc, Jr., ed. *The Czechoslovak Contribution to World Culture* (The Hague: Mouton & Company, 1964), pp. 45–48.

11. Kollár and Šafárik, like Štúr, were protestants educated abroad. For a discussion of religion and cultural-linguistic issues among the Slovaks see Ludovit Holotik, "The Slovaks: An Integrating or Disintegrating Force?" *Austrian History Yearbook* 3, Pt. 2 (1967), pp. 375–80.

12. Lorant Czigany, *The Oxford History of Hungarian Literature* (Oxford: The Clarendon Press, 1984), p. 101.

13. Joseph Remenyi, *Hungarian Writers and Literature* (New Brunswick, New Jersey: Rutgers University Press, 1964), for short studies of Vorosmarty (pp. 72–85), Arany (106–116), Petofi (84–105), and Jokai (pp. 165–77).

14. There was some use of Croatian in literature even in the fifteenth century. Franjo Trgograncic, "Literature, 1400–1835," in Eterovich, *Croatia* 2, p. 178.

15. One of the first modern Croatian books was a political pamphlet aimed at Croat delegates to the Hungarian diet. Bogdan Krizman, "The Croatians in the Habsburg Monarchy in the Nineteenth Century," *Austrian History Yearbook* 3, Pt. 2 (1967), p. 117.

16. On Kopitar see Edward Stankewicz, "Slovenian," in Schenker and Stankewicz, *The Slavic Literary Languages*, pp. 96–97.

17. The extreme francophiles were scornfully referred to as "bonjourist." See Campbell, *French Influence*, p. 81.

18. Charles A. Moser, *A History of Bulgarian Literature, 1855–1944* (The Hague: Mouton and Company, 1972), pp. 42–43.

19. For an excellent discussion of *Under the Yoke* see Clarence A. Manning and Roman Smal-Stocki, *The History of Modern Bulgarian Literature* (Westport, Connecticut: Greenwood Press, 1974), pp. 89–91.

Chapter 6—The Great War

1. Petrovich, *Serbia*, 2:618–20.

2. Wallace, *Czechoslovakia*, p. 111.

3. Piłsudski's proclamation upon the entrance of Polish troops into the Ukraine stated in part, "When the national government of the Ukrainian Republic will have established its authority, when the troops of the Ukrainian nation will have taken hold of its borders to protect their country against new intrusions, when the free nation itself will be in a position to decide its own destiny, then the Polish soldiers will withdraw behind the frontier of the free Republic of Poland." Josef Korbel, *Poland between East and West* (Princeton: Princeton University Press, 1963), p. 38.

Chapter 7—Interwar Eastern Europe

1. I. T. Berend and G. Ranki, *Hungary: A Century of Economic Development* (Newton Abbot: David & Charles Limited, 1974), p. 230. the figure is for Hungary, but the authors believe that it is a reasonable estimate for the entire area.

2. Walter Consuelo Langsam, *The World since 1914* (New York: Macmillan Company, 1940), p. 543.

3. An extensive discussion of the phenomenon of clearing is contained in Ivan T. Berend, and Gyorgy Ranki. *Economic Development in East-Central Europe in the 19th and 20th Centuries* (New York: Columbia University Press, 1974), pp. 265—84.

Chapter 8—Interior Poland

1. A significant issue was a German demand that Piłsudski and his followers transfer their allegiance from Austria-Hungary to Germany. Since the latter's treatment of Poles had been very harsh, Piłsudski was unwilling to accept, "If I were to go along with you, Germany would gain one man whilst I would lose a nation." Davies, *God's Playground,* 2:385.

2. Colin McEvedy and Richard Jones, *Atlas of World Population History* (New York: Penguin Books, 1980), p. 74.

3. George D. Jackson, Jr., *Comintern and Peasant in East Europe, 1919–1930* (New York: Columbia University Press, 1966), p. 7.

4. Ibid., p. 12.

5. Ibid., p. 11. Pages 3–25, "Peasant Societies in Transition," of Jackson's book offers an excellent summary of this topic.

6. Ibid.

7. Hugh Seton-Watson, *Eastern Europe between the Wars, 1918–1941* (New York: Harper and Row, Harper Torchbooks, 1967), p. 81.

8. Data are derived from McEvedy and Jones, *Atlas of Population,* pp. 55–60 and pp. 73–82. See also the sections on Poland and France in B. R. Mitchell, *European Historical Statistics, 1750–1970* (New York: Columbia University Press, 1976).

9. There was a slight influx of foreign (western) capital in 1927–28 but the total in Poland never exceeded about one-third. Richard M. Watt, *Bitter Glory: Poland and its Fate, 1918–1939* New York: (Simon and Schuster, 1982), p. 291.

10. Joseph Rothschild, *East Central Europe between the Two World Wars* (Seattle: University of Washington Press, 1974), p. 39. Looking at it another way, 58.7 percent of those engaged in commerce and insurance and 21.3 percent of those in industry and mining were Jews. Ibid., p. 40.

11. Ibid., p. 384. Janina Wojcicka gives a much higher figure, 21.6 percent; it is likely that the discrepancy in this estimate results at least in part from the use of data based on present-day frontiers, thereby excluding the Ukrainian peasantry. See "Education," in Oscar Halecki, ed., *Poland* (New York: Praeger, 1957), p. 193.

12. A summary list is provided in Leslie, *History of Poland,* pp. 153–154.

13. Watt, *Bitter Glory,* p. 205.

14. The already high level of public participation in industry increased as the government was forced to buy out many failing private industries. This amounted to 70 percent of iron and steel production and 80 percent of the chemical industry. Ibid., p. 297.

15. Dziewanowski, *Poland*, p. 99.
16. Ibid., p. 101.

Chapter 9—Interwar Czechoslovakia

1. Rothschild, *East Central Europe*, p. 91.
2. Czechoslovakia actually reduced the share of foreign ownership of capital in the period 1925–1931. Berend and Ranki, *Economic Development*, p. 237.
3. Josef Korbel, *Twentieth Century Czechoslovakia* (New York: Columbia University Press, 1977), pp. 46–47.
4. Jackson, *Comintern and Peasant*, p. 9.
5. Wilbert E. Moore, *Economic Demography of Eastern and Southern Europe*, (Geneva: League of Nations, 1945), p. 71.
6. Jackson, *Comintern and Peasant*, p. 269.
7. Population estimates are provided in Hugh Seton-Wastson, *Eastern Europe*, p. 414.
8. Electoral data for interwar Czechoslovakia are given in Rothschild, *East Central Europe*, pp. 102, 110, 116, and 126.
9. Had the strongly anticlerical Social Democrats been united it seems likely that the road to an agreement with the Church would have been much more difficult. For a discussion of the issues, see: Wallace, *Czechoslovakia*, pp. 178–79.

Chapter 10—Interwar Hungary

1. Rothschild, *East Central Europe*, p. 156.
2. Langsam, *The World since 1914*, p. 543.
3. Berend and Ranki, *Economic Development*, p. 230.
4. Jackson, *Comintern and Peasant*, p. 12.
5. Moore, *Economic Demography*, p. 71.
6. Real wages in 1929 were only 85–86 percent of the prewar level, and attained only about 95 percent in the strongest period of the 1930s. Berend and Ranki, *Economic Development*, pp. 158–59.
7. A concise description of the economic, social, and cultural status of the Jews in interwar Hungary is provided in C. A. Macartney, *October Fifteenth: A History of Modern Hungary, 1929–1945* (Edinburgh: Edinburgh University Press, 1957), 1:18–21.
8. In 1930 40 percent of university students were studying theology or law, and only 17 percent technology and business. Berend and Ranki, *Hungary*, p. 125.
9. The two major pieces of anti-Semitic legislation are summarized in *Macartney, October Fifteenth.*, 1:218–19, and 1:324–25.

Chapter 11—Interwar Romania

1. Moore, *Economic Demography*, p. 72.
2. Robert R. Gross, "Statistics on Eastern Europe," appendix to E. Garrison Walters, "The Other Europe" (Columbus, Ohio: unpublished photocopied text, 1982), p. 452.

3. Berend and Ranki, *Economic Development*, p. 106.

4. Antony Polonsky, *The Little Dictators* (London: Routledge & Kegan Paul, 1975), p. 179.

5. Berend and Ranki, *Economic Development*, p. 300.

6. Ibid., p. 282.

7. Bureaucrats outnumbered industrial workers even at the end of the interwar period. Lampe and Jackson, *Balkan Economic History*, p. 503.

8. Gross, "Statistics," p. 439.

9. Polonsky, *Little Dictators*, pp. 190–91.

10. Romania had 18 institutions of higher education, also more than Czechoslovakia. See: Rothschild, *East Central Europe*, p. 385.

11. Seton-Watson went on to say, "it was not the right issue on which to base the whole conflict between Democracy and Dictatorship. *Eastern Europe*, p. 204.

12. Hugh Seton-Watson summarizes Carol's role: "For a decade the history of Roumania consisted of this man's flamboyant gestures and cunning manouuvres, set against a drab background of peasant misery and police oppression." Ibid., p. 204.

13. Macartney and Palmer, *Independent Eastern Europe*, p. 335n.

Chapter 12—Interwar Yugoslavia

1. Bulgaria, the next country to be studied, belongs to this group as well.

2. Moore, *Economic Demography*, p. 72.

3. Gross, *Statistics*, p. 452.

4. Polonsky, *Little Dictators*, pp. 190–91.

5. By 1939, when Yugoslav leaders had come to look upon clearing as "an economic and political incubus of ugly proportions," it was too late to change. J. B. Hoptner, *Yugoslavia in Crisis, 1934–1941* (New York: Columbia University Press, 1962), p. 108.

6. Jozo Tomasevich, *Peasants, Politics, and Economic Change in Yugoslavia* (Stanford: Stanford University Press, 1955), p. 198.

7. Stavro Skendi, "Education," in Robert F. Byrnes, editor, *Yugoslavia* (New York: Praeger, 1957), p. 168.

8. The armed member of parliament was, appropriately, a Montengrin.

9. Ustaša leaders were offered refuge in Italy and Hungary both before and after the assassination. Fred Singleton, *Twentieth-Century Yugoslavia* (New York: Columbia University Press, 1976), p. 78.

Chapter 13—Interwar Bulgaria

1. Moore, *Economic Demography*, p. 26.

2. From another perspective, less than one percent of Bulgarian farm labor was hired help; a similar figure for Hungary was nearly 40 percent. Ibid., p. 234; p. 252.

3. Ibid., p. 71.

4. Gross, "Statistics," p. 452.

5. Polonsky, *Little Dictators*, p. 179.

6. Velchev was eventually arrested and imprisoned, but he continued political life

and was an important figure in the coup of 1944. Nissan Oren, *Bulgarian Communism* (New York: Columbia University Press, 1971), p. 33n.

Chapter 14—Interwar Albania

1. Moore, *Economic Demography*, p. 26.
2. Stavro Skendi, editor, *Albania* (New York: Frederick A. Praeger, 1957), p. 225.
3. The Italians also set up a National Bank of Albania, owned and controlled by Rome, which had the sole right to issue Albanian currency. L. S. Stavrianos, *The Balkans since 1453* (New York: Holt, Rinehart, and Winston, 1958), pp. 721–22.
4. As minister of the Interior Zog launched a successful campaign to disarm the lowlanders "a task both dangerous and formidable," but made no attempt to infringe similarly on the even more threatening highlanders. J. Swire, *Albania: The Rise of a Kingdom* (London: Unwin Brothers, Limited, 1929), p. 391.
5. J. Swire, *King Zog's Albania* (London: Robert Hale and Company, 1937), p. 217.

Chapter 15—Eastern Europe in World War I

1. As an example, M. K. Dziewanowski states that "for every 1,000 citizens of prewar Poland, 220 perished during the period from September 1, 1939, to May 8, 1945; in Yugoslavia the figures were 108 per 1,000 and in the USSR 40 per 1,000." Dziewanowski, *Poland*, p. 143. While total losses in Poland alone exceeded 6 million, military casualties (killed) for Britain, France, and the United States *combined* were about one million. See: Richard B. Morris and Graham W. Irwin, editors, *Harper Encyclopedia of the Modern World* (New York: Harper and Row, 1970, p. 513.
2. The hostility of Poland to the USSR, and the latter's potential and subsequent actual value as an ally against the Nazis, meant that the interests of the Poles, particularly in territory, were not of importance to the Allies, during the war. See Dziewanowski, *Poland*, p. 122–23.
3. Ibid., page 118.
4. J. K. Zawodny, *Death in the Forest* (South Bend: University of Notre Dame Press, 1962), pp. 9–10.
5. Ibid., p. 11.
6. Ibid., pp. 88–89.
7. Ibid., p. 5.
8. Dziewanowski, *Poland*, p. 143.
9. As a first step, Dr. Frank observed in 1940 that "the men capable of leadership whom we have found to exist in Poland must be liquidated." Zawodny, *Death in the Forest*, p. 79.
10. Dziewanoski, *Poland*, p. 143.
11. Total Polish killed in "a city of ruins and graves" are estimated at some 200,000; the surviving 800,000 were deported. Leslie *History of Poland*, p. 273.
12. Ibid., p. 272.
13. The Soviet Union also disassociated itself from what it described as an "ad-

venturist" undertaking. Arthur Bliss Lane, *I Saw Poland Betrayed* (New York: The Bobbs Merril Company, 1948), p. 50.

14. Lucy S. Dawidowicz, *The War against the Jews* (New York: Holt, Rinehart, and Winston, 1975), p. 339.

15. British recognition came in July of 1940. Wallace, *Czechoslavakia*, p. 225.

16. Ibid., p. 242. Beneš' desire to accommodate the Soviet Union was in part a consequence of his understanding of American policy developed during a visit to Washington earlier in 1943. Ibid., p. 232.

17. Dawidowicz, *The War*, p. 378.

18. Korbel, *Czechoslovakia*, p. 163.

19. Dawidowicz, *The War*, p. 378.

20. Ibid., p. 403.

21. Macartney, *October Fifteenth*, 2, pp. 30–31.

22. Ibid., II, pp. 27–28.

23. Ibid., II, pp. 120–23.

24. Macartney notes that, as the Soviet forces pushed into the Balkans, "at that moment the Hungarian Army was actually a negative factor in Hitler's war effort. Not only was it not fighting itself: it was preventing the Roumanians from doing so." Ibid., p. 222.

25. Ibid., 2, p. 415.

26. Ibid., 2, p. 135.

27. Ibid., 2, pp. 69–74.

28. Ibid., 2, p. 282.

29. Dawidowicz, *The War*, p. 403.

30. Stavrianos, *The Balkans*, p. 771.

31. Dawidowicz, *The War*, p. 392.

32. Singleton, *Twentieth-Century Yugoslavia*, p. 88.

33. Dawidowicz, *The War*, p. 392.

34. Stavrianos, *The Balkans*, p. 768.

35. It would be incorrect, however, to suggest that the communist leanings of the Partisans were a well-kept secret: as early as 1941 Partisan councils were emphasizing solidarity with the Soviet Union. Milovan Djilas, *Wartime* (New York: Harcourt, Brace, Jovanovich, 1977), pp. 56–57.

36. Robert Lee Wolf, *The Balkans in our Time* (New York: W. W. Norton and Company, 1967), p. 209.

37. The communist leader Djilas was of the opinion that Mihailovich was personally opposed to direct collaboration but that his failure to attack the German controlled Serbian forces amounted to the same thing. Djilas, *Wartime*, p. 99.

38. The speech was reported by a British liaison officer. Jozo Tomasevich, *The Chetniks* (Stanford: The Hoover Institution Press, 1975), pp. 291–92.

39. Djilas, *Wartime*, p. 4.

40. R. V. Burks, *The Dynamics of Communism in Eastern Europe* (Princeton: Princeton University Press, 1961), p. 79.

41. One of the British liaison officers who joined the Partisans in 1944 was Churchill's son, Randolph. Djilas, *Wartime*, p. 369.

42. The Iron Guard was even allowed to form its own police force. Nicholas M. Nagy-Talavera, *The Green Shirts and the Others* (Stanford: Hoover Institution Press, 1970), p. 312.

43. Antonescu, still unsure, waited until Hitler intervened personally to strike at the core of Sima's forces. In the interim, the Guardists directed incredible violence against the populace and especially on the Jews. Ibid., pp. 326–27.

44. Stavrianos, *The Balkans*, p. 767.

45. The weakness of the Romanian communists may owe something to the fact that their leader at the time was most probably a government agent. Robert R. King, *History of the Romanian Communist Party*, (Stanford: Hoover Institution Press, 1980), p. 43.

46. Rothschild, *East Central Europe*, p. 318.

47. Dawidowicz, *The War*, p. 385–86.

48. Ibid., p. 403.

49. Wolf, *The Balkans*, p. 246.

50. Although there was comparatively little native anti-Semitism and even a significant element of philo-Semitism in Bulgaria, a scholar who has studied the situation in detail argues that the ultimate reason for the survival of so many Jews was nothing more than the fact of Hitler's waning success on the battlefield. Frederick B. Chary, *The Bulgarian Jews and the Final Solution, 1940–1944* (Pittsburgh: University of Pittsburgh Press, 1972), p. 198.

51. Dawidowicz, *The War*, p. 403.

52. At the very end of the occupation the Germans undertook a vigorous campaign against those suspected of being pro-British. Wolf, *The Balkans*, p. 234.

Chapter 16—The Soviet Example

1. An excellent analysis of Lenin's thought is Alfred G. Meyer, *Leninism* (Cambridge: Harvard University Press, 1957).

2. An excellent overview of the structure and operation of the Soviet Union is John N. Hazard, *The Soviet System of Government* (Chicago: University of Chicago Press, 1980).

3. Robert Conquest, *The Great Terror* (New York: Macmillan Company, 1973), p. 275.

4. The Comintern's Fifth Congress (1924) "ordered a more vigorous subordination of the foreign communist parties to Moscow than had been achieved through the Twenty-one Conditions." Adam B. Ulam, *Expansion and Coexistence* (New York: Frederick A. Praeger, 1968).

Chapter 17—The East European Communist Parties to 1945

1. While the Bolsheviks had particular success in converting Hungarian prisoners of war (a small percentage, of course), it is also true that the Hungarian converts were unusually helpful to the Soviet cause during the revolution and civil war. Bennett Kovrig, *Communism in Hungary from Kun to Kadar* (Stanford: Hoover Institution Press, 1979), p. 23.

2. The communists' revolt was facilitated by public anger over the decision of the Paris Peace Conference to award Transylvania to Romania.

3. Kun, probably because of his Transylvanian upbringing, especially disliked the Romanians. Rothschild, *East Central Europe*, p. 145.

4. Kovrig, *Communism*, p. 52.

5. The various documents of the first meeting of the Comintern refer to the failures of Kun's rebellion specifically and repeatedly. Ibid., p. 79.

6. The same method was used to purge the small faction operating in Hungary proper. Ibid., p. 131.

7. The early history of the Communist Party of Poland is ably recounted in M. K. Dziewanowski, *The Communist Party of Poland* (Cambridge: Harvard University Press, 1959).

8. The purge extended even to Western Europe. A special organization was established by the Comintern in Paris with the ostensible objective of creating a new Polish party but with the actual task of finding and destroying remnants of the old. Jan B. de Weydenthal, *The Communists of Poland* (Stanford: Hoover Institution Press, 1978), p. 32.

9. M. K. Dziewanowski, *The Communist Party of Poland* (Cambridge: Harvard University Press, 1976), pp. 168—70.

10. Martin McCauley, *Marxism Leninism in the German Democratic Republic* (London: Macmillan Press Ltd., 1978), p. xii.

11. In 1930 the Comintern observed that the Romanian party suffered "a factional struggle devoid of all principle." Ghita Ionescu, *Communism in Romania* (London: Oxford University Press, 1964), p. 42.

12. Rakovsky was eventually swept up in the great purge and executed. The career of this fascinating individual—a Bulgarian national who was a founder of the Romanian Communist Party, head of the Ukrainian Soviet Republic and who died a Soviet citizen— is recounted in Joseph A. Rothschild, "Rakovsky," *St. Anthony's Papers on Soviet Affairs: St. Anthony's College, Oxford*, no. 18 (February 1955).

13. The membership of the RCP in 1944 is estimated at only about two thousand. King, *History of the Romanian*, p. 38.

14. The early history of the CPY is recounted in Ivan Avakumovic, *History of the Communist Party of Yugoslavia*, (Aberdeen: Aberdeen University Press, 1964).

15. The official Comintern line, which had to be drilled into the heads of the CPY leadership over and over again, was that Macedonia should become an autonomous part of a greater Balkan federation. The CPY supported this line, with an evident lack of enthusiasm, until the Comintern's "united front" line of 1935 allowed it to be soft-pedalled. Stoyan Pribichevich, *Macedonia* (University Park: Pennsylvania State University Press, 1982), pp. 144–45.

16. Rothschild, *East Central Europe*, p. 215.

17. An excellent history of the CPCS is Zdenek Suda, *Zealots and Rebels* (Stanford: Hoover Institution Press, 1980).

18. Suda estimates the initial membership to be about 350,000. Suda, *Zealots*, p. 50.

19. Party membership by the end of 1930 was estimated to be only about 30,000. Peter A. Toma, "The Communist Party of Czechoslovakia," in Stephen A. Fischer-Galati, editor, *The Communist Parties of Eastern Europe* (New York: Columbia University Press, 1979), p. 92.

20. Wallace, *Czechoslovakia*, p. 189; Korbel, *Twentieth-Century Czechoslovakia*, p. 74.

21. Joseph Rothschild, *The Communist Part of Bulgaria: Origins and Development*,

1883–1936 (New York: Columbia University Press, 1959), is an excellent treatment of this period.

22. The insanity of the purge is nowhere better illustrated than by the fact that some two hundred Bulgarian communists were arrested for allegedly plotting to annex the Ukraine to Bulgaria: Oren, *Bulgarian Communism*, p. 84.

23. Oren states that "the life of the Party came to a virtual stop." Ibid., p. 185.

24. Peter R. Prifti, *Socialist Albania since 1944* (Cambridge: The MIT Press, 1978), p. 14.

25. Ibid., p. 18.

26. R. V. Burks, *The Dynamics of Communism in Eastern Europe* (Princeton: Princeton University Press, 1961).

27. Ibid., p. 20.

28. Ibid., p. 26.

29. Ibid., p. 35.

30. Ibid., p. 53

31. Lewis S. Feuer, *The Conflict of Generations* (New York: Basic Books, 1969).

32. Burks, *Dynamics*, p. 72.

Suggestions for Further Reading

O NLY IN THE LAST FOUR DECADES has Eastern Europe received much attention from scholars at universities outside of the region. And, as one would expect, most of this interest has been directed toward the postwar period and the many controversies that surround the relations of the United States and Western Europe with the new regimes and their patron in Moscow. Still, the quality of available scholarship on Eastern Europe in the languages of Western Europe is quite high, and the coverage, although uneven, is remarkably good. The brief list that follows, like this text, is intended as an introduction rather than an exhaustive treatment. Preference has been given to books in English and to works which have not only intrinsic value but also good bibliographies of their own.

Overview of Eastern Europe

Economics

Berend, Ivan T., and Gyorgy Ranki. *Economic Development in East-Central Europe in the 19th and 20th Centuries.* New York: Columbia University Press, 1974. An excellent overview, particularly strong on the interwar period.

Kaiser, David E. *Economic Diplomacy and the Origins of the Second World War.* Princeton: Princeton University Press, 1980. The focus is on Eastern Europe. Useful.

Kaser, M. C. and Radice, E. A., editors. *The Economic History of Eastern Europe, 1919–1975* Oxford: The Clarendon Press, 1985. The first volume to appear, "Economic Structure and Performance between the Two Wars," is an invaluable analysis and reference.

408 FURTHER READINGS

Geography

Pounds, Norman J. G. *Eastern Europe.* Chicago: Aldine Publishing Company, 1969. A thorough study, but oriented toward professional geographers.

History

Halecki, Oscar. *Borderlands of Western Civilization.* New York: The Ronald Press Company, 1952. Both an essay and a text, the emphasis is on the northern tier and the period before 1900.

Palmer, Alan W. *The Lands Between: A History of Eastern-Central Europe Since the Congress of Vienna.* London: Weidenfeld and Nicholson, 1970. An excellent, well-balanced survey.

Sugar, Peter F., and Ivo J. Lederer, eds., *Nationalism in Eastern Europe.* Seattle: University of Washington Press, 1969. Solid studies of a crucial topic.

Eastern Europe: Areas and Special Topics

Balkans/Southeast Europe

Djordjevic, Dimitrije, and Stephen Fischer-Galati. *The Balkan Revolutionary Tradition.* New York: Columbia University Press, 1981. Insights into an area of importance.

Jelavich, Barbara. *History of the Balkans.* 2 vols. Cambridge: Cambridge University Press, 1983. The best survey of southeastern Europe.

Jelavich, Charles, and Barbara Jelavich. *The Establishment of the Balkan National States, 1804–1920.* Seattle: University of Washington Press, 1977. Similar to the above, but focusing on the nineteenth century.

Lampe, John R., and Marvin R. Jackson. *Balkan Economic History, 1550–1950.* Bloomington: Indiana University Press, 1982. Exceptional scholarship, but the organization and level of detail make it heavy going for the nonspecialist.

Stavrianos, Leften S. *The Balkans since 1453.* New York: Holt, Rinehart & Winston, 1963. A classic. Superseded to some extent by the work of Barbara Jelavich, but still an essential point of departure for the study of southeastern Europe.

Stoianovich, Traian. *A Study in Balkan Civilization.* New York: Knopf, 1967. An excellent essay.

Habsburg Empire

Jaszi, Oscar. *The Dissolution of the Habsburg Monarchy.* Chicago: University of Chicago Press, 1929. Out of date but still valuable because of the many insights which Jaszi brings to the topic.

Kann, Robert A. *A History of the Habsburg Empire, 1526–1918*. Berkeley: University of California Press, 1974. A solid short study.

———. *The Multinational Empire: Nationalism and National Reform in the Habsburg Monarchy, 1848–1918*. 2 vols. New York: Columbia University Press, 1950. Seminal, but difficult to read.

Kann, Robert A., and Zdenek V. David. *The Peoples of the Eastern Habsburg Lands, 1526–1918*. Seattle: University of Washington Press, 1984. One of the many outstanding volumes in the University of Washington series edited by Peter Sugar.

Macartney, C. A. *The Habsburg Empire, 1790–1918*. London: Weidenfeld and Nicolson, 1968. A detailed but readable survey of this period.

May, Arthur J. *The Habsburg Monarchy, 1867–1914*. New York: W. W. Norton, 1968. A solid introduction to the post-Ausgleich period.

Tapie, Victor. *The Rise and Fall of the Habsburg Monarchy*. Translated by Stephen Hardman. New York: Praeger, 1971. The best introductory survey.

The Jews

Dubnow, S. M. *History of the Jews in Russia and Poland*. 2 vols. Translated by I. Friedlaender. Philadelphia: The Jewish Publishing Society of America, 1916–1918. Very much out of date. A modern survey history of the Jews in Eastern Europe is urgently needed by historians of Eastern Europe.

The Slavs

Dvornik, Francis. *The Slavs: Their Early History and Civilization*. Boston: American Academy of Arts and Sciences, 1956. See below.

———. *The Slavs in European History and Civilization*. New Brunswick, New Jersey: Rutgers University Press, 1962. Solid scholarship and good writing make these two studies by Dvornik an invaluable introduction.

Portal, Roger. *The Slavs*. Translated by Patrick Evans. London: Weidenfeld and Nicolson, 1969. Includes Russia; simplistic and tendentious in parts.

National Histories

Albania

Logoreci, Anton. *The Albanians: Europe's Forgotten Survivors*. Boulder, Colorado, 1977. Good, but limited. A comprehensive, scholarly history of Albania has yet to appear.

Bulgaria

Kossev, D., H. Hristov, and D. Angelov. *A Short History of Bulgaria.* Sofia: Foreign Languages Press, 1963. An official (published in postwar Bulgaria) history. Very limited and biased, especially on the modern period.

Macdermott, Mercia. *A History of Bulgaria.* London: Allen & Unwin, 1962. As with Logoreci's book on Albania, this is just a first step toward a much-needed comprehensive, scholarly history of this country.

Czechoslovakia

Kerner, Robert J., ed. *Czechoslovakia.* Berkeley: University of California Press, 1940. A collection of essays that are out of date but still useful.

Seton-Watson, R.W. *A History of the Czechs and Slovaks.* London: Hutchinson, 1943. Out of date, but still valuable because of the author's direct observations.

Wallace, William V. *Czechoslovakia.* Boulder, Colorado: Westview Press, 1976. An excellent survey history.

Hungary

Macartney, C. A. *Hungary: A Short History.* Edinburgh: Edinburgh University Press, 1962. Solid, but very brief.

Pamlenyi, Ervin, ed. *A History of Hungary.* London: Collet's, 1975. A useful collection.

Sinor, Dennis. *A History of Hungary.* London: Allen and Unwin, 1959. Of limited value; Hungary also awaits a good comprehensive history.

Poland

Davies, Norman. *God's Playground: A History of Poland.* 2 vols. New York: Columbia University Press, 1984. Brilliant, insightful, and comprehensive. An extremely valuable contribution to the history of Eastern Europe.

Leslie, R. F., ed. *The History of Poland since 1863.* Cambridge: Cambridge University Press, 1980. An excellent study of this recent period.

Reddaway, W. J., ed. *The Cambridge History of Poland.* 2 vols. Cambridge: Cambridge University Press, 1941–1950. Coverage ends in the middle of the interwar period, but the scholarship is first rate.

Wandycz, Piotr S. *The Lands of Partitioned Poland.* Seattle: University of Washington Press, 1974. An invaluable study of the period from the partitions to the advent of independent Poland.

Romania

Chirot, Daniel. *Social Change in a Peripheral Society: The Creation of a Balkan Colony.* New York: Academic Press, 1976. A useful essay on sociological aspects of Romanian history.
Constantinescu, Miron, Constantin Daicoviciu, and Stefan Pascu. *Histoire de la Roumanie.* Paris: Editions Horvath, 1970. An official (published in postwar Romania) study. Erratic in its coverage and biased in many of its interpretations.
Seton-Watson, R. W. *A History of the Roumanians from Roman Times to the Completion of Unity.* Cambridge: Cambridge University Press, 1934. As with Seton-Watson's history of the Czechs and Slovaks, this study is out of date but still important because the author knew the subject so well and in some cases is reporting personal observations.

Yugoslavia

Auty, Phyllis. *Yugoslavia.* New York: Walker, 1965. An excellent short survey.
Clissold, Stephen, ed. *A Short History of Yugoslavia.* Cambridge: Cambridge University Press, 1966. Solid, but very brief.
Dedijer, Vladimir, Ivan Bozic, Sima Cirkovic, and Milorad Ekmecic. *History of Yugoslavia.* Translated by Kordija Kveder. New York: McGraw-Hill, 1974. By far the best of the national histories to be published by scholars employed in postwar Eastern Europe. Thorough and rarely polemical.
Eterovich, Francis H., ed. *Croatia: Land, People, Culture.* 2 vols. Toronto, University of Toronto Press, 1964–1970. A very valuable collection of essays covering many aspects of Croatia, including history and culture.
Petrovich, Michael B. *History of Serbia.* 2 vols. New York: Harcourt, Brace, Jovanovich, 1976. An excellent, scholarly survey. Exemplary of the kind of study still needed for most of the countries.
Pribichevich, Stoyan. *Macedonia: Its People and History.* University Park, Pennsylvania: The Pennsylvania State University Press, 1982. Brief, but a useful introduction.

Interwar/Twentieth-Century Eastern Europe

General

Jackson, George D., Jr. *Comintern and Peasant in East Europe, 1919–1930.* New York: Columbia University Pres, 1966. Excellent scholarship and fine writing; valuable beyond the narrow topic suggested by the title.

Macartney, C. A., and Alan W. Palmer. *Independent Eastern Europe*. New York: St. Martin's Press, 1966. Solid and informative, but not well balanced particularly on economic issues.

Polonsky, Anton. *The Little Dictators: The History of Eastern Europe since 1918*. London: Routledge & Kegan Paul, 1975. Insightful and very readable.

Rothschild, Joseph. *East Central Europe between the Two World Wars*. Seattle: University of Washington Press, 1974. An excellent, scholarly study. The best starting point for any analysis of this period.

Seton-Watson, Hugh. *Eastern Europe between the Wars, 1918–1941*. Third edition, revised. New York: Harper Torchbooks, 1967. A brilliant study by a scholar who knows Eastern Europe better than anyone. Originally published during the war and not significantly revised.

Albania

Fischer, Bernd Jurgen. *King Zog and the Struggle for Stability in Albania*. Boulder: East European Monographs, 1984. Scholarly and comprehensive; a major addition to the study of Albania.

Skendi, Stavro. *The Albanian National Awakening, 1878–1912*. Princeton: Princeton University Press, 1967. An excellent study of the period just before independence but crucial to an understanding of the period in question.

Swire, J. *Albania: The Rise of a Kingdom*. London: Williams and Ungate, 1929. Part history, part direct observation, this fascinating work covers only the first half of the interwar period.

———. *King Zog's Albania*. London: Robert Hale and Company, 1937. Continues the story to 1936.

Bulgaria

Bell, John D. *Peasants in Power*. Princeton: Princeton University Press, 1977. Excellent analysis of political and economic developments in the early part of the period.

Logio, G. C. *Bulgaria: Past and Present*. Manchester, England: Sherratt and Hughes, 1936. Useful for the first part of the period.

Czechoslovakia

Korbel, Josef. *Twentieth Century Czechoslovakia*. New York: Columbia University Press, 1977. Coverage of the interwar period is comparatively brief and superficial.

Mamatey, Victor S., and Radomir Luza, eds. *A History of the Czechoslovak Republic, 1918–1948.* Princeton: Princeton University Press, 1973. An excellent collection of studies.

Hungary

Berend, Tibor Ivan. *Hungary: A Century of Economic Development.* New York: Barnes and Nobel, 1974. Very useful.

Macartney, C. A. *October Fifteenth: A History of Modern Hungary, 1929–1945.* 2 vols. Edinburgh: Edinburgh University Press, 1956–57. A brilliant, highly analytical history.

Poland

Dziewanowski, M. K. *Poland in the Twentieth Century.* New York: Columbia University Press, 1977. Solid, but limited coverage.

Korbel, Josef. *Poland between East and West.* Princeton: Princeton University Press, 1963. An interesting perspective on diplomacy.

Polonsky, Anton. *Politics in Independent Poland, 1921–1939.* Oxford: The Clarendon Press, 1972. Scholarly and extremely well written.

Watt, Richard M. *Bitter Glory: Poland and its Fate, 1918–1939.* New York: Simon and Schuster, 1982. An outstanding history of this period.

Romania

Fischer-Galati, Stephen A. *Twentieth-Century Romania.* New York: Columbia University Press, 1970. Excellent, but like the other works in this series, the emphasis is on the postwar period.

Roberts, Henry L. *Rumania: Political Problems of an Agrarian State.* New York: Archon Books, 1969. A superb study of Romania between the wars.

Yugoslavia

Hoptner, J. B. *Yugoslavia in Crisis, 1934–1941.* New York: Columbia University Press, 1962. Excellent.

Singleton, Fred. *Twentieth-Century Yugoslavia.* New York: Columbia University Press, 1976. See the comments on Fischer-Galati's work above.

Tomasevich, Jozo. *Peasants, Politics, and Economic Change in Yugoslavia.* Stanford: Stanford University Press, 1955. An outstanding study.

World War II in Eastern Europe

General

Clissold, Stephen. *Whirlwind: An Account of Marshal Tito's Rise in Power.* London: 1949. An eyewitness account of Tito and the partisans during the war.

Gross, Jan T. *Polish Society Under German Occupation: General Government, 1939–1944.* Princeton: Princeton University Press, 1979. An excellent account of this grim topic.

Miller, Marshall Lee. *Bulgaria during the Second World War.* Stanford: Stanford University Press, 1975. An important contribution.

Roberts, Walter B. *Tito, Mihailovich, and the Allies: 1941–1945.* New Brunswick, New Jersey: Rutgers University Press, 1973. A critical view of the Allied decision to support the Partisans and drop the Chetniks.

Tomasevich, Jozo. *War and Revolution in Yugoslavia, 1941–45: The Četniks.* Stanford: Stanford University Press, 1975. Superb study by a fine scholar.

Holocaust

Dawidowicz, Lucy. *The War Against the Jews, 1933–1945.* New York: Bantam Books, 1976. Outstanding scholarship and clear, thoughtful writing make this an essential work.

Krakowski, Samuel. *The War of the Doomed: Jewish Armed Resistance in Poland, 1942–1944.* Translated by Orah Blaustein. New York: Holmes and Meier, 1983. Valuable on this limited topic.

Vago, Bela. *The Shadow of the Swastika.* London: Saxon House, 1975. Excellent scholarship. Includes many important documents from the British Foreign Office.

Communist Parties of Eastern Europe

General

Burks, R. V. *The Dynamics of Communism in Eastern Europe.* Princeton: Princeton University Press, 1961. A brilliant, pioneering study of a complex subject.

Fischer-Galati, Stephen, ed. *The Communist Parties of Eastern Europe.* New York: Columbia University Press, 1979. An extremely useful collection of studies.

Albanian

Institutes of the Party of Labor of Albania. *History of the Party of Labor of Albania*. Tirane: Naim Frasheri Publishing House, 1971. Obvious bias, but one of the few sources available.

Skendi, Stavro. "History of the Albanian Party of Labor," *News from Behind the Iron Curtain* 5, no. 1 (January, 1956):27–29. Useful.

Bulgarian

Oren, Nissan. *Bulgarian Communism: The Road to Power, 1934–1944*. New York: Columbia University Press, 1971. An excellent work; valuable as a general history as well.

Rothschild, Joseph. *The Communist Party of Bulgaria: Origins and Development, 1883–1936*. New York: Columbia University Press, 1959. Absolutely first rate. There is considerable irony in the disproportionate attention which western scholars have given to Bulgarian communism as opposed to Bulgarian history.

Czechoslovakia

Rupnik, Jacques. *Histoire du parti communiste Tchéco-slovacque*. Paris: Fondation Nationale des Sciences Politiques, 1981. Excellent.

Suda, Zdenek. *Zealots and Rebels*. Stanford: Hoover Institution Press, 1980. An insightful history.

Zinner, Paul E. *Communist Strategy and Tactics in Czechoslovakia, 1918–1948*. New York: Praeger, 1963. A solid study, but largely superseded by Rupnik's and Suda's works.

German

Leonhard, Wolfgang. *Child of the Revolution*. Chicago: Regnery, 1958. Brilliant.

Stern, Carola. *Ulbricht: A Political Biography*. New York: Praeger, 1965. A valuable profile of this long-time leader.

Hungarian

Kovrig, Bennett. *Communism in Hungary from Kun to Kádár*. Stanford: Stanford University Press, 1979. An excellent history.

Polish

de Weydenthal, Jan B. *The Communists of Poland: An Historical Outline.* Stanford: Hoover Institution Press, 1978. Like all of the histories in this series from the Hoover Institution Press, this is a major contribution.
Dziewanowski, M. K. *The Communist Party of Poland.* Cambridge: Harvard University Press, 1976. Valuable material, though a rather dry approach.

Romanian

Ionescu, Ghita. *Communism in Romania, 1944–1962.* London: Oxford University Press, 1964. Excellent, but contains comparatively little information on the early period.
King, Robert R. *History of the Romanian Communist Party.* Stanford: Hoover Institution Press, 1980. A political science rather than an historical approach, but still an important contribution from the latter perspective.

Yugoslav

Avakumovic, Ivan. *History of the Communist Party of Yugoslavia.* Aberdeen: Aberdeen University Press, 1964. A valuable albeit brief survey.

Principal Journals

Austrian History Yearbook
East European Quarterly
East Central Europe
Journal of Central European Affairs (no longer published)
Slavic Review
Slavonic and East European Review
Southeastern Europe

Index

Adrianople, Treaty of (1829), 41–42
Aehrenthal, Count, 96
Agrarian Party (Bulgaria), 256
Agrarian Party (Czechoslovakia), 198–99, 202
Agriculture: in interwar Albania, 262; in interwar Czechoslovakia, 191; in interwar Poland, 173–78; in interwar Romania, 220–22; in interwar Soviet Union, 319–20; in interwar Yugoslavia, 238–39
Albania, 24–25; diplomacy in, World War I, 142–43; diplomatic policy in interwar, 159–60; education in, 123; education in interwar, 264–65; geography of, 14–15; government and resistance in World War II, 307; history, 1848–1914, 107–9; history in 1800, 25; industrial development in, 262–63; Italian intervention in, 268; nationalism in, 42, 268; in Ottoman Empire, 1400–1800, 27–28, 42; social classes in interwar, 263–64
Albanians: and First Balkan War, 97; and interwar Yugoslavia, 243; in Macedonia, 94
Alecsandri, Vasile, 129
Alexander I, Tsar of Russia, 34, 49–52, 93
Alexander II, Tsar of Russia, 49–51
Alexander, King of Yugoslavia, 247–48, 290

Alexander, Prince of Bulgaria, 101–3
Alföld, See Great Plain
American-Albanian Agricultural School, 265
Andrássy, Gyula, 65
Anschlüss, 163–66
Anti-Fascist Council of National Liberation (Yugoslavia), 300–301 Anti-Semitism: and Béla Kun regime in Hungary, 208; in interwar Hungary, 215–18; in interwar Romania, 225–26, 234–36; in Russian Empire (1800–1848), 35–36; and wartime Czechoslovakia, 282
Antonescu, General Ion, 168, 301–5
Arany, János, 128
Arrowcross, 286–89
Ausgleich, 60–63, 71, 76–77, 79, 83–85, 89, 122
Austria, 3; industrial development in, 71; politics in (1867–1914), 68–75; and Romanians after Crimean War, 90; structure of (Imperial), 67–68
Austria-Hungary: alliance with Romania, 106; and Balkan politics, 96–97; and Bulgaria, 103; foreign policy and origins of World War I, 134; relations with Serbia, 98–100; structure of, 60–63, 65
Austrians, and siege of Vienna, 115
Austro-Prussian War (1866), 71, 105
Averescu, General Alexander, 230–31

417

Bach, Alexander, 59
Badeni, Count, 75
Bakunin, Mikhail, 324
Balaton, Lake, 6
Balkan Confederation, 350
Balkan Entente: and interwar Bulgaria,
    259–60; and interwar Yugoslavia,
    247
Balkan Mountains: geography of, 13
Balkan question: and Austria-Hungary,
    73–74; and Russia, 73–74
Balli Kombëtar: and Albanian commu-
    nism, 350; in World War II, 307
Baltic Sea, 112
Banat, 8. See also Romania
Bárdossy, László, 284–85
Bat'a factory, 190
Bektashis: and interwar Albania, 264
Belgrade (Beograd), 12
Bem, General Joseph, 46
Beneš, Edvard, 139–40, 204; and Mun-
    ich crisis, 164–65
Berlin, Congress of (1878), 74, 101
Bernstein, Edward, 312
Bessarabia, 152, 168; annexation by Ro-
    mania in World War II, 302–3, 305;
    education in, 226; landholding in in-
    terwar, 223; politics in interwar, 229;
    after Russo-Turkish War (1877–78),
    92
Bessarabian faction: in Romanian com-
    munism, 338–39
Bethlen, Count: government of, 214–16
Bismarck, Prince Otto von, 93–94, 112–
    13; and Polish rebellion of 1863, 54;
    and war of 1866, 60; dismissed, 134–
    35
Black Sea, 112
Blagoev, Dimiter, 345–46
Bohemia (Čechy): geography of, 4–5,
    18, 25, 68
Bohemian Forest. See Český Les
Böhme, General, 296
Boiars, 221
Bolshevik revolution, 150
Bolsheviks, and Polish prisoners, 138–
    39, 141
Boris III, King of Bulgaria, 255–56,
    258–60; in World War II, 306

Bosnia-Hercegovina, 96; and Austria-
    Hungary, 93; geography of, 11; revolt
    in, 73–74, 91; and Serb-Croat differ-
    ences, 242; and Serbia, 99–100
Bosniaks: and interwar Yugoslavia, 243
Botev, Christo, 101, 130
Brașov, 9
Brătianu family, 228
Brătianu, Ion C., 106, 141
Brătianu, Ionel, 228, 230–32
Brătianu, Vintila, 232–33
Bratislava, 5, 79, 82
Breslau. See Wrocław
Brest-Litovsk, Treaty of, 136–38
Britain: and interwar Hungary, 210; and
    Béla Kun regime in Hungary, 207; de-
    clares war on Germany, 16; foreign
    policy and origins of World War I,
    132–33; and interwar Bulgaria, 260;
    and interwar Romania, 222; and Ro-
    manians after Crimean War, 90; and
    wartime Poland, 271–72; and Yugos-
    lav resistance in World War II, 297
Brno (Brünn), 5
Broz, Josip. See Tito
Brünn. See Brno
Bucovina, 7–9, 29; annexed by Ro-
    mania in World War II, 302, 305
Budapest, 7, 61, 69
Bulgaria: and Austria-Hungary, 103;
    and Balkan Wars, 97; diplomacy in
    World War I, 141–42; diplomatic
    policy in interwar, 159–60; education
    in, 123, in 1800, 24; and First Balkan
    War, 97; foreign policy in interwar,
    259–60; and German attack on
    Greece, 169–70; geography of, 12–
    14; government in World War II,
    305–6; industrial development in in-
    terwar, 253; and Macedonian ques-
    tion, 95; nationalism in, 42;
    nationality issues in, 254–55; and Ot-
    toman Empire (1400–1800), 28; poli-
    tics in interwar, 255–60; social classes
    in interwar, 253–54
Bulgarian Communist Party (BCP), 255–
    58
Bulgarian language, 19
Bulgarian literature, 130

Bulgarian Orthodox Church, 100; and Holocaust, 307; and Macedonia, 94
Bulgarian Plain: geography of, 13
Bulgarian-Serb War of 1885, 93, 102
Bulgarians: early history to 1400, 20–21; history (1848–1914), 100–4; in Ottoman Empire (1800–1848), 42; in Ottoman Empire, 1848–1914, 90 and revolt in Bosnia-Hercegovina, 73
Burks, R. V., 353, 355–56
Byelorussian language, 19
Byelorussians: in interwar Poland, 182
Byzantium, 25

Cargiale, Ion Luca, 130
Carol I, King of Romania, 105–6, 168, 227
Carol II, King of Romania, 232–36, 301
Carpathian Mountains, 1–3, 5–9, 87
Carpatho-Ruthenia, 193; in Austria-Hungary, 87, 165; Ukrainians in, 57–58; and wartime Czechoslovakia, 280. See also Czechoslovakia
Cavour, Count, 59
Čechy. See Bohemia
Celts, 16
Česky Les (Bohemian Forest), 4
Četniks, 294–300
Chamberlain, Neville, 164
Charles of Habsburg: as claimant to Hungarian throne, 208, 214
Charles University, 196
Cheka, 316, 328; and Béla Kun regime in Hungary, 208
Chopin, Frederyk, 127
Christian Socialist Party, 75, 81–82
Christian Union Party (Hungary), 214
Church Slavonic, 21
Churchill, Winston: and Yugoslav resistance in World War II, 294, 299; and wartime Poland, 272
Ciano, Count, 168
Clearing agreements: and German economic policy, 157–58; and interwar Yugoslavia, 240
Climate of Eastern Europe, 15, 111–12
Coburgs, 194

Codreanu, Corneliu, 235–36, 301
Comenius, John, 124
Comintern, 322–23, 329, 356–57; and Albanian communism, 350; and Bulgarian communism, 346–47, 349; and Czechoslovak communism, 343–44; and Czechoslovak Communist Party, 197–98; and German communism, 335; and Polish communism, 332; and Romanian communism, 337–39; and Yugoslav communism, 340; and Yugoslavia in World War II, 298
Communism, in Greece, 351–52; in Russia, 48–50
Communist Party of Albania (CPA): in World War II, 307, 349–51
Communist Party of Bulgaria (CPB), 345–49
Communist Party of Czechoslovakia (CPCS), 202–3, 343–45
Communist Party of Germany (KPD), 333–37
Communist Party of Hungary (CPH), 206, 325–30
Communist Party of Poland (CPP), 330–33; in World War II, 276, 283
Communist Party of Yugoslavia (CPY), 295–96, 339–42
Congress of Lushnjë, 262, 265
Conquest, Robert, 321
Conservative Party (Romania), 227–28
Constanţa, 9
Constantinople, 91. See also Istanbul
Copernicus, 119
Corfu Agreement (1917), 142, 237
Cossacks, 57
Counter-Reformation, 124–27
Cracow (Kraków), 2
Cracow, University of, 23, 126
Crimean War, 47, 90; Polish views on, 51
Croatia, 24, 96; education in, 122; geography of 10–11; and Imperial Hungary, 63–64. See also Yugoslavia
Croatian literature, 128–29
Croatian Peasant Party, 86, 99
Croatians: in Austria-Hungary, 85–87; in 1848 45–46; in Habsburg Empire (1800–1848), 39–40; nationalism in,

39–40, 78; and revolutions of 1848, 59; and Slovenes, 84
Crownlands of St. Stephen, 22, 45, 141, 327
Cuza, Alexander (Prince of Romania), 105
Czech Lands: early industrialization in, 117; education in, 122; Germans in 81; and Habsburg Empire (1400–1800), 30; population of, 76. *See also* Bohemia, Moravia
Czech language, 19
Czech literature, 124–25
Czechoslovak National Council, 189
Czechoslovakia: church-state relations in interwar, 199–200; diplomacy in World War I, 139–40; diplomatic policy in interwar, 159–61; education in interwar, 196; in 1800, 23; foreign policy in interwar, 199 geography of, 4–5; government and military in World War II, 279–81; industrial development in, 190–91, 200; land reform in, 191–92; nationality issues in, 194–96, 200–202; policy toward interwar Poland, 187; politics in interwar, 197–204; social classes in interwar, 192–94; World War I, damage in, 190; World War II, resistance in, 282–83
Czechs: in Austria-Hungary, 75–78; and Austrian parliament, 70; and Franco-Prussian War, 72; in Habsburg Empire (1800–1848), 36–37; nationalism in, 36–37; and revolutions of 1848, 59; and siege of Vienna, 115; and Slovaks in Habsburg Empire, 82; and Taaffe ministry, 75

Dacia, 17
Dacians, 17
Dalmatia, 10–11, 29; annexed by Italy in World War II, 290
Danube River, 1, 6–8, 13, 112
Danubian principalities. *See* Romania
Danzig, 166, 179; as free city, 185. *See also* Gdánsk

Deák, Istvan, 65; and Croats, 85
Deutscher, Isaac, 332
Dielli, 265
Dimitrov, Georgi, 346–48
Dinaric Mountains, 10–11, 14
Dmowski, Roman, 54–55, 138–39, 172
Dobrogea, 8–9
Dobrogeanu-Gherea, C., 337–38
Drava River, 10
Dual Alliance, 74, 92; and Romania, 106
Dual Monarchy. *See* Austria-Hungary
Dvořak, Antonín, 125
Dzerzhinsky, Felix, 316

Eastern Rumelia, 101–2
Economic development: in interwar Eastern Europe, 154–58
Education: in Eastern Europe, 120–23
Eminescu, Mihai, 129–30
Eötvös, Jozsef, 65
Estherházy family, 64, 68

Fascism: in interwar Hungary, 215; in interwar Romania 234–36; in interwar Yugoslavia, 249
Fatherland Front (Bulgaria), 306
Ferdinand I, King of Romania, 227–28, 232
Ferdinand, King of Bulgaria, 103, 255
Feudal system, 26
Feudalism, in Eastern Europe, 116; in Western Europe, 113–14
Feuer, Louis, 355
First Balkan War, 96; and Albania, 109
Fiume, 85. *See* Rijeka
Five-Year Plan, in the Soviet Union, 317–19
France: and Béla Kun regime in Hungary, 207; as center of nationalism, 33; and Czechoslovakia, 199; declares war on Germany, 167; diplomatic policy and interwar Eastern Europe, 158, 160–61; and economic policy in interwar Eastern Europe, 155; foreign

policy and origins of World War I, 133; and interwar Bulgaria, 260; and interwar Hungary 210; and interwar Poland, 185; and interwar Romania, 222; and interwar Yugoslavia, 240; policy toward interwar Poland 187; and Romanians after Crimean War, 90; and war of 1859, 59–60; and wartime Poland, 271

Franco-Prussian War, 72, 77

Frank, Hans, 277

Franz-Ferdinand, Archduke: assassination of, 135–36

Franz-Joseph, Emperor, 45, 59–61, 63, 66–67, 71–75, 77–78

Frashëri, Sami, 109

French Revolution: nationalism in, 33

Front of National Resistance, 236

Gaj, Ljudevit, 129

Galicia, 22, 29, 54, 56, 68–69, 76, 87, 138, 172; 1846 revolt in, 88–89, geography of, 2–3; Ukrainians in, 57

Gdansk, 4. See also Danzig

Gdynia, 4, 187

German Christain Social Party (Czechoslovakia), 199

German Farmer Party (Czechoslovakia), 199

German invasion of Poland, 167

German liberals, 69–71, 82, 85; and aspirations of Czechs, 77–78; and occupation of Bosnia-Hercegovina, 74

German universities, 122; nationalism in, 33, 39

Germans, 29, 80; in Austria-Hungary, 80–82; as colonists in Czech and Slovak lands 23; as colonists in Poland, 23; as colonists in Transylvania, 23, in Czech lands, 81; in Habsburg Empire (1800–48), 39; in Hungary (1867–1914), 65; in interwar Czechoslovakia, 196, 202–4; in interwar Poland, 181–82; in interwar Romania, 220; Invasion of Poland, 167; nationalism and, 39; in Transylvania, 81

Germany: and economic policy in interwar Eastern Europe, 157–58, 163; foreign policy and origins of World War I, 133–35; and interwar Hungary, 215, 217–18; and interwar Poland 185; and interwar Yugoslavia, 240; policy toward interwar Poland, 187

Gheg, 17

Gheorghiu-Dej, Gheorghe, 304, 339

Goga, Octavian, 235

Gömbös, Gyula government of, 217

Gomułka, Władisław, 333

Gottwald, Klement, 344–45

Government Party (Hungary), 214

Great Plain (Alföld), 7

Greece: and First Balkan War 97; and interwar Albania, 262; nationalism in, 41; and Macedonian question, 94; resistance to Italian invasion, 169; revolt in Bosnia-Hercegovina, 73

Greeks: and early Eastern Europe, 16–19; in Macedonia, 94; and nationalism, 33; in Ottoman Empire (1800–48), 41–42; in Ottoman Empire (1848–1914), 90

Green International, 257

Gypsies, and Holocaust, 271

Habsburg Empire: history (1400–1800), 29–30; history (1848–1914), 58–90

Habsburg family, 25, 29

Habsburgs, and Serbs, 41

Hacha, Emil, 279–80

Hajduks, 27

Helen, Princess of Greece, 232

Henlein, Konrad, 164–66

Heydrich, Reinhard, 282

High Tatra Mountains, 2

Hilandar Monastery, 130

Hitler, Adolf: and Bulgaria in World War II, 306; and Czechoslovakia, 204; and German communism, 336; and Hungary in World War II, 285–87; and interwar Bulgaria, 260; and Munich crisis, 166; and Romania in World War II, 301–2; and Yugoslavia in World War II, 292

Hlinka, Msgr., 202

Hohenwart, Count: ministry of, 75, 77–78
Holland: and interwar Romania, 222
Holocaust: in Bulgaria, 306–7; in Czechoslovakia, 283–84; in Hungary, 208, 288–90; in Poland, 271, 279; in Romania, 304–5; in Yugoslavia, 291–92
Home Army, 278–79
Horthy, Admiral Miklós, 208, 213, 216–18; in World War II, 284–89
Hoxha, Enver, 350
Hungarian language, 19
Hungarian literature, 127–28
Hungarians: and aspirations of Czechs, 77–78; in Austria-Hungary, 78–80; and Croats, 85–86; in 1848, 45; in Habsburg Empire (1800–48), 38–39; in interwar Czechoslovakia, 195; in interwar Romania, 220; and nationalism, 33, 38–39; and revolutions of 1848, 59; and Romanians in Transylvania, 83–84
Hungary: and assassination of King Alexander, 248; and Czechoslovakia, 199; diplomacy in World War I, 140–41 diplomatic policy in interwar, 159–60; early history to 1400, 21–22; early industrialization in, 117; economic development in, 209–11; education in, 122; in 1800, 23–24; geography of, 6–7; and German attack on Greece, 169; government and military in World War II, 284–88 and Ottoman Empire (1400–1800), 29; politics in, 213–18; politics in (1867–1914), 64–67; population changes in, 211; social classes in, 212; structure of (Imperial), 63–67; World War I losses in, 208–9; World War II resistance in, 288
Hus, Jan, 30, 192

Iancu, Avram, 45
Illyrian movement, 129. See also Yugoslav idea
Illyrians, 17

IMRO (Internal Macedonian Revolutionary Organization), 95; and assassination of King Alexander, 248; in interwar Bulgaria, 257–60
Industrial revolution in Western Europe, 117–18
Industrialization in Russia, 47–48
International Brigade, 296
Iorga, Nicolae, 301
Iron Gates, 112
Iron Guard, 235–36, 301–2
Islam: in Albania, 107; and interwar Albania, 264–65; and Serb-Croat differences, 241–42
Istanbul, 26–27, 123. See also Constantinople
Italians: and Austrian parliament, 70; in Habsburg Empire (1800–1848), 40; and revolutions of 1848, 59
Italy, 60; and assassination of King Alexander, 248; and economic policy in interwar Eastern Europe, 163; and interwar Albania, 261–62; and interwar Hungary, 210; and interwar Yugoslavia, 240; nationalism in 40; and settlement of World War I, 144; surrender in World War II, 297–98
Izvolsky, A. P., 96

Jajce, Congress of (1943), 300
Jelačić, General, 45
Jews, 271; and communism 355; in Hungary (1867–1914), 65; in interwar Czechoslovakia, 195; in interwar Poland, 181–82, 187; in interwar Romania, 220, 223, 226; nationalism and, 35–36; in Poland 52; and Poles 89; and Polish National Democrats, 55; Russian attitudes to, 48; in Russian Empire (1800–48), 35–36

Kállay, Miklós, 285–86
Karadžić, Vuk, 96, 128

Karageorgevich dynasty, 98–99, 142, 237
Karageorgevich, Peter, 99
Karavelov, Ljuben, 101, 130
Károlyi, Mihály: government of, 205–6
Katowice, 3, 178
Katyn Forest Massacre, 272–76
Kingdom of Serbs, Croats, and Slovenes, 237. See also Yugoslavia
Književni Dogovor, 129
Kochanowski, Jan, 126
Kolarov, Vasil, 346–48
Kollár, Ján, 127, 129
Königgrätz, Battle of, 60
Konstantinov, Aleko, 130
Kopitar, Jernej, 128
Kosovo, 12, 109; and Albanian communism, 351; annexation by Albania in World War II, 290, 293; geography of, 12
Kosovo Polje, Battle of (1389), 24, 26, 28, 40
Kossuth, Louis, 64–65, 140, 215, 327; and Croats, 85; in 1848, 45–46; and Serbs, 79
Kraków. See Cracow
Kramář, Karel, 198
Kulturkampf in Prussian Poland, 56
Kun, Béla, 206–8, 325–29; and revolution in Hungary, 162; and Romanian communism, 338

Lakatos, Géza, 286, 289
Land reform, in interwar Poland, 173–74; in interwar Romania, 220–21
Langsam, Walter C., 362
League of Nations, 160; and Hungary, 210; and interwar Albania, 262
League of Prizren, 108–9
League of the Archangel Michael. See Iron Guard
Lenin's Boys, 328
Lenin, V. I., 139, 358; and Béla Kun regime in Hungary, 208
Leninism, 308–12
Lesser Poland. See Małopolska
Leuger, Karl, 82

Levski, Vasil, 101, 130
Liberal Party (Romania), 104–5, 227–33; and World War II, 303
Lichtenstein family, 194
Lidice, Nazi atrocities in, 282
Liebknecht, Karl, 334–35
Liszt, Ferenc, 128
Literature, in Eastern Europe, 124–31
Lithuania, 22; and Polish Socialists, 55
Little Entente, 160, 164, 187; and Czechoslovakia, 199; formation of, 207; and interwar Yugoslavia, 247
Locarno Treaties, and Poland, 185
Łódź, 3; industry in, 178
Lombardy: and war of 1859, 60
Lower Austria, 69
Lublin, 3
Lukács, György, 329
Lupescu, Magda, 232–36
Luxemburg, Rosa, 331, 334–36, 358

Macartney, C. A., 285
Macedonia, 24, 96; annexation by Bulgaria in World War II, 290, 293; and First Balkan War, 97; geography of, 11–12
Macedonian Communist Party, 300
Macedonian language, 19–20
Macedonian question, 91; and Bulgaria, 103–4; and Bulgarian communism, 349; in interwar Bulgaria, 257–60; in interwar Yugoslavia, 243; history of, 1848–1914, 94–95; and Yugoslav communism 340
Macedonians, and revolt in Bosnia-Hercegovina, 73
Maček, Vladimir, 249–50
MacGahan, J. A., and revolt in Bulgaria, 91
Magyar. See Hungarian
Magyarization, 79–80; and Carpatho-Ruthenians, 87–88; in Romanian lands, 83–84; and Serbs, 87
Maiorescu, Titu, 130

Małopolska ("Lessor Poland"): geography of, 2. *See also* Galicia
Maniu, Iuliu, 229–31, 234
Manorial system: in Eastern Europe, 116; in Western Europe, 113–14
Maramureş, 8
Maritsa Valley, geography of, 13
Marx, Karl, 308–12
Marxism, in Russia, 48–50
Masaryk, Tamáš G., 125, 139–40, 189, 204
Mazovia, geography of, 3
Mazowsze. *See* Mazovia
Mazzini, Giuseppe, 151
Metternich, Prince, 36, 44
Michael II, King of Romania, 301, 303–4
Michael, Prince of Serbia, 98
Michelet, Jules, 126
Mickiewicz, Adam, 126–27
Mihailović, Draža, 294–300
Milan, Prince of Serbia, 98
Miracle of Warsaw, 146
Miskolc, 7
Mlada Bosna, 135
Moldavia, 8–9, 18, 152. *See also* Romania
Molotov-Ribbentrop pact, 166
Mongols: invasion of Europe by, 114
Montenegrins: in Ottoman Empire (1848–1914), 90
Montenegro, 24; and Albania, 108; and Balkan Wars, 97; geography of, 11; and Ottoman Empire (1400–1800), 27; and revolt in Bosnia-Hercegovina, 73, 91; and Serbia, 98; in World War I, 142
Moravia (Morava), 18, 68; geography of, 4–5
Moravian state: early history to 1400 of, 21
Moslems, 26–27
Mugoša, Dušan, 350
Munich Agreements (1938), 165, 204
Munţii Apuseni, 8. *See also* Western Mountains
Mureş River, 8
Muscovite state, 31
Mussolini, Benito: invades Greece, 169

Nagodba, 63–64, 85–86
Napoleon I: nationalism and, 33
Narutowicz, Gabriel, 184
National Christian Party (Romania), 235
National Democrat Party (Czechoslovakia), 198
National Democrat Party (Poland), 54–55, 172, 183–84
National Liberation Movement (Albania), 350
National Party (Romania), 229–31
National Peasant Party (Romania), 232; and World War II, 303
National Socialist Party (Czechoslovakia), 199
Nationalism, 32–44, 151–52; in Eastern Europe, 118; in Western Europe, 118
Nationality Law of 1868 (Hungary), 83
Nationality policy, in the Soviet Union, 312–13
Neretva River, 11
Neuilly, Treaty of, 143, 251, 257, 259–60
Nicholas I, Tsar of Russia, 35, 51, 96
NKVD (Soviet secret police; later KGB), 342; and Katyn Forest Massacre, 274–75; and Polish communism, 333
Noli, Bp. Fan, 265–67
Northern Mountains, 7

Obrenovich dynasty, 98–99
Oder (Odra) River, 2
Odessa, and Romanian forces in World War II, 302
Ohrid, Lake, 11, 14
"Old Czechs," 76–77
Operation Barbarossa, 170; Romanian participation in, 301
Opole, 3
Ore Mountains, 4
Organic Statute (1832), 35
Orthodox Church, 20; and education, 120–21; and interwar Albania, 264–65; and Macedonia, 94; in Romanian lands, 83; and Serb-Croat differences, 241
Ostrava, 5

Ottoman Empire, and Balkan peoples
(1848–1914), 90–109; and Balkan
Wars, 97; nature of rule in Balkans,
26–27; peoples of (1800–48), 40–43;
and Serbs, 87; Young Turk movement
in, 96
Ottoman Turks, 65; history (1400–
1800), 25–29; invasion of Europe,
114

Paisi, Father, 130
Palacký, František, 76, 125
Pan-Slavism, 48, 100; and Czechs, 37,
76, 129
Pannonia, 18
Paris: nationalism in, 33
Paris Peace Conference (1919), 238
Partisans (Albania), 307, 350–51
Partisans (Yugoslavia), 295–300, 342
Pašić, Nikola, 245, 247
Pătrășcanu, Lucrețiu, 304
Pauker, Marcel, 338
Paul, Prince of Yugoslavia, 248–50
Pavelić, Ante, 249, 290–91
Peasant Party (Croatia), 245, 247, 249
Peasant Party (Romania), 228–29
Peasant Revolt of 1907 in Romania, 107
People's Party (Slovene), 245–47
Peter, King of Yugoslavia, 290–91, 294,
300
Petöfi, Sándor, 128
Phanariots, 43
Piast Party (Poland), 183, 185
Piedmont-Sardinia: and war of 1859,
59–60
"Pig War" (1906), 99
Piłsudski, Józef, 55, 138–39, 171–72,
182–87, 201; and Polish communism,
331
Pittsburgh Agreement, 201
Pleven: siege of, 92
Poland: and Czechoslovakia, 199; diplo-
macy in World War I, 138–39; diplo-
matic policy in interwar, 159, 161–
62; early history to 1400, 21; early
industrialization in, 117; education in,
121–22; education in interwar, 182;

in 1800, 22–23; foreign capital in interwar, 179–80; foreign policy in interwar, 185, 187–88; geography of,
1–4; government and military in
World War II, 271–77; and Habsburg
Empire (1400–1800), 30–31; indus-
tial development in interwar, 178–79;
nationality issues in interwar, 181–82;
partitions of (1772, 1793, 1795), 31;
politics in interwar, 182–87; population changes in, 177; under Prussian
(German) rule, 56; rebellion of 1863
in, 53–54; in Russian Empire (1848–
1914), 50–56; social classes in interwar, 180–81; World War losses in,
172–73; in World War I, 136–37;
World War II resistance in, 277–79
Poland-Lithuania, 30
Poles: in Austria-Hungary, 88–90; and
Austrian parliament, 69–70; as na-
tionalist leaders, 33–34; and revolu-
tions of 1848, 59; and Roman
Catholic Church, 70; Russian atti-
tudes, to 48; in Russian Empire, 34–
35; and siege of Vienna, 115; and
Taaffe ministry, 75
Polish corridor, 185
Polish kingdom: disappearance of, 116
Polish language, 19
Polish literature, 125–27
Polish Socialist Party (PPS), 55, 184, 331
Polish Workers' Party See Communist
Party of Poland
Polish-Soviet relations: in World War II,
271–76
Polish-Soviet War (1920–21), 162
Pomerania (Pomorze), 22, 56; annexa-
tion by Germany in World War II,
277; geography of, 3
Pomorze. See Pomerania
Popović, Miladin, 350
Populist Party (Czechoslovakia), 199
Posen (Poznán): annexed by Germany in
World War II, 277; geography of, 3
Prague, 77
Praha. See Prague
Prešeren, France, 129
Prespa, Lake, 11, 14
Pressburg. See Bratislava

Protestant Churches: in Czech lands, 30; and education, 120–21; influence on literary languages; 124–27
Prus, Bolesław, 127
Prussia, 29, 31, 60; and Polish rebellion of 1863, 54; and Romanians after Crimean War, 90
Prussian Poland, 54
Prut River, 9

Radić, Stjepan, 86, 245, 247–48
Radical-Democratic Party (Serbian), 245, 247
Rădulescu, Ion Heliade, 129
Rákosi, Mátyás, 329–30
Rakovski, George, 101
Rakovsky, Christian G., 337–38
Rapallo agreements, 160
Red Army: and Bulgaria in World War II, 306; and resistance in wartime Poland, 278–79; and Romania in World War II, 303–4; and Yugoslavia in World War II, 298
Reformation, 124
Rej, Mikołaj, 126
Renaissance, 124–27
Revolution of 1848: in Habsburg lands, 44–46
Revolutionary movements: in Russia, 48–50
Rhodope Mountains: geography of, 12–14
Ribbentrop, Baron von, 168
Rijeka, 85–86
Robert College, 123
Roman Catholic Church: in Austria, 70; and Czech Protestants, 30; and education, 120–21; and Germans, 80; and interwar Albania, 264–65; in Poland, 51–52; and Polish National Democrats, 55; and Serb-Croat differences, 241; and Slovenia, 246; and Taaffe ministry, 75
Romania: and Bulgarian revolutionaries, 100; diplomacy in World War I, 141; diplomatic policy in interwar, 159–60; early history to 1400, 22; educa-

tion in, 122; in 1800, 25; fascism in interwar, 234–36; foreign capital in, 222; geography of, 7–9; and German attack on Greece, 169; government and military in World War II, 301–4; industrial development in, 239–40; industrial development in interwar, 222; and invasion of Poland, 167; and Macedonian question, 95; nationalism in, 43; nationality issues in interwar, 223–25; Peasant Revolt of 1907 in, 107; politics in interwar, 226–36; population changes in, 223; and Ottoman Empire (1400–1800), 28; and revolt in Bosnia-Hercegovina, 73; social classes in, 222–23; in World War II, 37
Romanian Communist Party (RCP): and World War II, 304, 337–39
Romanian language, 18
Romanian literature, 129–30
Romanian Orthodox Church, 43
Romanians: in Austria-Hungary, 83; in 1848, 45–46; in Habsburg Empire (1800–48), 40; history (1848–1914), 104–7; and revolutions of 1848, 59; in Ottoman Empire (1800–48), 43; and Russo-Turkish War (1877–78), 92;
Romans: and early Eastern Europe, 17–18
Roosevelt, Franklin D.: and Yugoslav resistance in World War II, 294, 299; and wartime Poland, 272
Ruse, 13
Russia, 31, 87; and Balkan politics, 96–97; and Bulgarian politics (1878–1914), 102–4; and Bulgarian revolutionaries, 101; and Bulgarian students, 123; and control of Ukraine, 57; and Germany before World War I, 135; and Romanians after Crimean War, 90; and Serbia, 98; and Serbs, 41
Russian Empire: history of (1848–1914), 47–58
Russian language, 19
Russian Poland, 54
Russians: nationalism of, 33

Russo-Turkish War (1829), 43; and
 Serbs, 41
Russo-Turkish War (1877–78), 73–74;
 and Albania, 108 and Romania, 106
Ruthenians, See Ukrainians

Šafárik, Pavel, 127
San Stefano, Treaty of, 74, 92, 101; and
 Albania, 108
Sava River, 10
Schacht, Hjalmar: and interwar Yugo-
 slavia, 240
Schwarzenberg family, 194
Scutari, Lake, 14
Scythians, 16–17
Sebian Radical Party, 99
Second Balkan War, 97
Second Vienna Award, 168
Sejm, 182–84
Serb-Bulgarian War of 1885, 93, 102
Serbia: early history to 1400, 22; educa-
 tion in, 122–23; geography of, 12;
 and First Balkan War, 97; history
 (1848–1914), 97–100; nationalism in,
 40–41; and Ottoman Empire (1400–
 1800), 27; and revolt in Bosnia-Her-
 cegovina, 73; and revolt in Bosnia-
 Hercegovina, 91; and Russo-Turkish
 War (1877–78), 92; and Yugoslav
 idea, 96; in World War I, 137
Serbian literature, 128
Serbian Orthodox Church, 40
Serbo-Croatian language, 19
Serbs, 28; in Austria-Hungary, 87; and
 Croats in Austria-Hungary, 86; in
 Habsburg Empire (1800–48), 40; and
 Kossuth, 79; in Ottoman Empire
 (1800–48), 40–41; in Ottoman Em-
 pire (1848–1914), 90; and Slovenes,
 84
Seton-Watson, Hugh, 176, 234
Sevastopol: and Romanian forces in
 World War II, 302
Sibiu, 9
Sienkiewicz, Henryk, 127
Sikorski, General, 271–72
Silesia, 22, 29, 56, 68, 178; annexation

by Germany in World War II, 277;
 geography of, 2
Silesian War, 116
Sima, Horia, 301–2
Simeon II, King of Bulgaria: in World
 War II, 306
Siret River, 9
Skanderbeg, 107
Skarga, Piotr, 126
Škoda Works, 166, 190, 281
Skupština, 245
Śląsk. See Silesia
Slaveykov, Pencho, 130
Slavic languages, 19–20
Slavs, early history, 18–20
Slovak language, 19
Slovak literature, 127
Slovak National Council, 283
Slovak People's Party, 202
Slovakia, 18, 87, 165; and Béla Kun re-
 gime in Hungary, 207; early history to
 1400, 21; education in, 122; geog-
 raphy of, 5; and Hungarian commu-
 nism, 328; independence in World
 War II, 281–82
Slovaks, 78; in Austria-Hungary, 82–83;
 in 1848, 45–46; in Habsburg Empire
 (1800–48), 37–38; nationalism and,
 37–38; and revolutions of 1848, 59
Slovene language, 19
Slovene literature, 129
Slovene Peoples Party, 84
Slovenes: in Austria-Hungary, 84–85;
 and Austrian parliament, 70; in Habs-
 burg Empire (1800–48), 39; national-
 ism in, 39; and revolutions of, 1848,
 59; and Roman Catholic Church, 70
Slovenia, 24: annexation by Germany in
 World War II, 290
Smallholders Party, 213
Šmeral, Bohumín, 344
Smetana, Bedřich, 125
Smith, Jr., Jeremiah: and interwar Hun-
 gary, 210
Sobranie, 255
Social Democratic Party (Austria-Hun-
 gary), 82
Social Democratic Party (Czechoslova-
 kia), 197

428 INDEX

Social Democratic Party (Germany), 197, 203, 334–36
Social Democratic Party (Hungary), 326
Social Democratic Party (Poland and Lithuania, SDKPL), 330–32
Social Democratic Party (Romania), 338–39
Someş River, 8
Soviet Union: and economic policy in interwar Eastern Europe, 162–63; and interwar Czechoslovakia, 199; and interwar Poland, 185
Spanish Civil War, 296
Spartacus League, 334–36
Spoleto, Duke of, 290
Sporazum, 249–50
St. Germain, Treaty of, 143
"Stakhanovism", 319
Stalin, J. V.: and Bulgarian communism, 348; and Communist Party of the Soviet Union, 314–15; and German communism, 335–36; and Katyn Forest Massacre, 273–75; and Polish communism, 332; and purges in the Soviet Union, 315–16, 320–22; and Romanian communism, 339; and Trotsky, 313–14; and Yugoslavia in World War II, 298–99
Stalingrad, Battle of: and Romanian forces in World War II, 303; Hungarian army and, 287
Stambuliski, Alexander: Bulgarian communists and, 346–47; 256–58
Stambulov, Stefan, 103
Stettin, 118. See also Szczecin
Stoyadinović, Milan: government of, 249
Strossmayer, Bp., 96
Štúr, Ludovít, 127, 129
Šubašić, Ivan, 300
Sudeten Germans, 164–66
Sudeten Mountains, 13–4
Sudetenland, 199, 204
Šumava Mountains, 4
Swire, J.: and interwar Albania, 267–68
Szálasi, Ferenc, 286–89
Szczecin (Stettin), 4

Szlachta (Polish nobility), 50–52, 54; in Galicia, 89
Sztójay, Döme 285–87, 289

Taaffe, Count: ministry of, 74–75, 78, 84
Tannenberg, Battle of, 172
Tatry Wysokie. See High Tatra Mountains
Teleki, Count, 284
Ten-Year Agreements: in Austria-Hungary, 63, 66
Teschen Silesia, 22, 145, 165; geography, of 5
Teutonic Knights, 22
Thälmann, Ernst, 33, 63, 58
Thirty Years War, 30
Thracians, 17
Timişoara, 9
Tiranä, 15
Tiranä, Treaty of (1926), 267
Tirnovo Constitution, 101–2, 255
Tiso, Msgr. Joseph, 280–84
Tisza River, 7
Tisza, Kálmán, 65–66
Tito (Josip Broz), 295–301, 341–42; and Albanian communism, 350
Tosk, 17
Trade unions: in interwar Czechoslovakia, 200; in interwar Hungary, 212–13
Trajan, 18
Transdanubia (Dunántúl): geography of, 6
Transnistria: annexation by Romania in World War II, 302
Transylvania, 8, 97, 168, 271; in Austria-Hungary, 83–84; education in, 122, 226; in 1848, 46; Germans and Hungarians in interwar, 224; history of (1848–1914), 104–7; Hungarian rule in, 92–93; landholding in interwar, 223; politics in interwar, 229; Uniate Church in, 43; united with Hungary, 64. See also Romania, 8–9

Transylvanian faction: in Romanian communism, 338–39
Trialism: in Austria-Hungary, 86, 135–36
Trianon, Treaty of, 143, 207, 215
Trieste, 85, 118
Trotsky, Leon: and Polish communism, 332; and Stalin, 313–14
Turkey: and First Balkan War, 97
Turks: in Macedonia, 94. See also Ottomans
Twenty-One conditions, 197; and Czechoslovak communism, 343; and Hungarian communism, 329

Ukraine, 53; nationalism in, 58; and Poland-Lithuania, 30–31; and Polish Socialists, 55
Ukrainian language, 19
Ukrainians in Galicia, 88; in interwar Czechoslovakia, 196; in interwar Poland, 182, 187; and Poles, 89; and revolutions of 1848, 59; in the Russian Empire (1848–1914), 56–58; Russian attitudes toward, 48
Uniate Church, 43; in Austria, 70; and Carpatho-Ruthenians, 87; in Romanian lands, 83; in Ukraine, 58
Union of Polish Patriots, 333
United States: and Béla Kun regime in Hungary, 207; and interwar Hungary, 210; and interwar Romania, 222; and wartime Poland, 271–72
Ustaša: and assassination of King Alexander, 248; in World War II, 291–92, 299

Vaida-Voievod, Alexandru, 229–31
Vardar River, 11
Varna, 13
Vatican: and Yugoslavia in World War II, 292; and wartime Czechoslovakia, 283
Vatra, 265

Vazov, Ivan, 130
Velchev, Damian, 258–60
Venetia: and war of 1859, 60
Versailles, Treaty of, 143
Vidovdan Constitution, 245–48
Vienna, 27, 61, 69, 80, 82; siege of (1529), 115; siege of (1683), 115; sieges of, 29
Vienna, Congress of (1815), 34
Vikings: in Western Europe, 113
Vistula (Wisła) River, 2
Vistulaland, 54
Vlachs: in interwar Albania, 264; in Macedonia, 94
Vladika, 27
Vojvodina: annexation by Hungary in World War II, 292–93; geography of, 12
Voronezh, Battle of: Hungarian army and, 287
Vörösmarty, Mihály, 127–28
Vrchlický, Jaroslav, 125
Vysoke Tatry. See High Tatra Mountains

Wallachia (Tara Romaneasca), 8, 9, 18, 152; 1848 revolution in, 90. See also Romania
Wallenberg, Raul, 290
Warsaw (Warszawa), 3
Warszawa. See Warsaw
Western Mountains, 219. See also Munții Apuseni
White Mountain, Battle of, 30, 78, 124, 192
Wielkopolska, 3, 22, 56
Wilhelm zu Wied (Prince of Albania), 109, 261
Wilson, Woodrow, 143–44; and interwar Albania, 262
Winter War (1939–40), 167
Wisła. See Vistula
Witos, Wincenty, 183, 185
World War I: peace settlement, 143–49
World War II: Czechoslovak forces in, 280–81; Polish forces in, 276

Wrangel, General: and interwar Albania, 266
Wrocław (Breslau), 3
Wyzwolenie (Liberation) Party (Poland), 183

Xoxe, Koci, 350

Yalta Conference: and Bulgaria in World War II, 306
Yezhovschina, 321–22; and Bulgarian communism, 348; and German communism, 337; and Polish communism, 332–33; and Yugoslav communism, 341–42
Young Czechs, 76–78
Young Turk movement, 96

Yugoslav idea, 94, 95–96, 142; and Slovenes in Austria-Hungary, 84
Yugoslavia: diplomacy in World War I, 142–43; diplomatic policy in interwar, 159–60; education in interwar, 244; in 1800, 24; foreign policy in, 246–47; formation of a communist state, 298–301; geography of, 10–12; and German attack on Greece, 170; and interwar Albania, 262, 266; and invasion of Poland, 167; nationality issues in, 240–44; occupation and administration in World War II, 290–93; politics in interwar, 244–50; social classes in interwar, 240; World War II resistance in, 293–98

Zagreb, 10, 86
Zawodny, J. K., 275
Zog, King Ahmet I, 266–68
Zveno Party (Bulgaria), 258–59

THE OTHER EUROPE
was composed in 10 on 12 Sabon on a Mergenthaler Linotron 202
by Worldcomp;
printed by sheet-fed offset on 50-pound, acid-free Glatfelter Natural Smooth,
Smyth-sewn and bound over binder's boards in Holliston Roxite C,
also notch bound with paper covers
by Braun-Brumfield, Inc.;
with paper covers printed in 2 colors
by Braun-Brumfield, Inc.;
and published by
Syracuse University Press
Syracuse, New York 13244-5160